FESTERING
ROMANCE

To Dayna,
Thanks bunches!

Published by Oni Press, Inc.

Joe Nozemack · publisher

James Lucas Jones · editor in chief

Randal C. Jarrell · managing editor

Cory Casoni · marketing director

Keith Wood · art director

Jill Beaton · assistant editor

Douglas E. Sherwood · production assistant

ONI PRESS, INC.
1305 SE Martin Luther King Jr. Blvd.
Suite A
Portland, OR 97214
USA

www.onipress.com
www.fridgewithfeet.com

First edition: July 2009
ISBN-13: 978-1-934964-18-7

1 3 5 7 9 10 8 6 4 2
PRINTED IN CANADA.

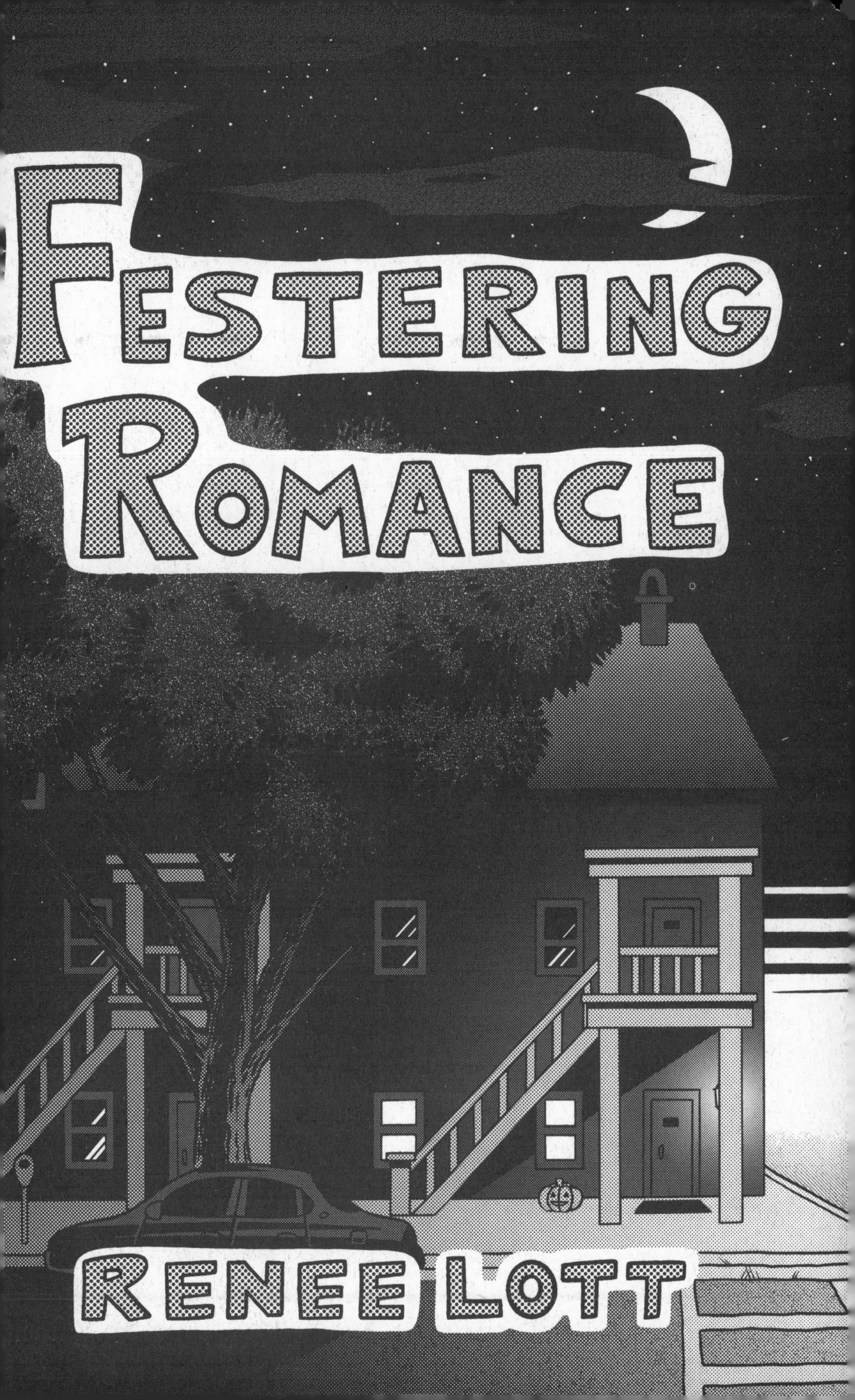
Festering
Romance
Renee Lott

Chapter 1

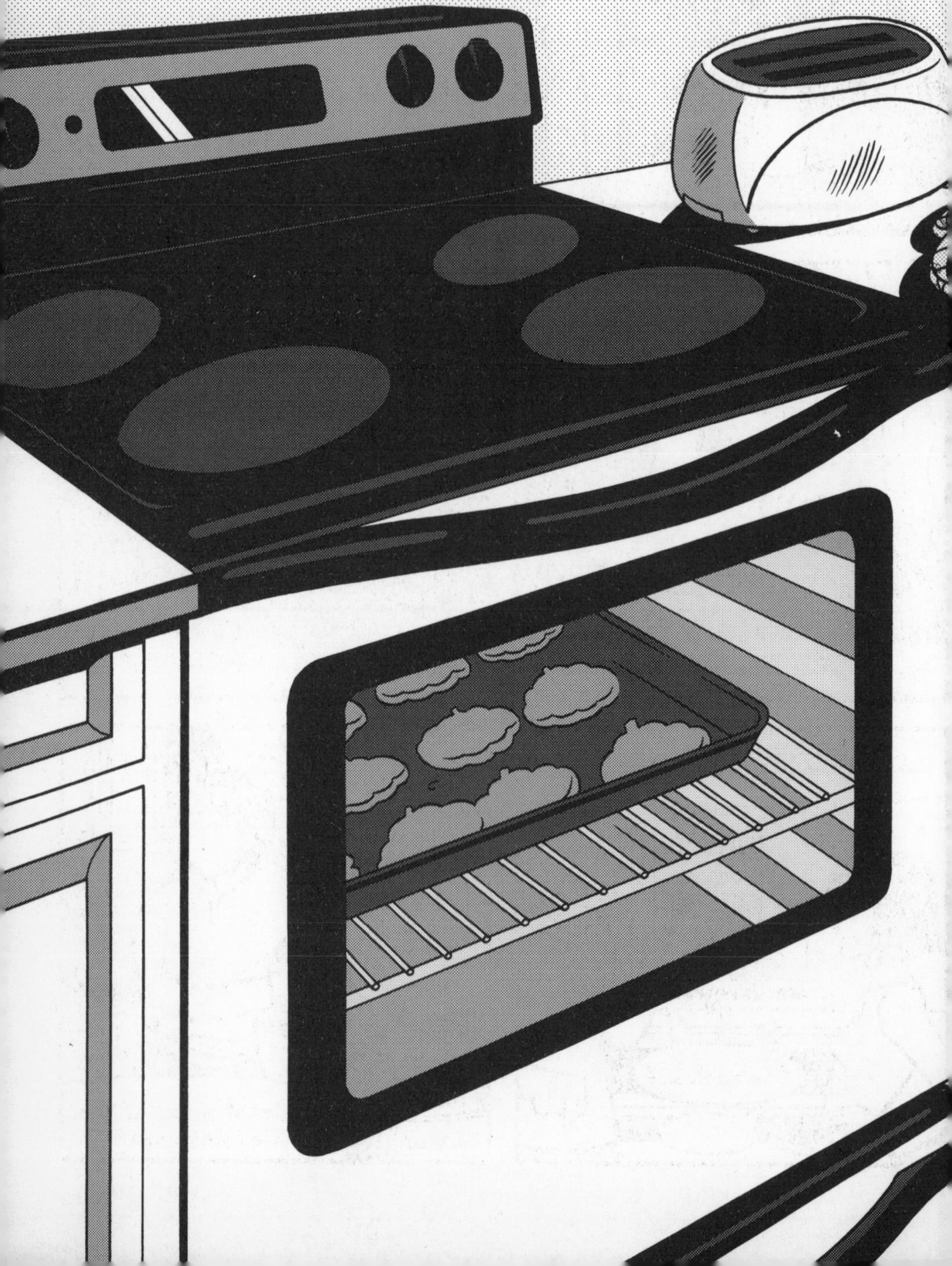

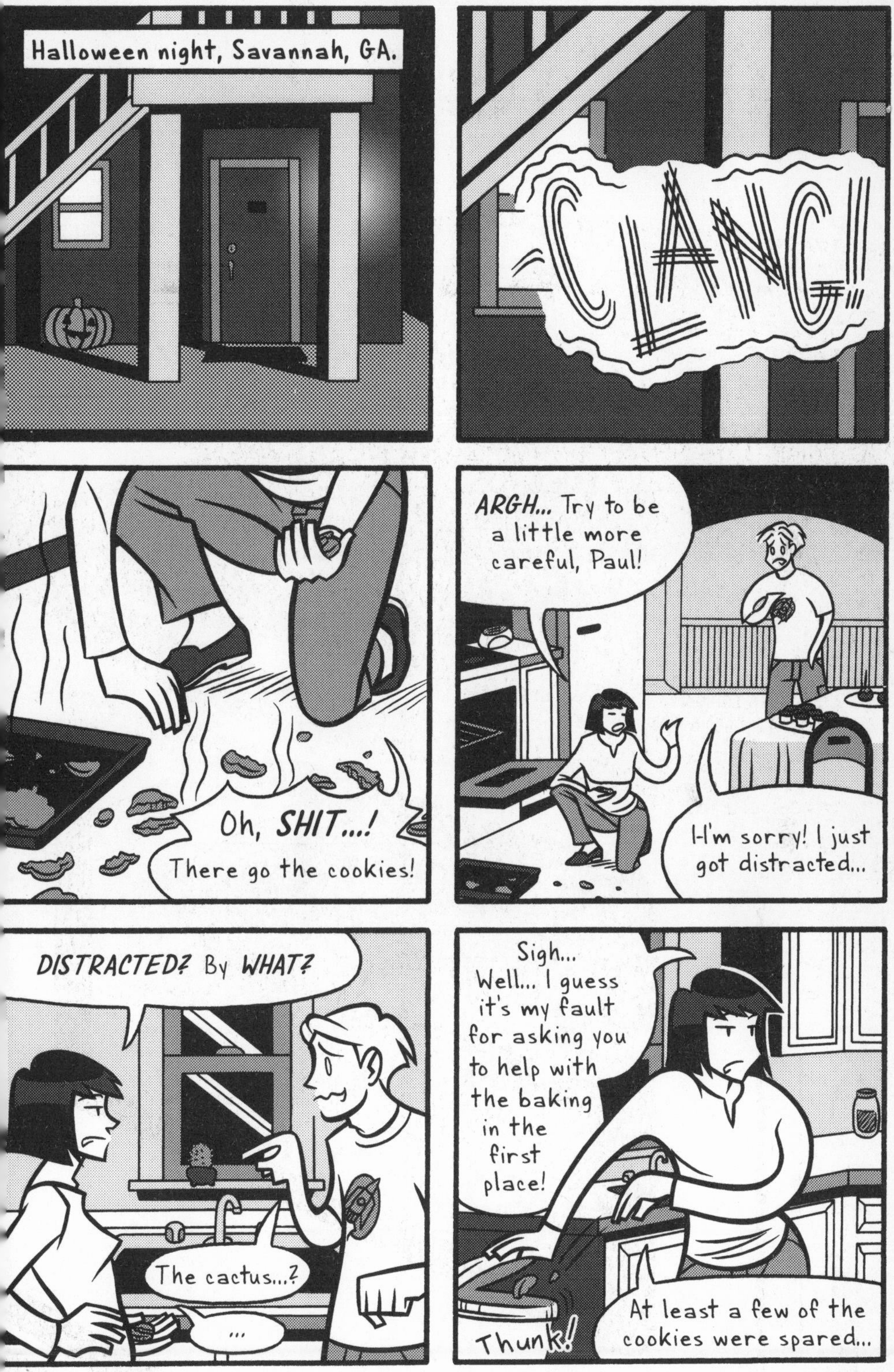
Halloween night, Savannah, GA.
CLANG!!
Oh, SHIT...! There go the cookies!
ARGH... Try to be a little more careful, Paul!
I-I'm sorry! I just got distracted...
DISTRACTED? By WHAT?
The cactus...?
...
Sigh... Well... I guess it's my fault for asking you to help with the baking in the first place!
Thunk!
At least a few of the cookies were spared...

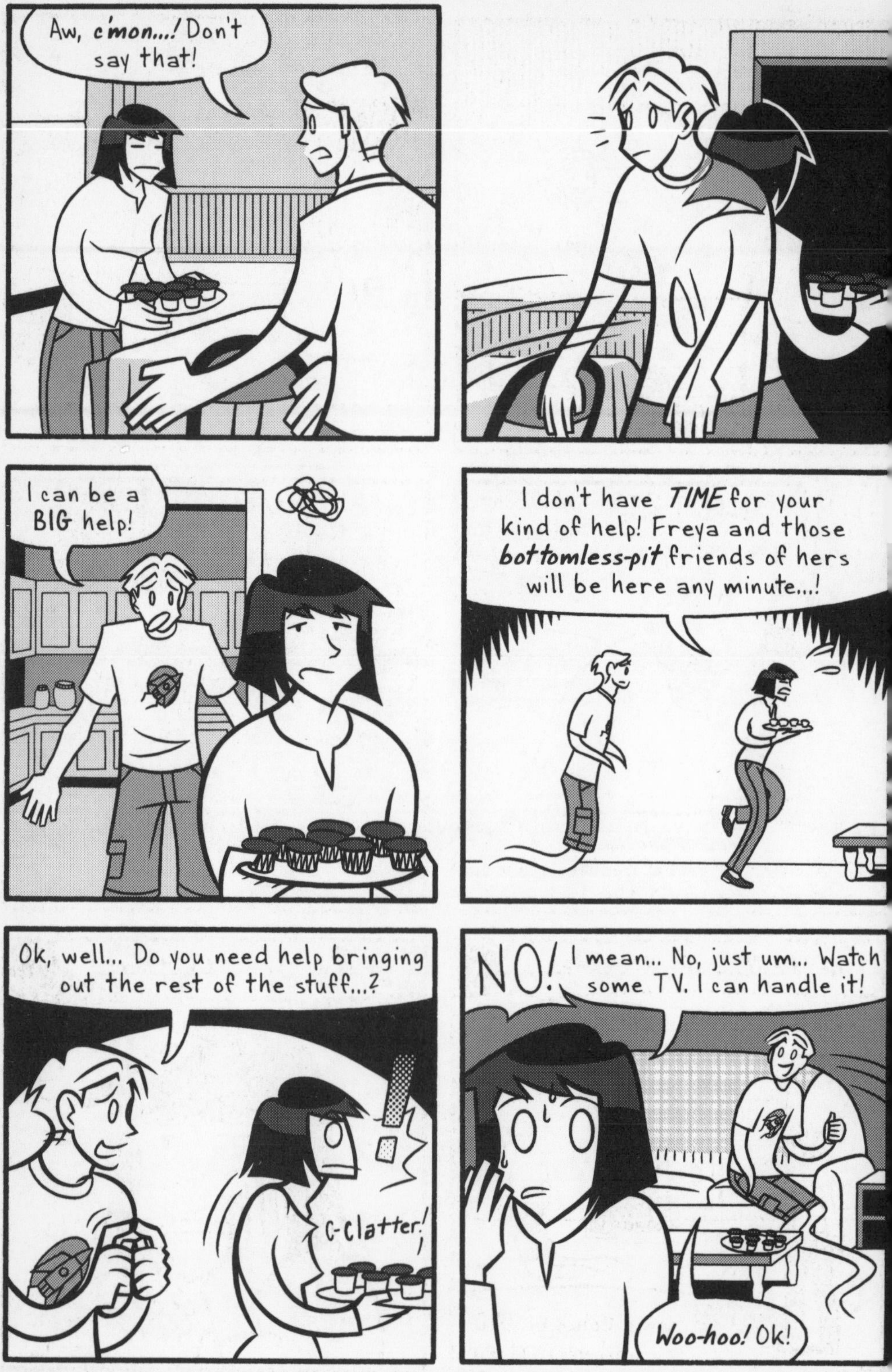
Aw, c'mon...! Don't say that!
I can be a BIG help!
I don't have TIME for your kind of help! Freya and those bottomless-pit friends of hers will be here any minute...!
Ok, well... Do you need help bringing out the rest of the stuff...?
C-Clatter!
NO! I mean... No, just um... Watch some TV. I can handle it!
Woo-hoo! Ok!

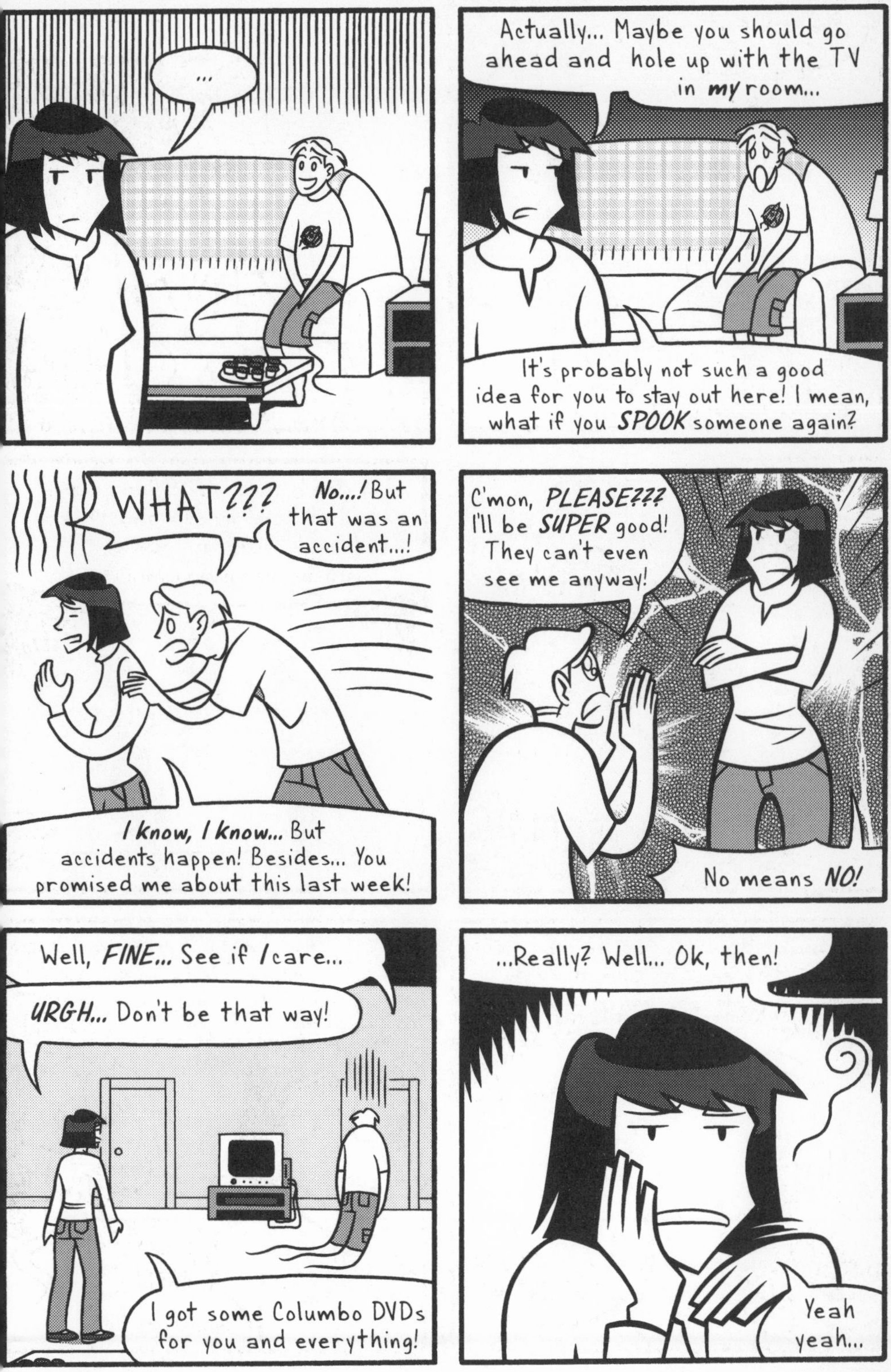
...
Actually... Maybe you should go ahead and hole up with the TV in my room...
It's probably not such a good idea for you to stay out here! I mean, what if you SPOOK someone again?
WHAT???
No...! But that was an accident...!
I know, I know... But accidents happen! Besides... You promised me about this last week!
C'mon, PLEASE??? I'll be SUPER good! They can't even see me anyway!
No means NO!
Well, FINE... See if I care...
URGH... Don't be that way!
I got some Columbo DVDs for you and everything!
...Really? Well... Ok, then!
Yeah yeah...

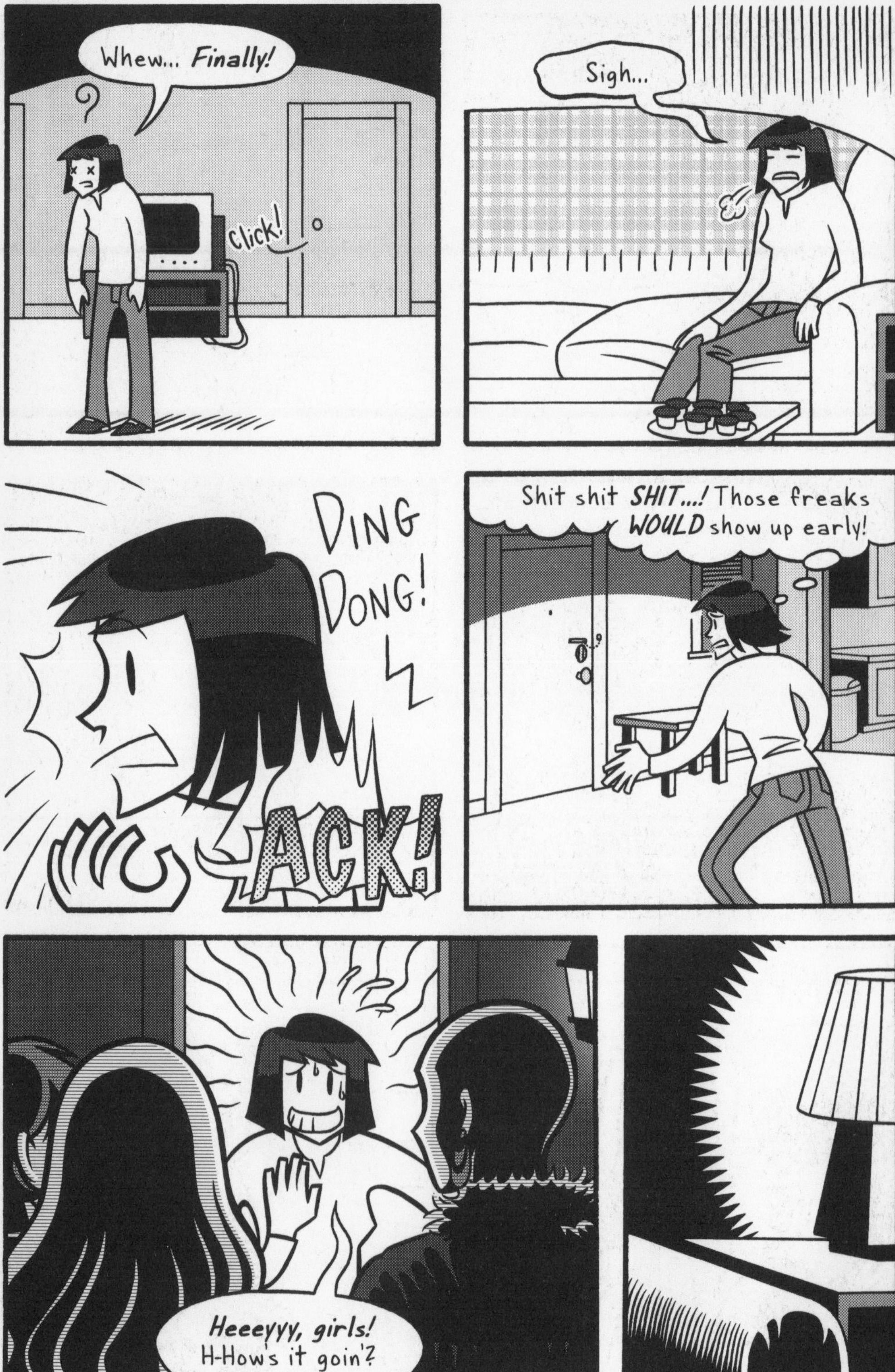
Whew... Finally!
Click!
Sigh...
DING DONG!
ACK!
Shit shit SHIT...! Those freaks WOULD show up early!
Heeeyyy, girls!
H-How's it goin'?

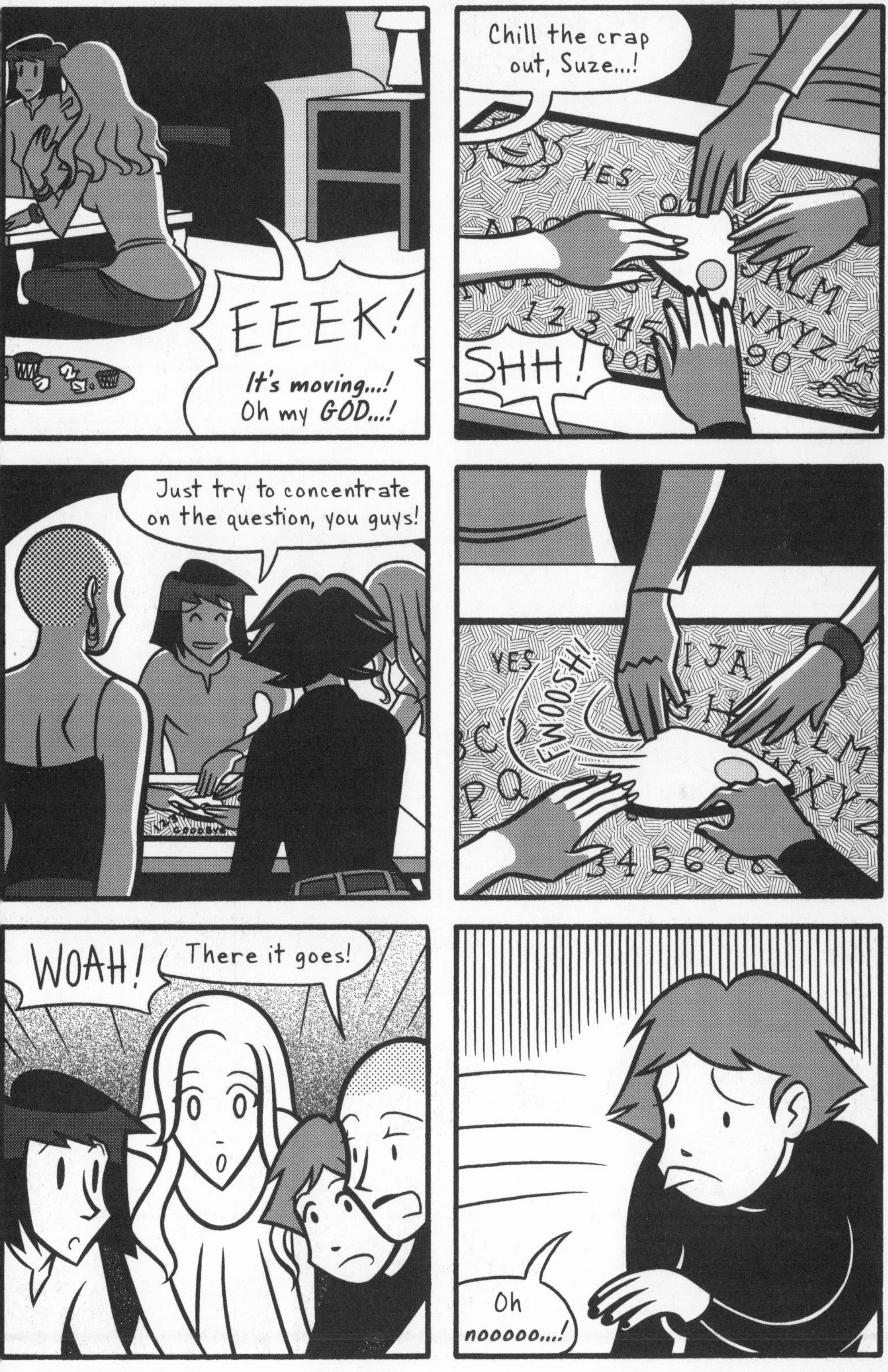
EEEK!
It's moving...! Oh my GOD...!
Chill the crap out, Suze...!
SHH!
Just try to concentrate on the question, you guys!
WOOSH!
WOAH!
There it goes!
Oh nooooo...!

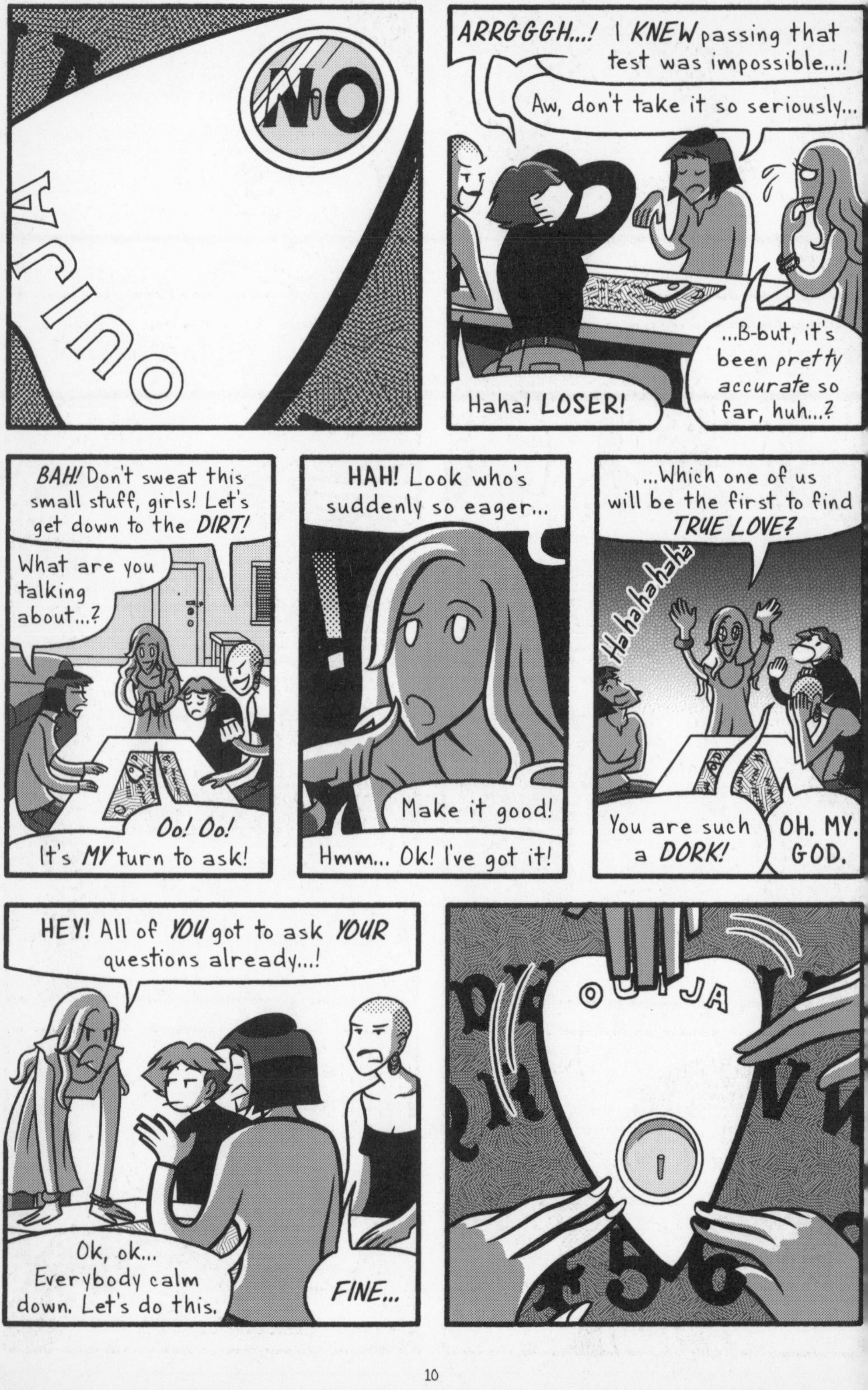
NO
OUIJA
ARRGGGH...! I KNEW passing that test was impossible...!
Aw, don't take it so seriously...
Haha! LOSER!
...B-but, it's been pretty accurate so far, huh...?
BAH! Don't sweat this small stuff, girls! Let's get down to the DIRT!
What are you talking about...?
Oo! Oo!
It's MY turn to ask!
HAH! Look who's suddenly so eager...
Make it good!
Hmm... Ok! I've got it!
...Which one of us will be the first to find TRUE LOVE?
Hahahahaha
You are such a DORK!
OH. MY. GOD.
HEY! All of YOU got to ask YOUR questions already...!
Ok, ok... Everybody calm down. Let's do this.
FINE...
OUIJA

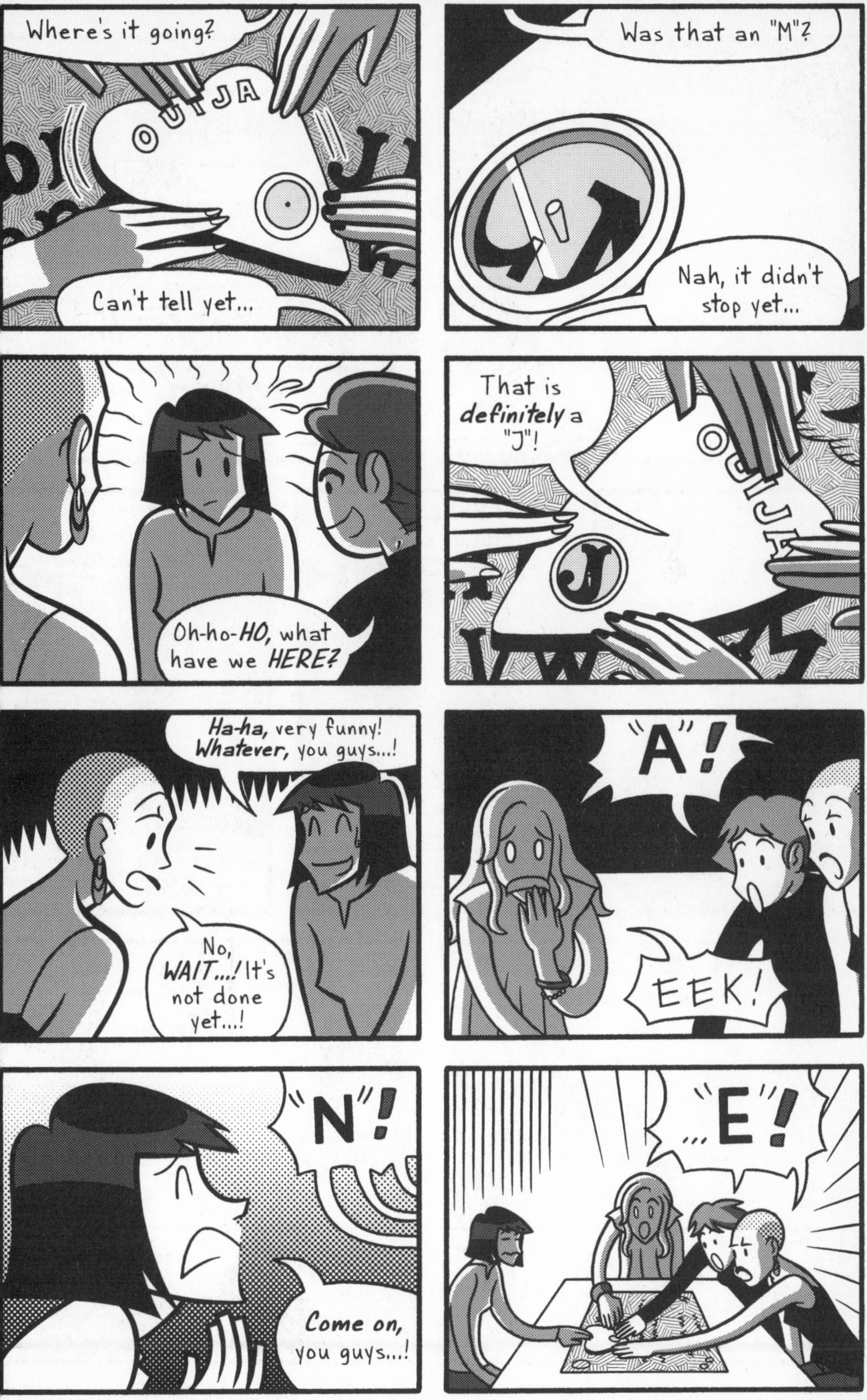
Where's it going?
OUIJA
Can't tell yet...
Was that an "M"?
Nah, it didn't stop yet...
Oh-ho-HO, what have we HERE?
That is definitely a "J"!
Ha-ha, very funny! Whatever, you guys...!
No, WAIT...! It's not done yet...!
"A"!
EEK!
"N"!
Come on, you guys...!
..."E"!

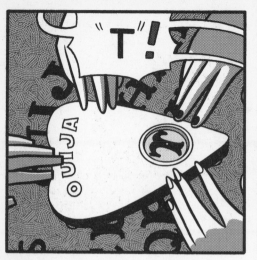

"T"!

"JANET"!

Aw, *LUCKY*... And Janet doesn't even *HAVE* a boyfriend...

Wahahaha!

...sigh.

Hmm...

Hey, wait—! Y'know...

?

...I'd say this bodes well for that BLIND DATE I set you up on...

Twitch!

...*huh*, Janet-baby?

WHAT?!

Is *that* what this is all about?!

Leave me out of your MACHINATIONS! You... You...

GAH!!

...GAME FIXER!

NOW who's taking this too seriously...?!

C-calm down Janet...!

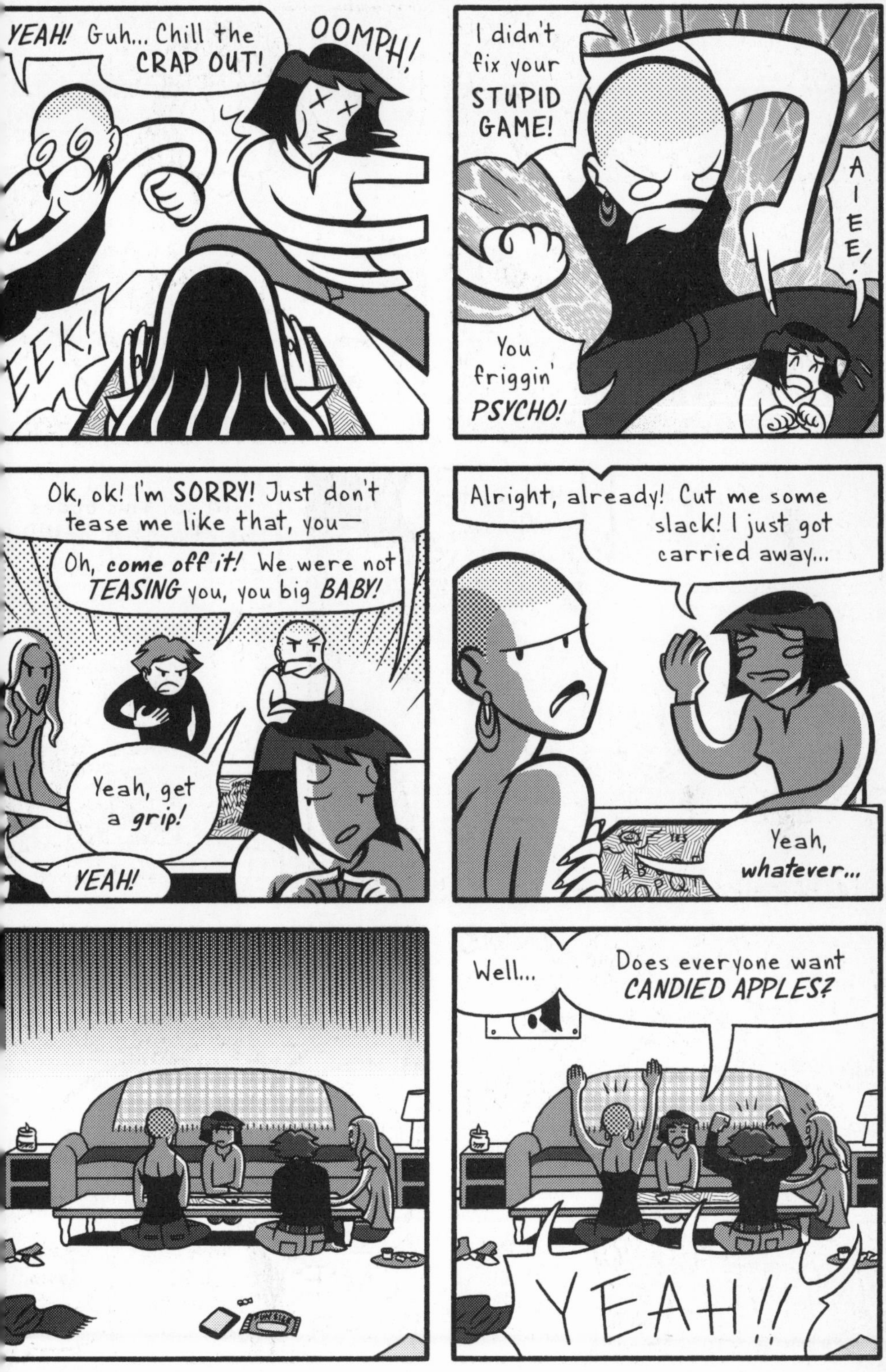
YEAH! Guh... Chill the CRAP OUT!
OOMPH!
EEK!
I didn't fix your STUPID GAME!
AIEE!
You friggin' PSYCHO!
Ok, ok! I'm SORRY! Just don't tease me like that, you—
Oh, come off it! We were not TEASING you, you big BABY!
Yeah, get a grip!
YEAH!
Alright, already! Cut me some slack! I just got carried away...
Yeah, whatever...
Well...
Does everyone want CANDIED APPLES?
YEAH!!

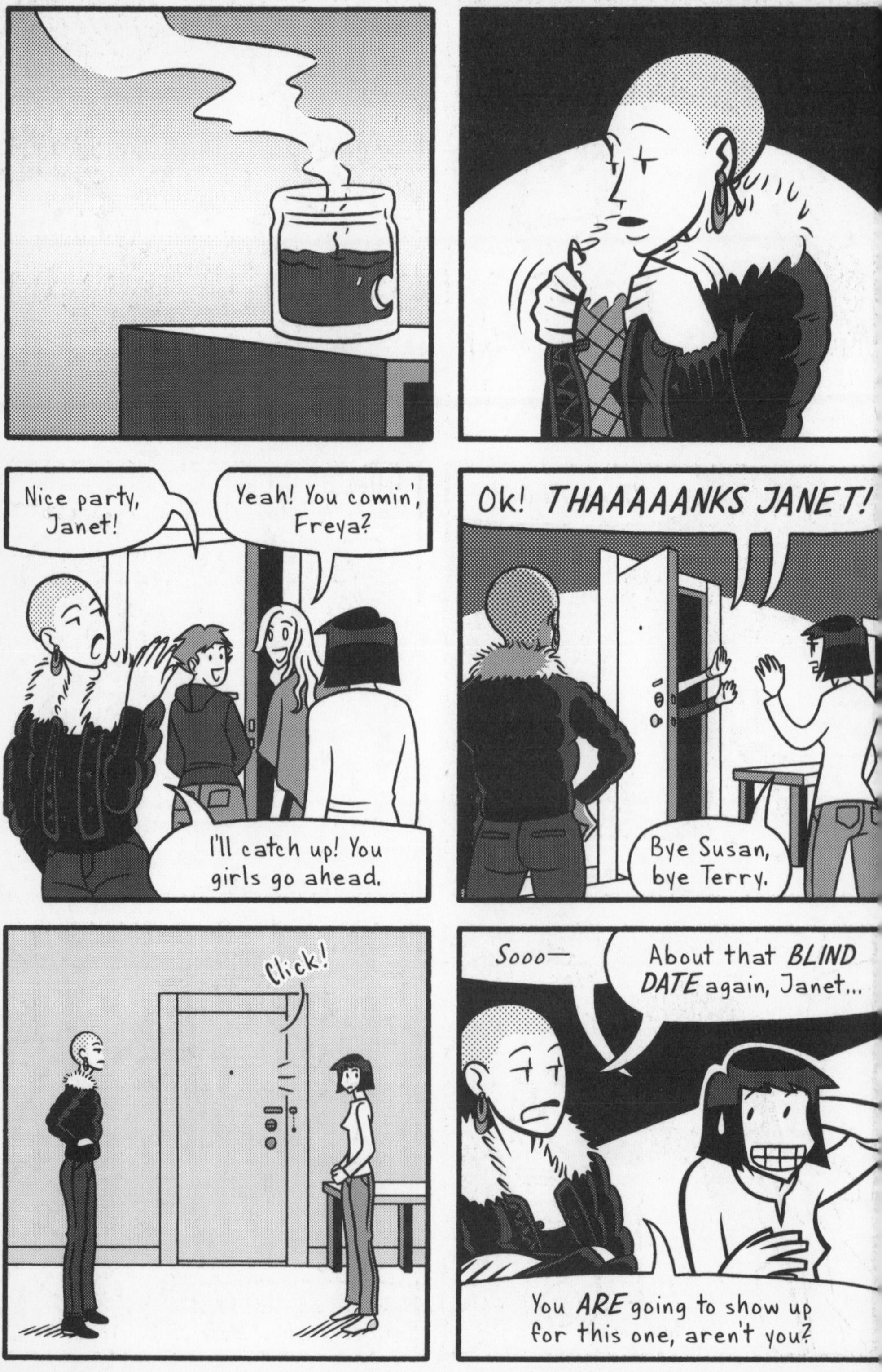
Nice party, Janet!
Yeah! You comin', Freya?
I'll catch up! You girls go ahead.
Ok! THAAAAANKS JANET!
Bye Susan, bye Terry.
Click!
Sooo—
About that BLIND DATE again, Janet...
You ARE going to show up for this one, aren't you?

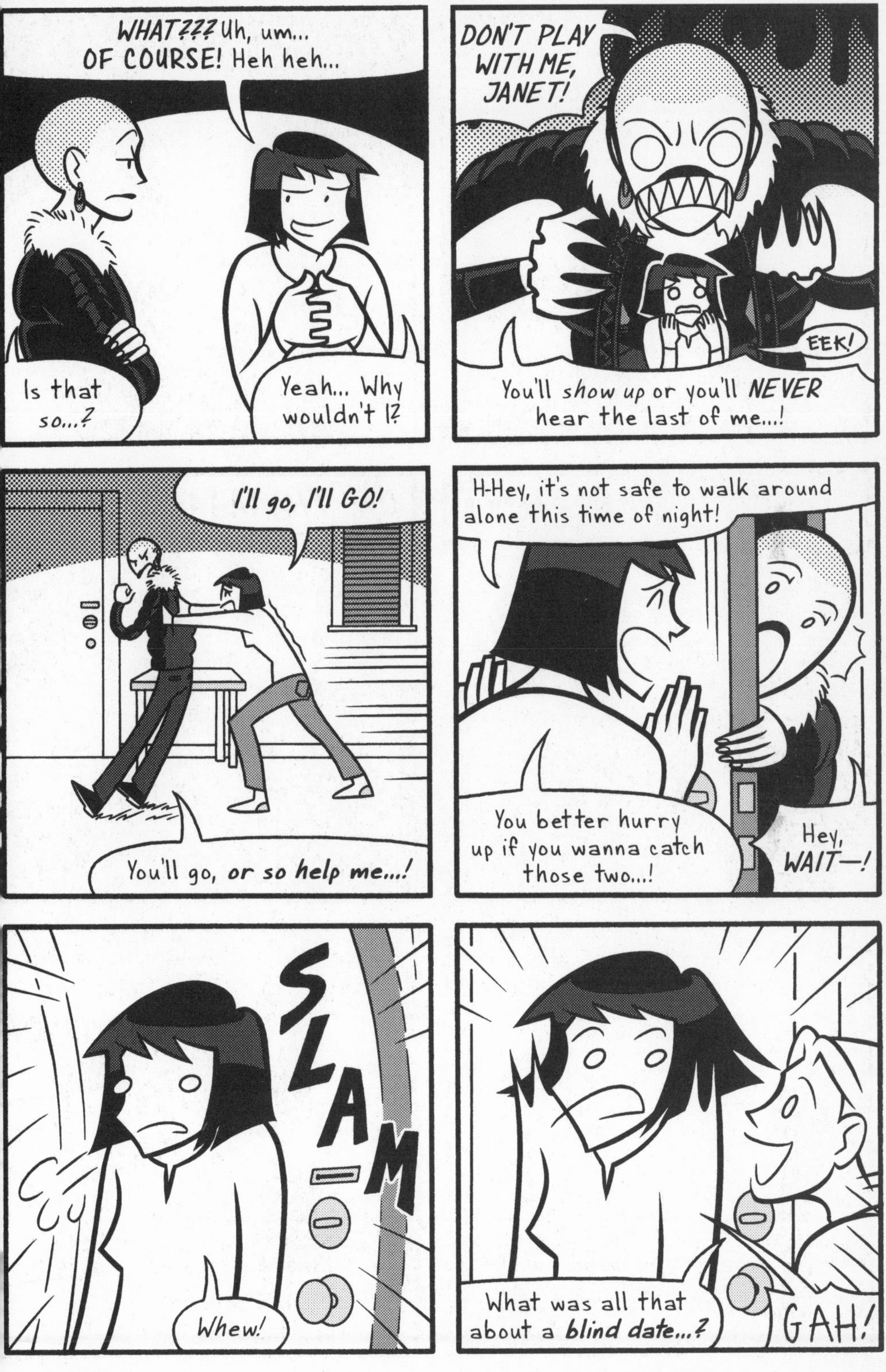
WHAT??? Uh, um... OF COURSE! Heh heh...
Is that so...?
Yeah... Why wouldn't I?
DON'T PLAY WITH ME, JANET!
EEK!
You'll *show up* or you'll **NEVER** hear the last of me...!
I'll go, I'll GO!
You'll go, **or so help me...!**
H-Hey, it's not safe to walk around alone this time of night!
You better hurry up if you wanna catch those two...!
Hey, WAIT—!
SLAM
Whew!
What was all that about a **blind date...?**
GAH!

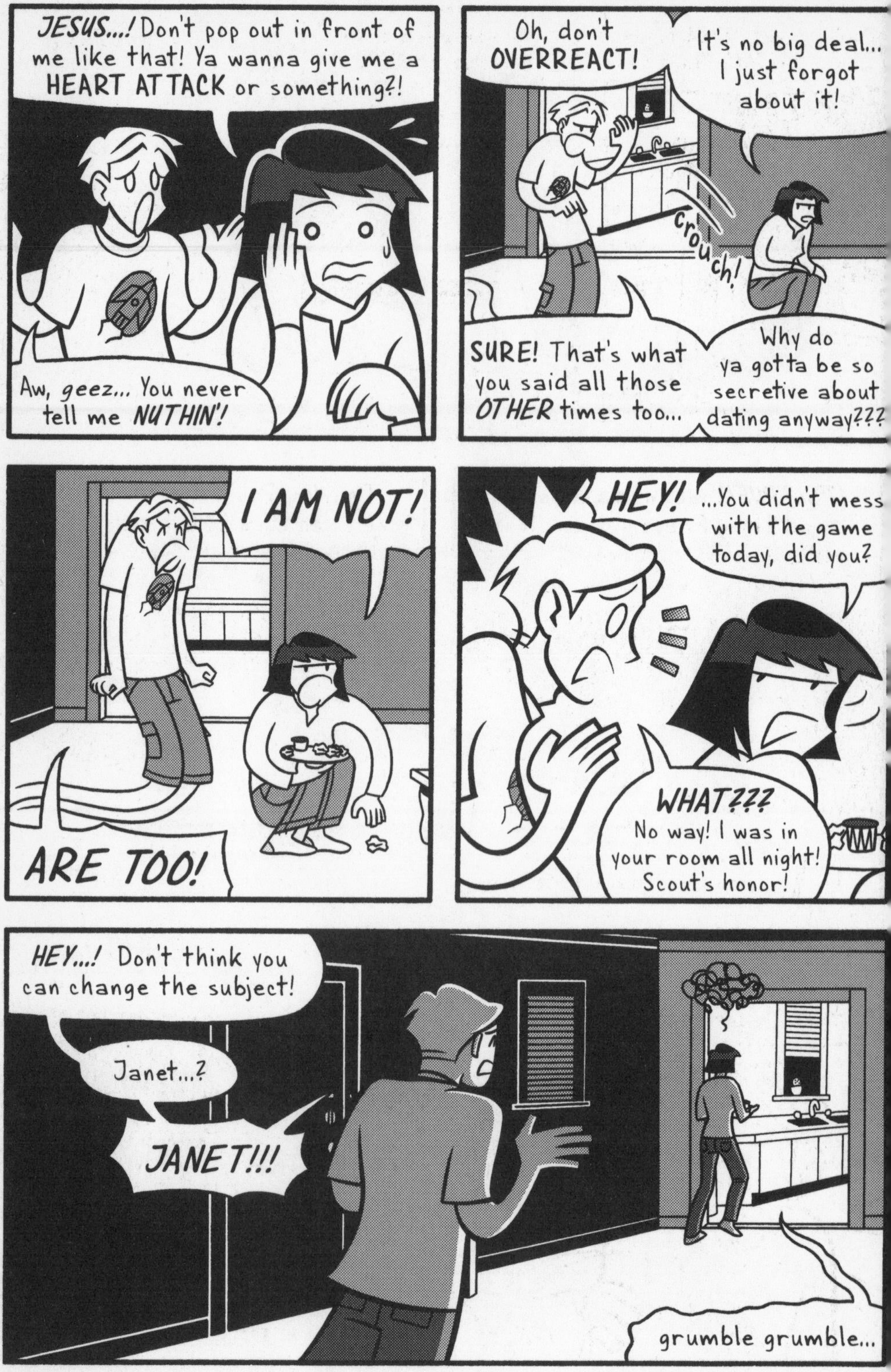
JESUS...! Don't pop out in front of me like that! Ya wanna give me a HEART ATTACK or something?!
Aw, geez... You never tell me NUTHIN'!
Oh, don't OVERREACT!
It's no big deal... I just forgot about it!
crouch!
SURE! That's what you said all those OTHER times too...
Why do ya gotta be so secretive about dating anyway???
I AM NOT!
ARE TOO!
HEY!
...You didn't mess with the game today, did you?
WHAT??? No way! I was in your room all night! Scout's honor!
HEY...! Don't think you can change the subject!
Janet...?
JANET!!!
grumble grumble...

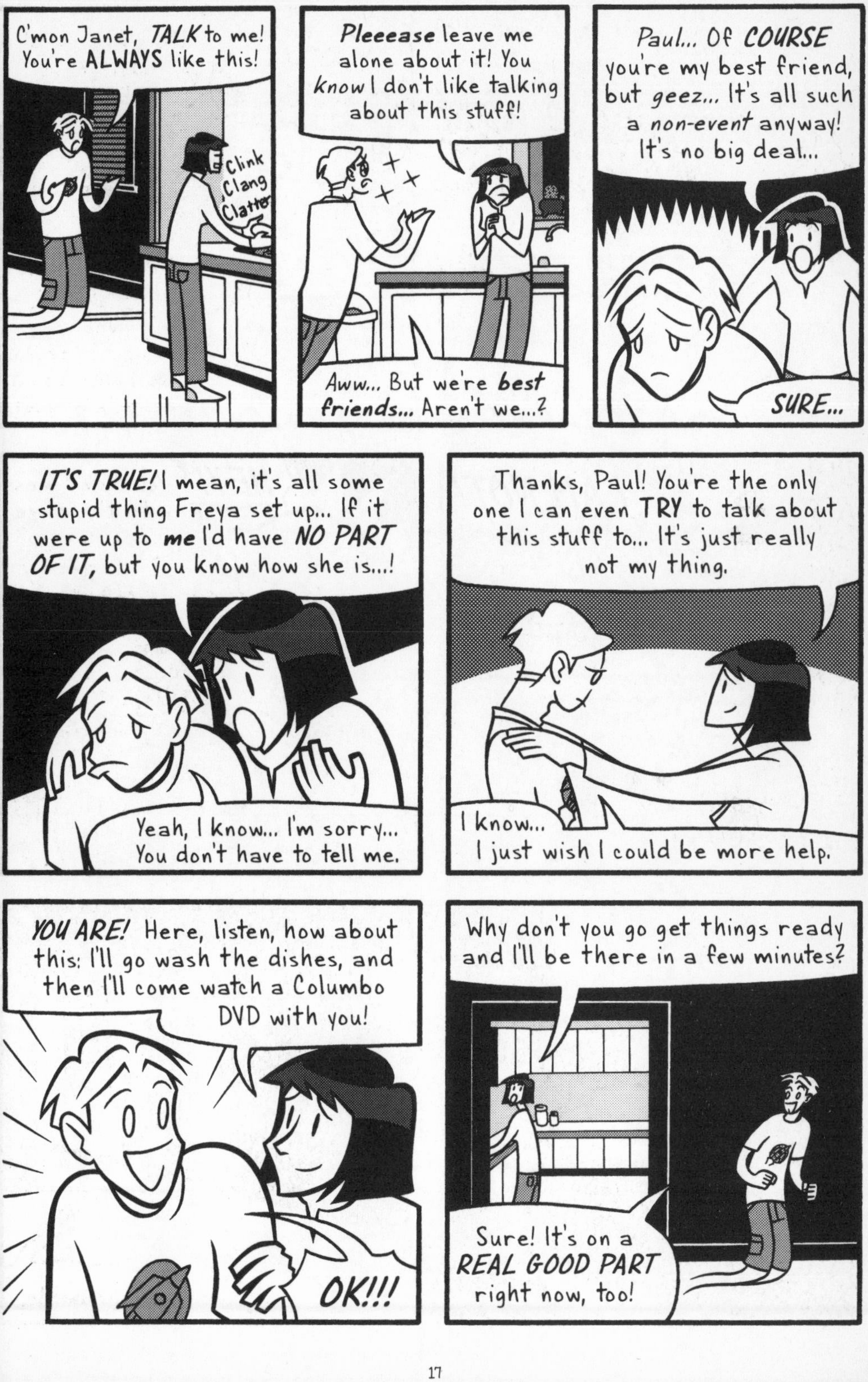
C'mon Janet, TALK to me! You're ALWAYS like this!
Clink Clang Clatter
Pleeease leave me alone about it! You know I don't like talking about this stuff!
Aww... But we're best friends... Aren't we...?
Paul... Of COURSE you're my best friend, but geez... It's all such a non-event anyway! It's no big deal...
SURE...
IT'S TRUE! I mean, it's all some stupid thing Freya set up... If it were up to me I'd have NO PART OF IT, but you know how she is...!
Yeah, I know... I'm sorry... You don't have to tell me.
Thanks, Paul! You're the only one I can even TRY to talk about this stuff to... It's just really not my thing.
I know... I just wish I could be more help.
YOU ARE! Here, listen, how about this: I'll go wash the dishes, and then I'll come watch a Columbo DVD with you!
OK!!!
Why don't you go get things ready and I'll be there in a few minutes?
Sure! It's on a REAL GOOD PART right now, too!

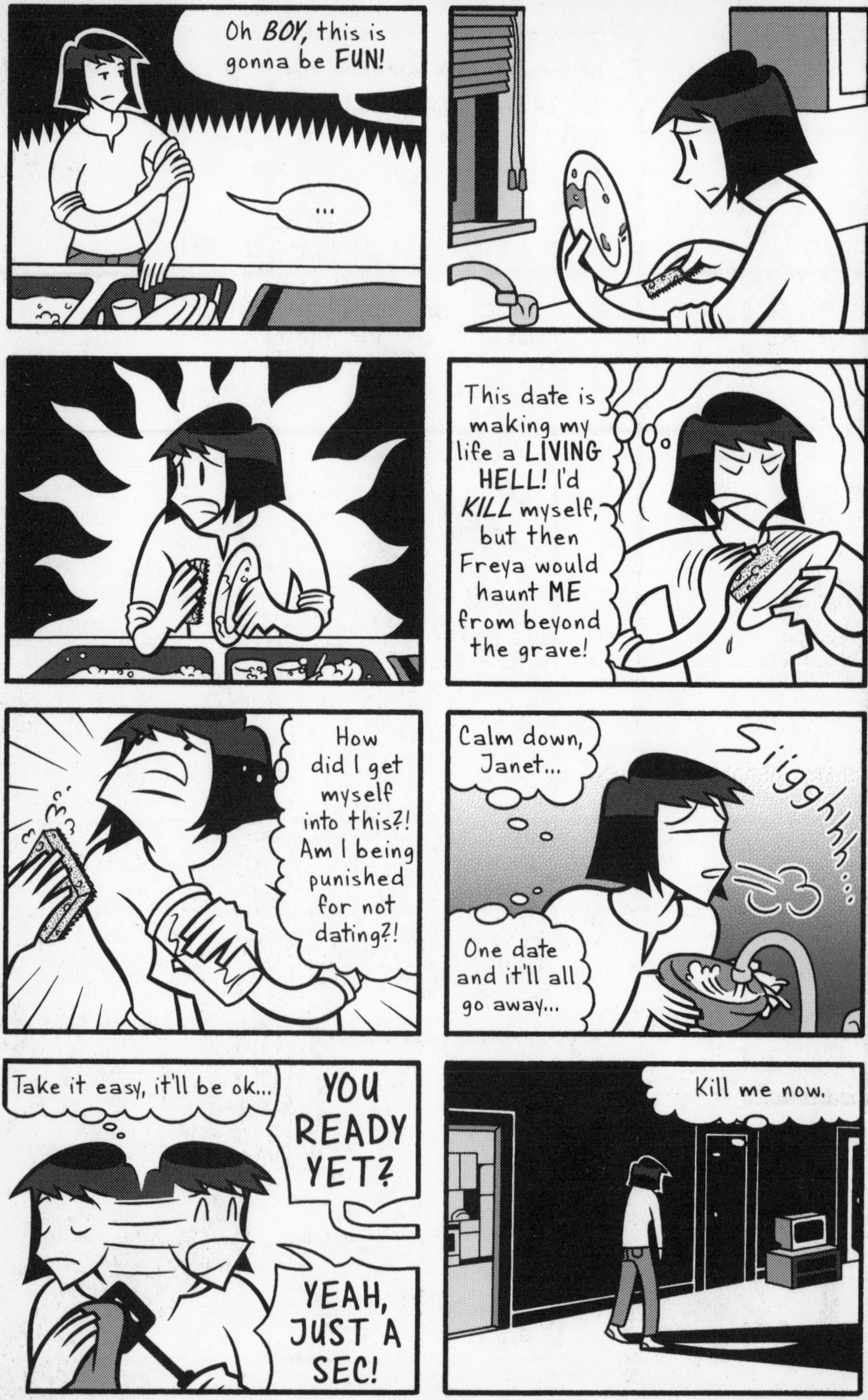
Oh BOY, this is gonna be FUN!
...
This date is making my life a LIVING HELL! I'd KILL myself, but then Freya would haunt ME from beyond the grave!
How did I get myself into this?! Am I being punished for not dating?!
Calm down, Janet...
Siigghhh...
One date and it'll all go away...
Take it easy, it'll be ok...
YOU READY YET?
YEAH, JUST A SEC!
Kill me now.

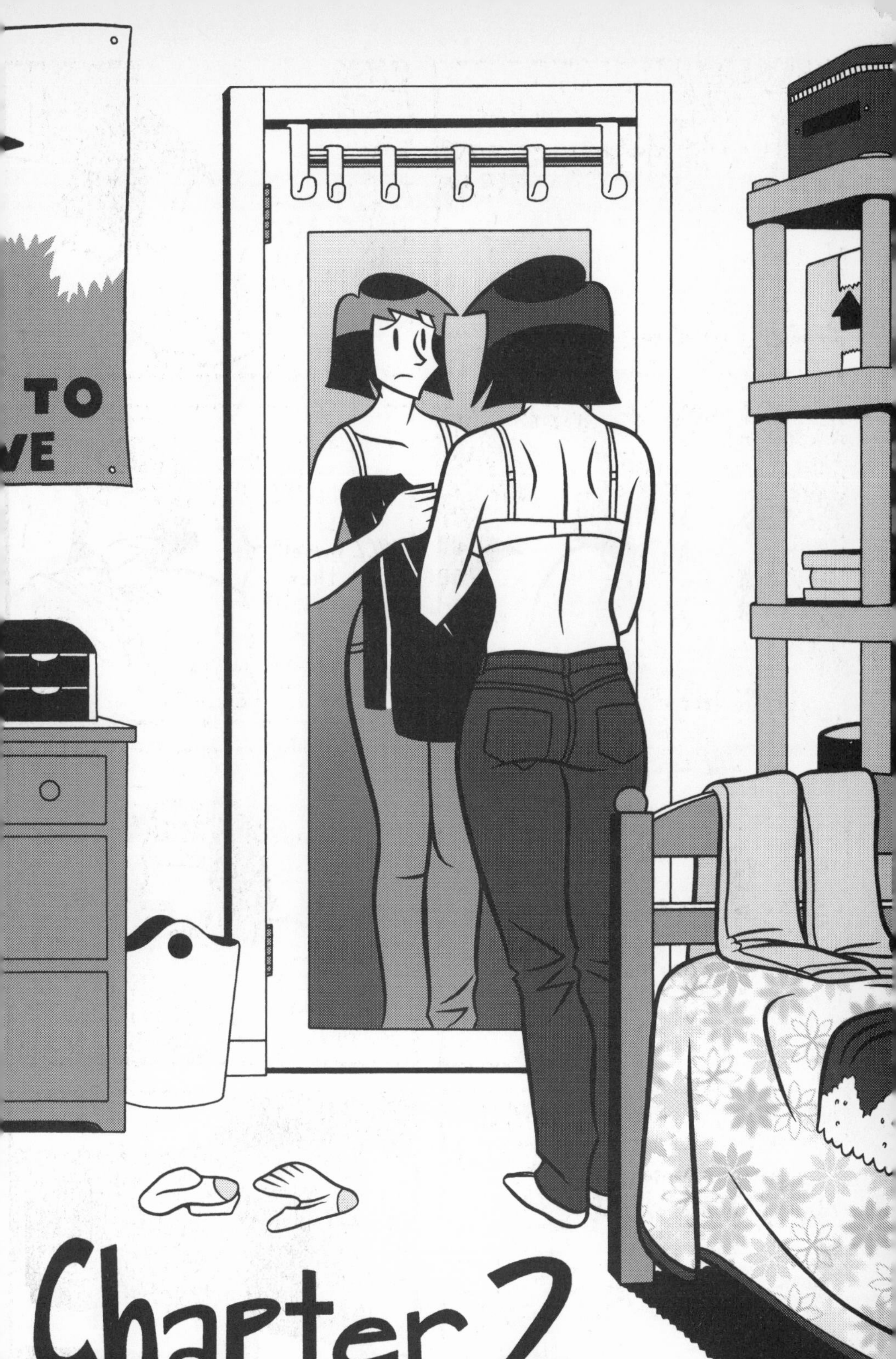
TO

Chapter 2

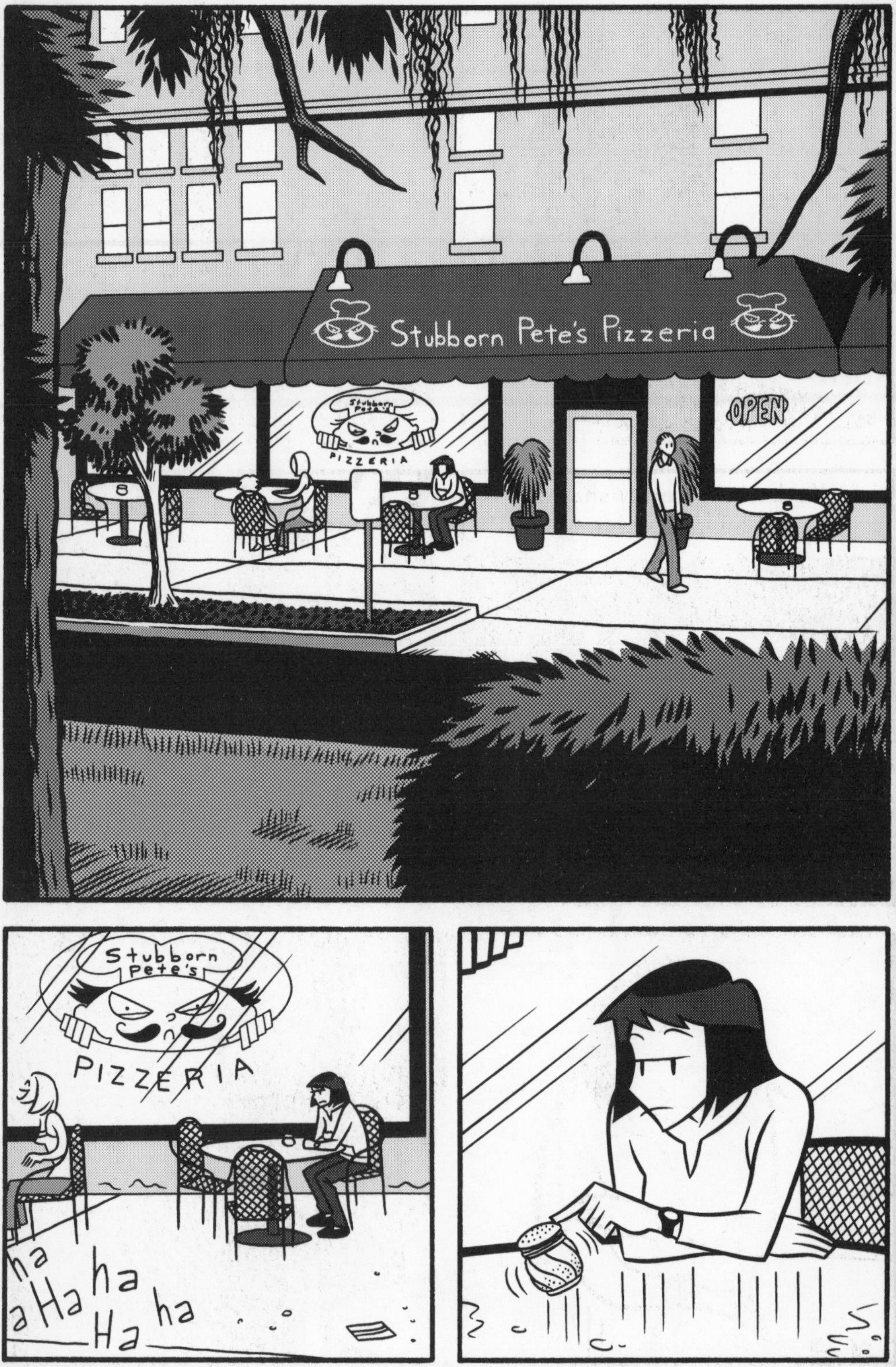
Stubborn Pete's Pizzeria
PIZZERIA
OPEN
Stubborn Pete's
PIZZERIA
ha
aHa ha
Ha ha

Why did we have to go out for *lunch?* I'm too nauseous to eat! I'll *PUKE* before I eat! I haven't puked in years...!

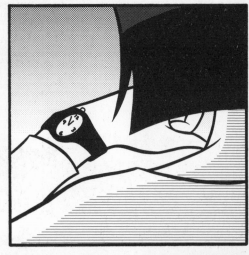

Maybe he already showed up and left! I'd never know!

If I was smart, I'd leave now too!

If he doesn't show up by 1, I'm leaving! I should just get out of here right now!

Hi, um... Are you Janet?

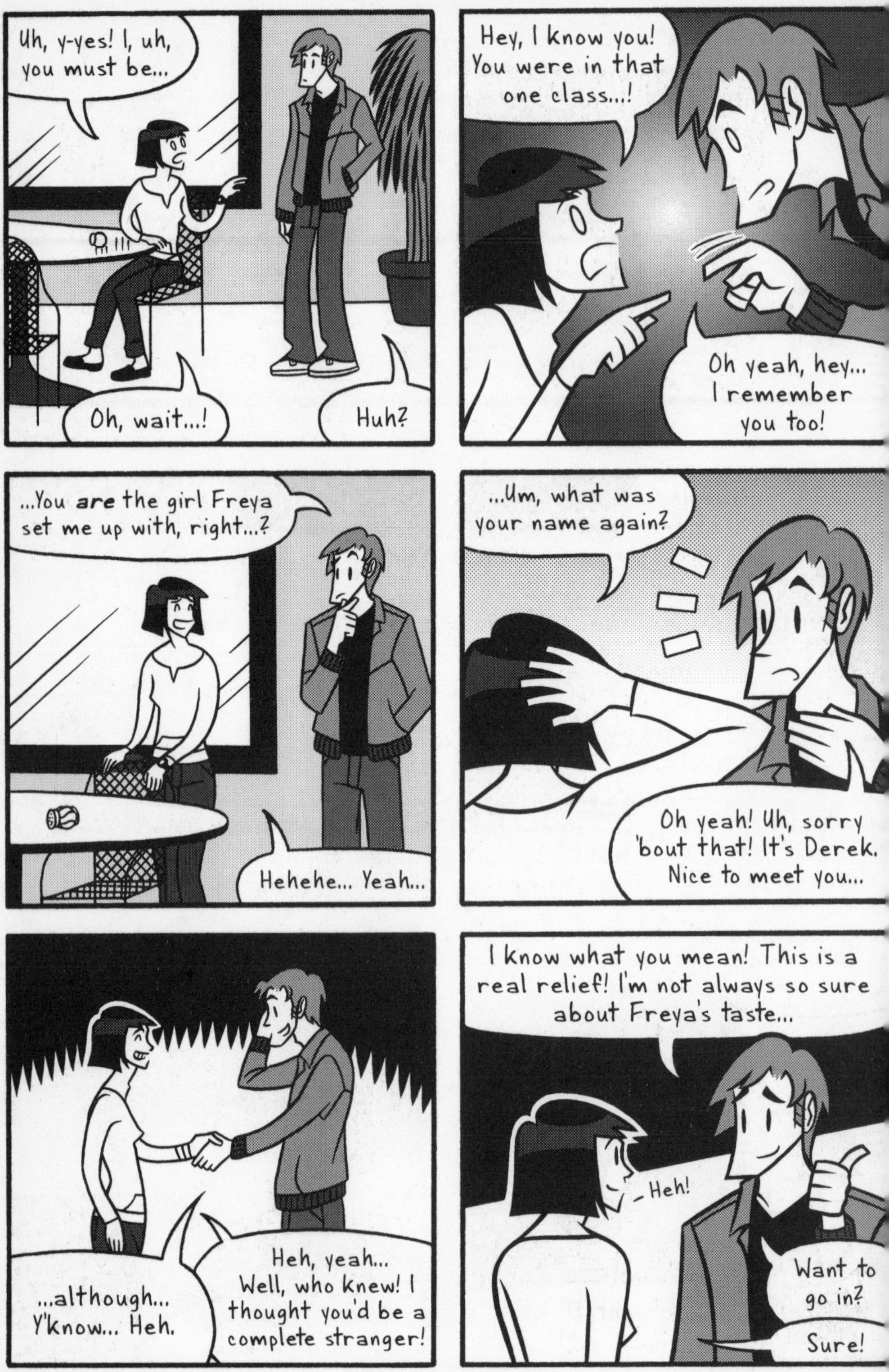
Uh, y-yes! I, uh, you must be...
Oh, wait...!
Huh?
Hey, I know you! You were in that one class...!
Oh yeah, hey... I remember you too!
...You **are** the girl Freya set me up with, right...?
Hehehe... Yeah...
...Um, what was your name again?
Oh yeah! Uh, sorry 'bout that! It's Derek. Nice to meet you...
...although... Y'know... Heh.
Heh, yeah... Well, who knew! I thought you'd be a complete stranger!
I know what you mean! This is a real relief! I'm not always so sure about Freya's taste...
-Heh!
Want to go in?
Sure!

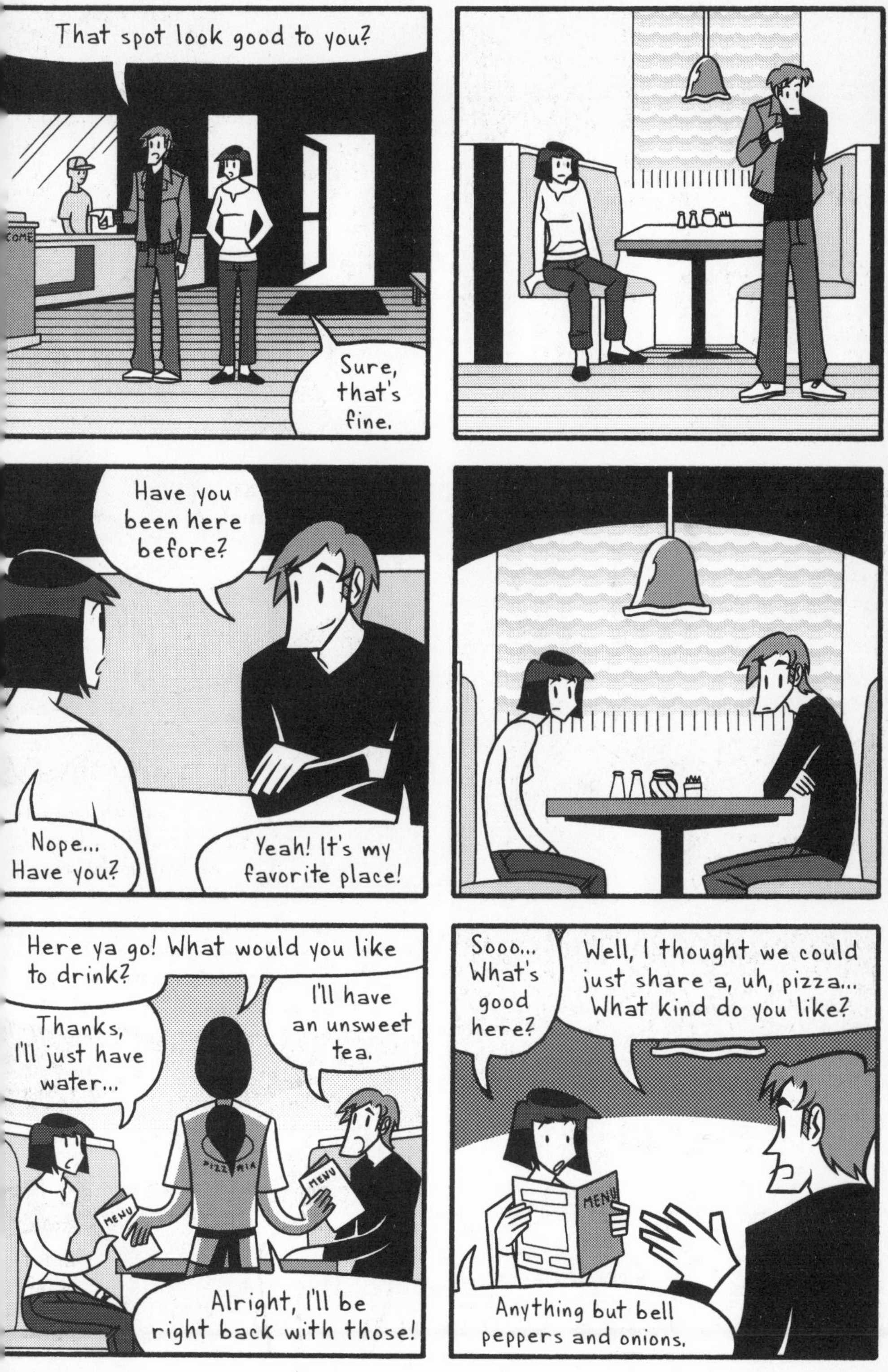
That spot look good to you?
Sure, that's fine.
Have you been here before?
Nope... Have you?
Yeah! It's my favorite place!
Here ya go! What would you like to drink?
Thanks, I'll just have water...
I'll have an unsweet tea.
MENU
PIZZERIA
MENU
Alright, I'll be right back with those!
Sooo... What's good here?
Well, I thought we could just share a, uh, pizza... What kind do you like?
MENU
Anything but bell peppers and onions.

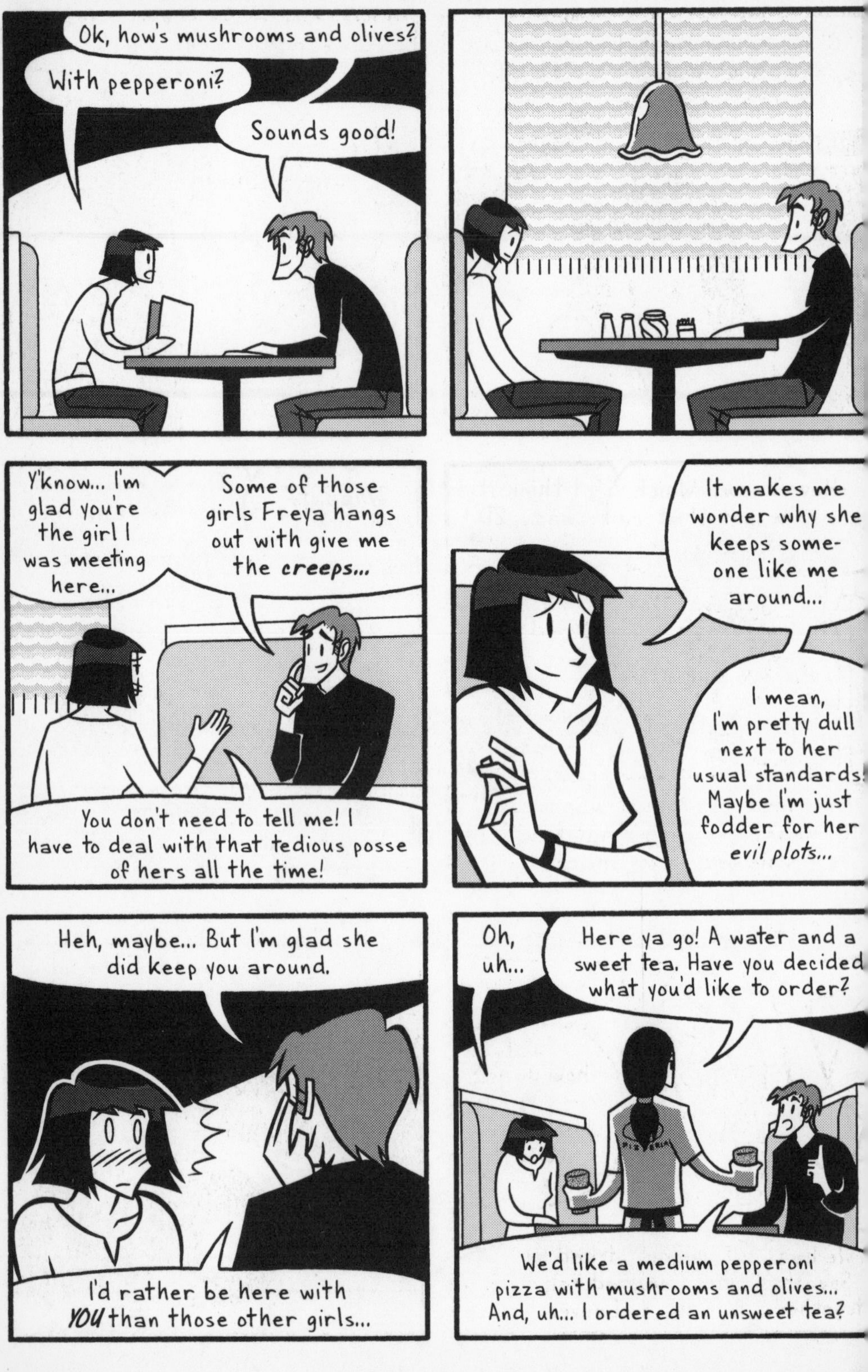
Ok, how's mushrooms and olives?
With pepperoni?
Sounds good!
Y'know... I'm glad you're the girl I was meeting here...
Some of those girls Freya hangs out with give me the *creeps...*
You don't need to tell me! I have to deal with that tedious posse of hers all the time!
It makes me wonder why she keeps someone like me around...
I mean, I'm pretty dull next to her usual standards! Maybe I'm just fodder for her *evil plots...*
Heh, maybe... But I'm glad she did keep you around.
I'd rather be here with *YOU* than those other girls...
Oh, uh...
Here ya go! A water and a sweet tea. Have you decided what you'd like to order?
We'd like a medium pepperoni pizza with mushrooms and olives... And, uh... I ordered an unsweet tea?

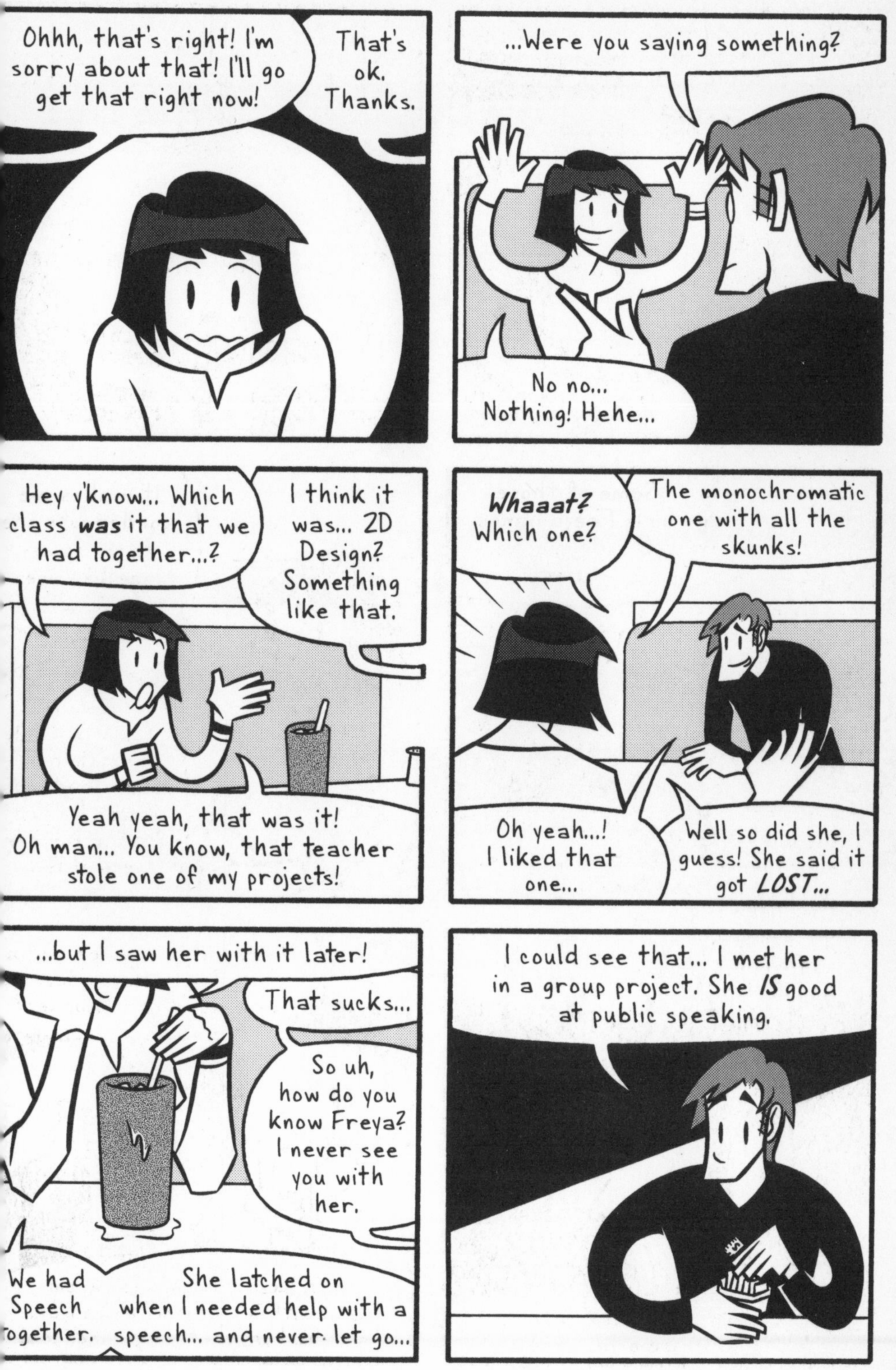
Ohhh, that's right! I'm sorry about that! I'll go get that right now!
That's ok. Thanks.
...Were you saying something?
No no... Nothing! Hehe...
Hey y'know... Which class **was** it that we had together...?
I think it was... 2D Design? Something like that.
Yeah yeah, that was it! Oh man... You know, that teacher stole one of my projects!
Whaaat? Which one?
The monochromatic one with all the skunks!
Oh yeah...! I liked that one...
Well so did she, I guess! She said it got ***LOST***...
...but I saw her with it later!
That sucks...
So uh, how do you know Freya? I never see you with her.
We had Speech together.
She latched on when I needed help with a speech... and never let go...
I could see that... I met her in a group project. She ***IS*** good at public speaking.

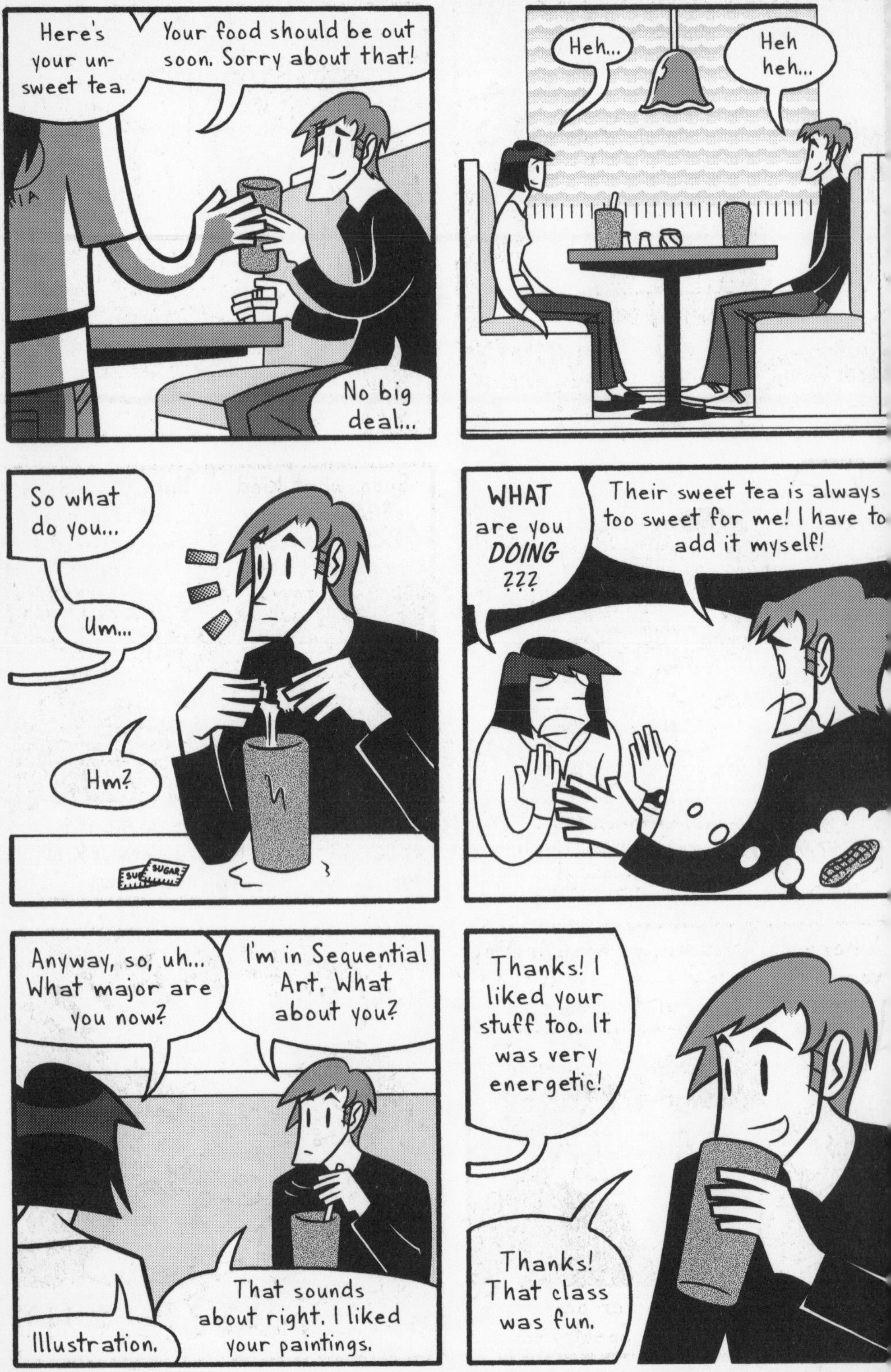
Here's your un-sweet tea.
Your food should be out soon. Sorry about that!
No big deal...
Heh...
Heh heh...
So what do you...
Um...
Hm?
SUGAR
WHAT are you DOING ???
Their sweet tea is always too sweet for me! I have to add it myself!
Anyway, so, uh... What major are you now?
I'm in Sequential Art. What about you?
Illustration.
That sounds about right. I liked your paintings.
Thanks! I liked your stuff too. It was very energetic!
Thanks! That class was fun.

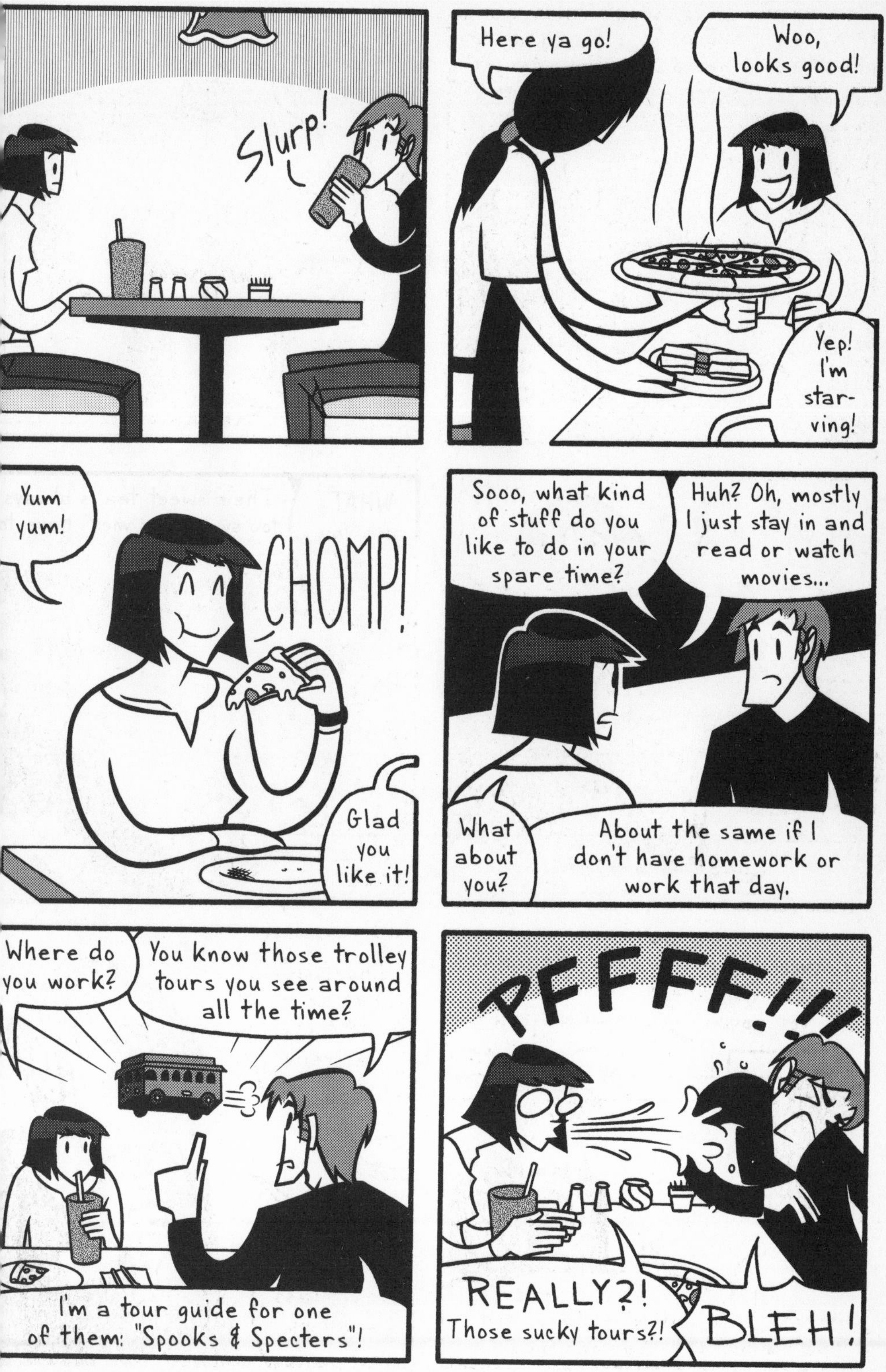
Slurp!
Here ya go!
Woo, looks good!
Yep! I'm star-ving!
Yum yum!
CHOMP!
Glad you like it!
Sooo, what kind of stuff do you like to do in your spare time?
Huh? Oh, mostly I just stay in and read or watch movies...
What about you?
About the same if I don't have homework or work that day.
Where do you work?
You know those trolley tours you see around all the time?
I'm a tour guide for one of them: "Spooks & Specters"!
PFFFF!!!
REALLY?! Those sucky tours?!
BLEH!

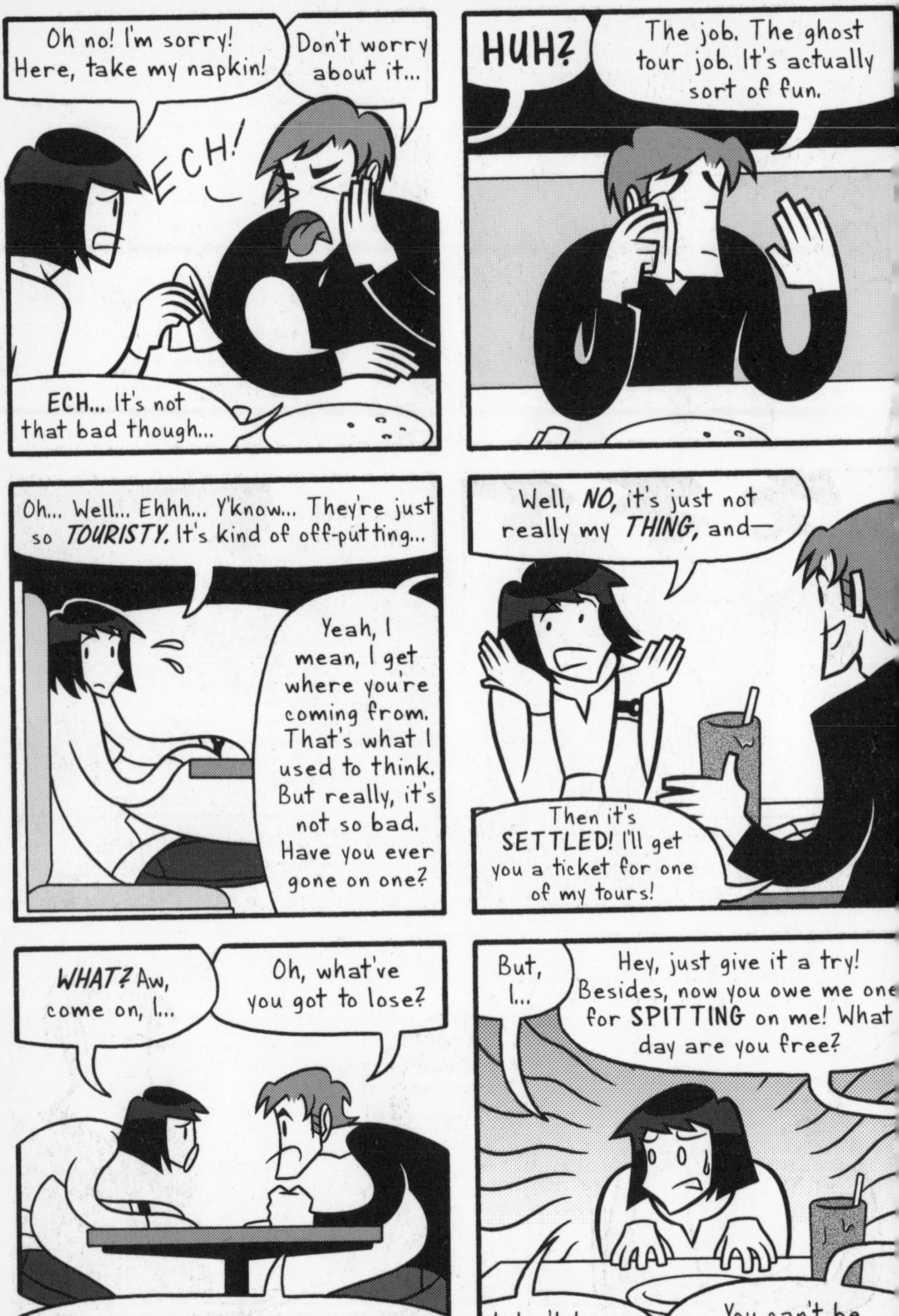
Oh no! I'm sorry! Here, take my napkin!
Don't worry about it...
ECH!
ECH... It's not that bad though...
HUH?
The job. The ghost tour job. It's actually sort of fun.
Oh... Well... Ehhh... Y'know... They're just so TOURISTY. It's kind of off-putting...
Yeah, I mean, I get where you're coming from. That's what I used to think. But really, it's not so bad. Have you ever gone on one?
Well, NO, it's just not really my THING, and—
Then it's SETTLED! I'll get you a ticket for one of my tours!
WHAT? Aw, come on, I...
Oh, what've you got to lose?
It's free, easy to get there, they run like EVERY night... WHY NOT? It'll be fun!
But, I...
Hey, just give it a try! Besides, now you owe me one for SPITTING on me! What day are you free?
I don't know really, uh...
You can't be busy EVERY day!

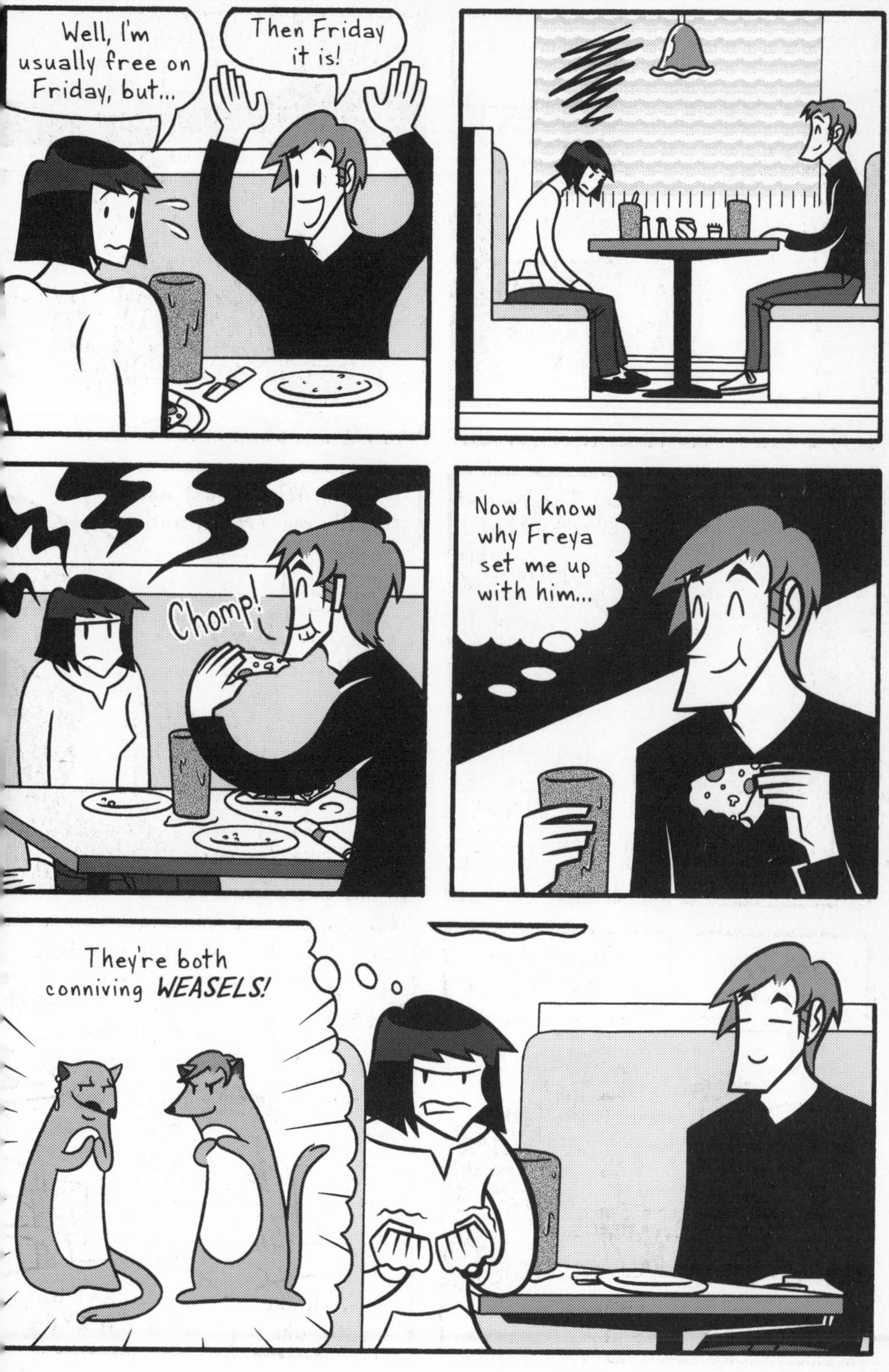
Well, I'm usually free on Friday, but...
Then Friday it is!
Chomp!
Now I know why Freya set me up with him...
They're both conniving WEASELS!

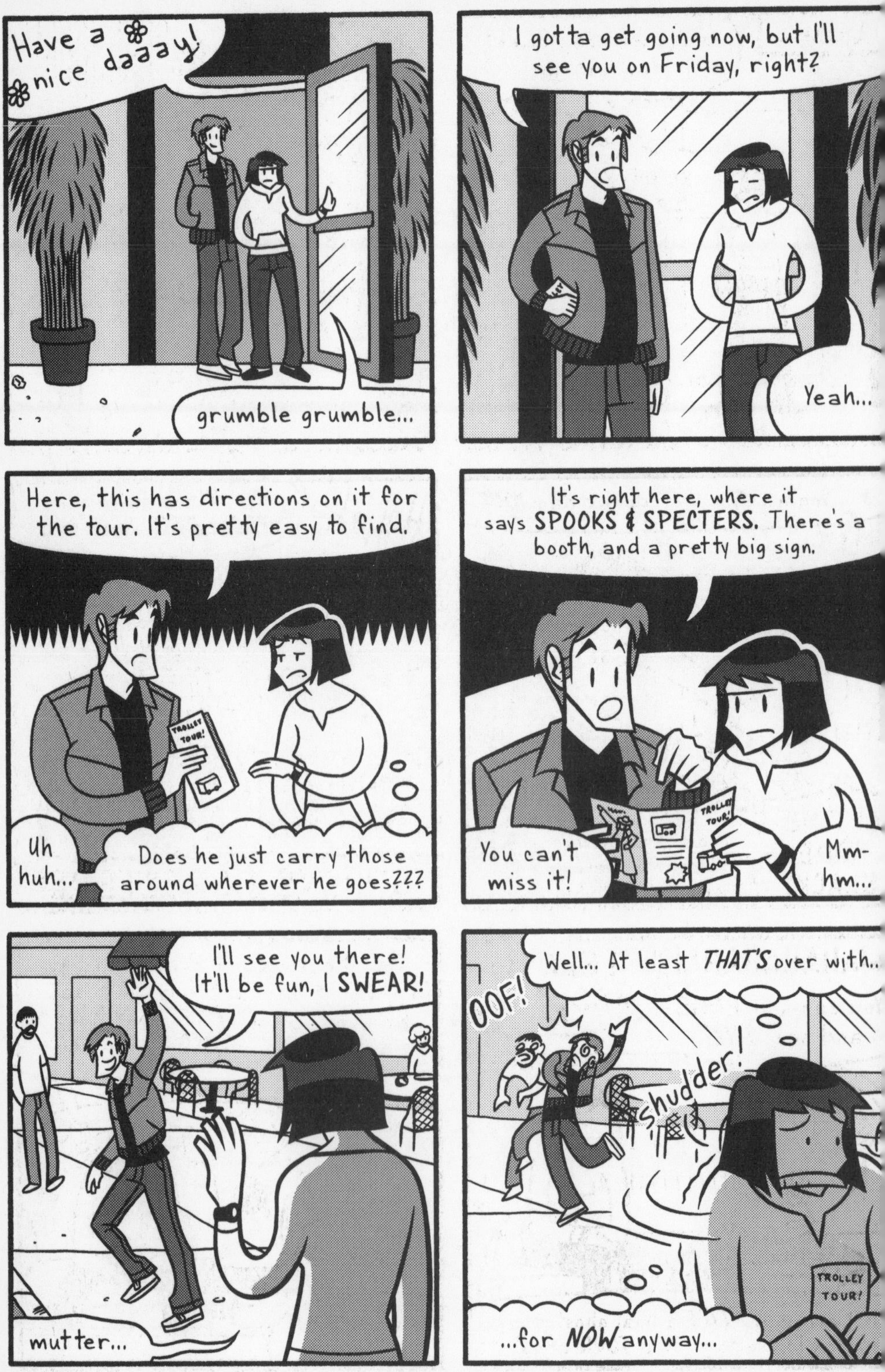
Have a nice daaay!
grumble grumble...
I gotta get going now, but I'll see you on Friday, right?
Yeah...
Here, this has directions on it for the tour. It's pretty easy to find.
TROLLEY TOUR!
Uh huh...
Does he just carry those around wherever he goes???
It's right here, where it says SPOOKS & SPECTERS. There's a booth, and a pretty big sign.
TROLLEY TOUR!
You can't miss it!
Mm-hm...
I'll see you there! It'll be fun, I SWEAR!
mutter...
Well... At least THAT'S over with...
OOF!
shudder!
TROLLEY TOUR!
...for NOW anyway...

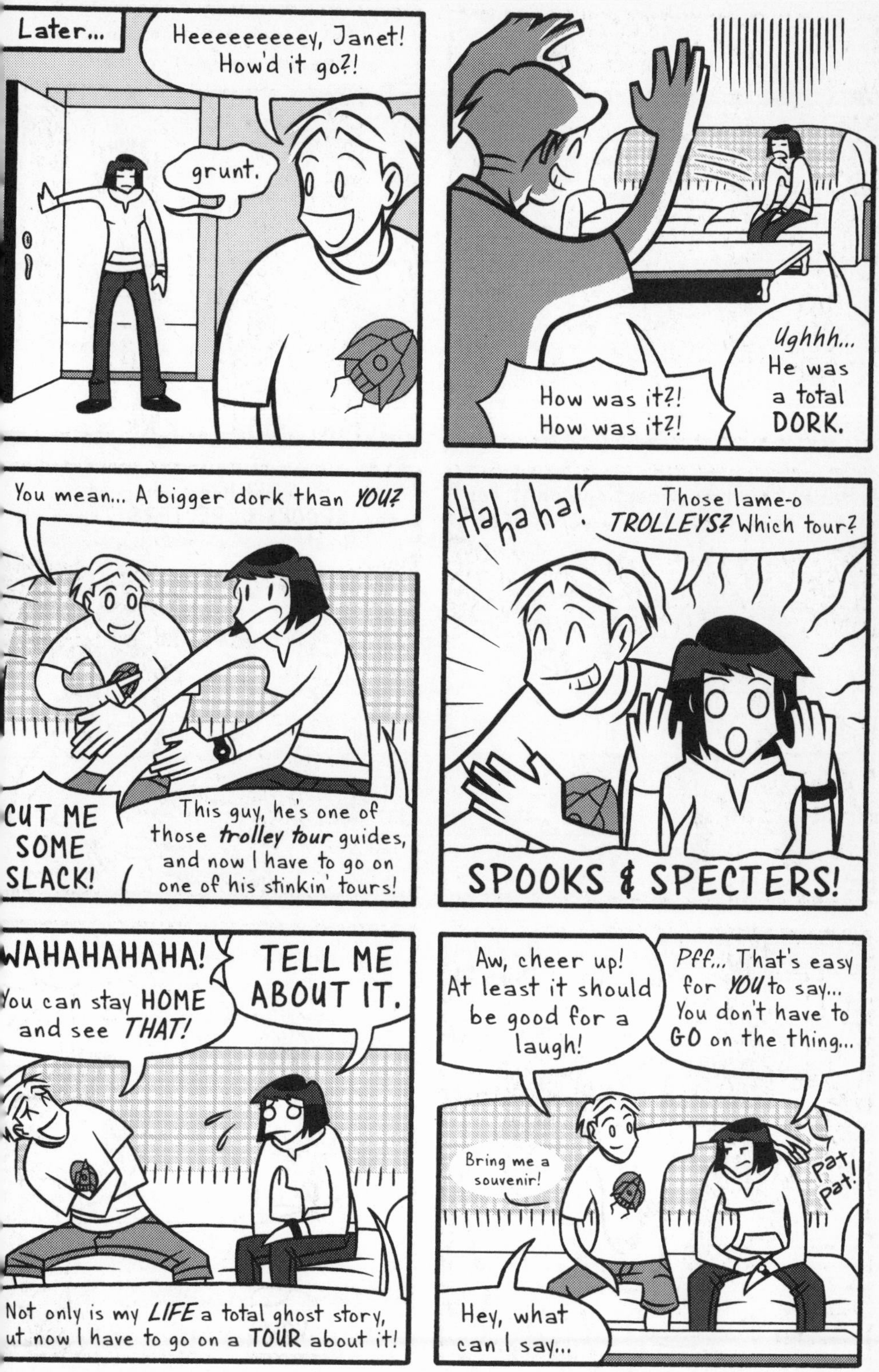
Later...
Heeeeeeeeey, Janet! How'd it go?!
grunt.
How was it?! How was it?!
Ughhh... He was a total DORK.
You mean... A bigger dork than YOU?
CUT ME SOME SLACK!
This guy, he's one of those trolley tour guides, and now I have to go on one of his stinkin' tours!
Hahaha!
Those lame-o TROLLEYS? Which tour?
SPOOKS & SPECTERS!
WAHAHAHAHA! You can stay HOME and see THAT!
TELL ME ABOUT IT.
Not only is my LIFE a total ghost story, ut now I have to go on a TOUR about it!
Aw, cheer up! At least it should be good for a laugh!
Pff... That's easy for YOU to say... You don't have to GO on the thing...
Bring me a souvenir!
Pat pat!
Hey, what can I say...

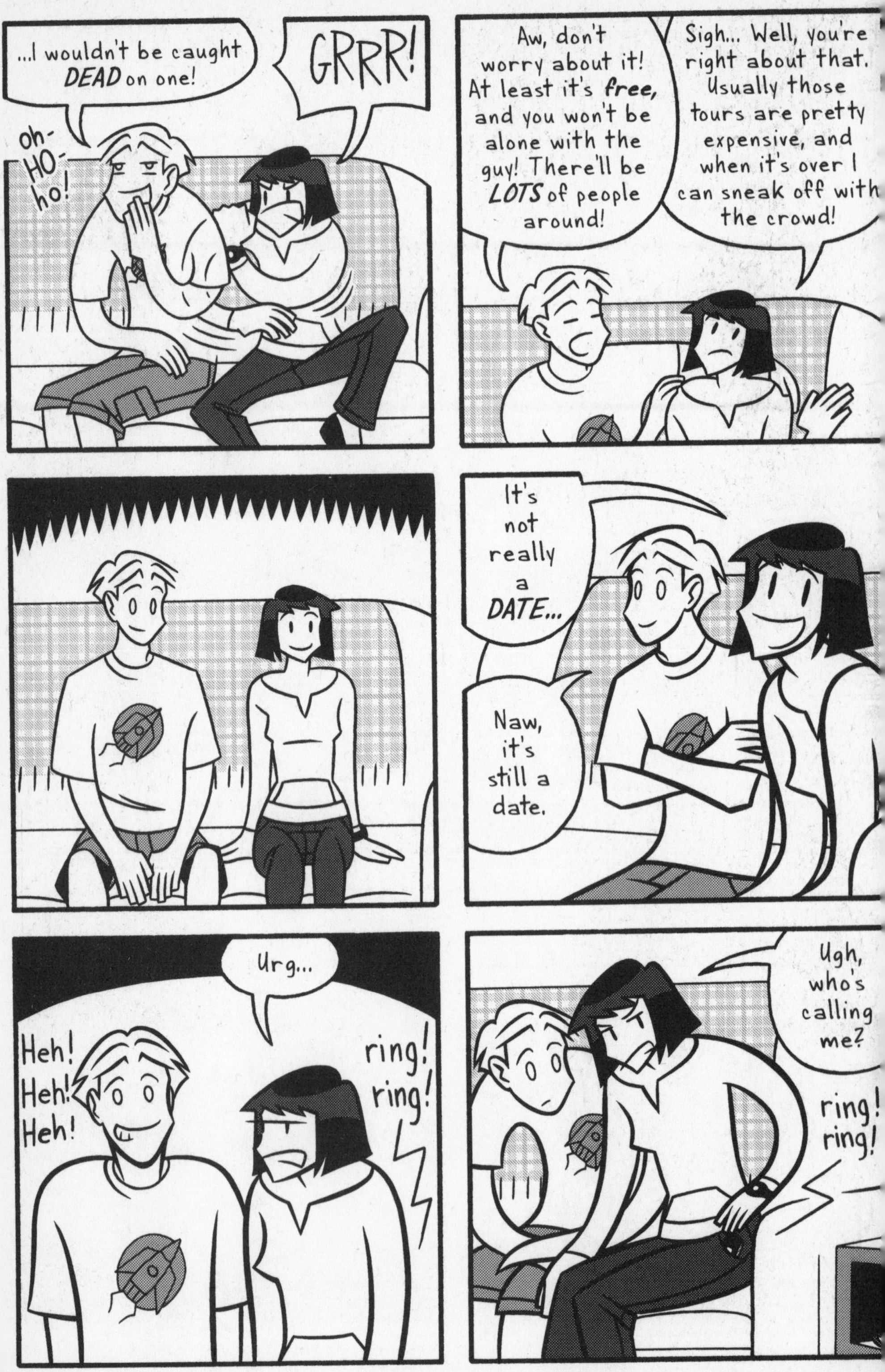
...I wouldn't be caught DEAD on one!
oh-HO-ho!
GRRR!
Aw, don't worry about it! At least it's free, and you won't be alone with the guy! There'll be LOTS of people around!
Sigh... Well, you're right about that. Usually those tours are pretty expensive, and when it's over I can sneak off with the crowd!
It's not really a DATE...
Naw, it's still a date.
Urg...
Heh! Heh! Heh!
ring! ring!
Ugh, who's calling me?
ring! ring!

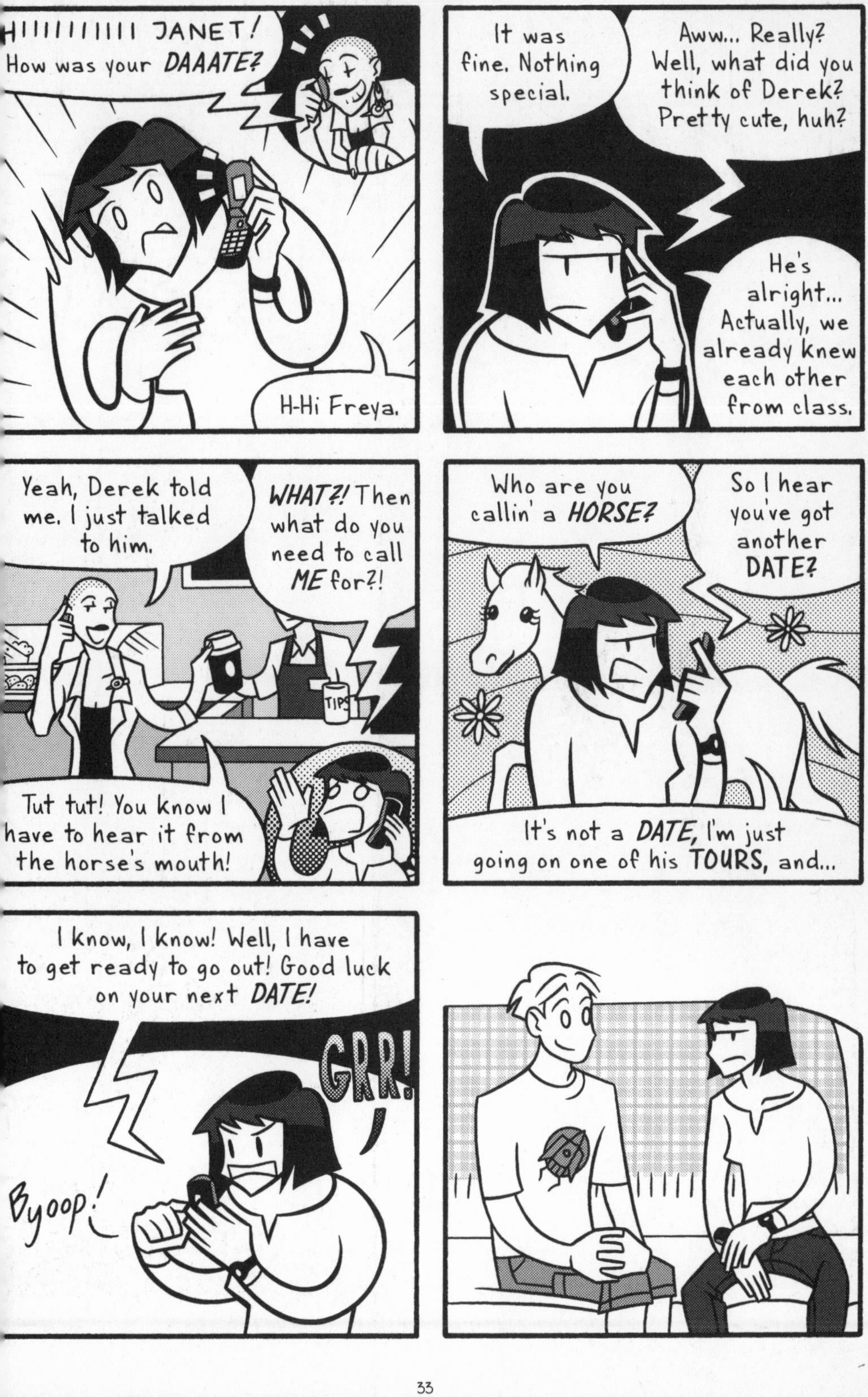

HIIIIIIIIII JANET! How was your *DAAATE?*
H-Hi Freya.
It was fine. Nothing special.
Aww... Really? Well, what did you think of Derek? Pretty cute, huh?
He's alright... Actually, we already knew each other from class.
Yeah, Derek told me. I just talked to him.
WHAT?! Then what do you need to call *ME* for?!
TIPS
Tut tut! You know I have to hear it from the horse's mouth!
Who are you callin' a *HORSE?*
So I hear you've got another DATE?
It's not a *DATE,* I'm just going on one of his TOURS, and...
I know, I know! Well, I have to get ready to go out! Good luck on your next *DATE!*
GRR!
Byoop!

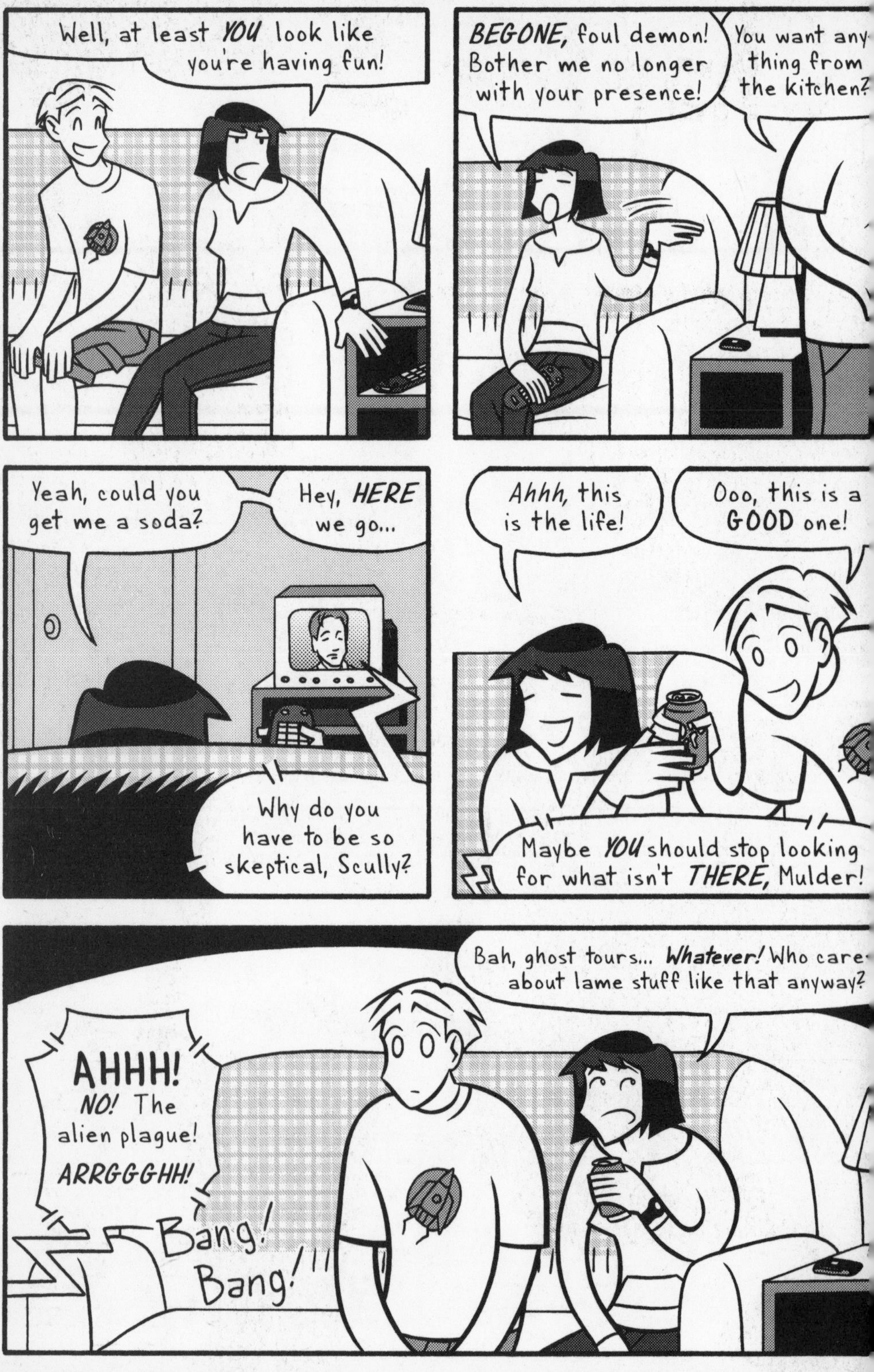

Well, at least YOU look like you're having fun!
BEGONE, foul demon! Bother me no longer with your presence!
You want anything from the kitchen?
Yeah, could you get me a soda?
Hey, HERE we go...
Why do you have to be so skeptical, Scully?
Ahhh, this is the life!
Ooo, this is a GOOD one!
Maybe YOU should stop looking for what isn't THERE, Mulder!
Bah, ghost tours... Whatever! Who cares about lame stuff like that anyway?
AHHH! NO! The alien plague! ARRGGGHH!
Bang! Bang!

Chapter 3

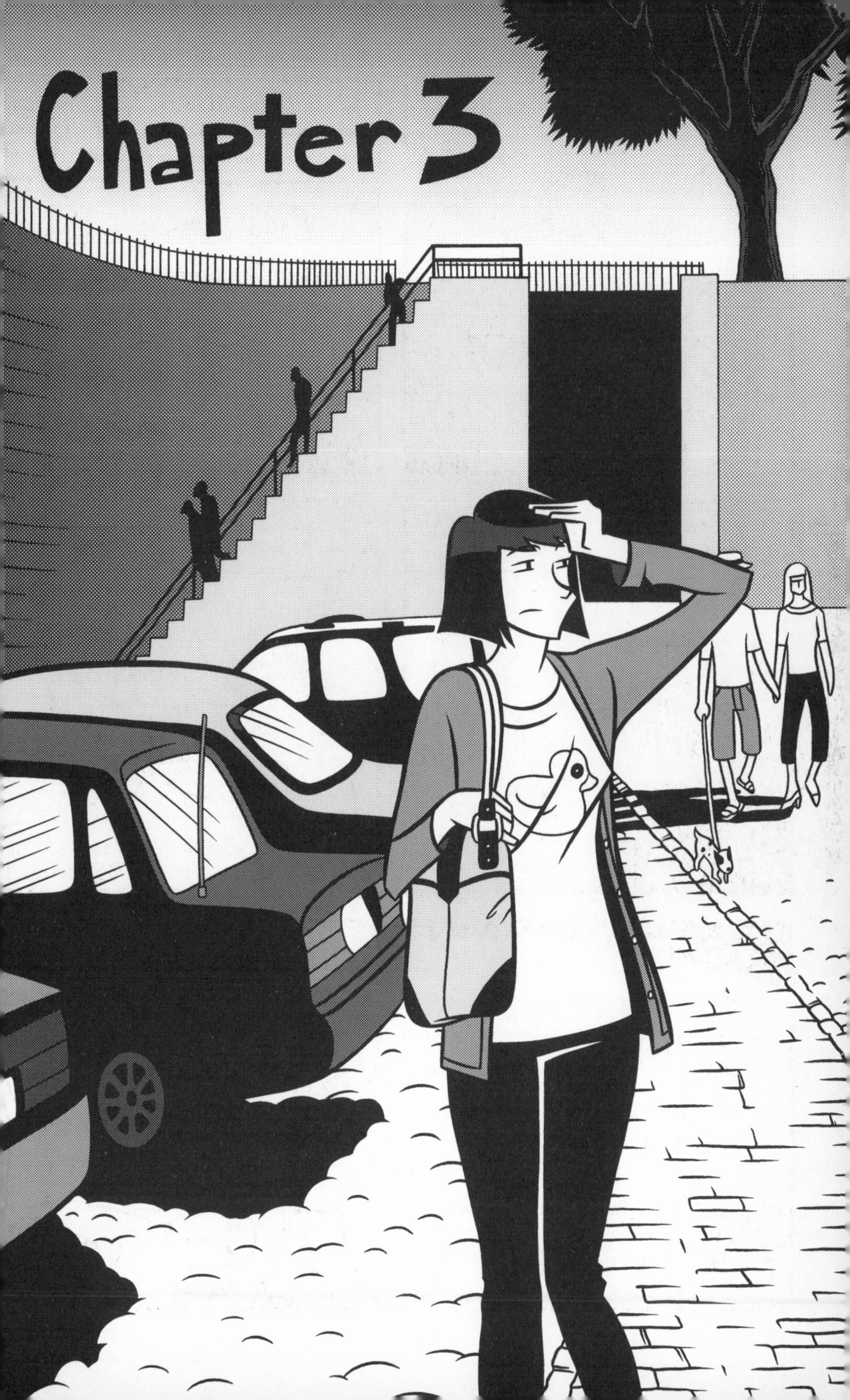

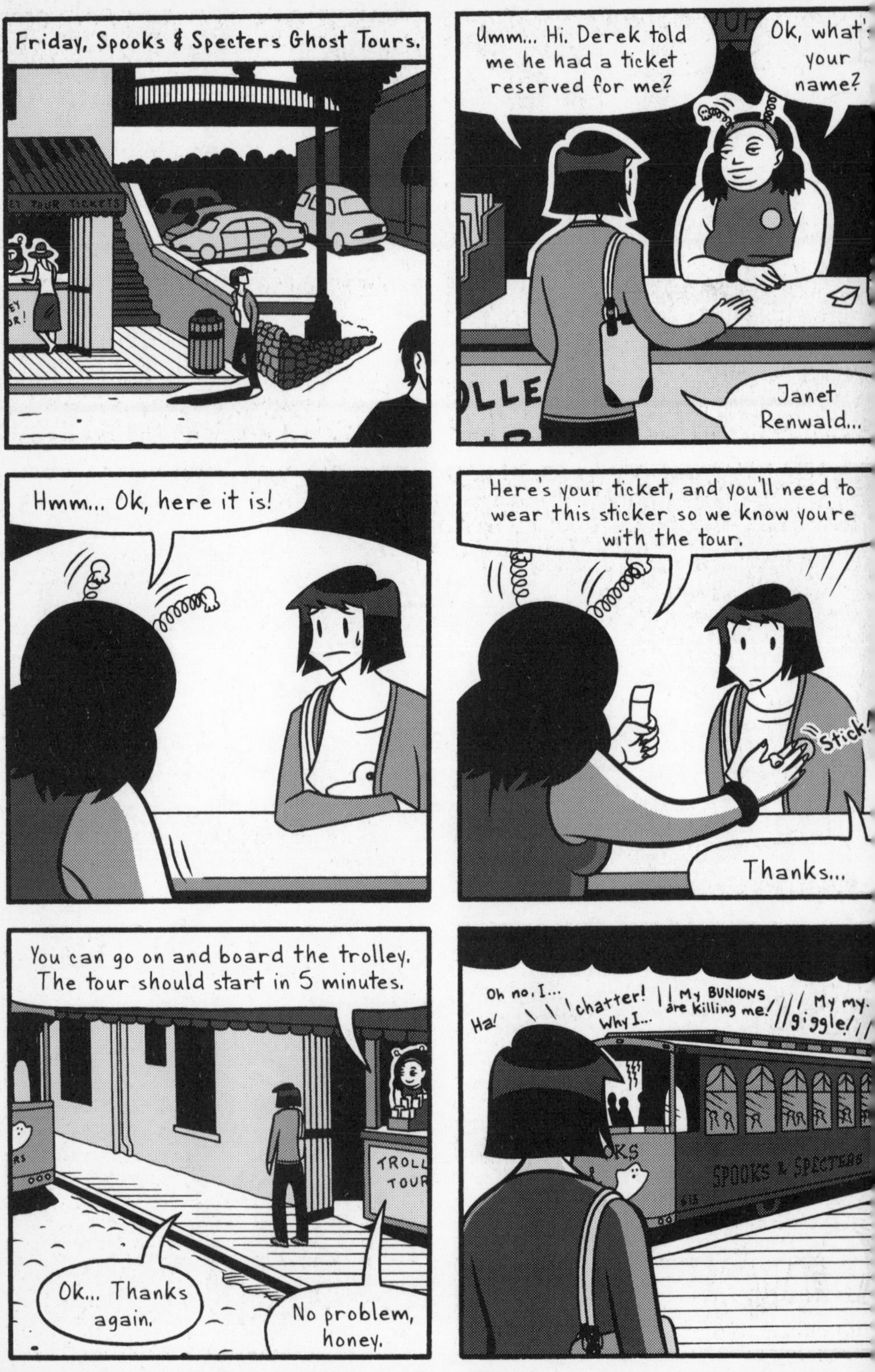
Friday, Spooks & Specters Ghost Tours.
Umm... Hi. Derek told me he had a ticket reserved for me?
Ok, what's your name?
Janet Renwald...
Hmm... Ok, here it is!
Here's your ticket, and you'll need to wear this sticker so we know you're with the tour.
Stick!
Thanks...
You can go on and board the trolley. The tour should start in 5 minutes.
Ok... Thanks again.
No problem, honey.
Oh no, I...
Ha!
chatter!
Why I...
My BUNIONS are killing me!
My my.
giggle!
SPOOKS & SPECTERS

chatter! chatter!

mutter! mutter!

Why, hello there dear! Please sit down!

Uh, h-hi. Thanks.

Where are you from, young lady? My husband and I came all the way from Colorado, and boy, I must say, the climate DOES agree with us! Why, we're relocating! I just a... salty... seagulls, the... Why, even so many sh... the and fried chic...

First, I kill Derek... Next, Freya...

Uh-huh...

We're much fonder of the warm weather here, and it really helps my arthritis! I love these palm trees and that MOSS! It's BEAUTI-... blah... blah...

No... way...

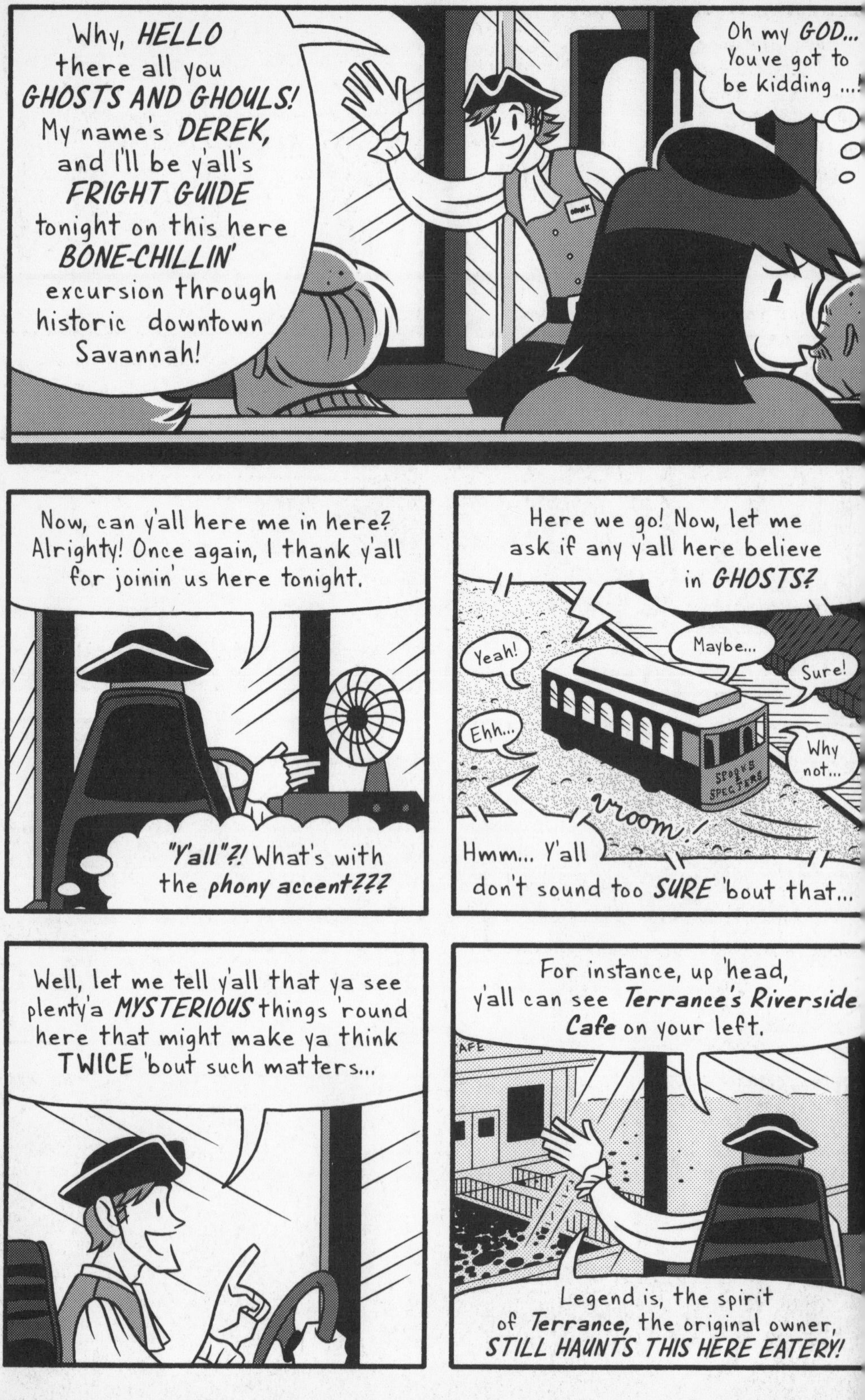

Why, HELLO there all you GHOSTS AND GHOULS! My name's DEREK, and I'll be y'all's FRIGHT GUIDE tonight on this here BONE-CHILLIN' excursion through historic downtown Savannah!
Oh my GOD... You've got to be kidding ...!
Now, can y'all here me in here? Alrighty! Once again, I thank y'all for joinin' us here tonight.
"Y'all"?! What's with the phony accent???
Here we go! Now, let me ask if any y'all here believe in GHOSTS?
Yeah!
Maybe...
Sure!
Ehh...
Why not...
vroom!
Hmm... Y'all don't sound too SURE 'bout that...
Well, let me tell y'all that ya see plenty'a MYSTERIOUS things 'round here that might make ya think TWICE 'bout such matters...
For instance, up 'head, y'all can see Terrance's Riverside Cafe on your left.
Legend is, the spirit of Terrance, the original owner, STILL HAUNTS THIS HERE EATERY!

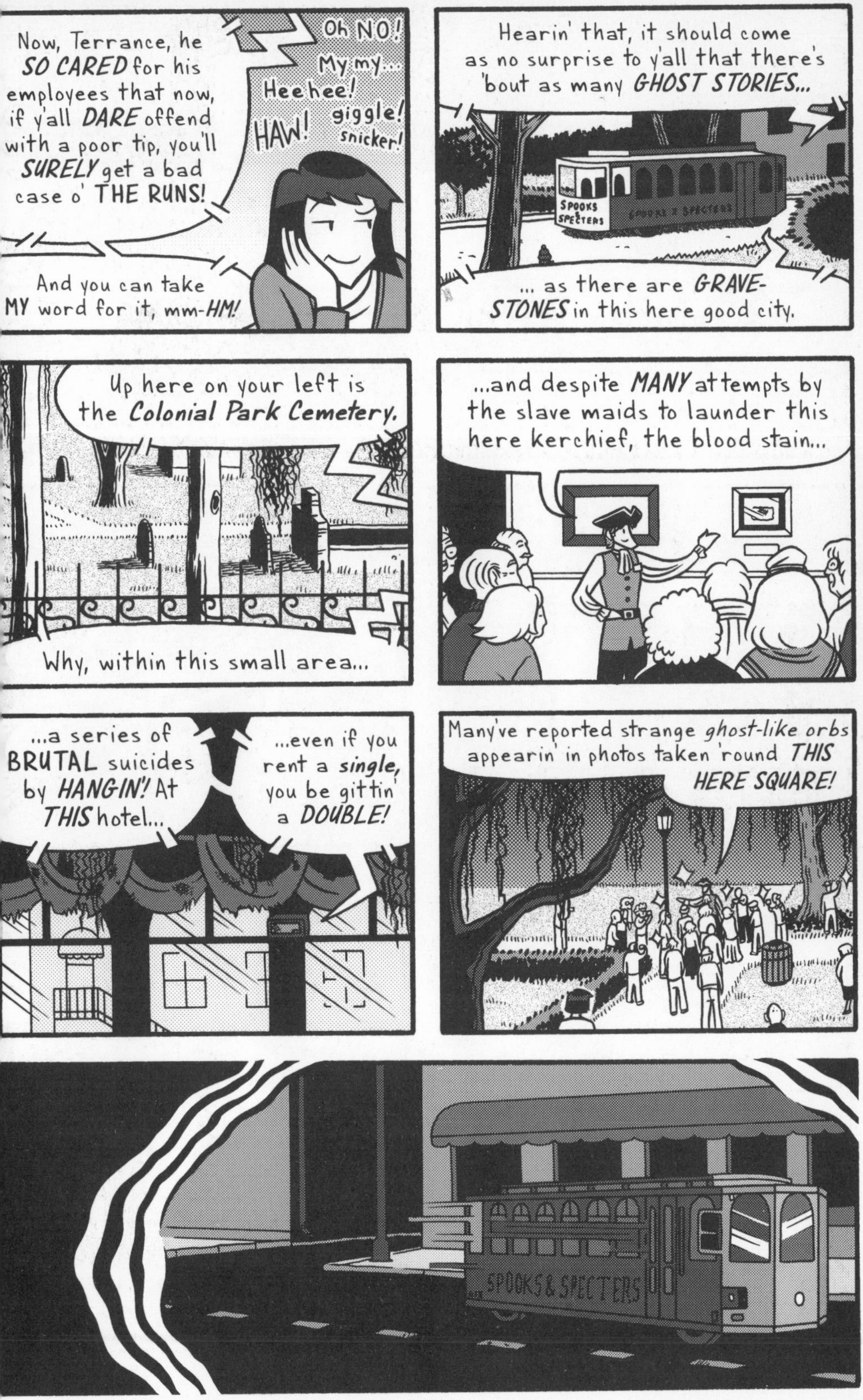
Now, Terrance, he SO CARED for his employees that now, if y'all DARE offend with a poor tip, you'll SURELY get a bad case o' THE RUNS!
Oh NO!
My my...
Hee hee!
giggle!
HAW!
snicker!
And you can take MY word for it, mm-HM!
Hearin' that, it should come as no surprise to y'all that there's 'bout as many GHOST STORIES...
SPOOKS & SPECTERS
... as there are GRAVE-STONES in this here good city.
Up here on your left is the Colonial Park Cemetery.
Why, within this small area...
...and despite MANY attempts by the slave maids to launder this here kerchief, the blood stain...
...a series of BRUTAL suicides by HANGIN'! At THIS hotel...
...even if you rent a single, you be gittin' a DOUBLE!
Many've reported strange ghost-like orbs appearin' in photos taken 'round THIS HERE SQUARE!
SPOOKS & SPECTERS

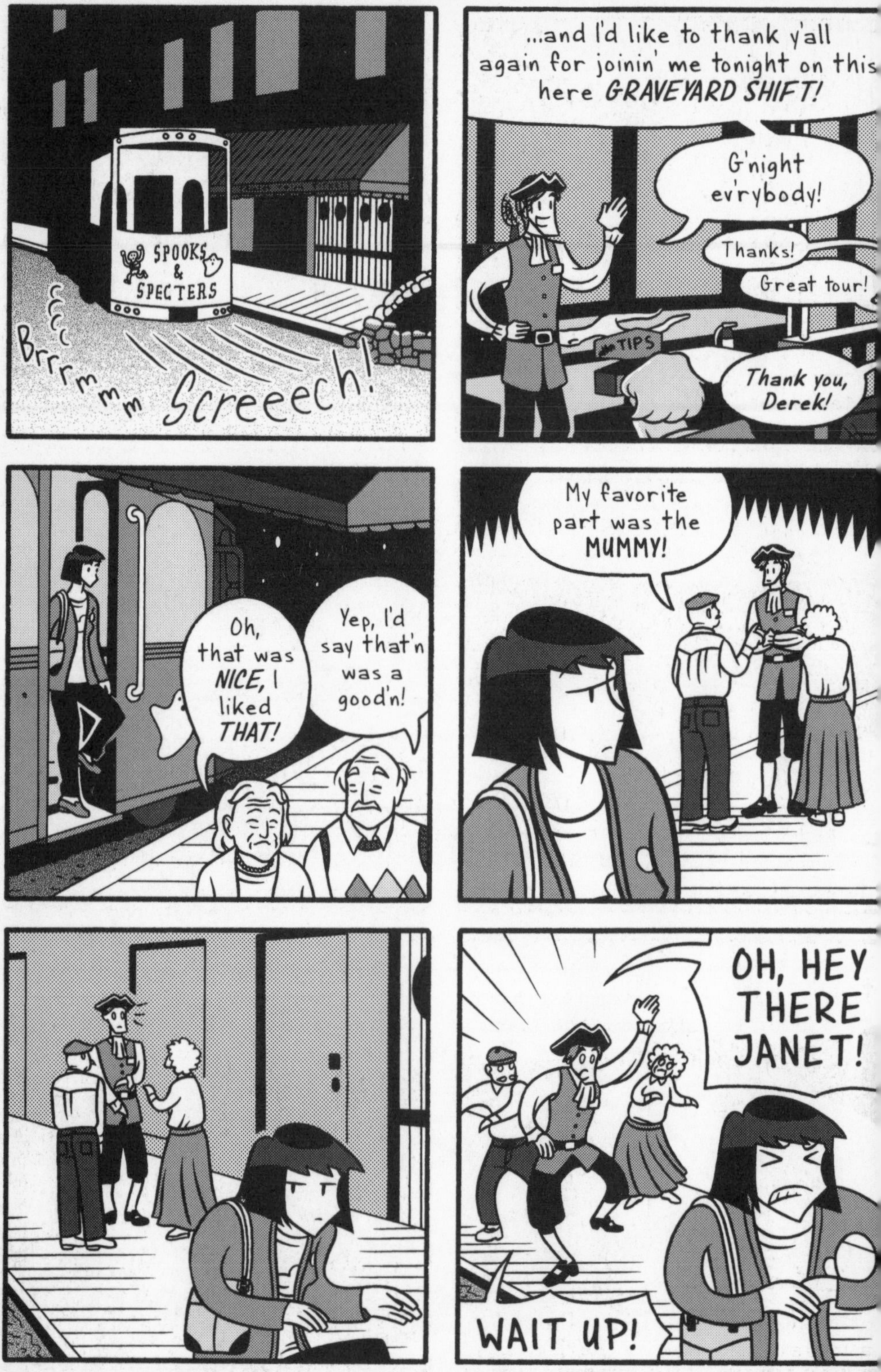
SPOOKS & SPECTERS
Brrrmmm
Screeech!
...and I'd like to thank y'all again for joinin' me tonight on this here GRAVEYARD SHIFT!
G'night ev'rybody!
Thanks!
Great tour!
TIPS
Thank you, Derek!
Oh, that was NICE, I liked THAT!
Yep, I'd say that'n was a good'n!
My favorite part was the MUMMY!
OH, HEY THERE JANET!
WAIT UP!

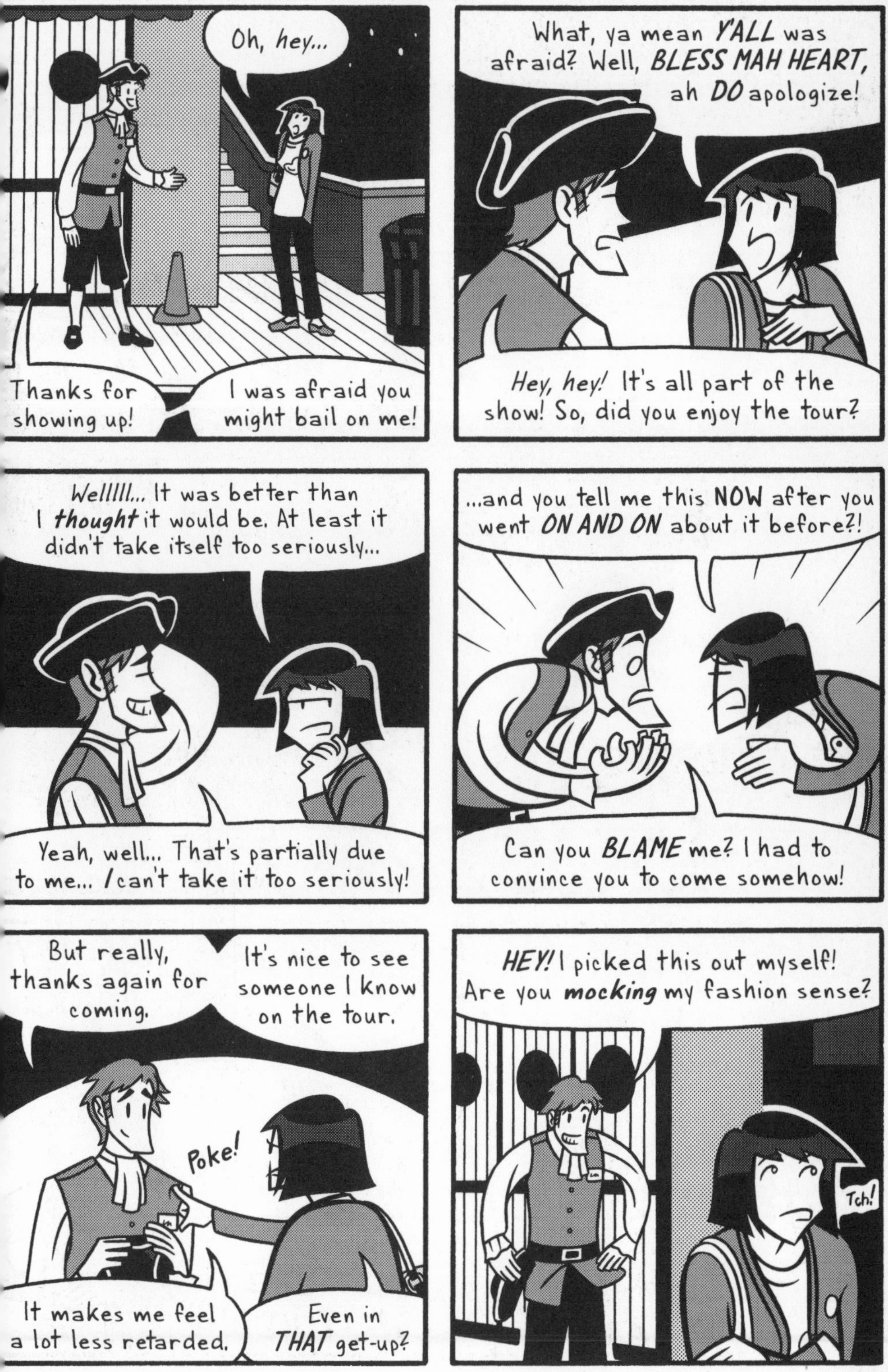
Oh, hey...
Thanks for showing up!
I was afraid you might bail on me!
What, ya mean Y'ALL was afraid? Well, BLESS MAH HEART, ah DO apologize!
Hey, hey! It's all part of the show! So, did you enjoy the tour?
Wellllll... It was better than I thought it would be. At least it didn't take itself too seriously...
Yeah, well... That's partially due to me... I can't take it too seriously!
...and you tell me this NOW after you went ON AND ON about it before?!
Can you BLAME me? I had to convince you to come somehow!
But really, thanks again for coming.
It's nice to see someone I know on the tour.
Poke!
It makes me feel a lot less retarded.
Even in THAT get-up?
HEY! I picked this out myself! Are you mocking my fashion sense?
Tch!

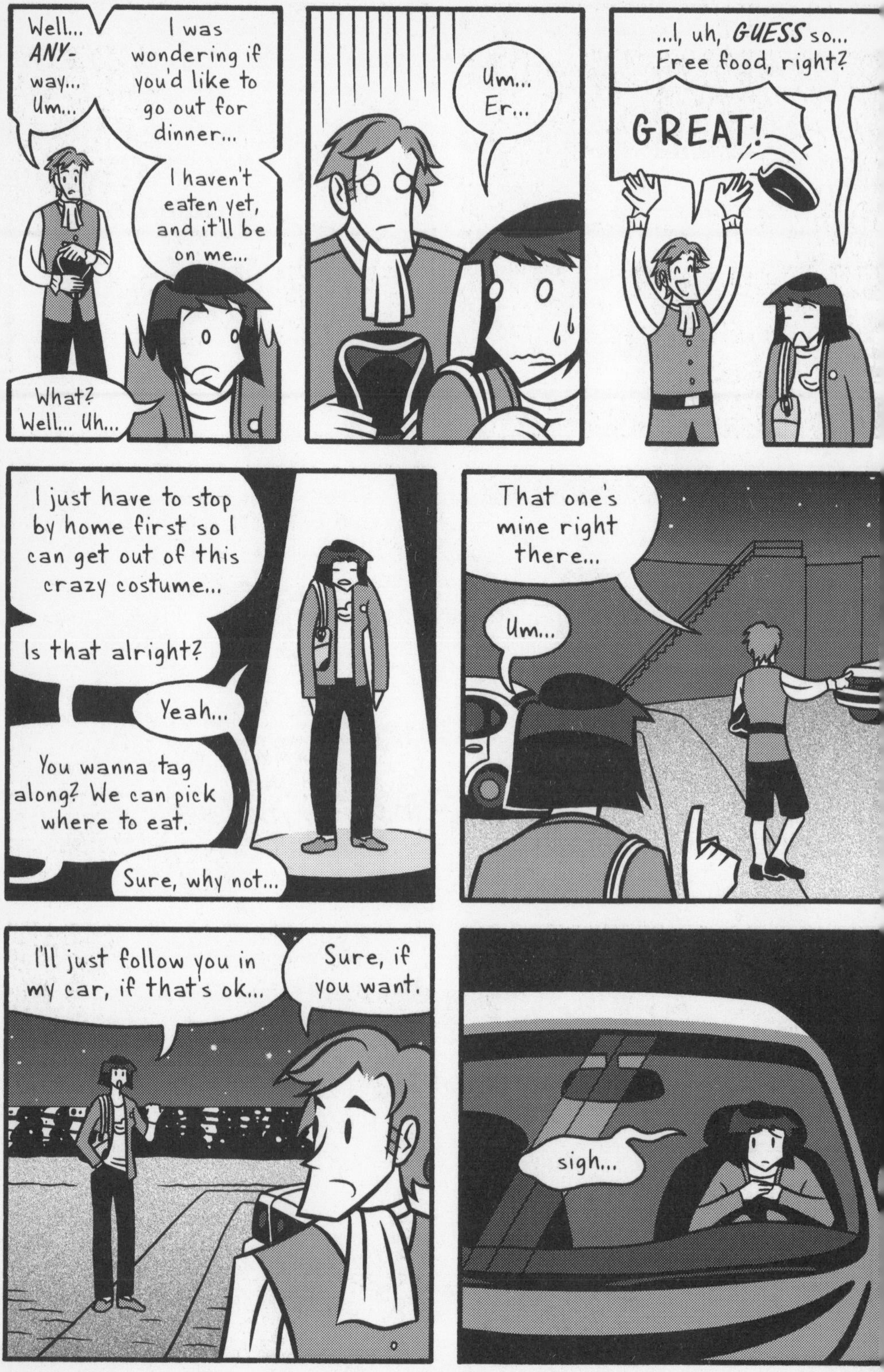

Well... ANY-way... Um...
I was wondering if you'd like to go out for dinner...
I haven't eaten yet, and it'll be on me...
What? Well... Uh...
Um... Er...
...I, uh, GUESS so... Free food, right?
GREAT!
I just have to stop by home first so I can get out of this crazy costume...
Is that alright?
Yeah...
You wanna tag along? We can pick where to eat.
Sure, why not...
That one's mine right there...
Um...
I'll just follow you in my car, if that's ok...
Sure, if you want.
sigh...

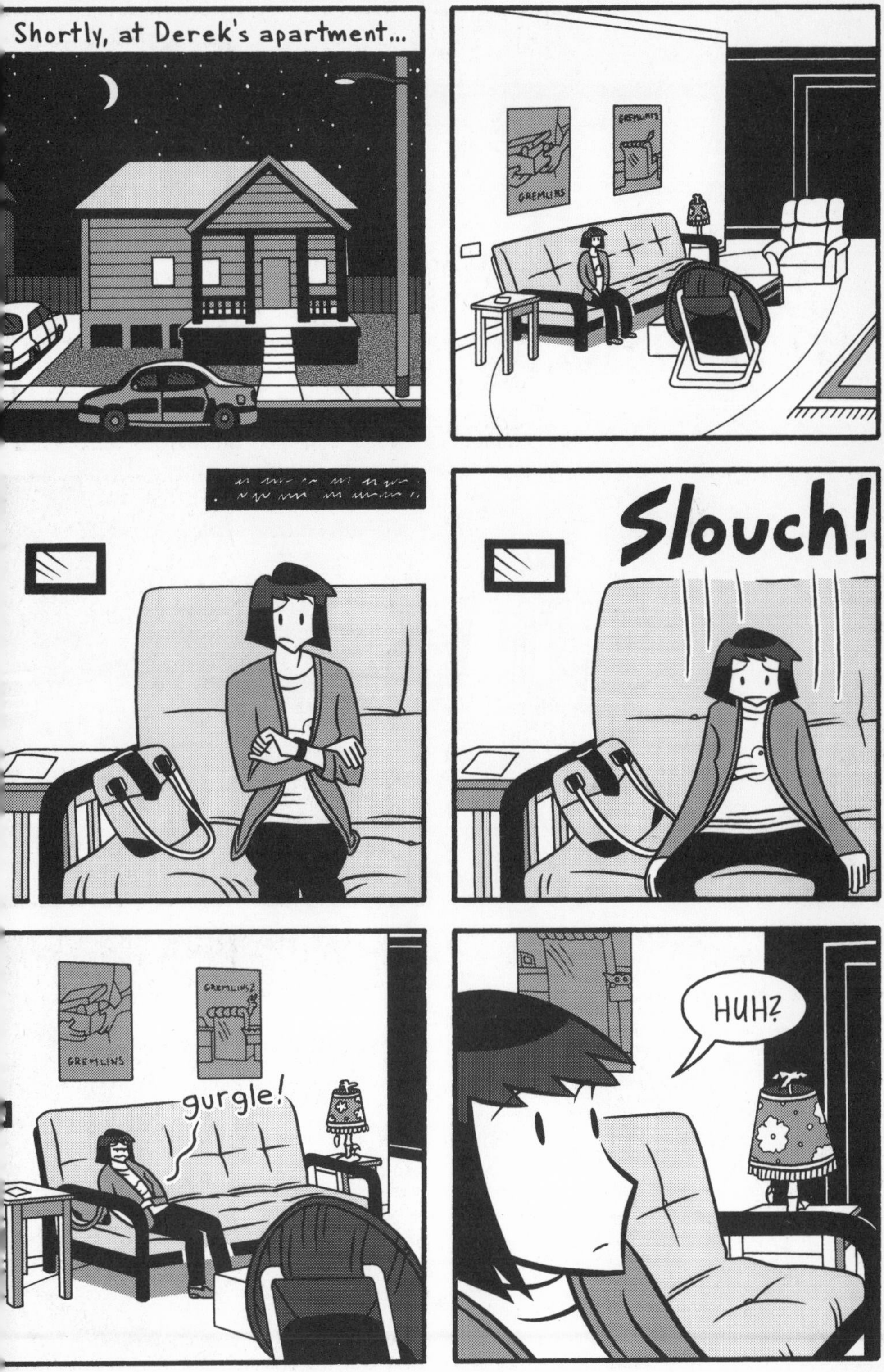
Shortly, at Derek's apartment...
GREMLINS
GREMLINS 2
Slouch!
GREMLINS
GREMLINS 2
gurgle!
HUH?

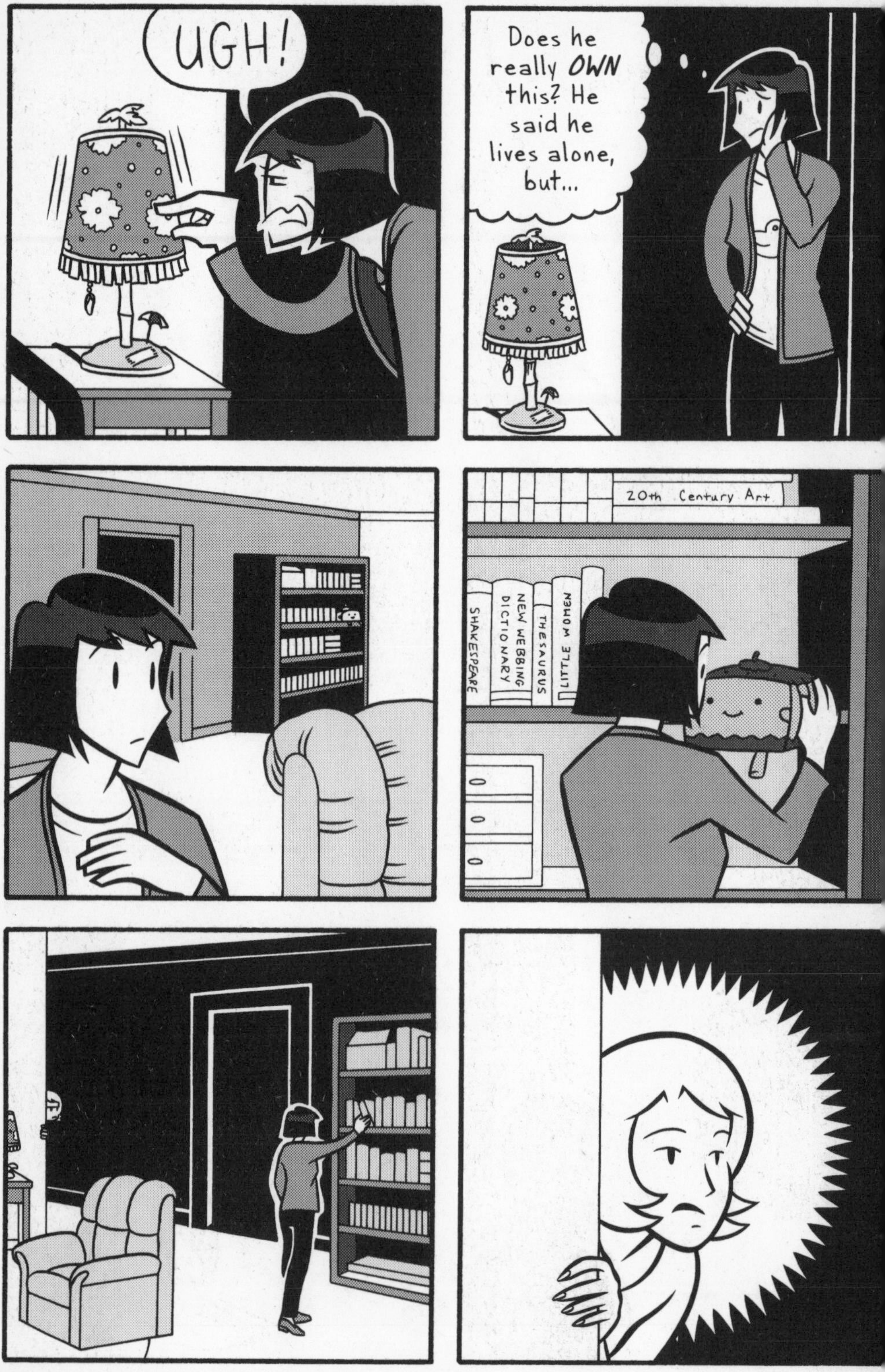
UGH!
Does he really OWN this? He said he lives alone, but...
20th Century Art
SHAKESPEARE
NEW WEBBING DICTIONARY
THESAURUS
LITTLE WOMEN

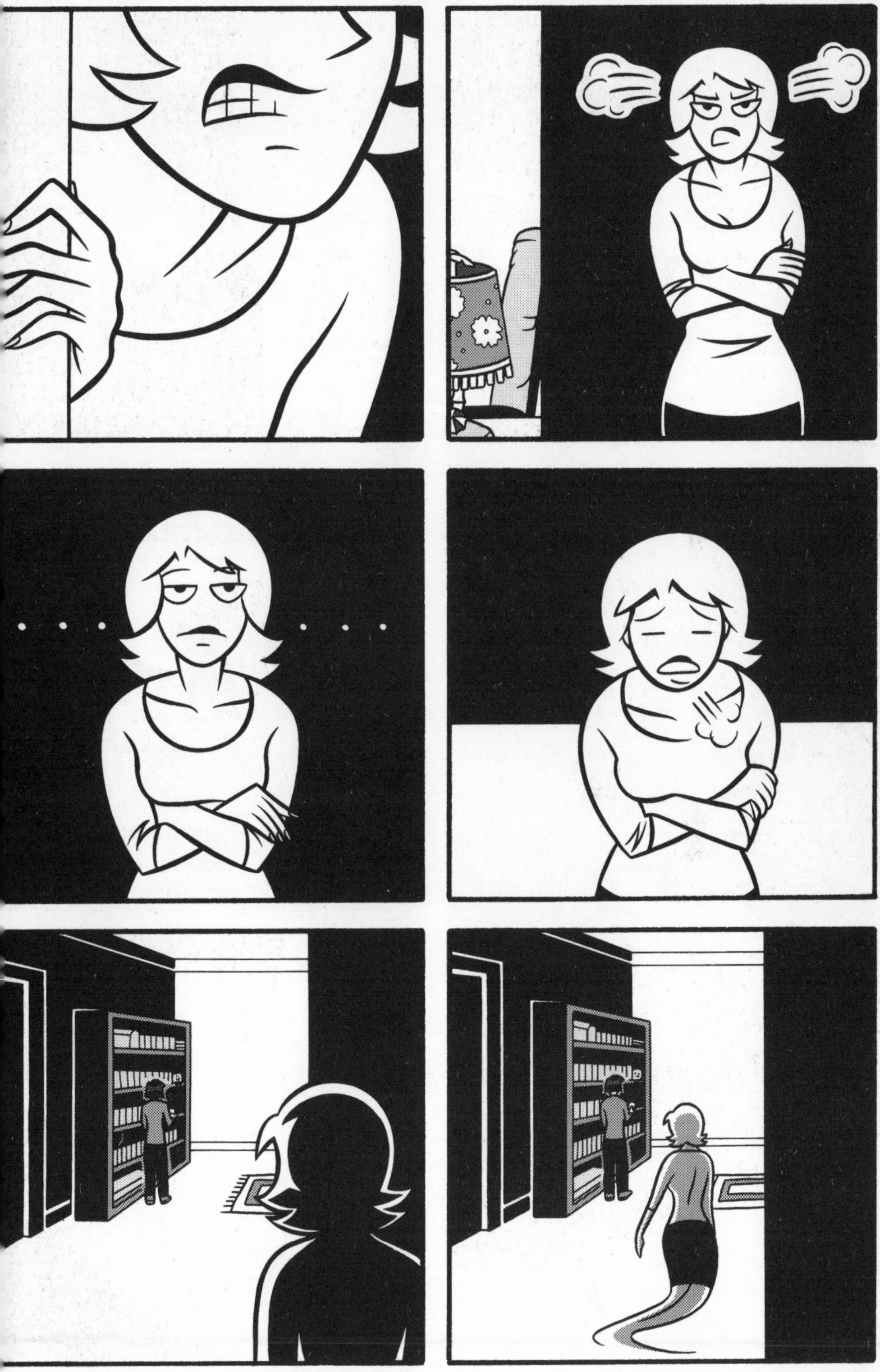

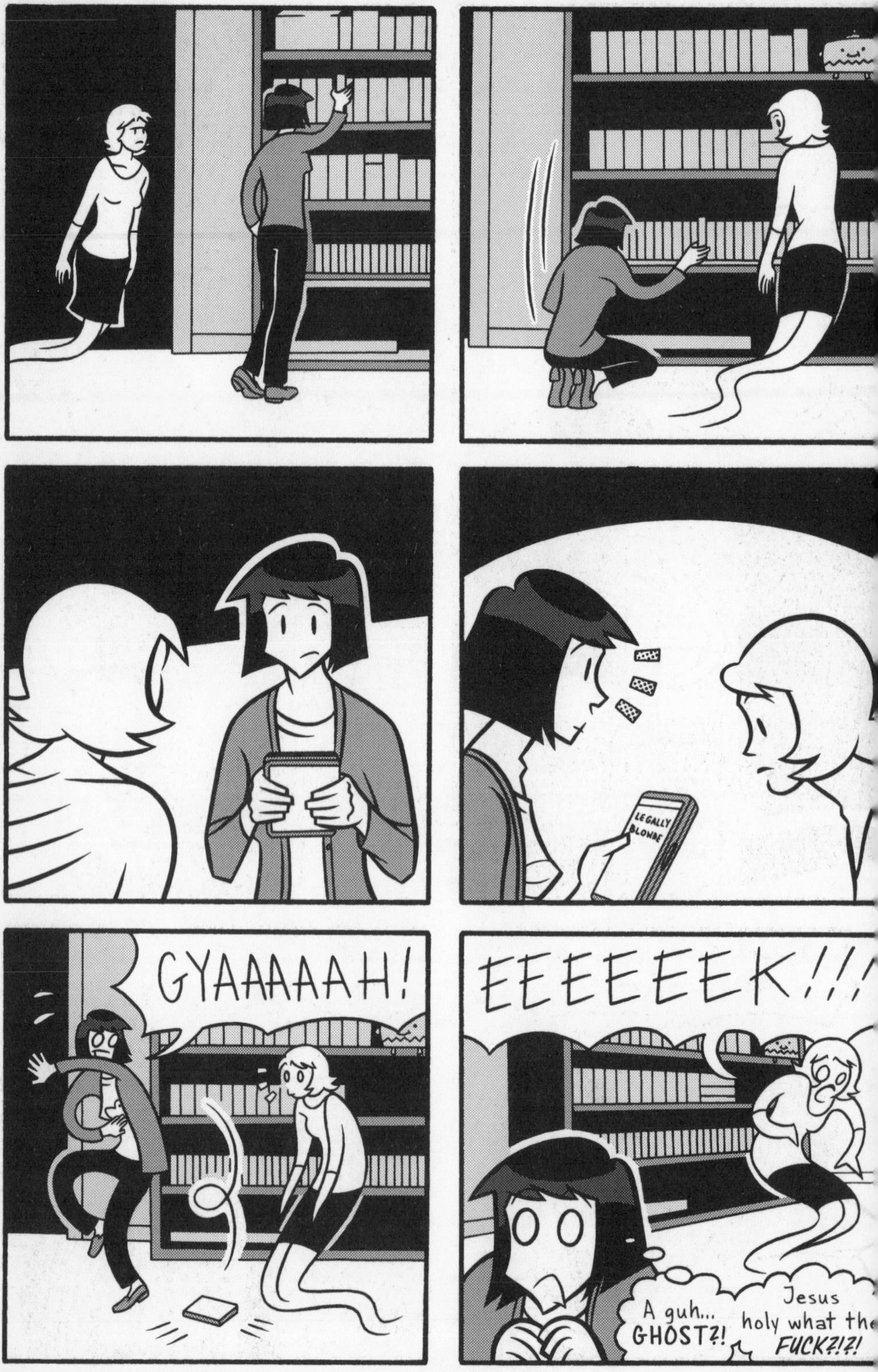
LEGALLY BLONDE
GYAAAAAAH!
EEEEEEK!!!
A guh... GHOST?!
Jesus holy what the FUCK?!?!

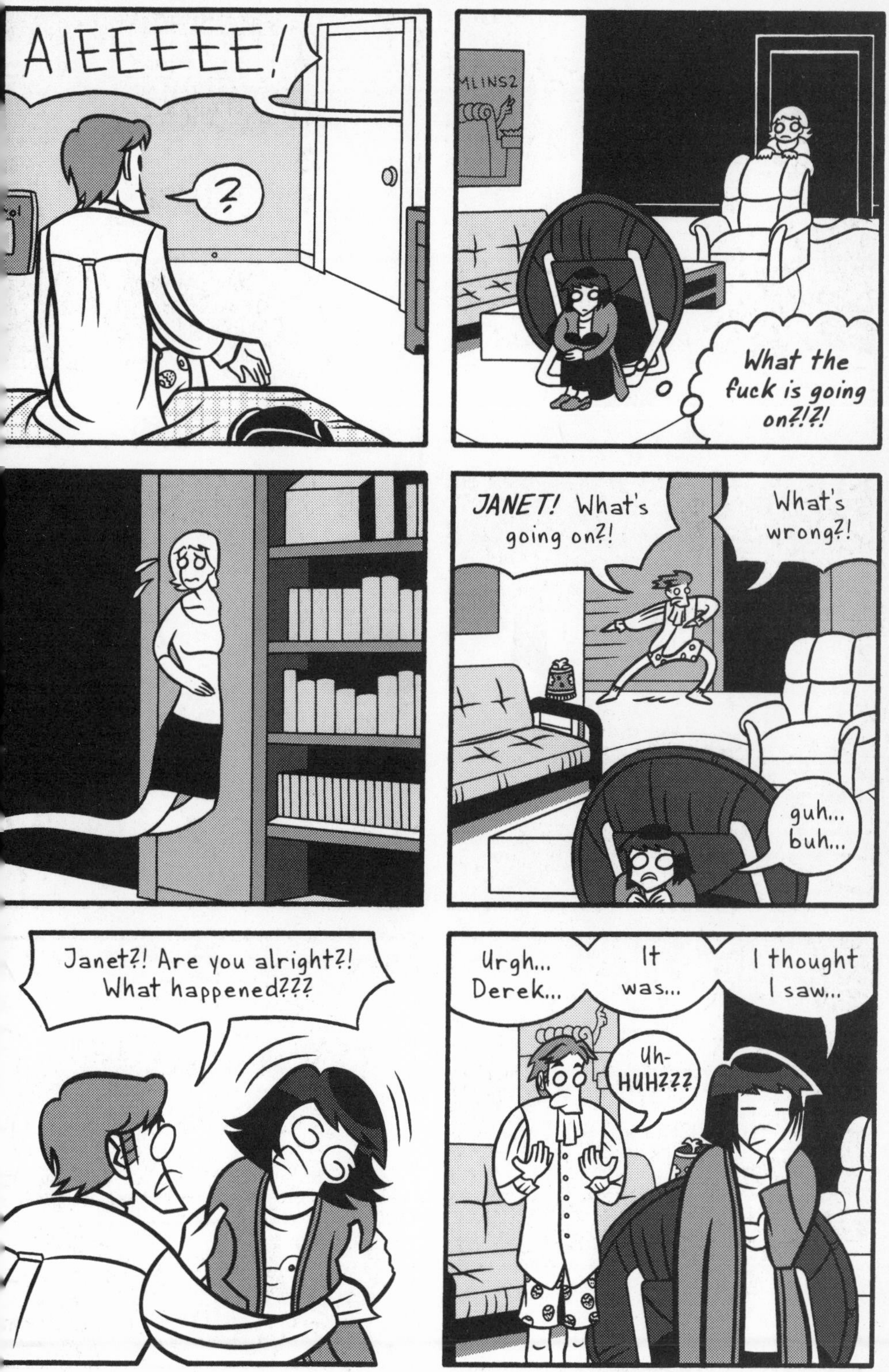
AIEEEEE!
?
What the fuck is going on?!?!
JANET! What's going on?!
What's wrong?!
guh... buh...
Janet?! Are you alright?! What happened???
Urgh... Derek...
It was...
I thought I saw...
Uh-HUH???

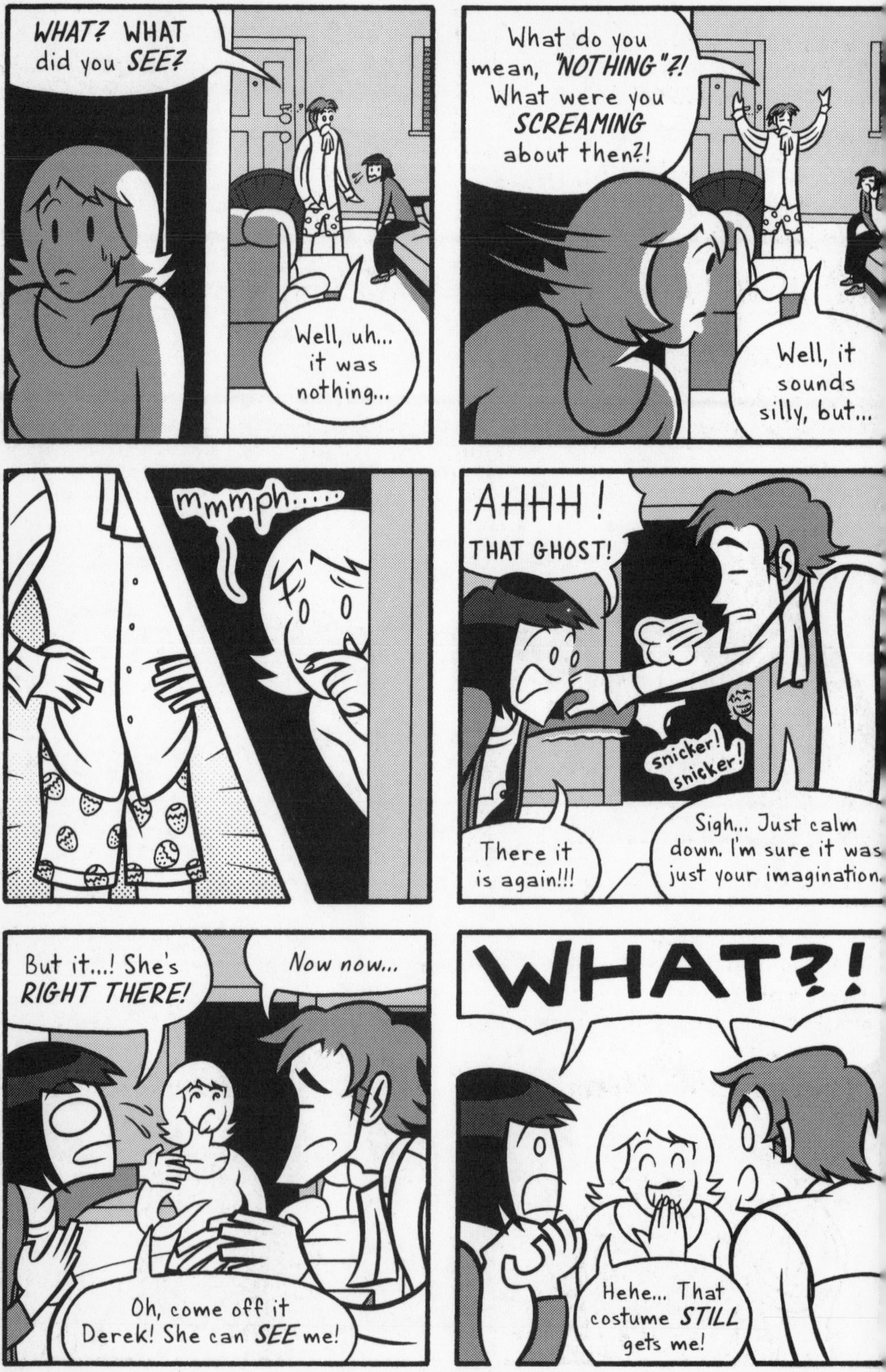
WHAT? WHAT did you SEE?
Well, uh... it was nothing...
What do you mean, "NOTHING"?! What were you SCREAMING about then?!
Well, it sounds silly, but...
mmmph.....
AHHH! THAT GHOST!
snicker! snicker!
There it is again!!!
Sigh... Just calm down. I'm sure it was just your imagination.
But it...! She's RIGHT THERE!
Now now...
Oh, come off it Derek! She can SEE me!
WHAT?!
Hehe... That costume STILL gets me!

What do you mean, *"just my imagination"?!* You can see her *TOO?!*

Wow...! You can really see her? Really???

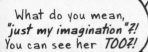
sigh.

OF COURSE I CAN! OBVIOUSLY!

This is *too weird...!*

You're telling *ME!* No one else has ever seen Carol before!

YEAH! How come *SHE* can see me?

GYAH!

...Who *ARE* you, anyway? Derek, who *IS* this girl?

This is JANET, remember? The girl Freya set me up with!

Ooohhh... *THAT* girl... Well, Freya sure can *PICK* 'em!

I'm sorry, are you alright, Janet?

Sure... Never been better...

pff!

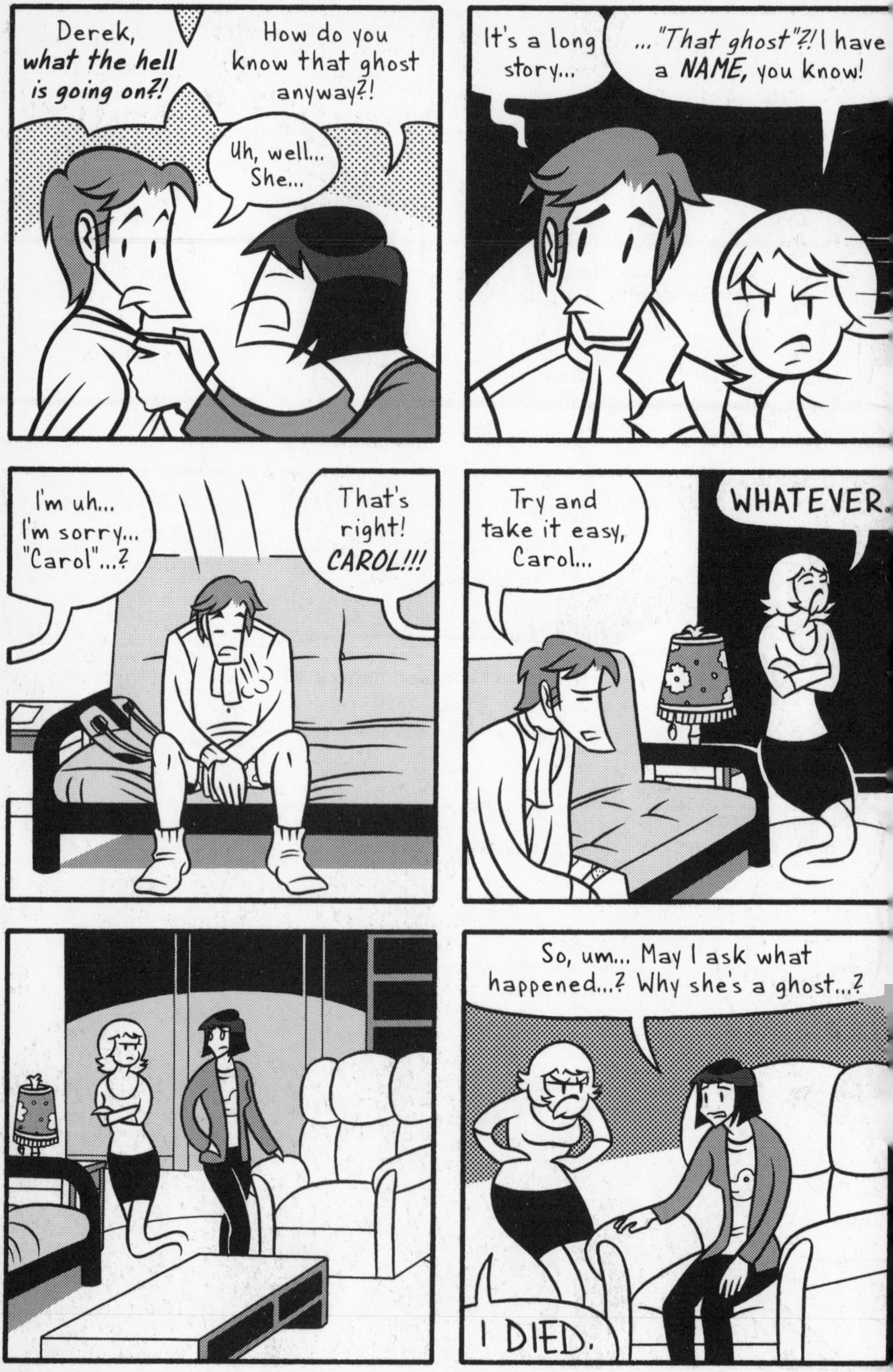
Derek, what the hell is going on?!
How do you know that ghost anyway?!
Uh, well... She...
It's a long story...
..."That ghost"?! I have a NAME, you know!
I'm uh... I'm sorry... "Carol"...?
That's right! CAROL!!!
Try and take it easy, Carol...
WHATEVER.
So, um... May I ask what happened...? Why she's a ghost...?
I DIED.

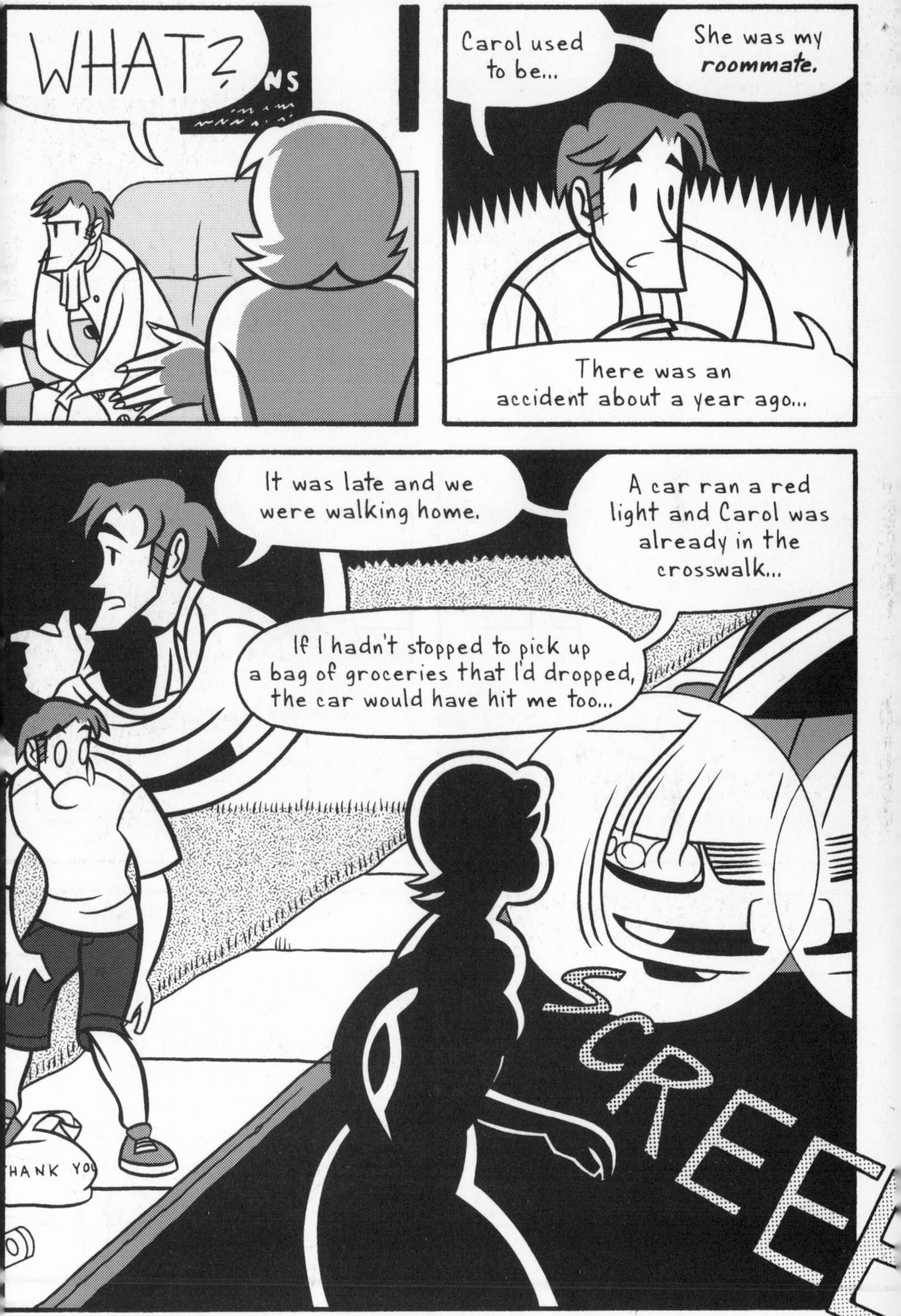
WHAT?
Carol used to be...
She was my *roommate.*
There was an accident about a year ago...
It was late and we were walking home.
A car ran a red light and Carol was already in the crosswalk...
If I hadn't stopped to pick up a bag of groceries that I'd dropped, the car would have hit me too...
SCREEE
THANK YO

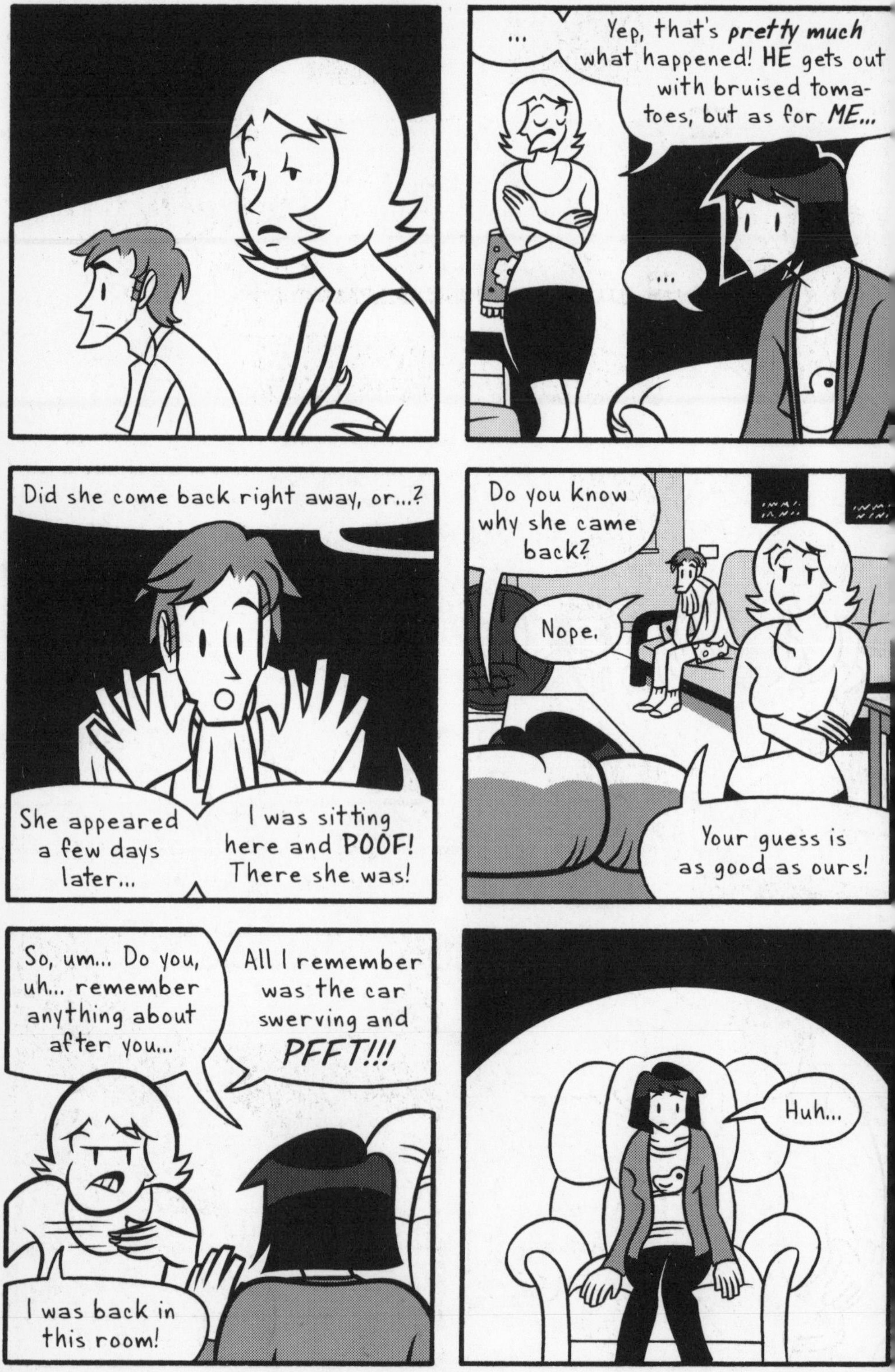
...
Yep, that's *pretty much* what happened! HE gets out with bruised tomatoes, but as for *ME*...
...
Did she come back right away, or...?
She appeared a few days later...
I was sitting here and POOF! There she was!
Do you know why she came back?
Nope.
Your guess is as good as ours!
So, um... Do you, uh... remember anything about after you...
All I remember was the car swerving and *PFFT!!!*
I was back in this room!
Huh...

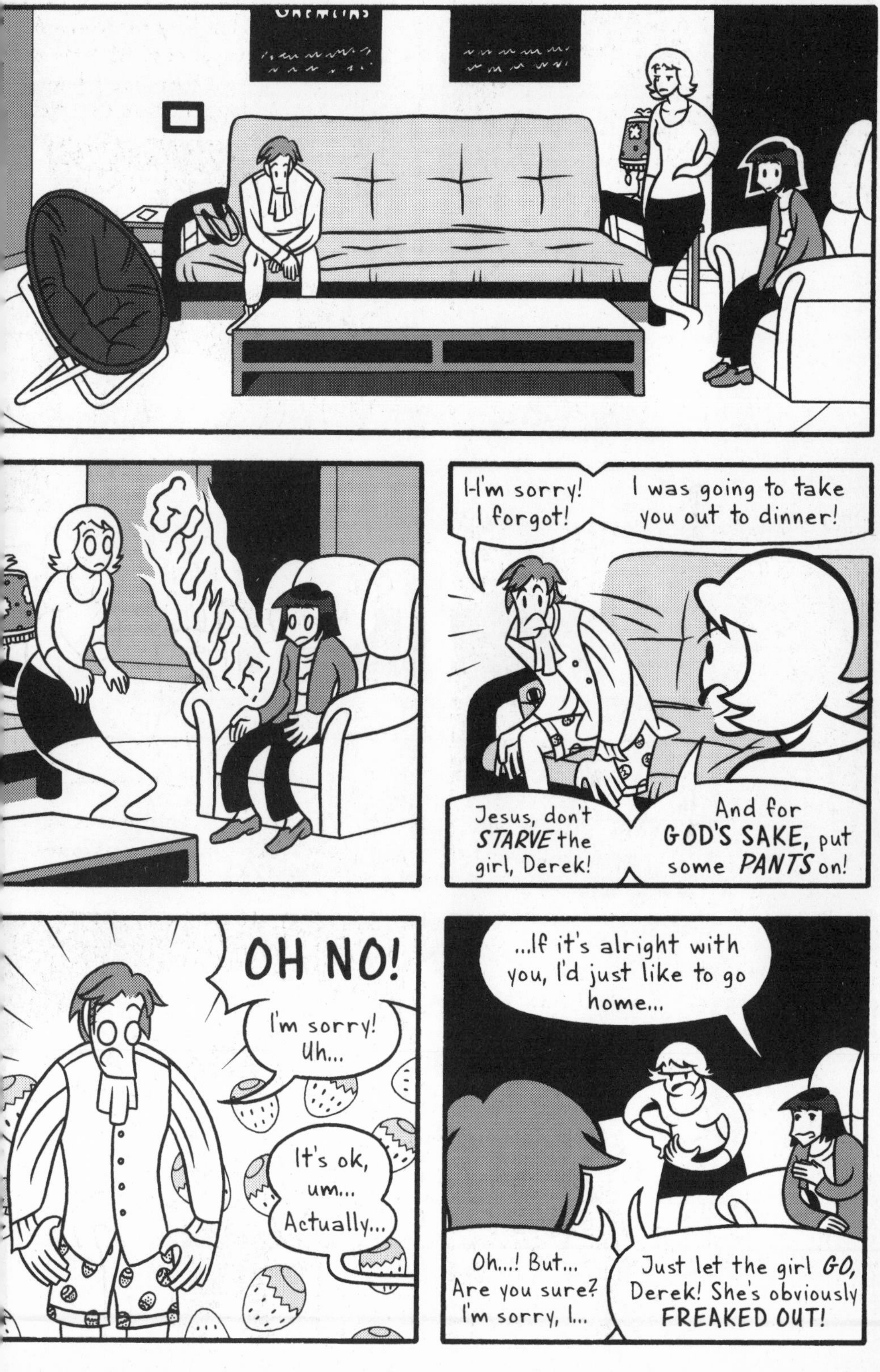

GRUMBLE!
I-I'm sorry! I forgot!
I was going to take you out to dinner!
Jesus, don't STARVE the girl, Derek!
And for GOD'S SAKE, put some PANTS on!
OH NO!
I'm sorry! Uh...
It's ok, um... Actually...
...If it's alright with you, I'd just like to go home...
Oh...! But... Are you sure? I'm sorry, I...
Just let the girl GO, Derek! She's obviously FREAKED OUT!

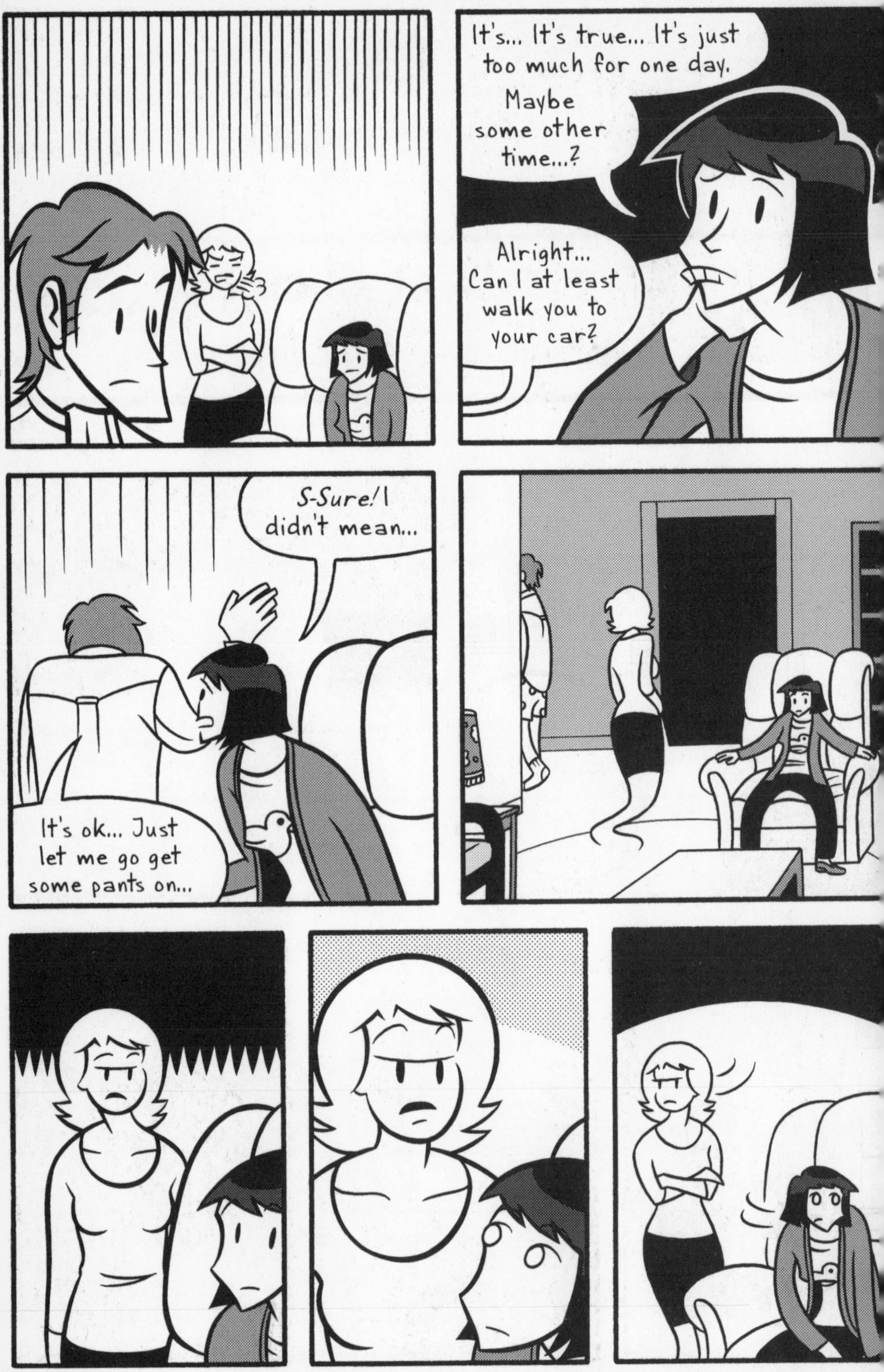
It's... It's true... It's just too much for one day.
Maybe some other time...?
Alright... Can I at least walk you to your car?
S-Sure! I didn't mean...
It's ok... Just let me go get some pants on...

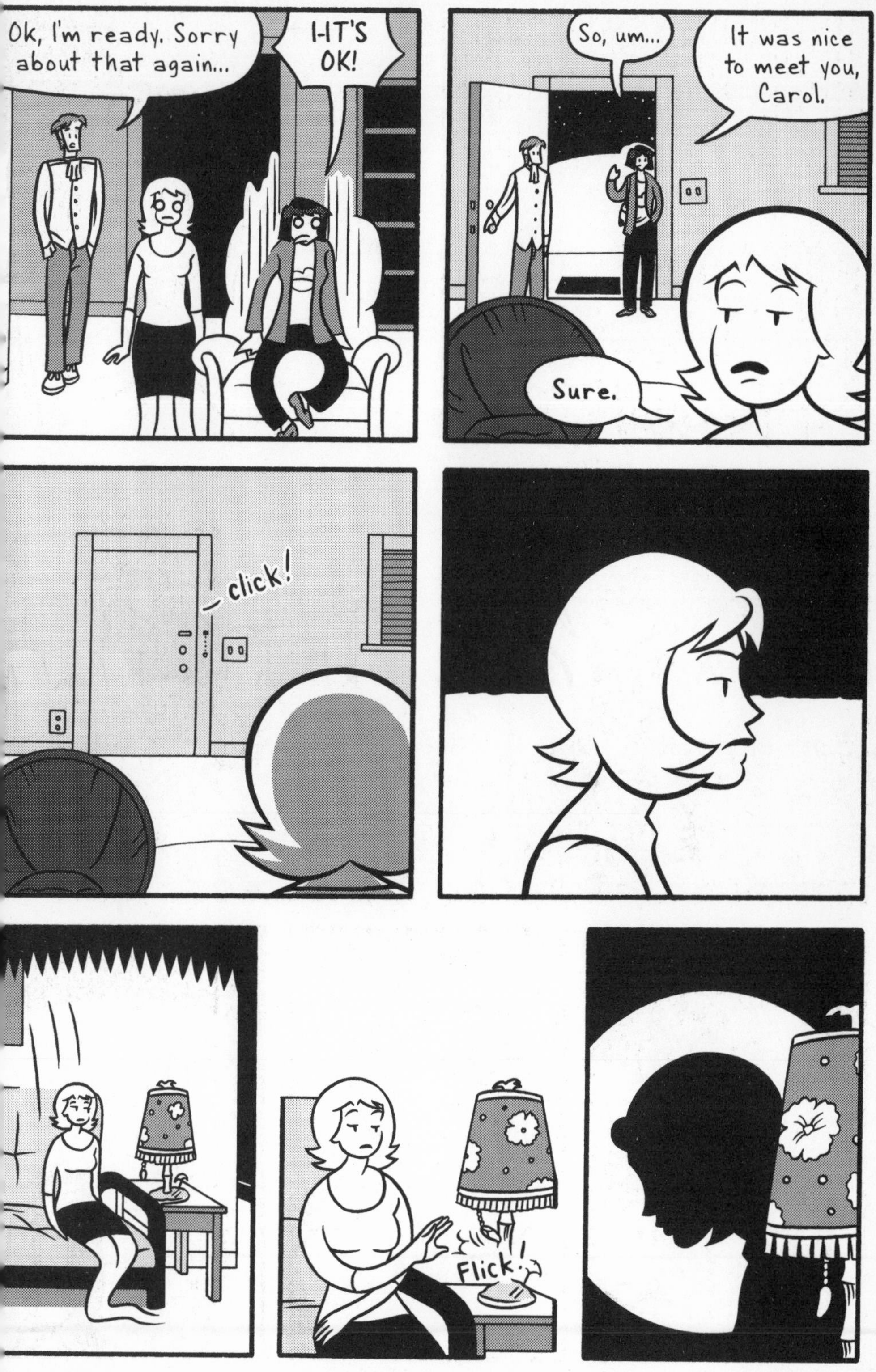
Ok, I'm ready. Sorry about that again...
I-IT'S OK!
So, um...
It was nice to meet you, Carol.
Sure.
click!
Flick!

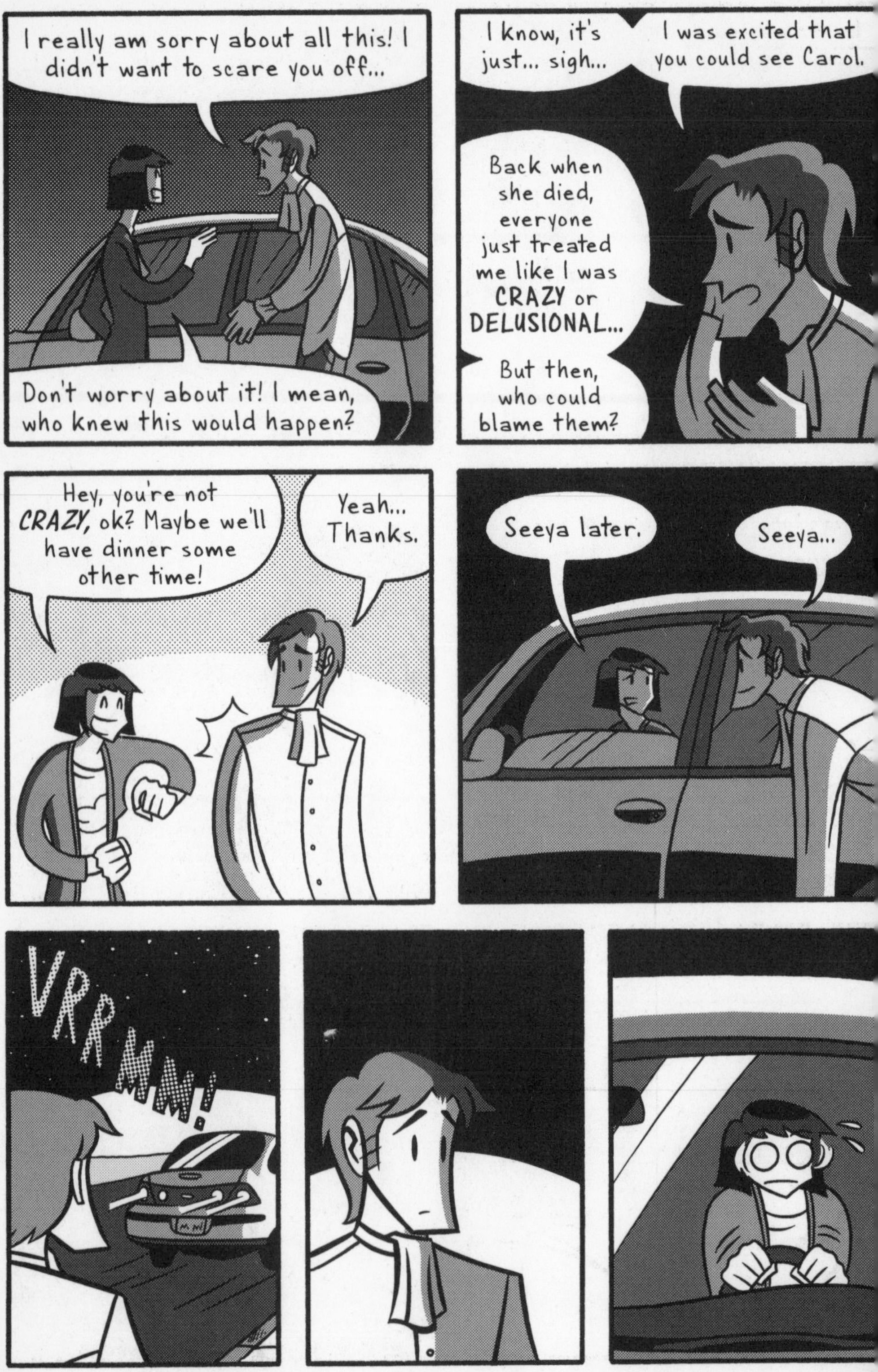
I really am sorry about all this! I didn't want to scare you off...
Don't worry about it! I mean, who knew this would happen?
I know, it's just... sigh...
I was excited that you could see Carol.
Back when she died, everyone just treated me like I was CRAZY or DELUSIONAL...
But then, who could blame them?
Hey, you're not CRAZY, ok? Maybe we'll have dinner some other time!
Yeah... Thanks.
Seeya later.
Seeya...
VRRMMM!

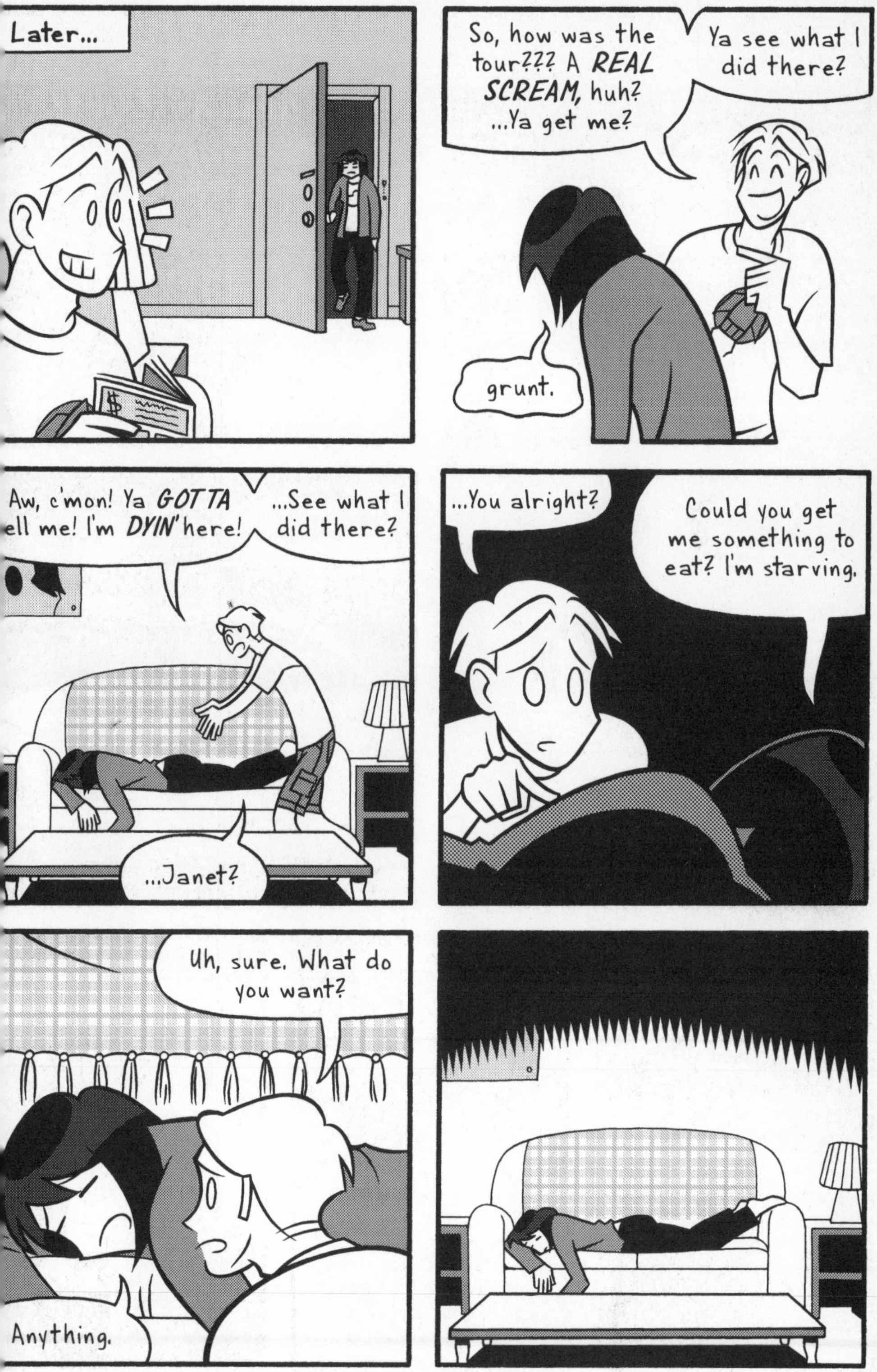
Later...
So, how was the tour??? A REAL SCREAM, huh? ...Ya get me?
Ya see what I did there?
grunt.
Aw, c'mon! Ya GOTTA ell me! I'm DYIN' here!
...See what I did there?
...Janet?
...You alright?
Could you get me something to eat? I'm starving.
Uh, sure. What do you want?
Anything.

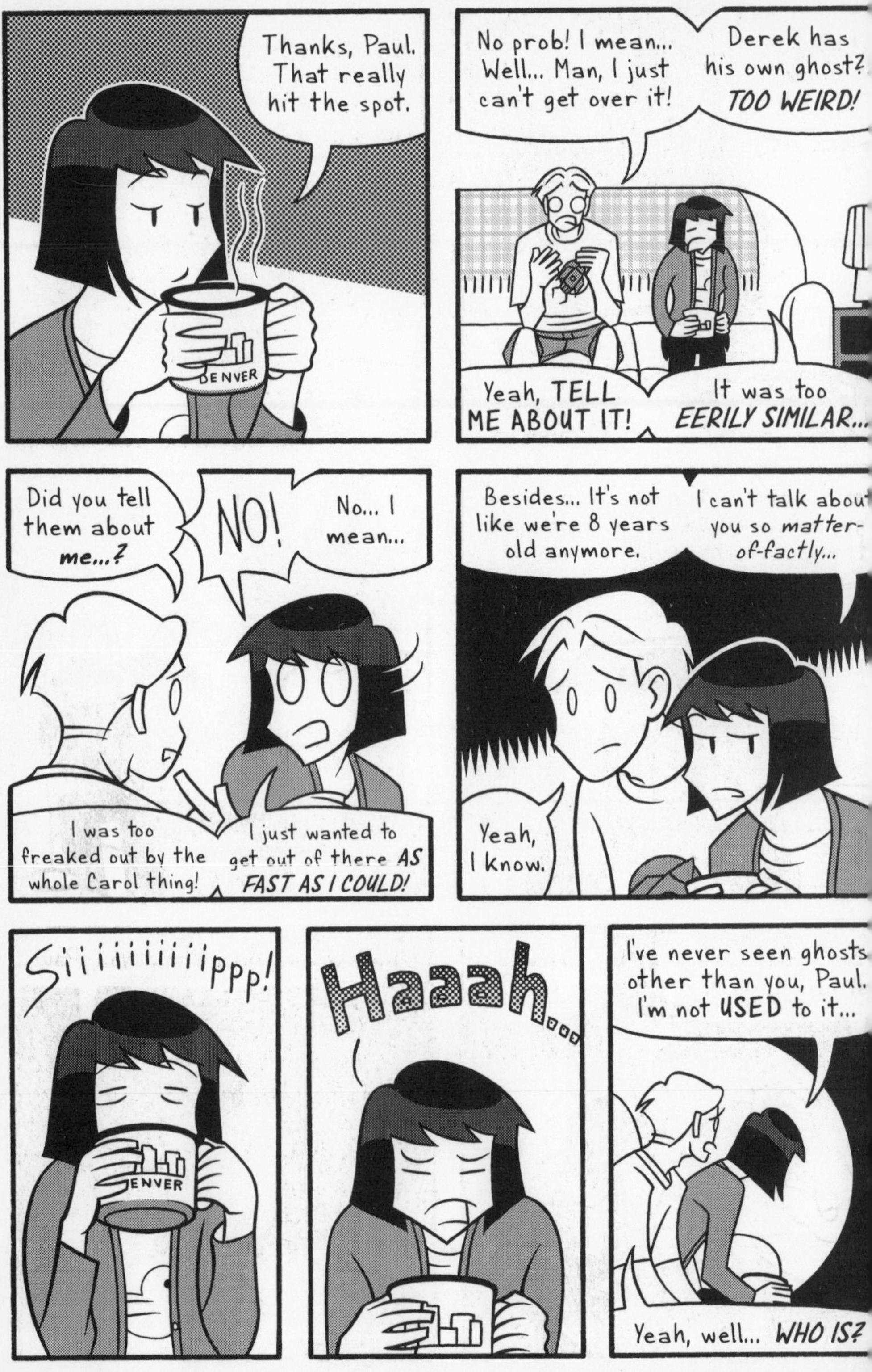
Thanks, Paul. That really hit the spot.
DENVER
No prob! I mean... Well... Man, I just can't get over it!
Derek has his own ghost? TOO WEIRD!
Yeah, TELL ME ABOUT IT!
It was too EERILY SIMILAR...
Did you tell them about me...?
NO!
No... I mean...
I was too freaked out by the whole Carol thing!
I just wanted to get out of there AS FAST AS I COULD!
Besides... It's not like we're 8 years old anymore.
I can't talk about you so matter-of-factly...
Yeah, I know.
Siiiiiiiiiippp!
ENVER
Haaah...
I've never seen ghosts other than you, Paul. I'm not USED to it...
Yeah, well... WHO IS?

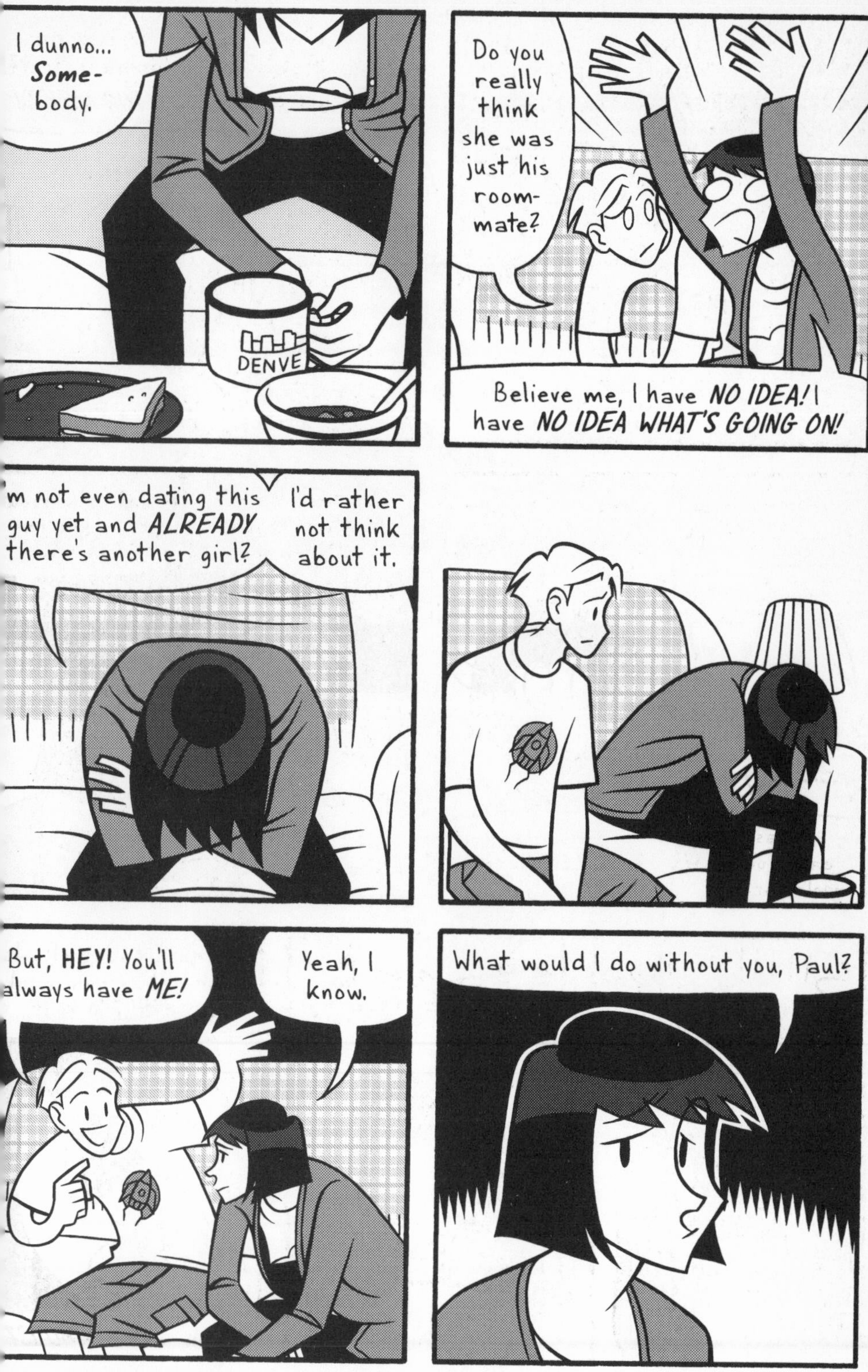
I dunno... **Some-**body.
DENVE
Do you really think she was just his room-mate?
Believe me, I have ***NO IDEA!*** I have ***NO IDEA WHAT'S GOING ON!***
m not even dating this guy yet and ***ALREADY*** there's another girl?
I'd rather not think about it.
But, **HEY!** You'll always have ***ME!***
Yeah, I know.
What would I do without you, Paul?

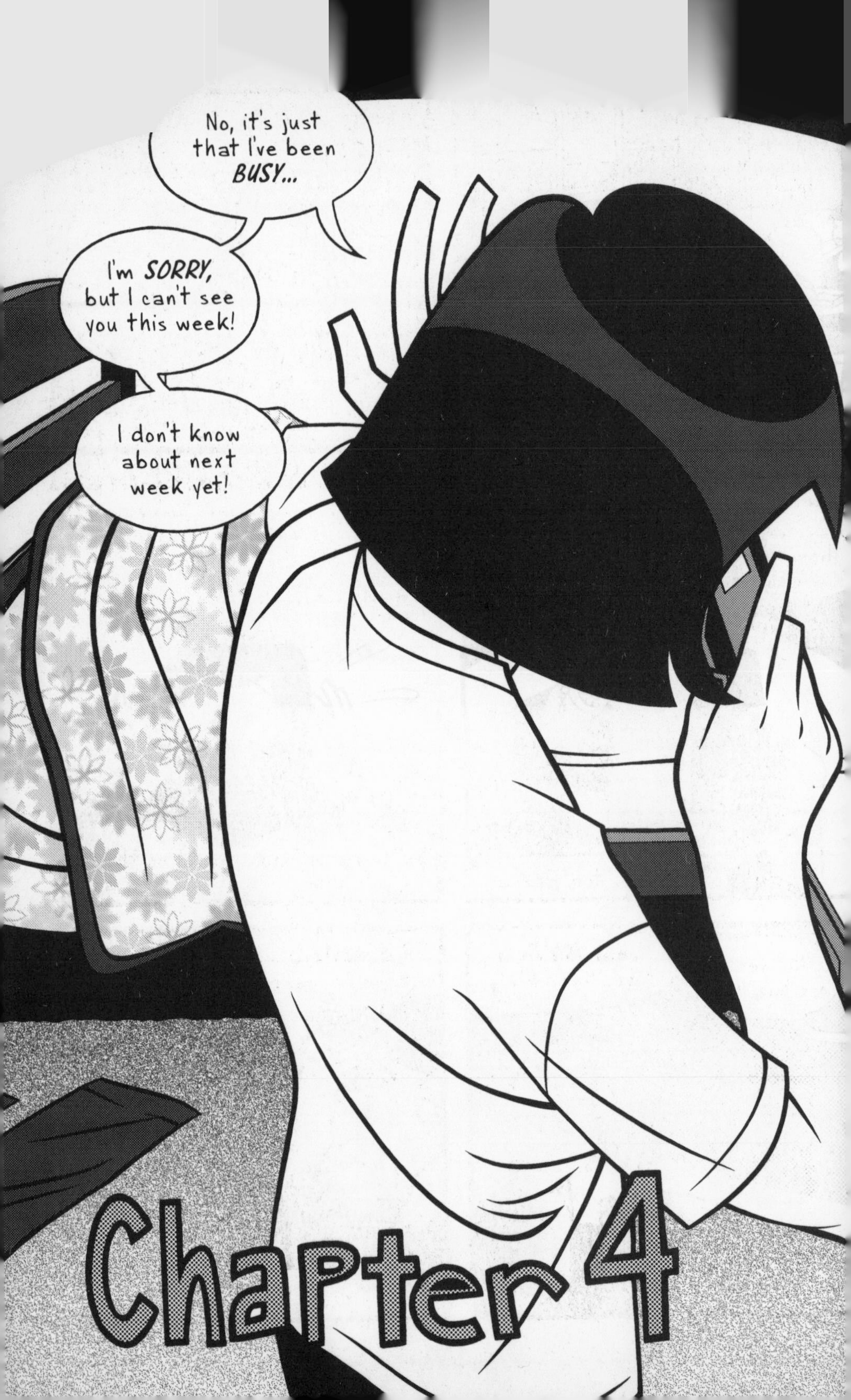
No, it's just that I've been *BUSY*...
I'm *SORRY*, but I can't see you this week!
I don't know about next week yet!
Chapter 4

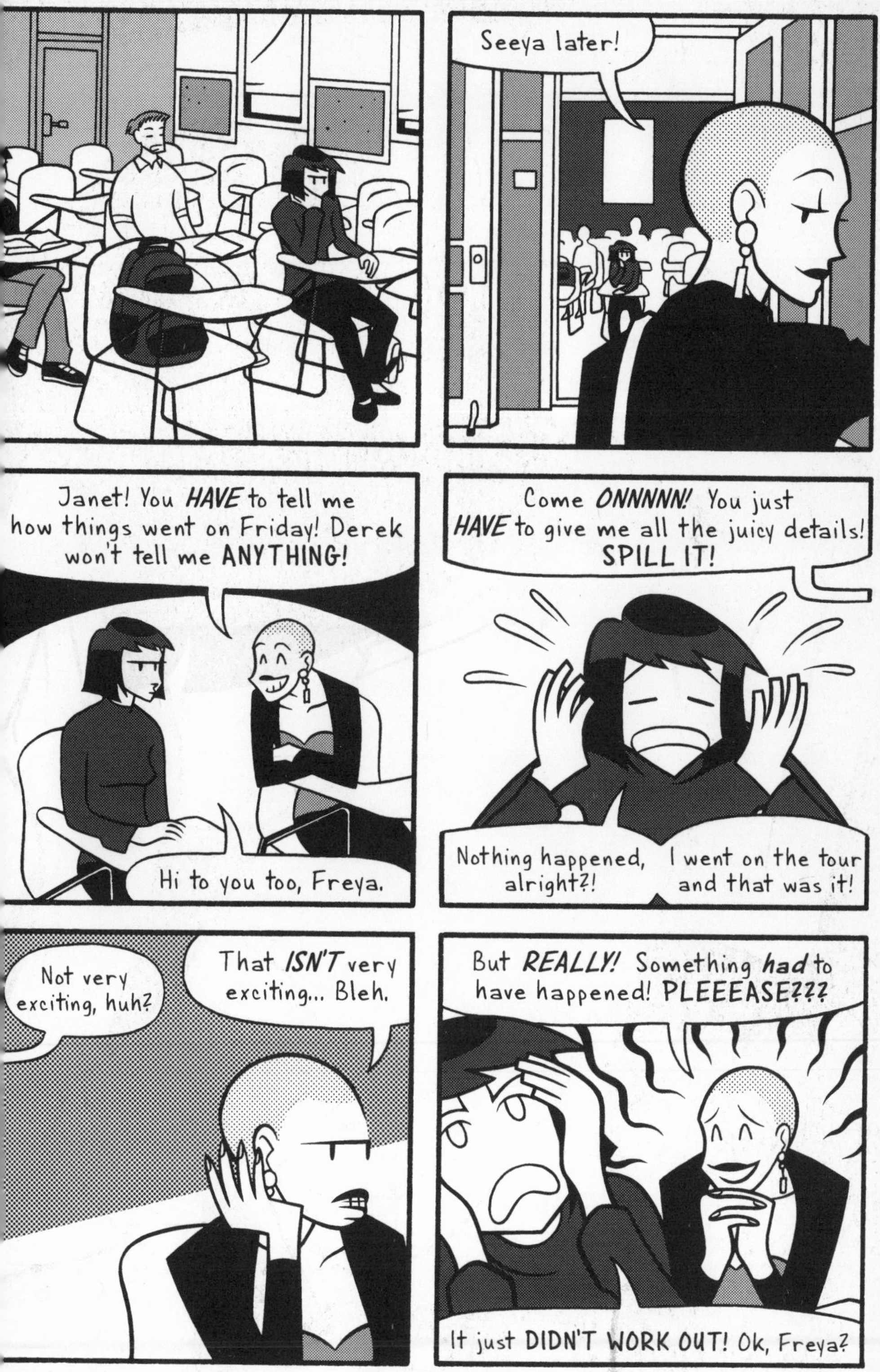
Seeya later!
Janet! You HAVE to tell me how things went on Friday! Derek won't tell me ANYTHING!
Hi to you too, Freya.
Come ONNNNN! You just HAVE to give me all the juicy details! SPILL IT!
Nothing happened, alright?!
I went on the tour and that was it!
Not very exciting, huh?
That ISN'T very exciting... Bleh.
But REALLY! Something had to have happened! PLEEEASE???
It just DIDN'T WORK OUT! Ok, Freya?

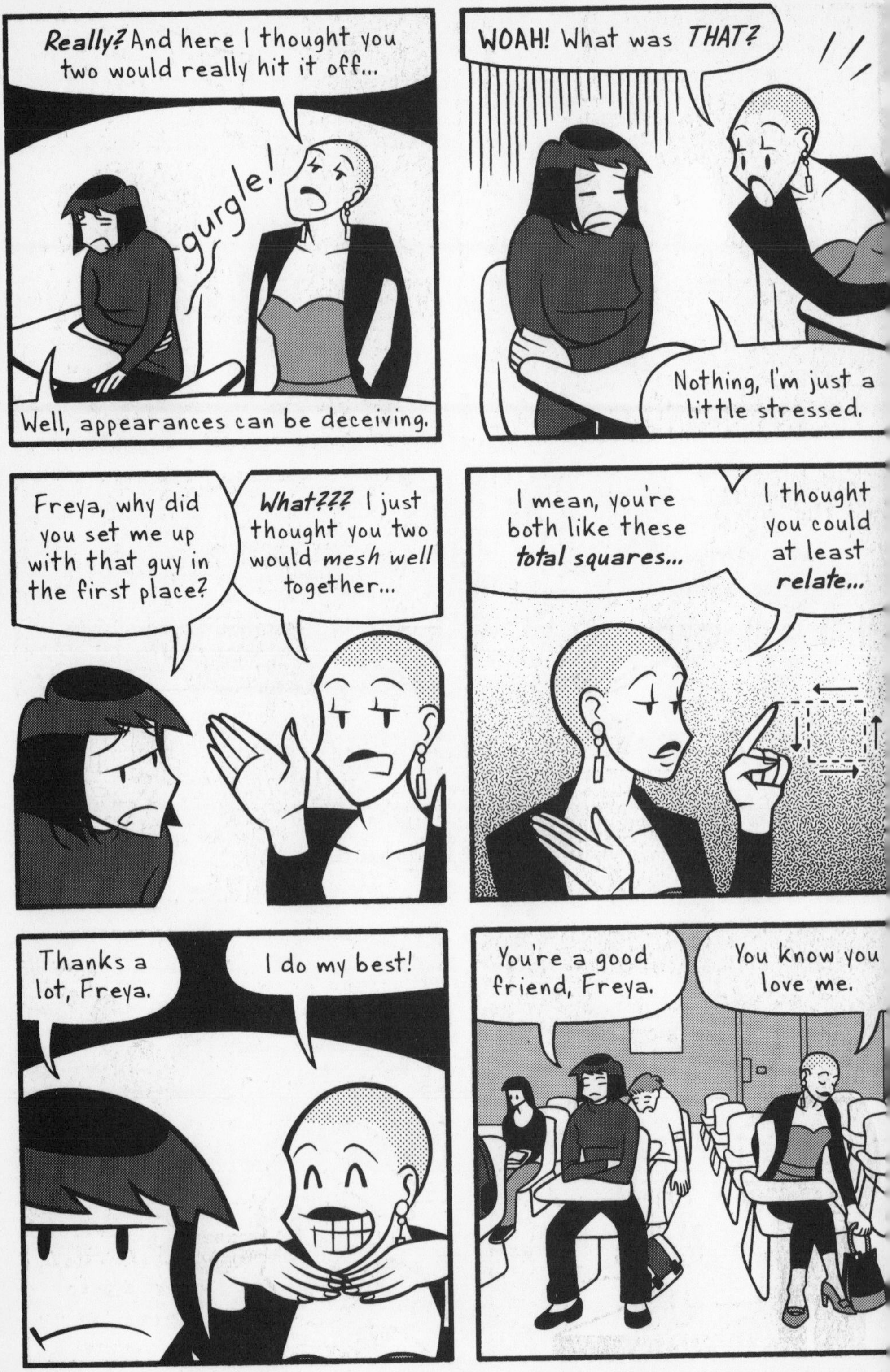
Really? And here I thought you two would really hit it off...
gurgle!
Well, appearances can be deceiving.
WOAH! What was THAT?
Nothing, I'm just a little stressed.
Freya, why did you set me up with that guy in the first place?
What??? I just thought you two would mesh well together...
I mean, you're both like these total squares...
I thought you could at least relate...
Thanks a lot, Freya.
I do my best!
You're a good friend, Freya.
You know you love me.

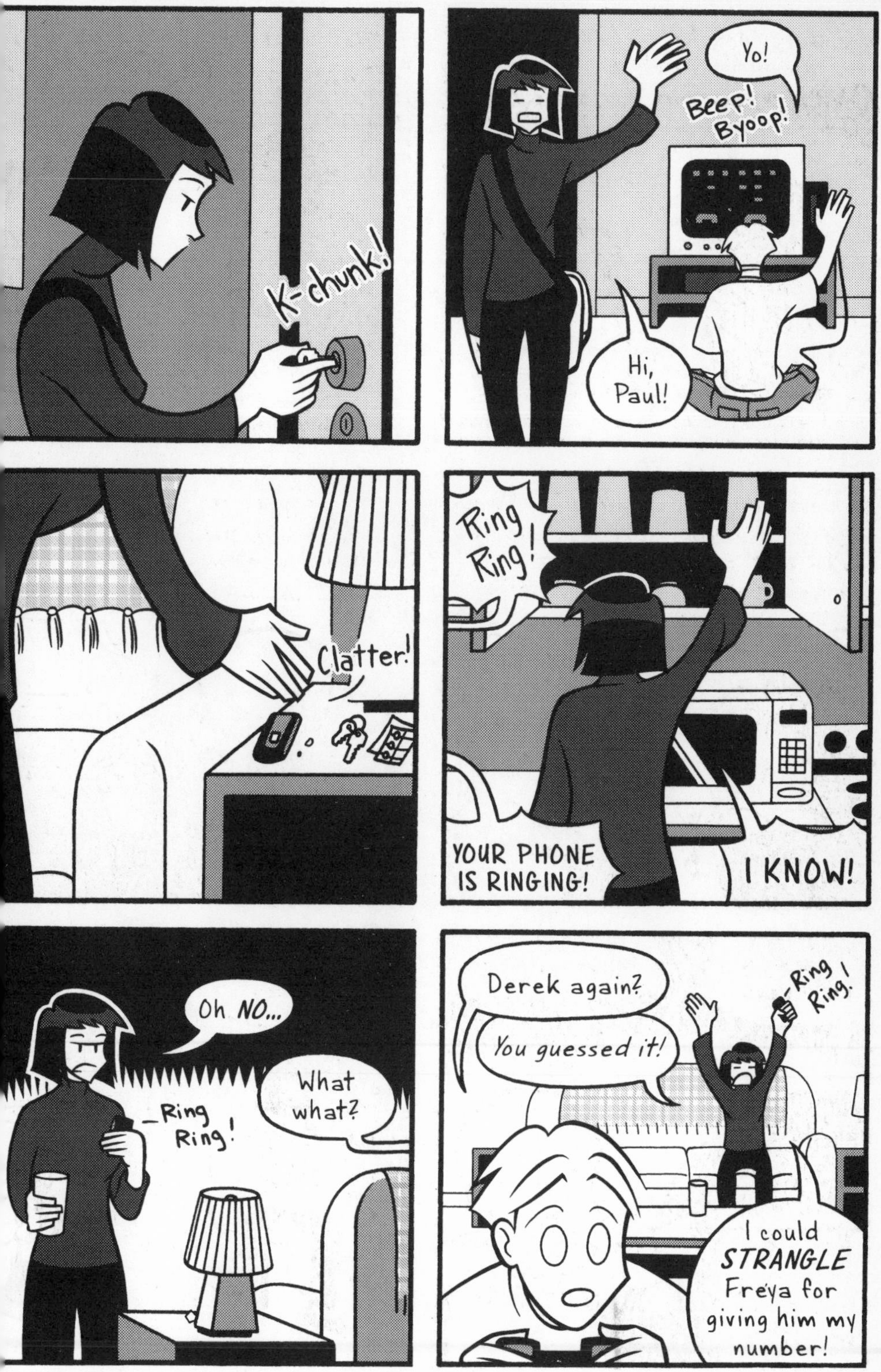
K-chunk!
Yo!
Beep! Byoop!
Hi, Paul!
Clatter!
Ring Ring!
YOUR PHONE IS RINGING!
I KNOW!
Oh NO...
Ring Ring!
What what?
Derek again?
You guessed it!
Ring Ring!
I could STRANGLE Freya for giving him my number!

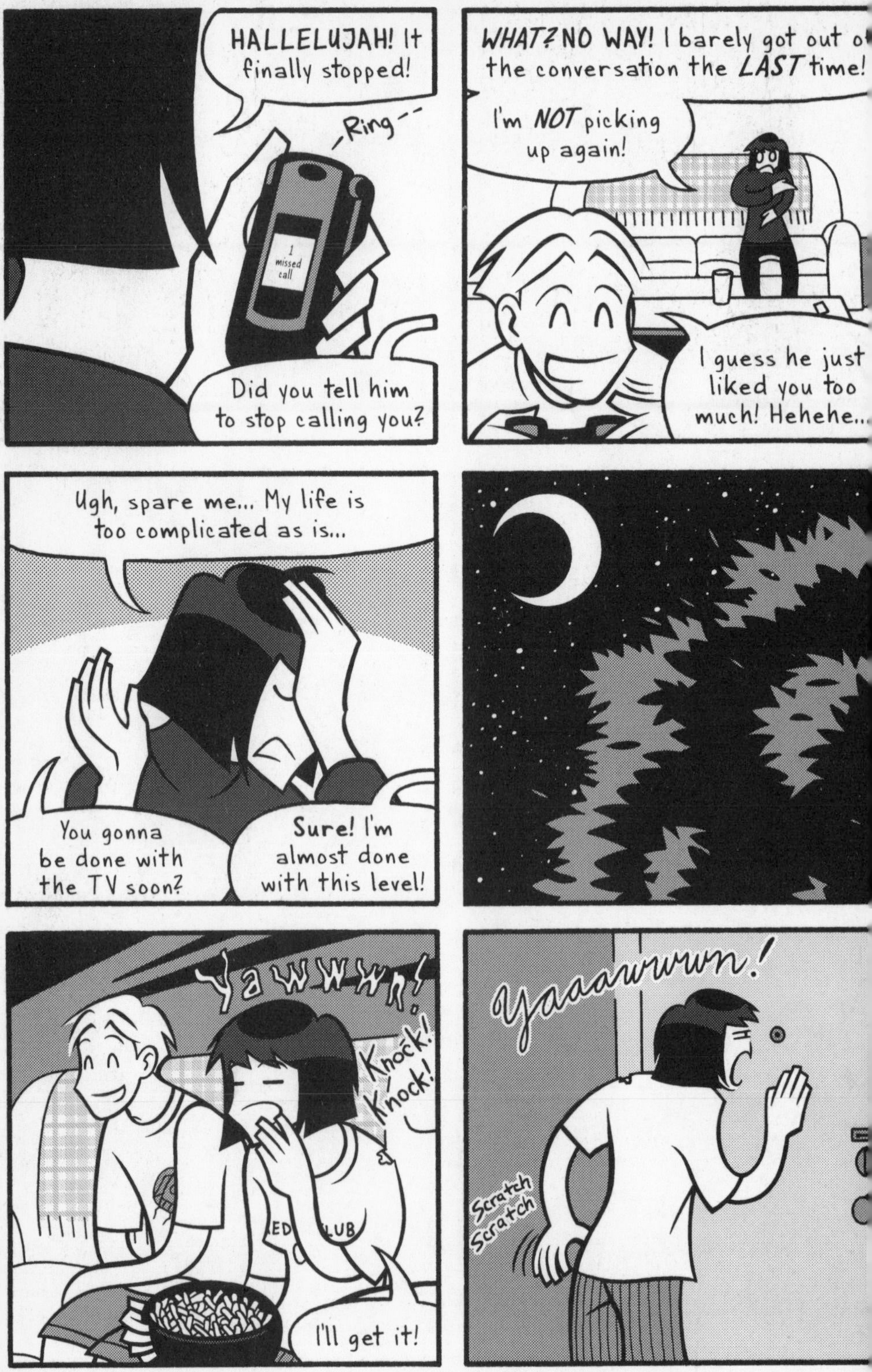
HALLELUJAH! It finally stopped!
Ring
1 missed call
Did you tell him to stop calling you?
WHAT? NO WAY! I barely got out of the conversation the LAST time!
I'm NOT picking up again!
I guess he just liked you too much! Hehehe...
Ugh, spare me... My life is too complicated as is...
You gonna be done with the TV soon?
Sure! I'm almost done with this level!
Yawwwn!
Knock! Knock!
I'll get it!
Yaaawwwn!
Scratch Scratch

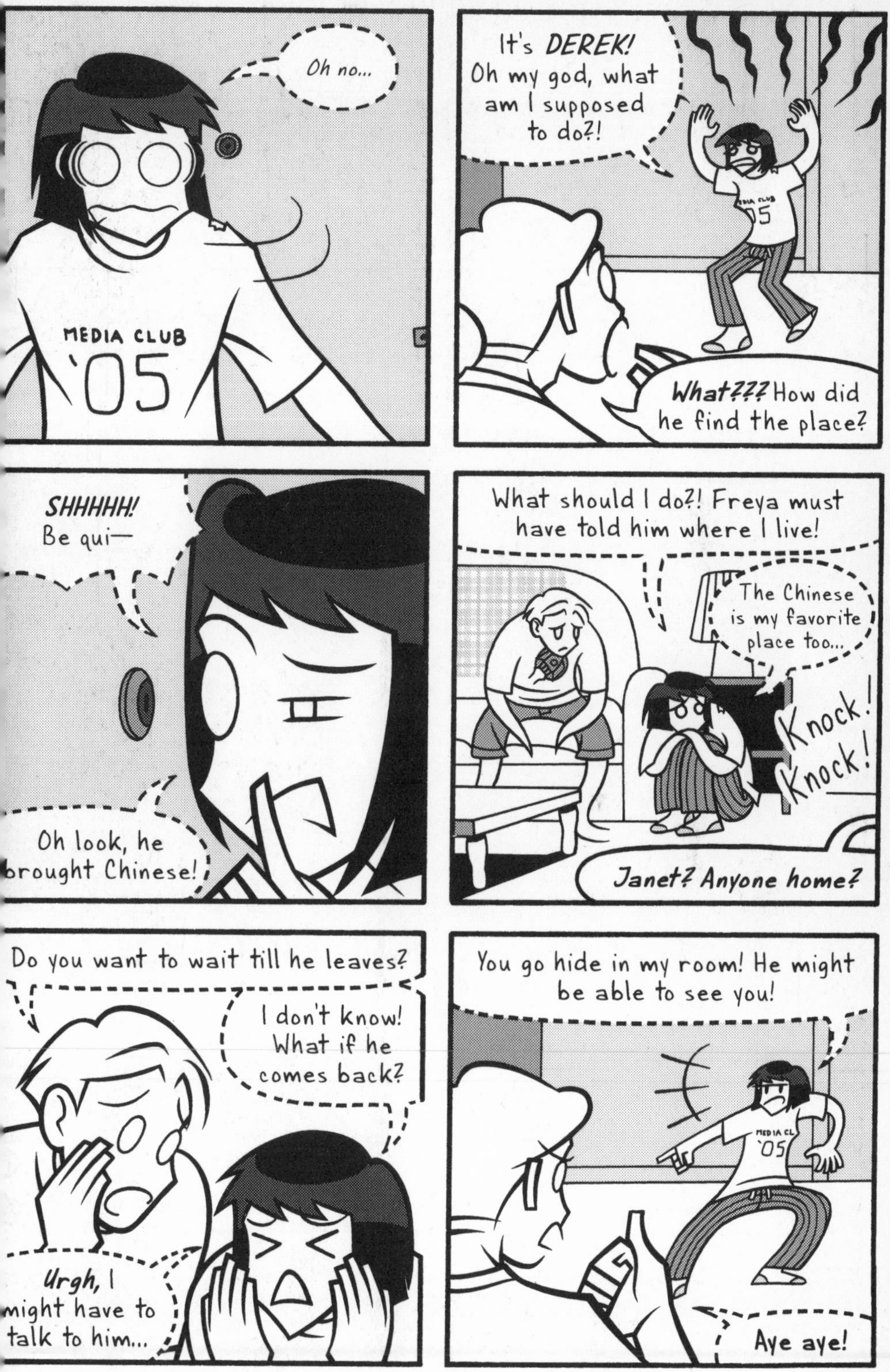
Oh no...
It's DEREK! Oh my god, what am I supposed to do?!
What??? How did he find the place?
SHHHHH! Be qui—
Oh look, he brought Chinese!
What should I do?! Freya must have told him where I live!
The Chinese is my favorite place too...
Knock! Knock!
Janet? Anyone home?
Do you want to wait till he leaves?
I don't know! What if he comes back?
Urgh, I might have to talk to him...
You go hide in my room! He might be able to see you!
Aye aye!

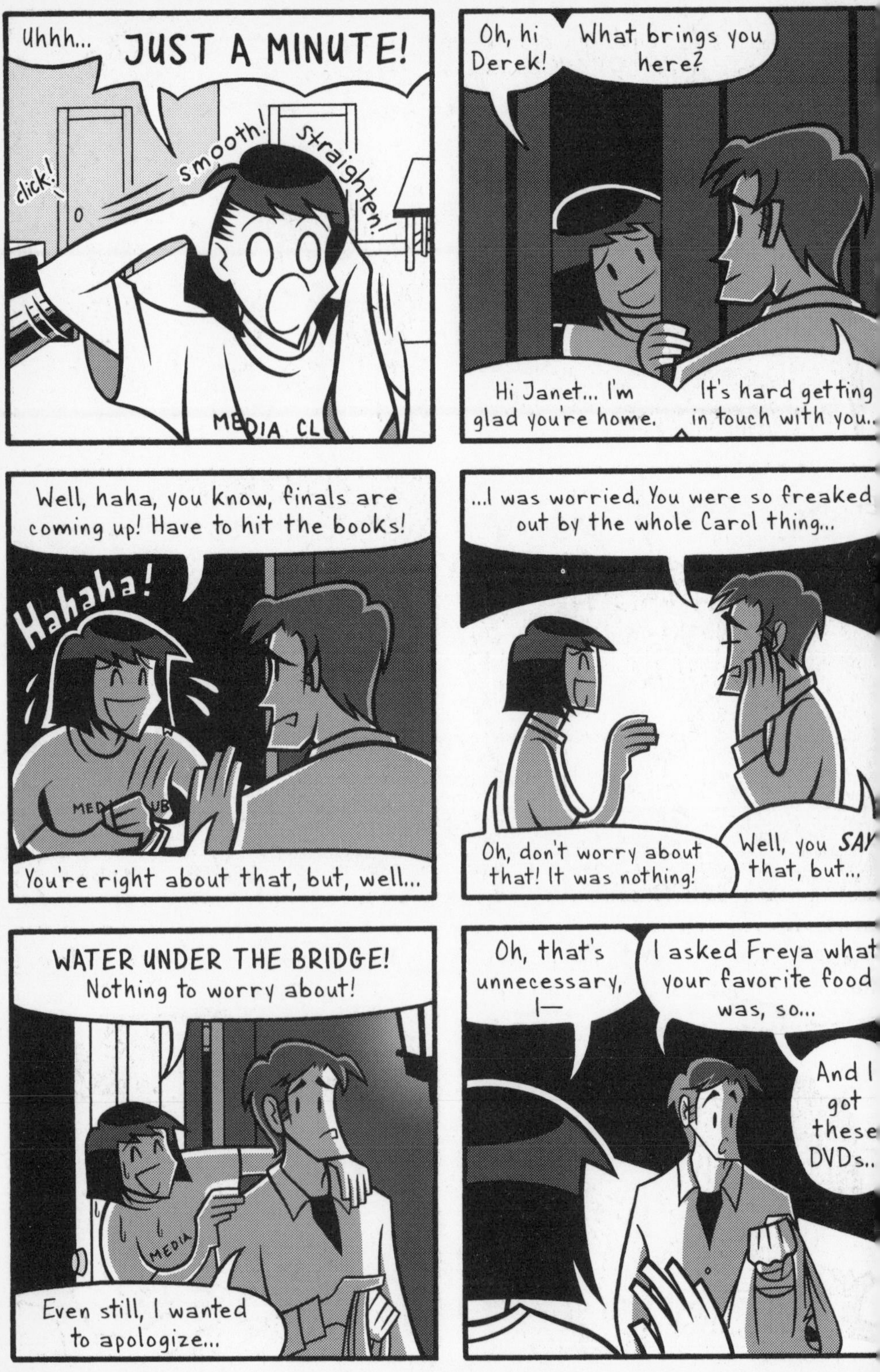
Uhhh...
JUST A MINUTE!
click!
smooth!
straighten!
MEDIA CL
Oh, hi Derek!
What brings you here?
Hi Janet... I'm glad you're home.
It's hard getting in touch with you..
Well, haha, you know, finals are coming up! Have to hit the books!
Hahaha!
MEDI UB
You're right about that, but, well...
...I was worried. You were so freaked out by the whole Carol thing...
Oh, don't worry about that! It was nothing!
Well, you SAY that, but...
WATER UNDER THE BRIDGE!
Nothing to worry about!
MEDIA
Even still, I wanted to apologize...
Oh, that's unnecessary, I—
I asked Freya what your favorite food was, so...
And I got these DVDs..

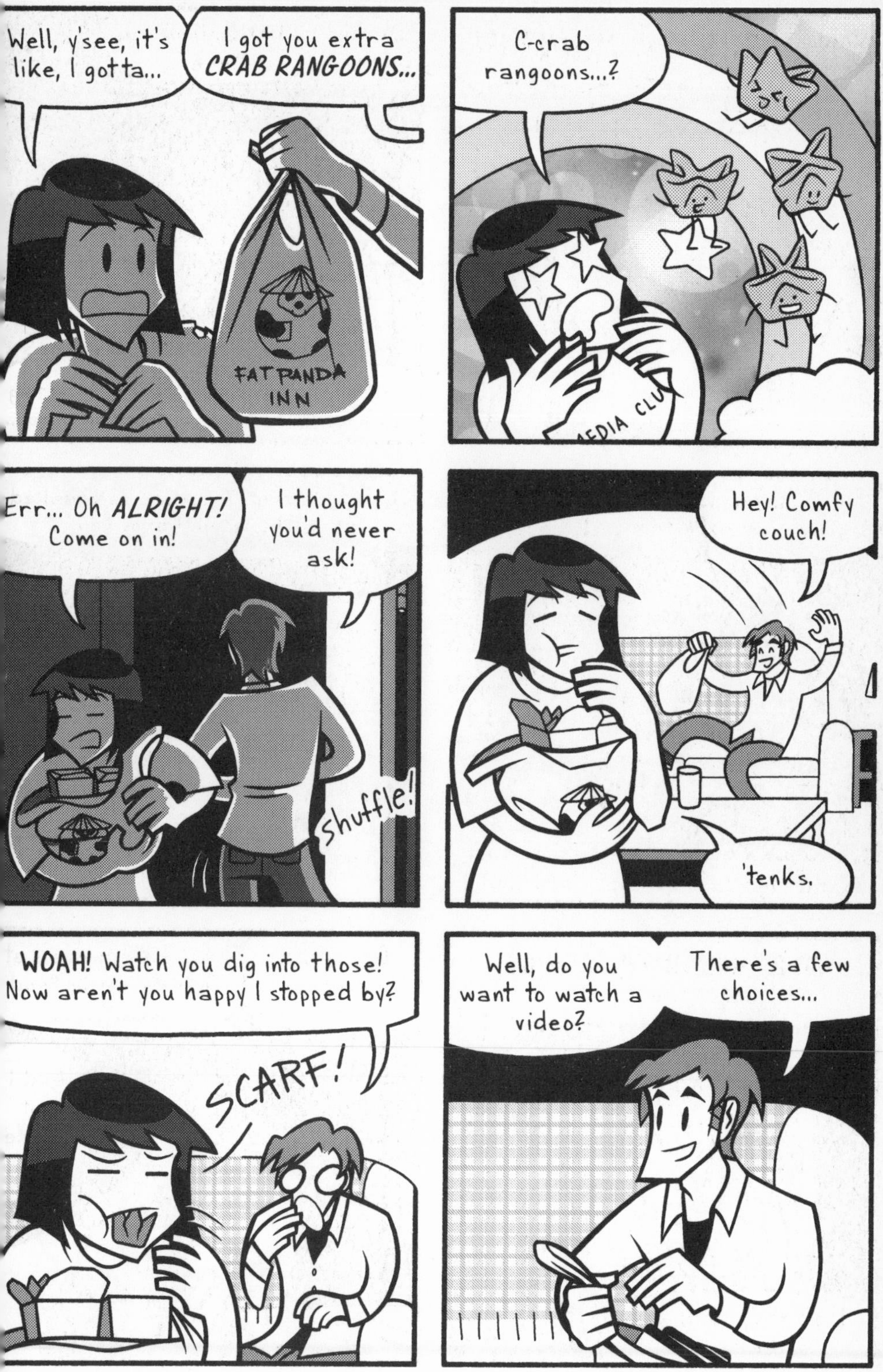
Well, y'see, it's like, I gotta...
I got you extra CRAB RANGOONS...
FAT PANDA INN
C-crab rangoons...?
MEDIA CLU
Err... Oh ALRIGHT! Come on in!
I thought you'd never ask!
shuffle!
Hey! Comfy couch!
'tenks.
WOAH! Watch you dig into those! Now aren't you happy I stopped by?
SCARF!
Well, do you want to watch a video?
There's a few choices...

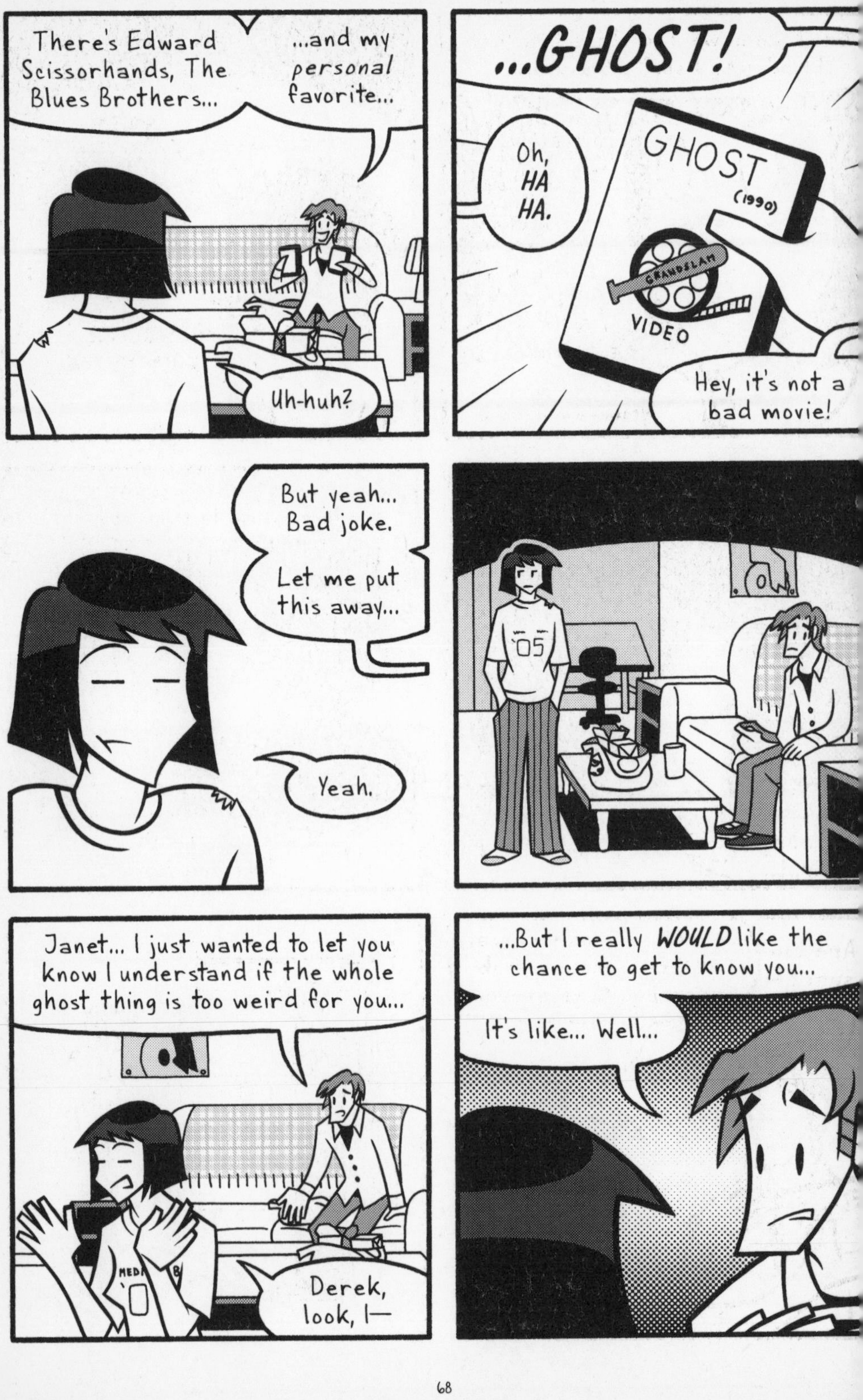
There's Edward Scissorhands, The Blues Brothers...
...and my personal favorite...
Uh-huh?
...GHOST!
Oh, HA HA.
GHOST
(1990)
GRANDSLAM
VIDEO
Hey, it's not a bad movie!
But yeah... Bad joke.
Let me put this away...
Yeah.
'05
Janet... I just wanted to let you know I understand if the whole ghost thing is too weird for you...
Derek, look, I—
...But I really *WOULD* like the chance to get to know you...
It's like... Well...

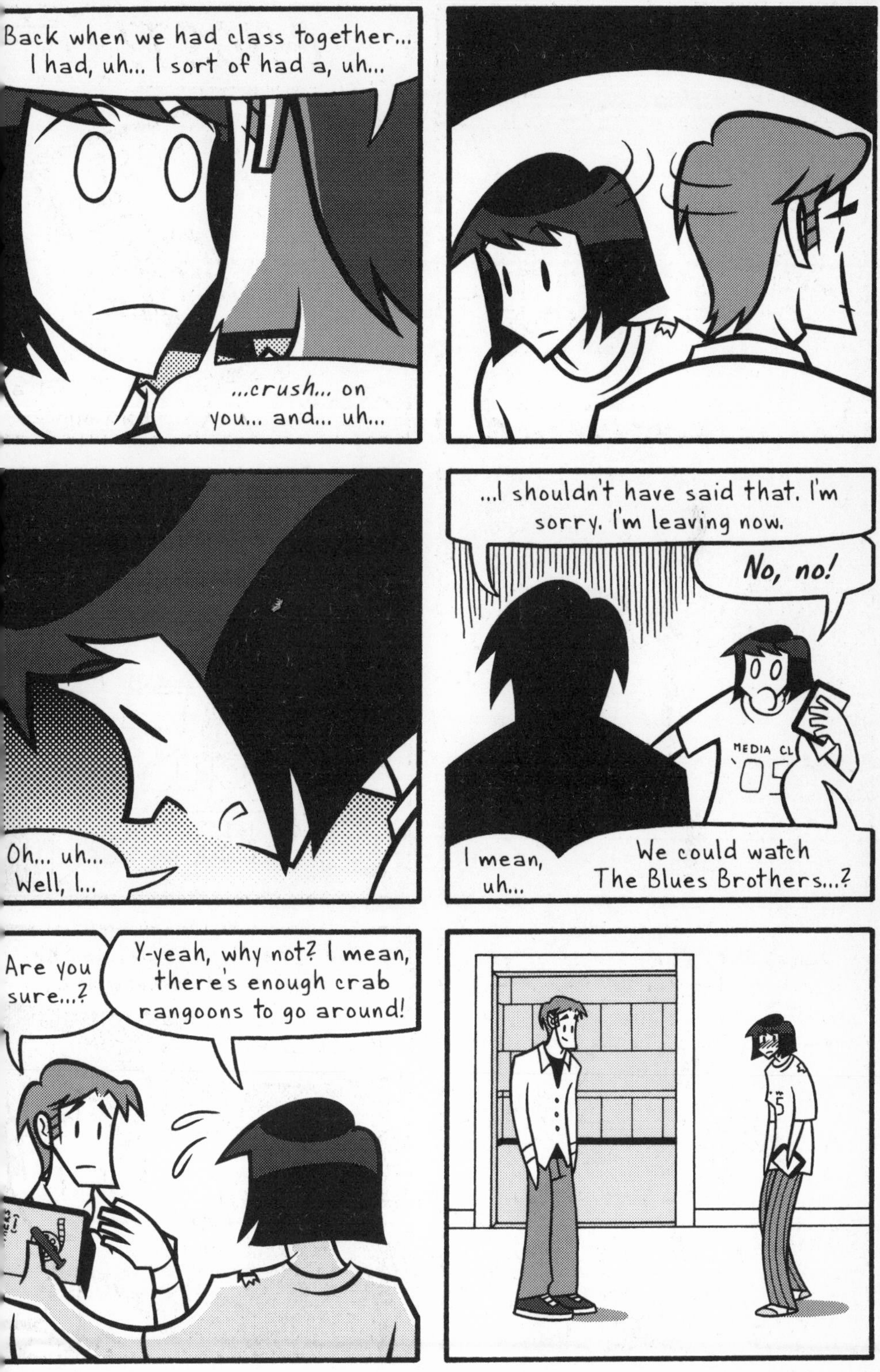
Back when we had class together...
I had, uh... I sort of had a, uh...
...crush... on you... and... uh...
Oh... uh... Well, I...
...I shouldn't have said that. I'm sorry. I'm leaving now.
No, no!
MEDIA CL
'05
I mean, uh...
We could watch The Blues Brothers...?
Are you sure...?
Y-yeah, why not? I mean, there's enough crab rangoons to go around!

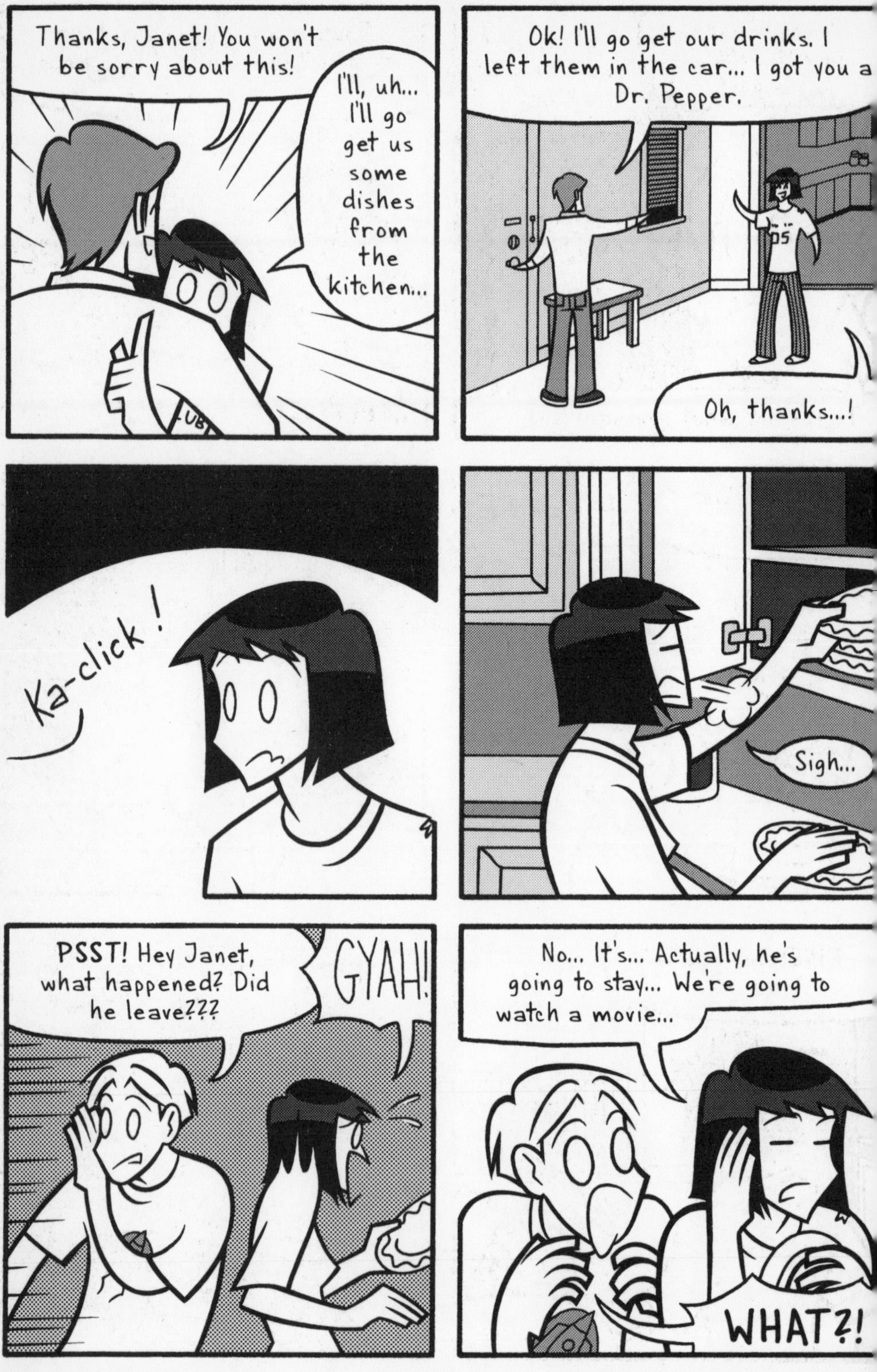

Thanks, Janet! You won't be sorry about this!
I'll, uh... I'll go get us some dishes from the kitchen...
Ok! I'll go get our drinks. I left them in the car... I got you a Dr. Pepper.
Oh, thanks...!
Ka-click!
Sigh...
PSST! Hey Janet, what happened? Did he leave???
GYAH!
No... It's... Actually, he's going to stay... We're going to watch a movie...
WHAT?!

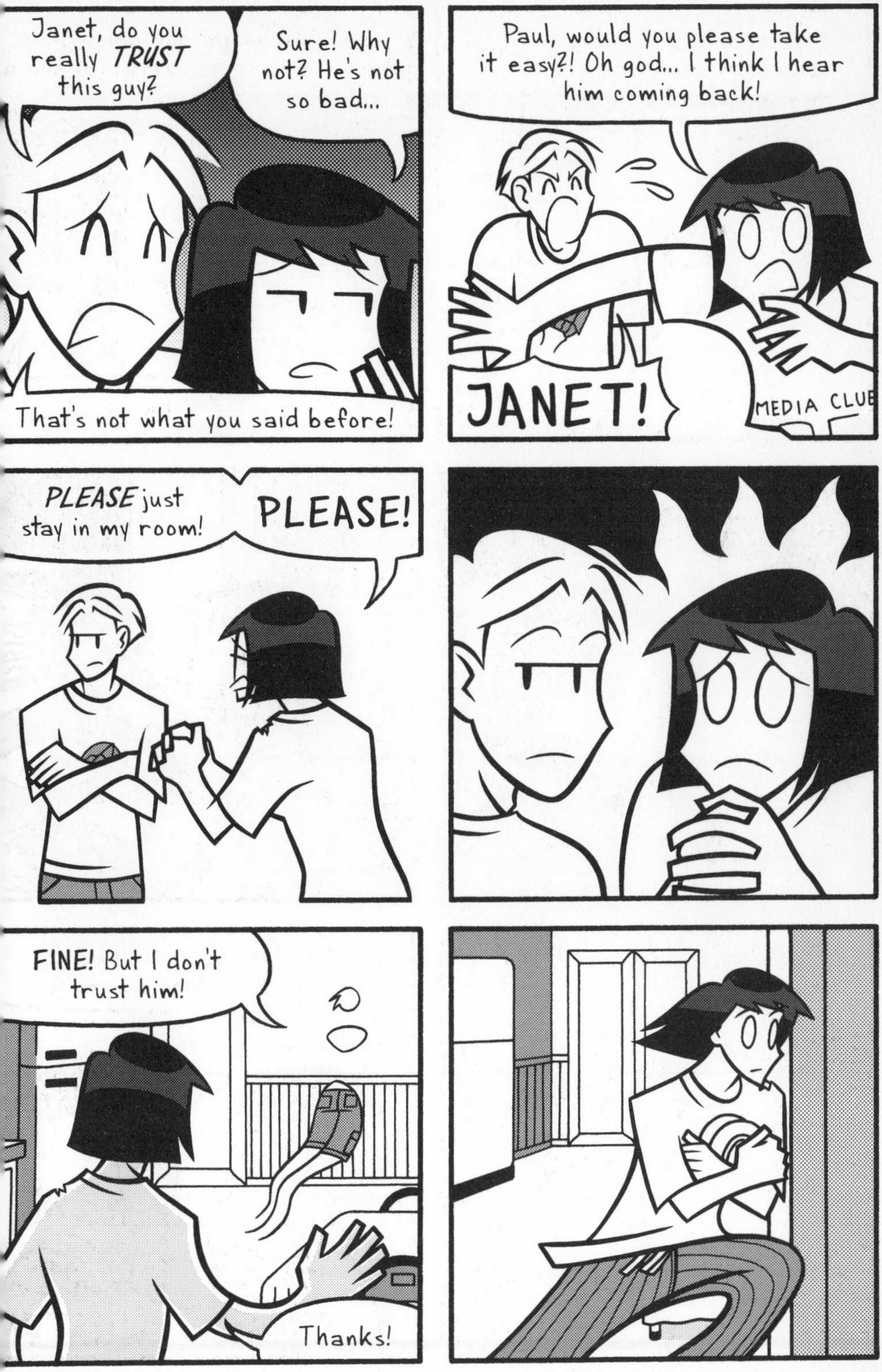

Janet, do you really TRUST this guy?
Sure! Why not? He's not so bad...
That's not what you said before!
Paul, would you please take it easy?! Oh god... I think I hear him coming back!
JANET!
MEDIA CLUB
PLEASE just stay in my room!
PLEASE!
FINE! But I don't trust him!
Thanks!

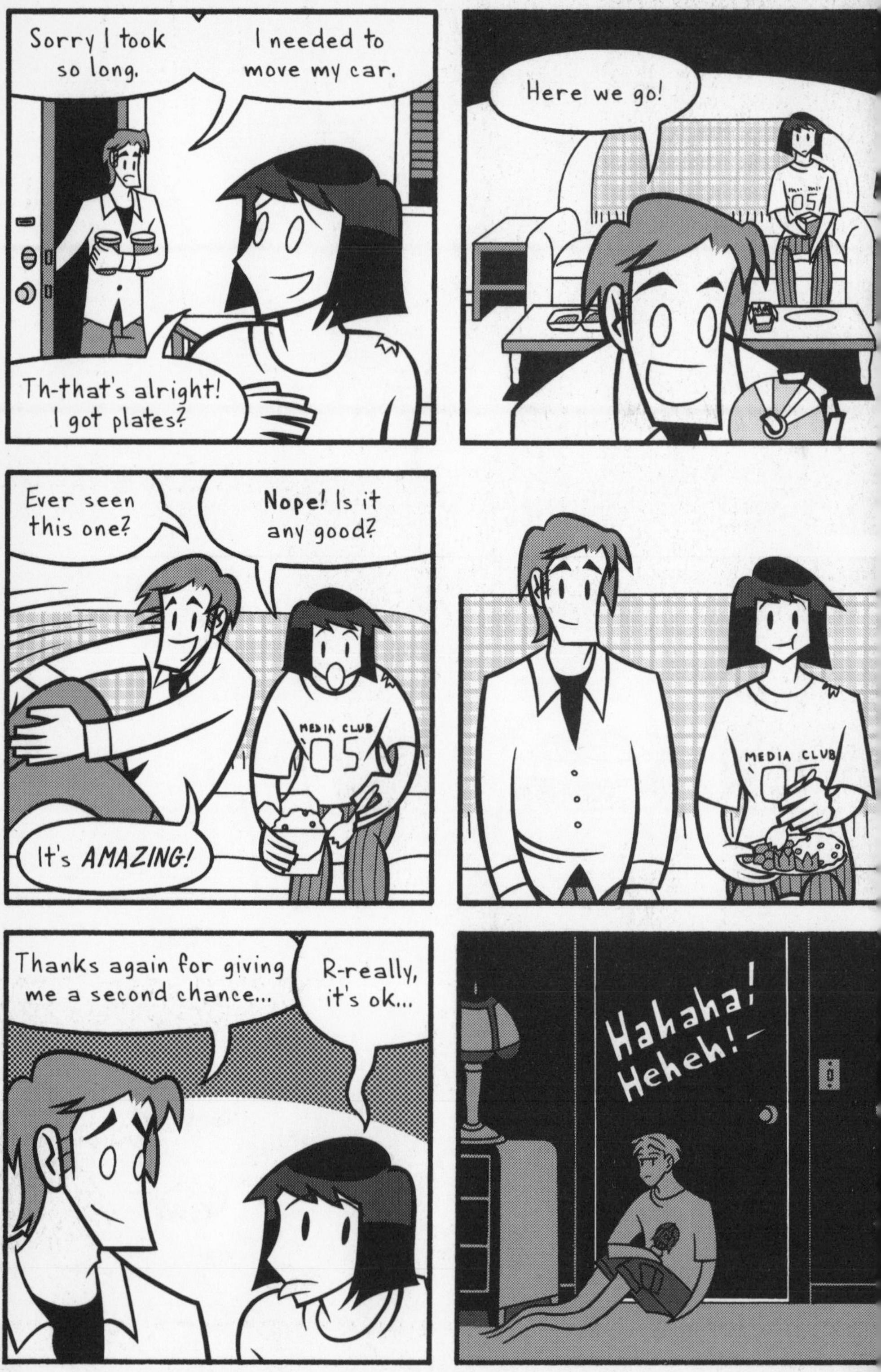
Sorry I took so long.
I needed to move my car.
Th-that's alright! I got plates?
Here we go!
Ever seen this one?
Nope! Is it any good?
It's AMAZING!
MEDIA CLUB '05
MEDIA CLUB
Thanks again for giving me a second chance...
R-really, it's ok...
Hahaha! Heheh!

Chapter 5

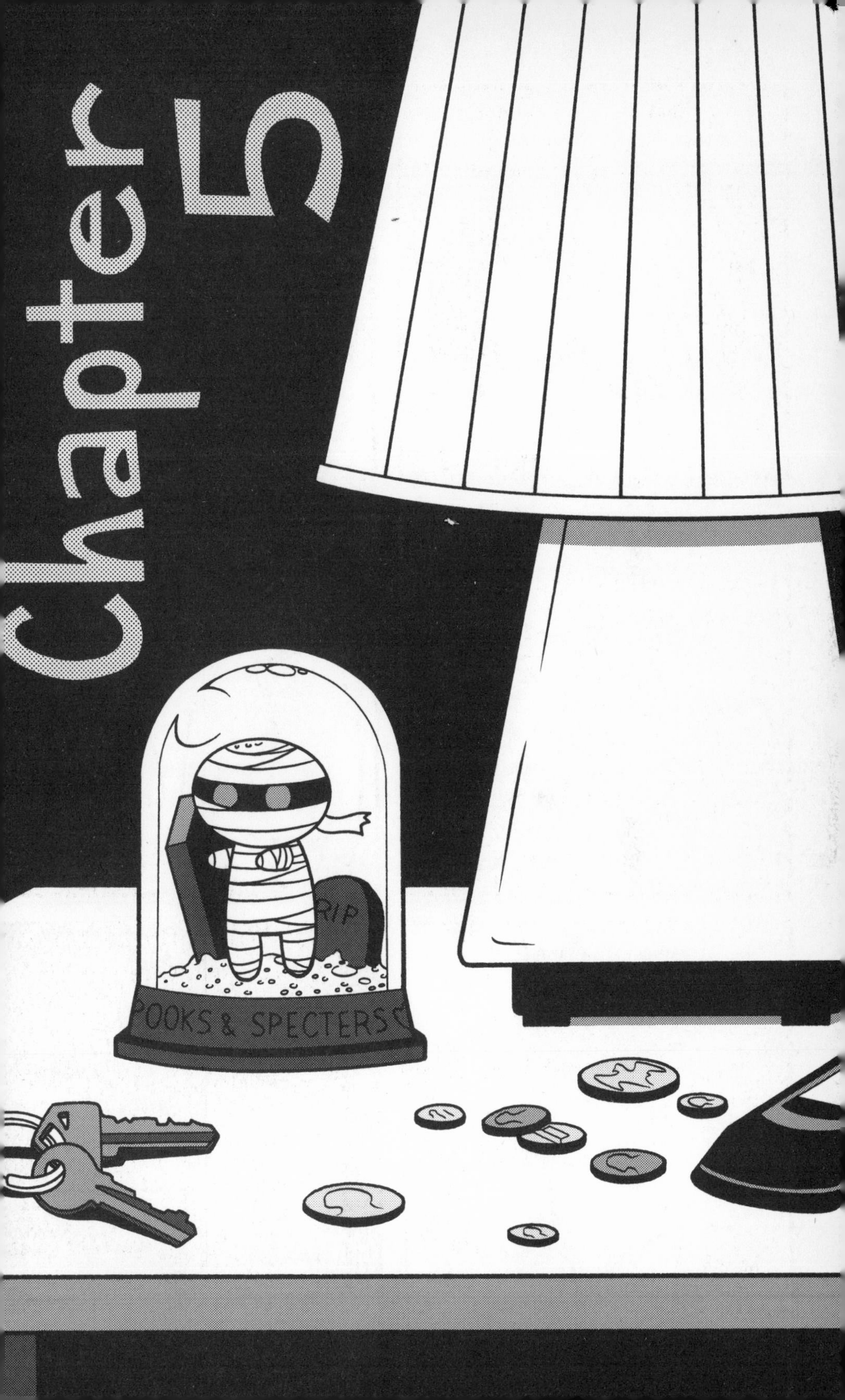
RIP
POOKS & SPECTERS

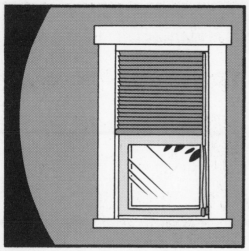

Another date with Derek?

Yep! We're making dinner at his place today!

Carol gonna be there too?

Dunno... I guess so.

Why do you ask?

No reason... Just curious!

Hmm... Well...

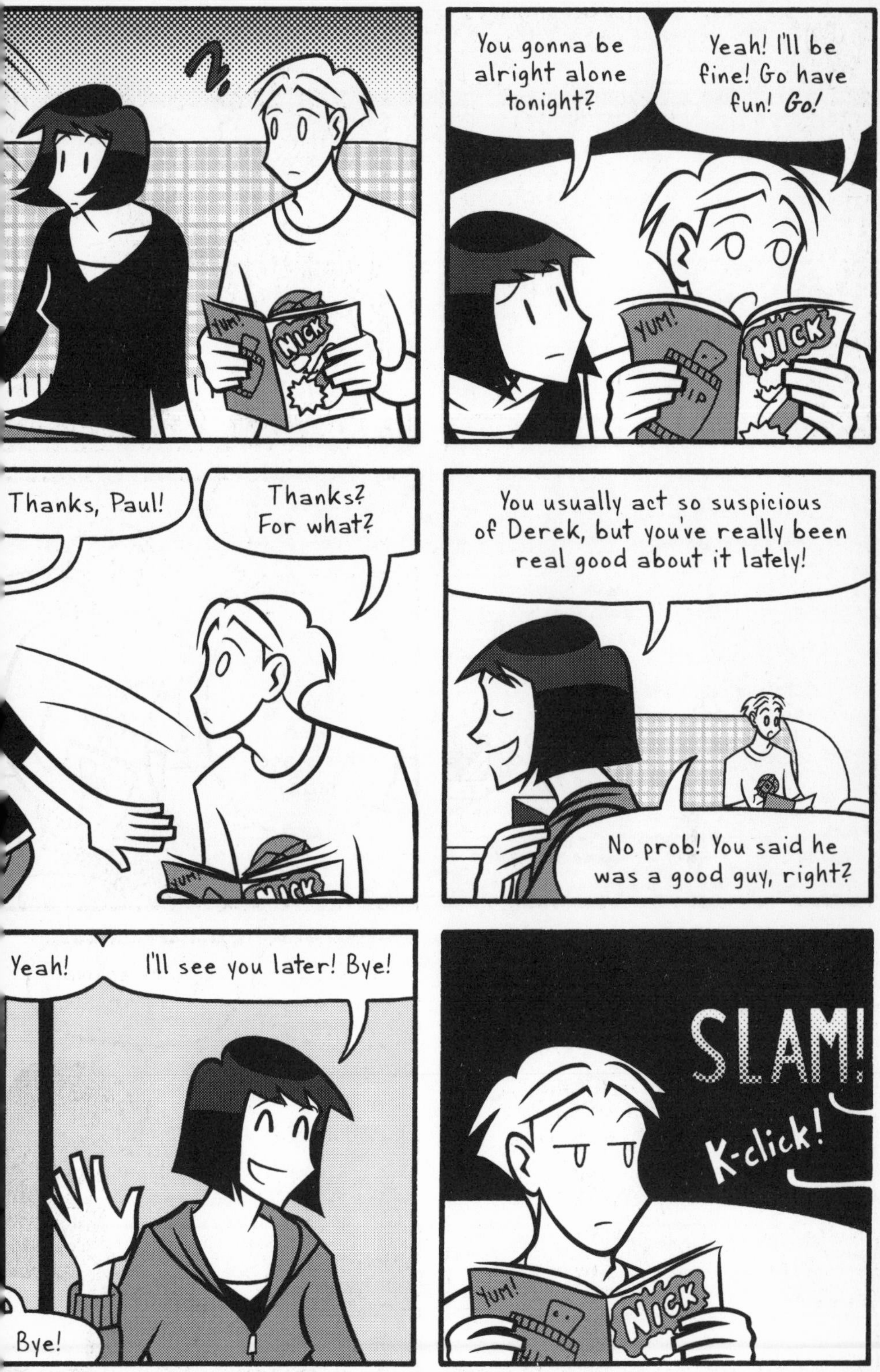
?
YUM!
NICK
You gonna be alright alone tonight?
Yeah! I'll be fine! Go have fun! *Go!*
Thanks, Paul!
Thanks? For what?
You usually act so suspicious of Derek, but you've really been real good about it lately!
No prob! You said he was a good guy, right?
Yeah!
I'll see you later! Bye!
Bye!
SLAM!
K-click!

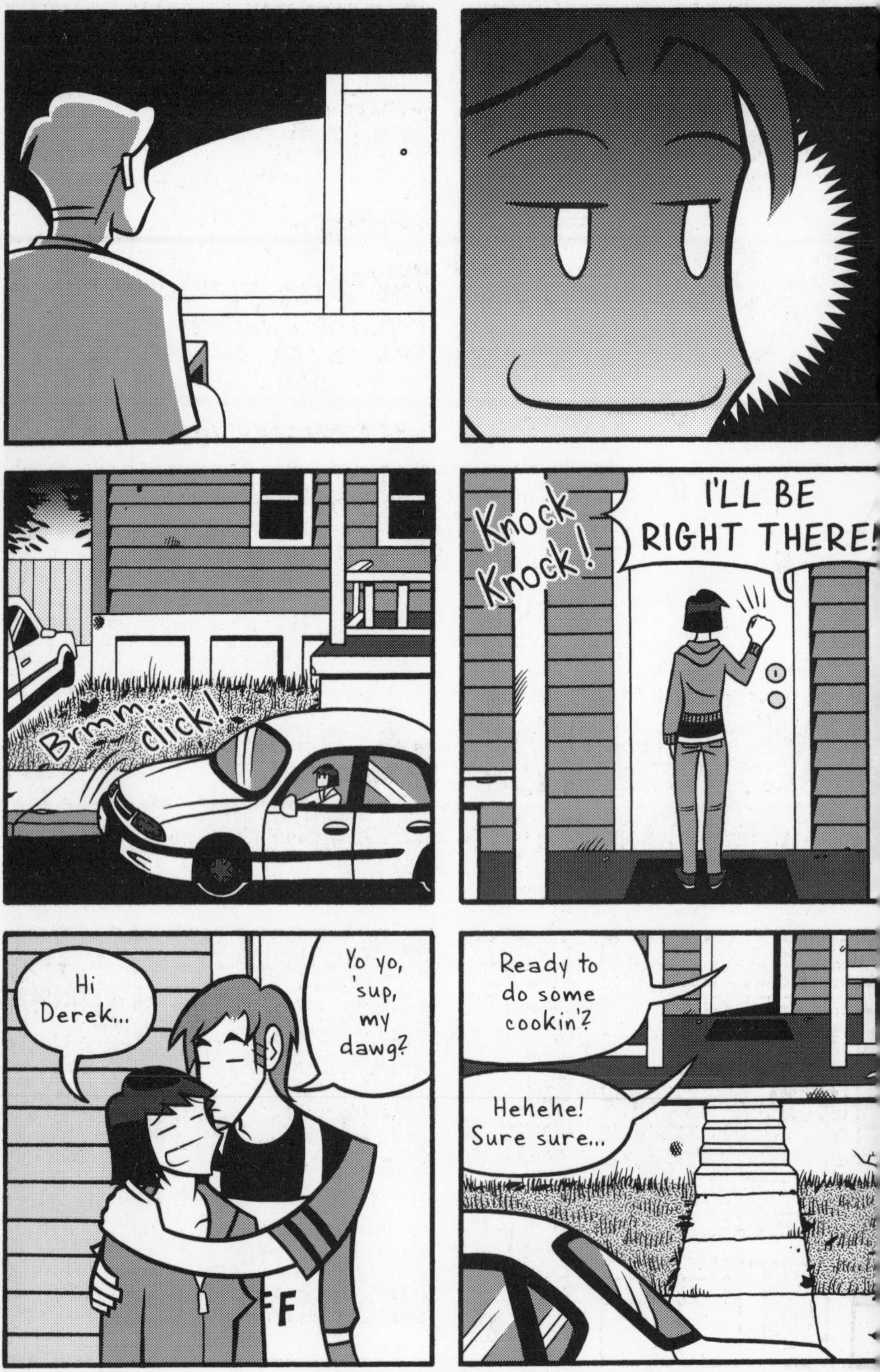
Knock Knock!
I'LL BE RIGHT THERE!
Brmm... click!
Hi Derek...
Yo yo, 'sup, my dawg?
Ready to do some cookin'?
Hehehe! Sure sure...

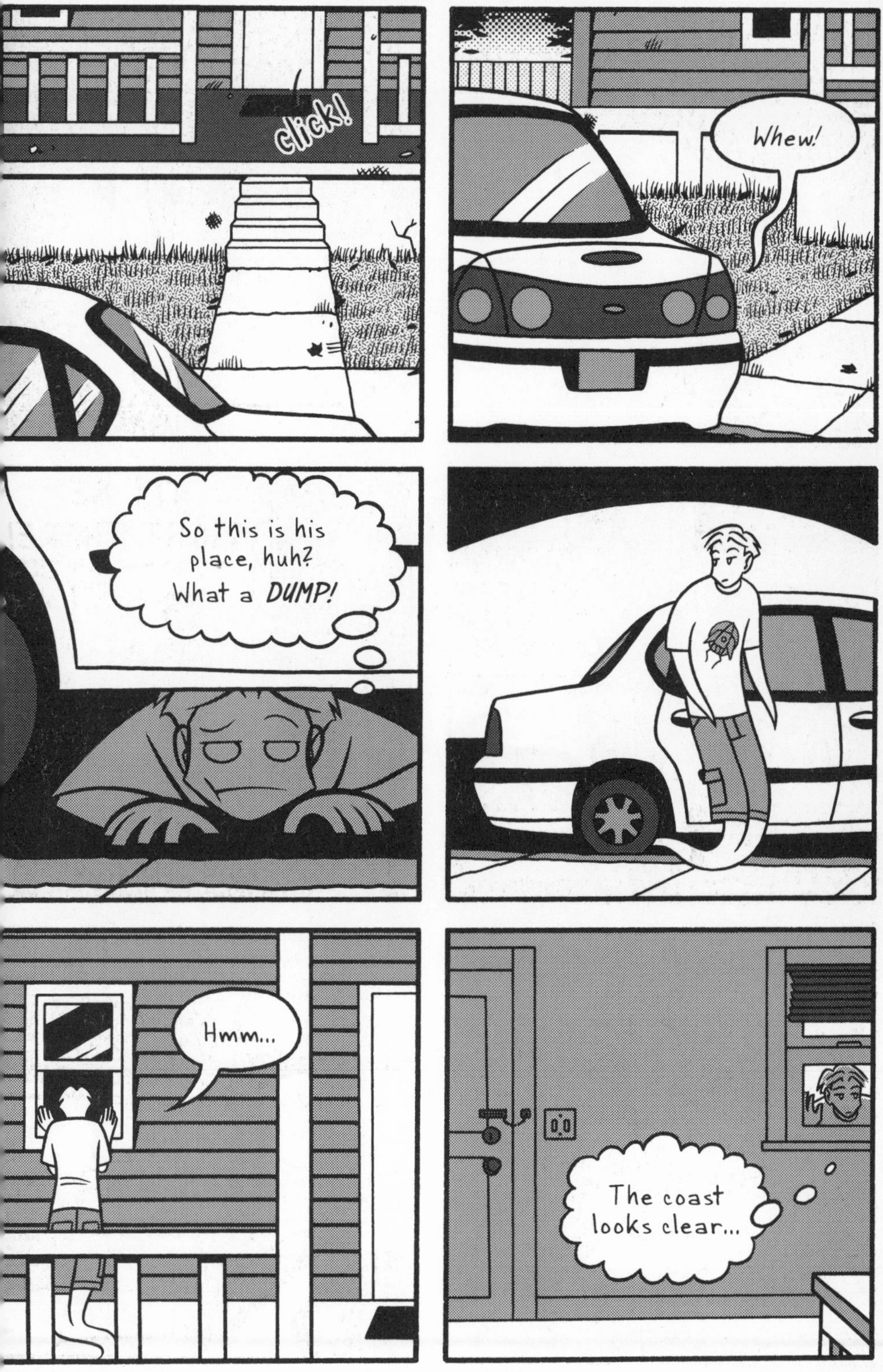
click!
Whew!
So this is his place, huh? What a DUMP!
Hmm...
The coast looks clear...

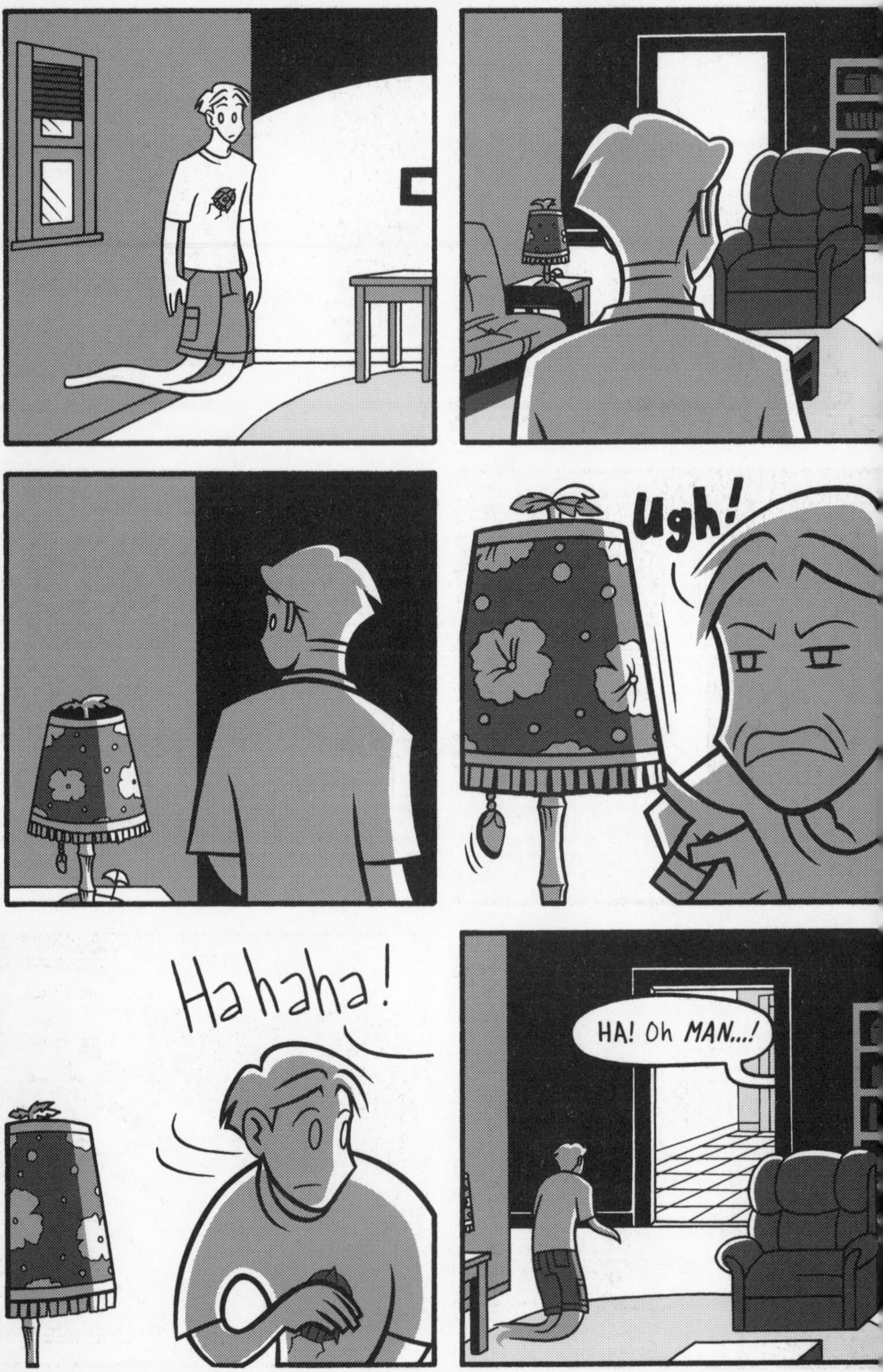
Ugh!
Hahaha!
HA! Oh MAN...!

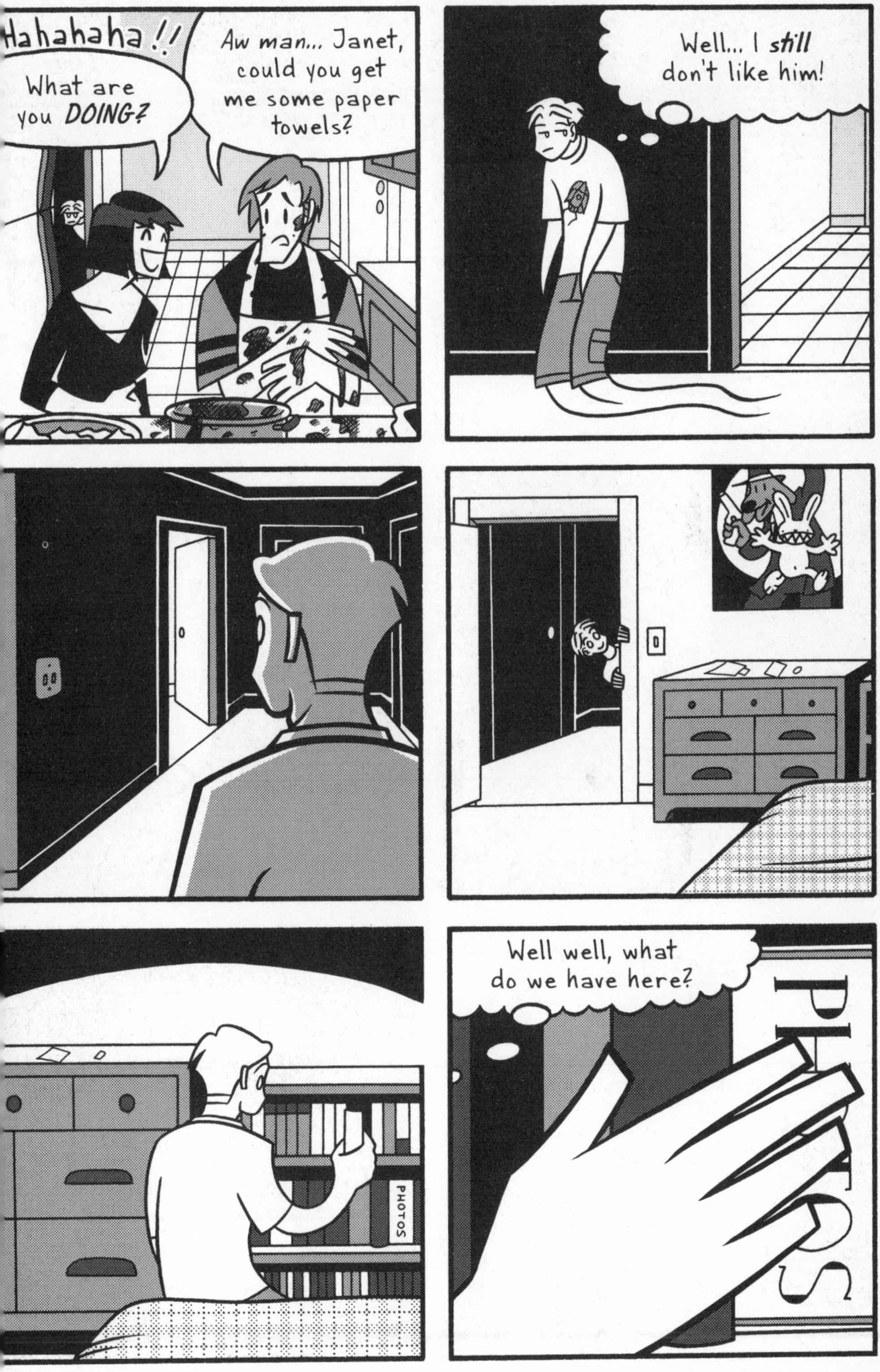
Hahahaha!!
What are you DOING?
Aw man... Janet, could you get me some paper towels?
Well... I still don't like him!
PHOTOS
Well well, what do we have here?
PHOTOS

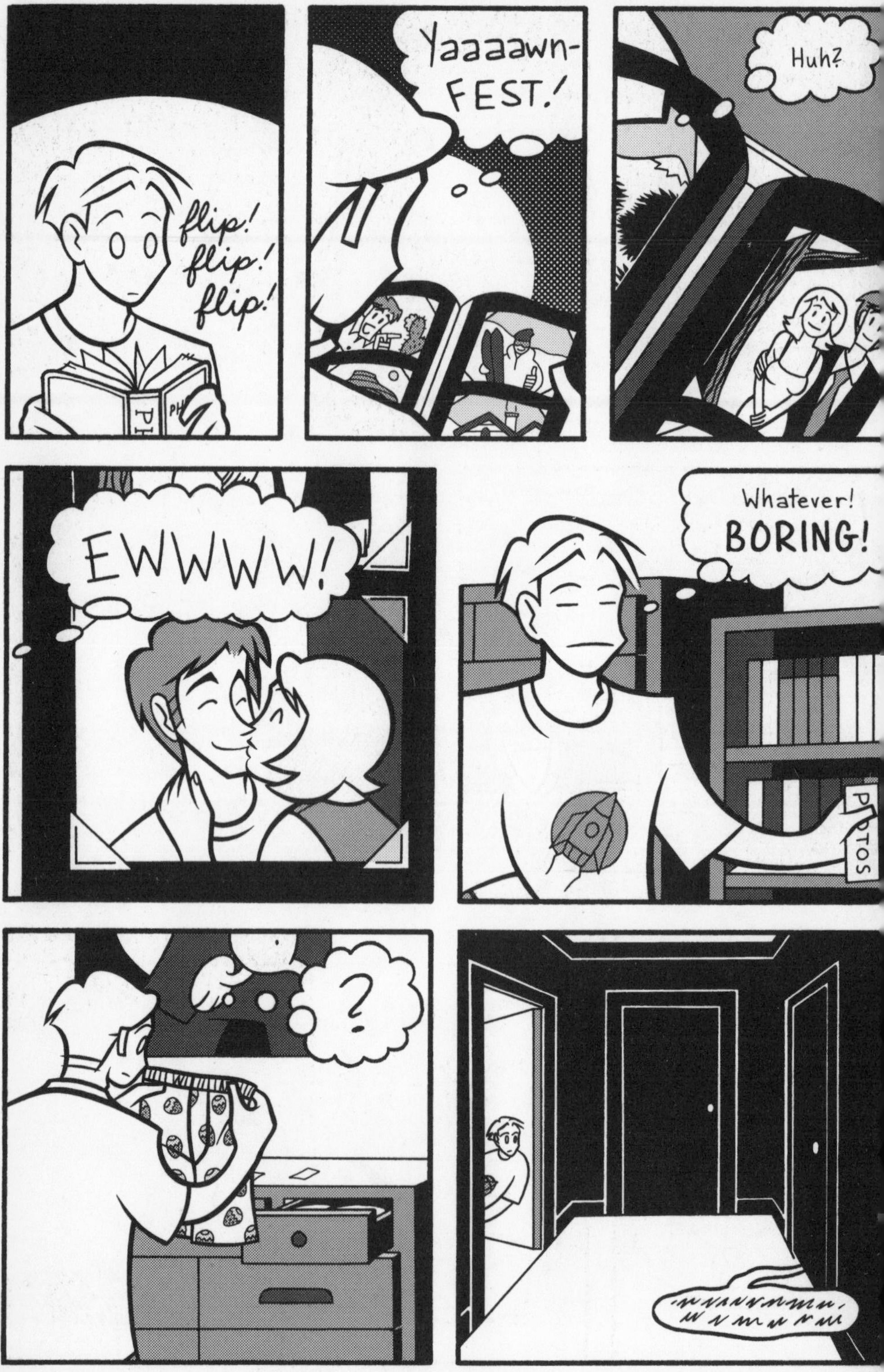
flip! flip! flip!
Yaaaawn-FEST.!
Huh?
EWWWW!
Whatever! BORING!
?

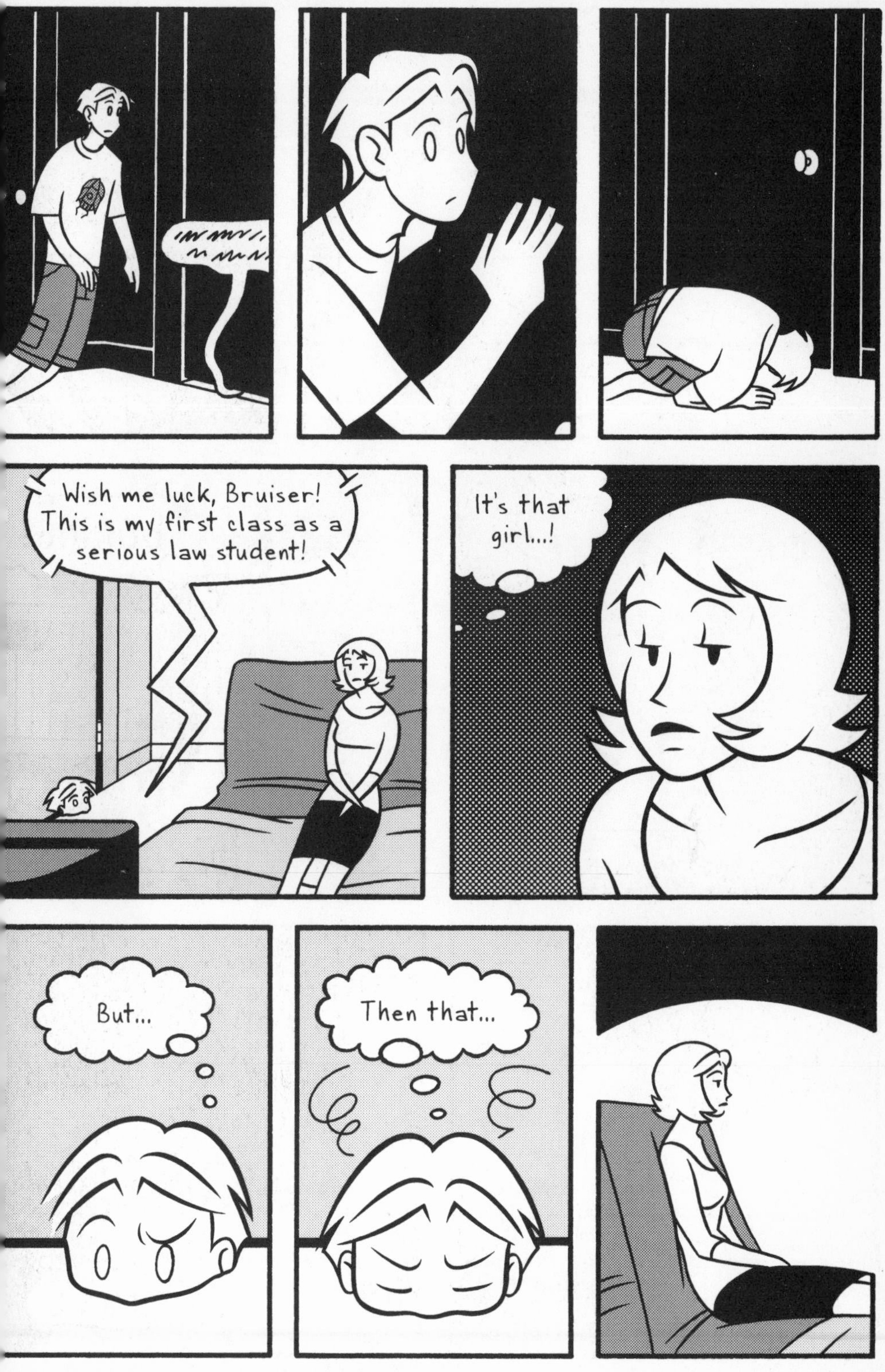
Wish me luck, Bruiser! This is my first class as a serious law student!
It's that girl...!
But...
Then that...

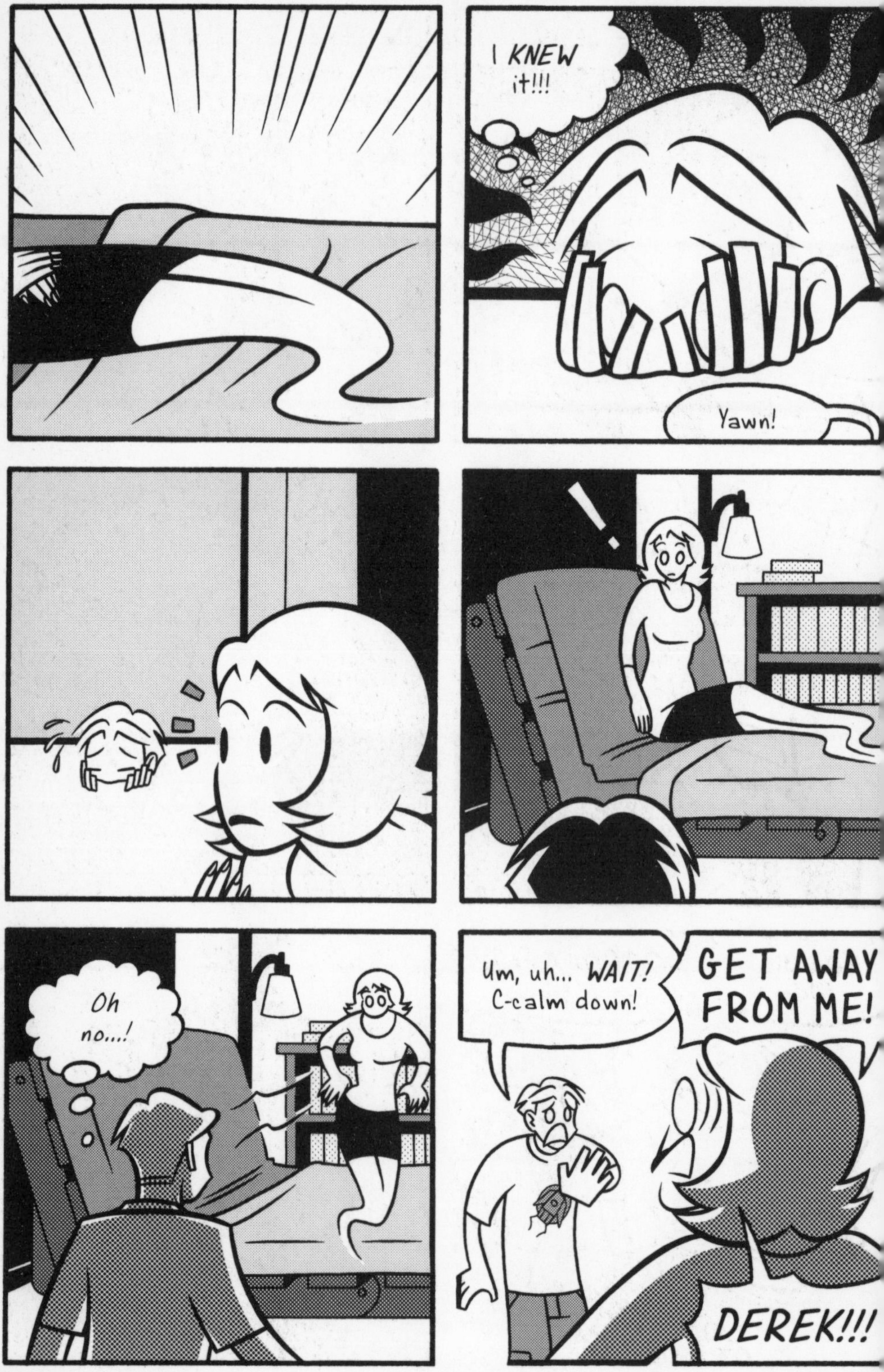
I KNEW it!!!
Yawn!
!
Oh no...!
Um, uh... WAIT! C-calm down!
GET AWAY FROM ME!
DEREK!!!

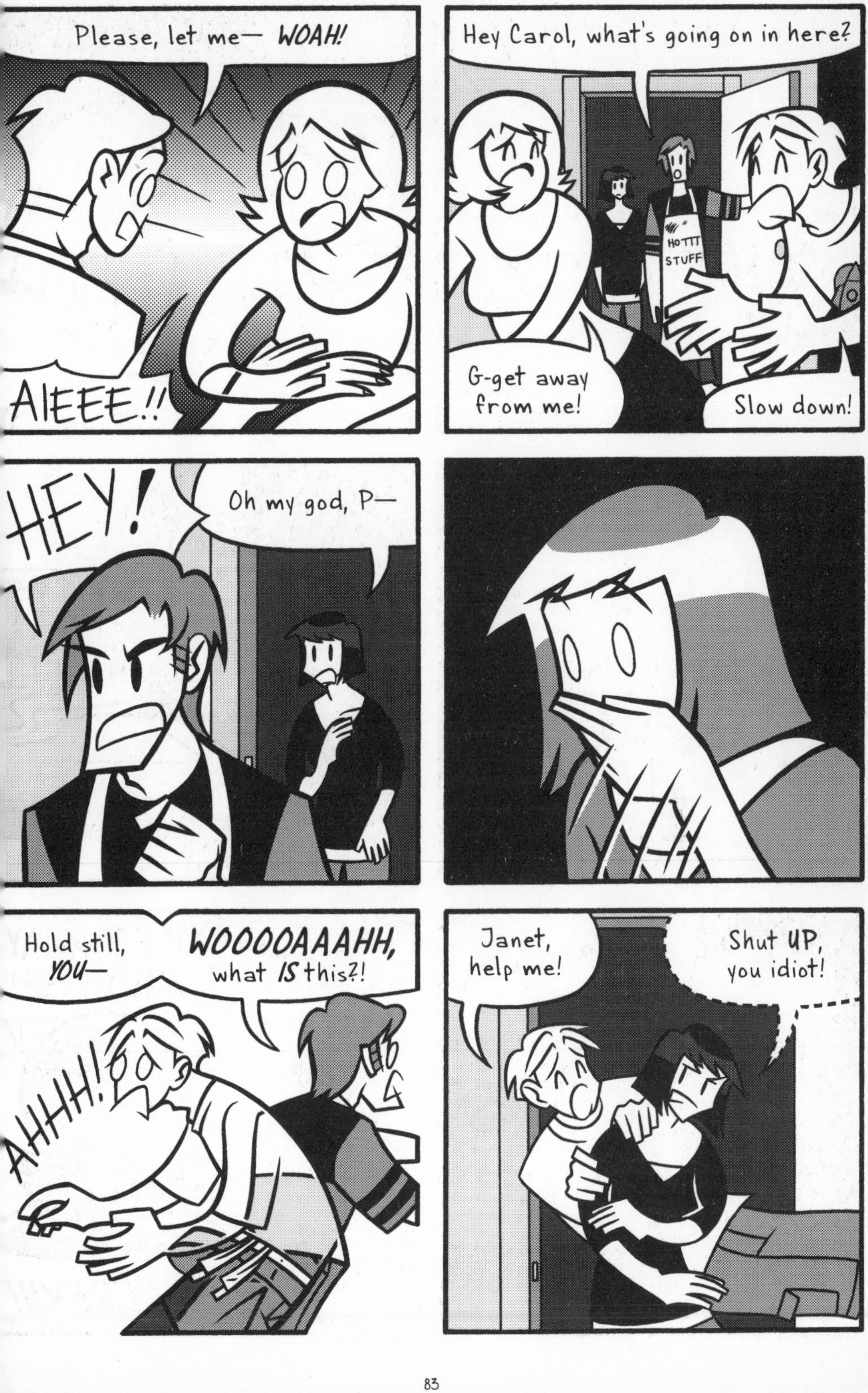

Please, let me— WOAH!
AIEEE!!
Hey Carol, what's going on in here?
HOTTT STUFF
G-get away from me!
Slow down!
HEY!
Oh my god, P—
Hold still, YOU—
WOOOOAAAHH, what IS this?!
AHHH!
Janet, help me!
Shut UP, you idiot!

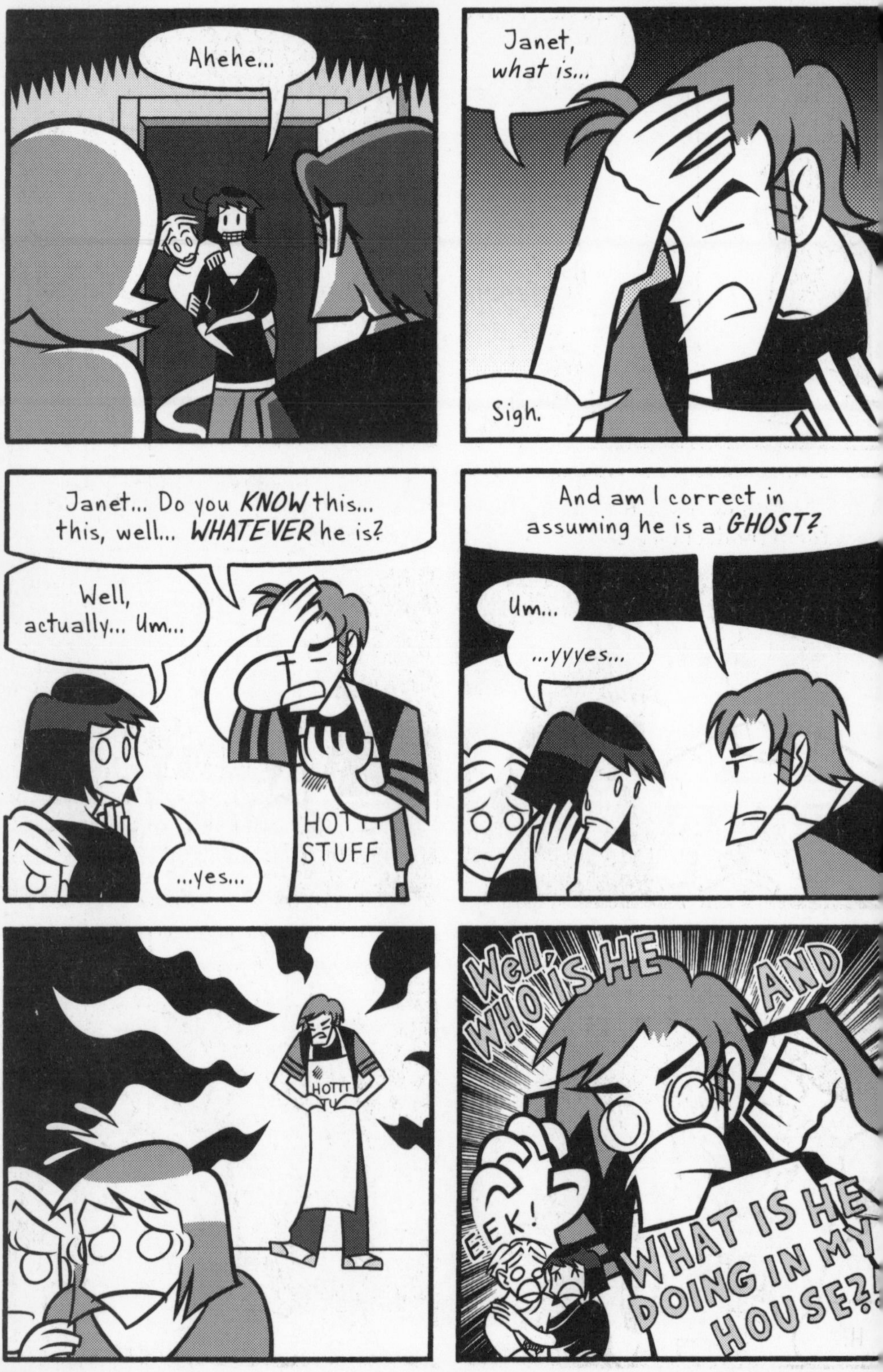
Ahehe...
Janet, what is...
Sigh.
Janet... Do you KNOW this... this, well... WHATEVER he is?
Well, actually... Um...
...yes...
HOTT STUFF
And am I correct in assuming he is a GHOST?
Um...
...yyyes...
HOTTT
Well, WHO IS HE AND
EEK!
WHAT IS HE DOING IN MY HOUSE?!

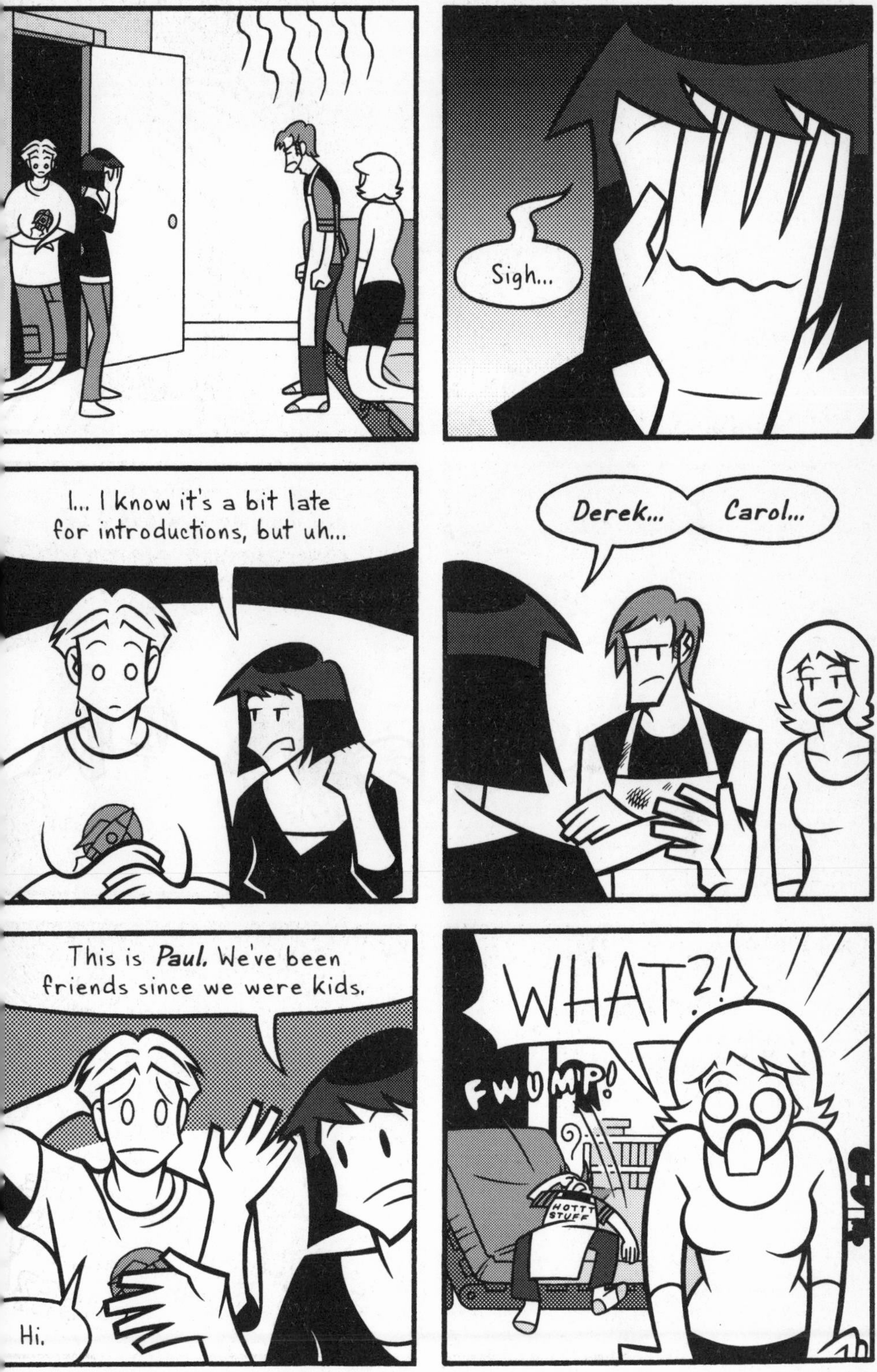
Sigh...
I... I know it's a bit late for introductions, but uh...
Derek...
Carol...
This is Paul. We've been friends since we were kids.
Hi.
WHAT?!
FWUMP!
HOTTT STUFF

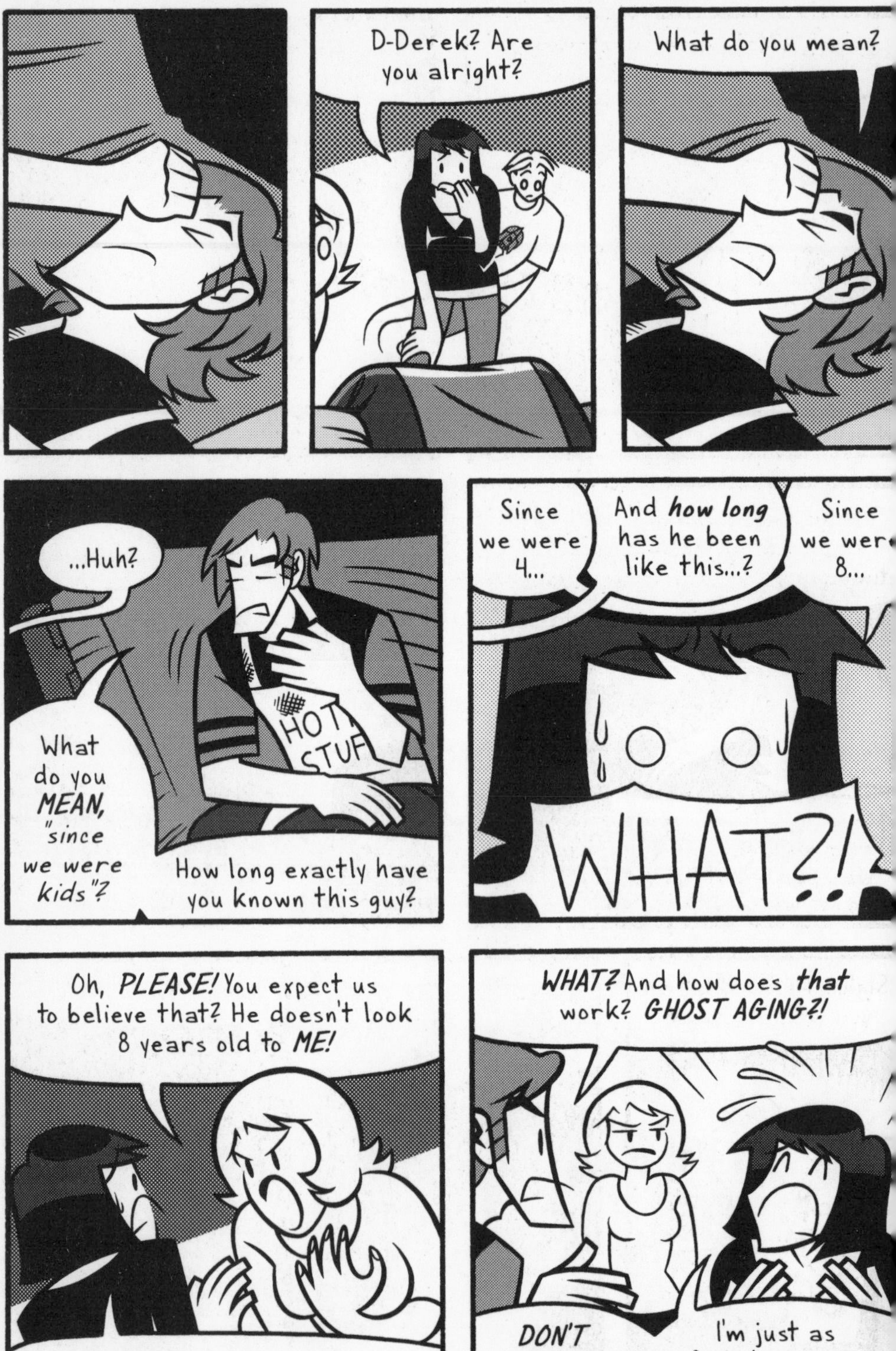
D-Derek? Are you alright?
What do you mean?
...Huh?
What do you MEAN, "since we were kids"?
How long exactly have you known this guy?
HOT STUF
Since we were 4...
And how long has he been like this...?
Since we wer 8...
WHAT?!
Oh, PLEASE! You expect us to believe that? He doesn't look 8 years old to ME!
W-Well, he's aged with me...
WHAT? And how does that work? GHOST AGING?!
DON'T ASK ME!
I'm just as confused as you are

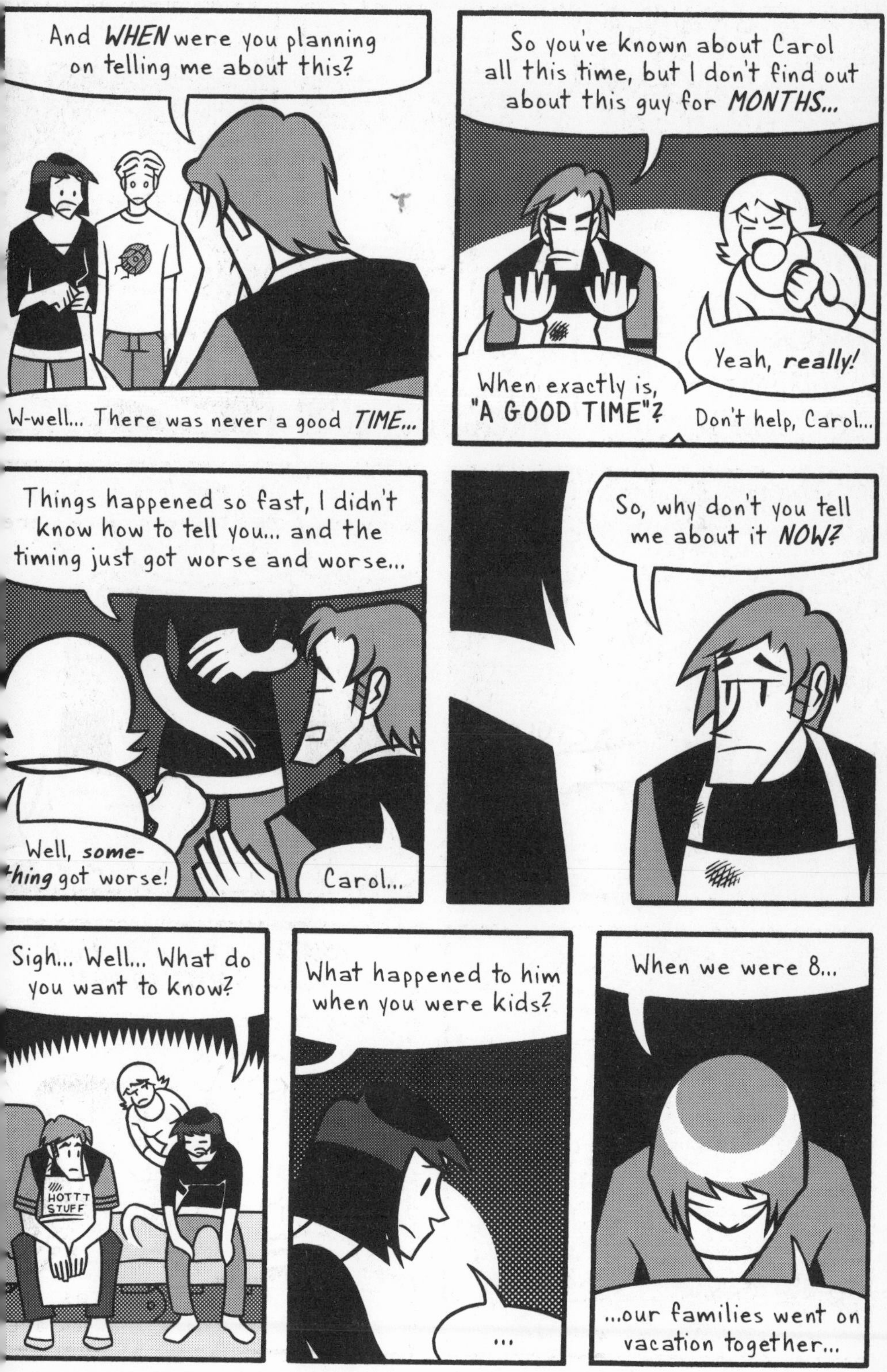
And WHEN were you planning on telling me about this?
W-well... There was never a good TIME...
So you've known about Carol all this time, but I don't find out about this guy for MONTHS...
When exactly is, "A GOOD TIME"?
Yeah, really!
Don't help, Carol...
Things happened so fast, I didn't know how to tell you... and the timing just got worse and worse...
Well, something got worse!
Carol...
So, why don't you tell me about it NOW?
Sigh... Well... What do you want to know?
HOTTT STUFF
What happened to him when you were kids?
...
When we were 8...
...our families went on vacation together...

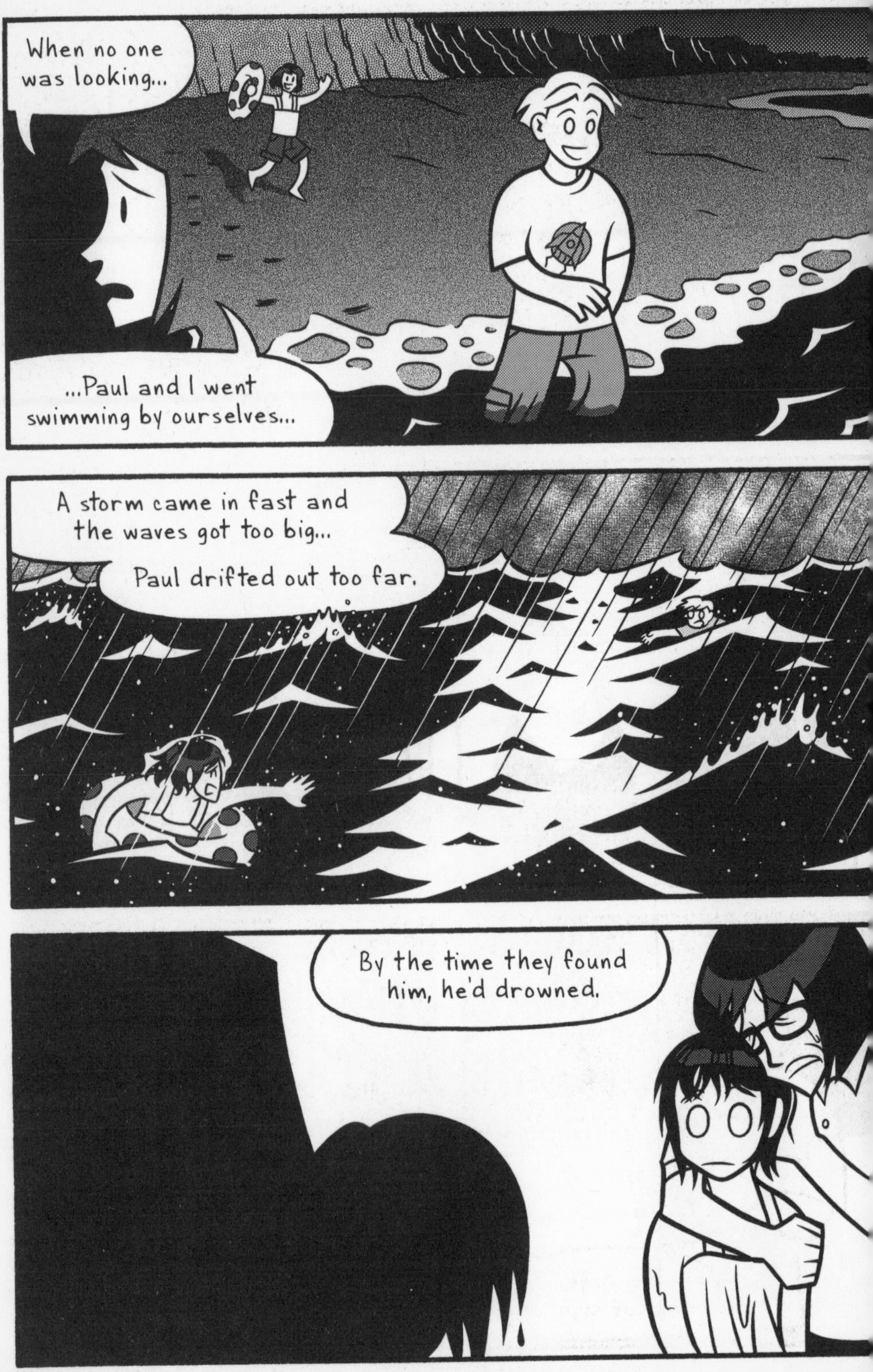
When no one was looking...
...Paul and I went swimming by ourselves...
A storm came in fast and the waves got too big...
Paul drifted out too far.
By the time they found him, he'd drowned.

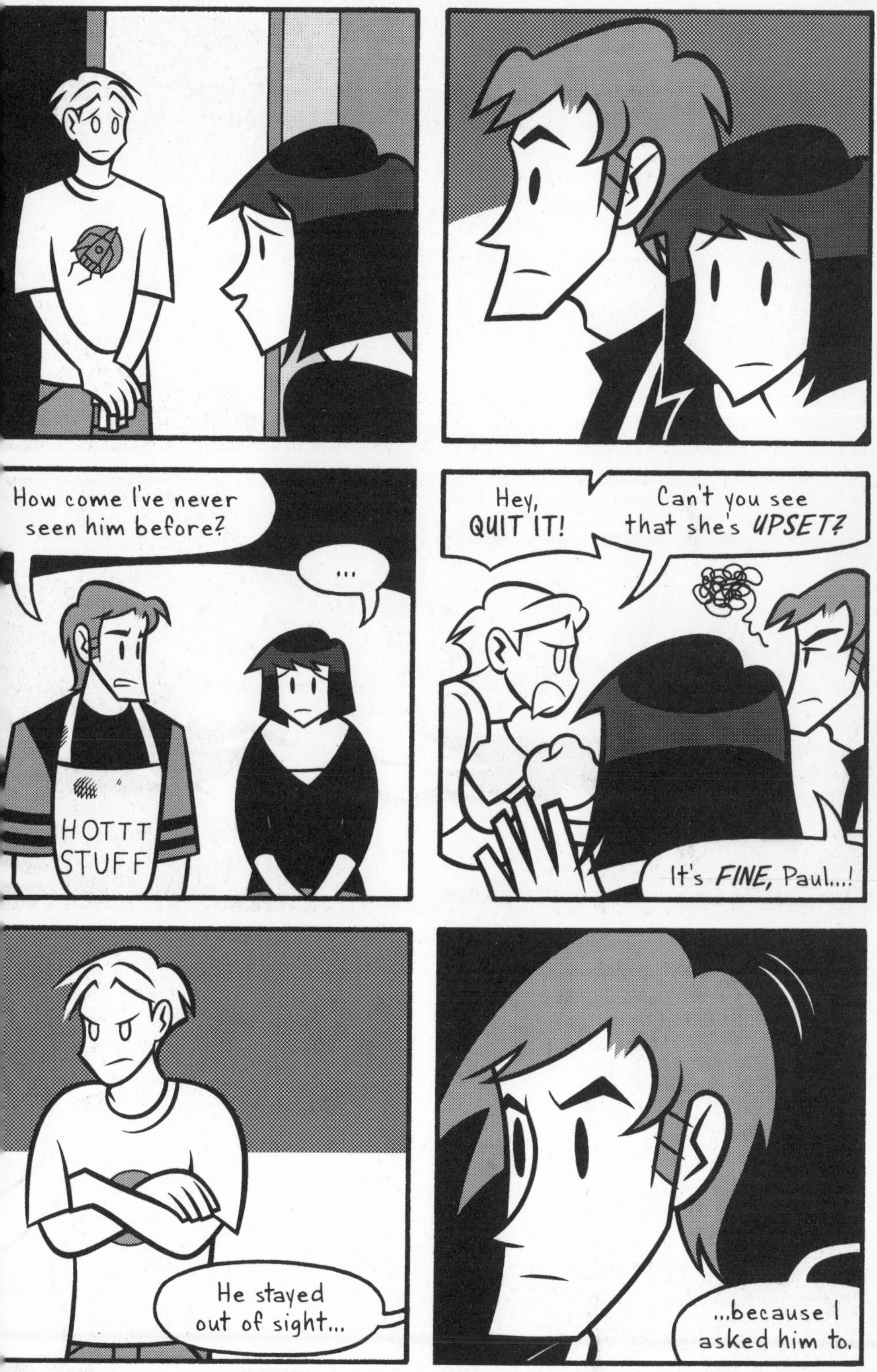
How come I've never seen him before?
...
Hey, QUIT IT!
Can't you see that she's UPSET?
It's FINE, Paul...!
HOTTT STUFF
He stayed out of sight...
...because I asked him to.

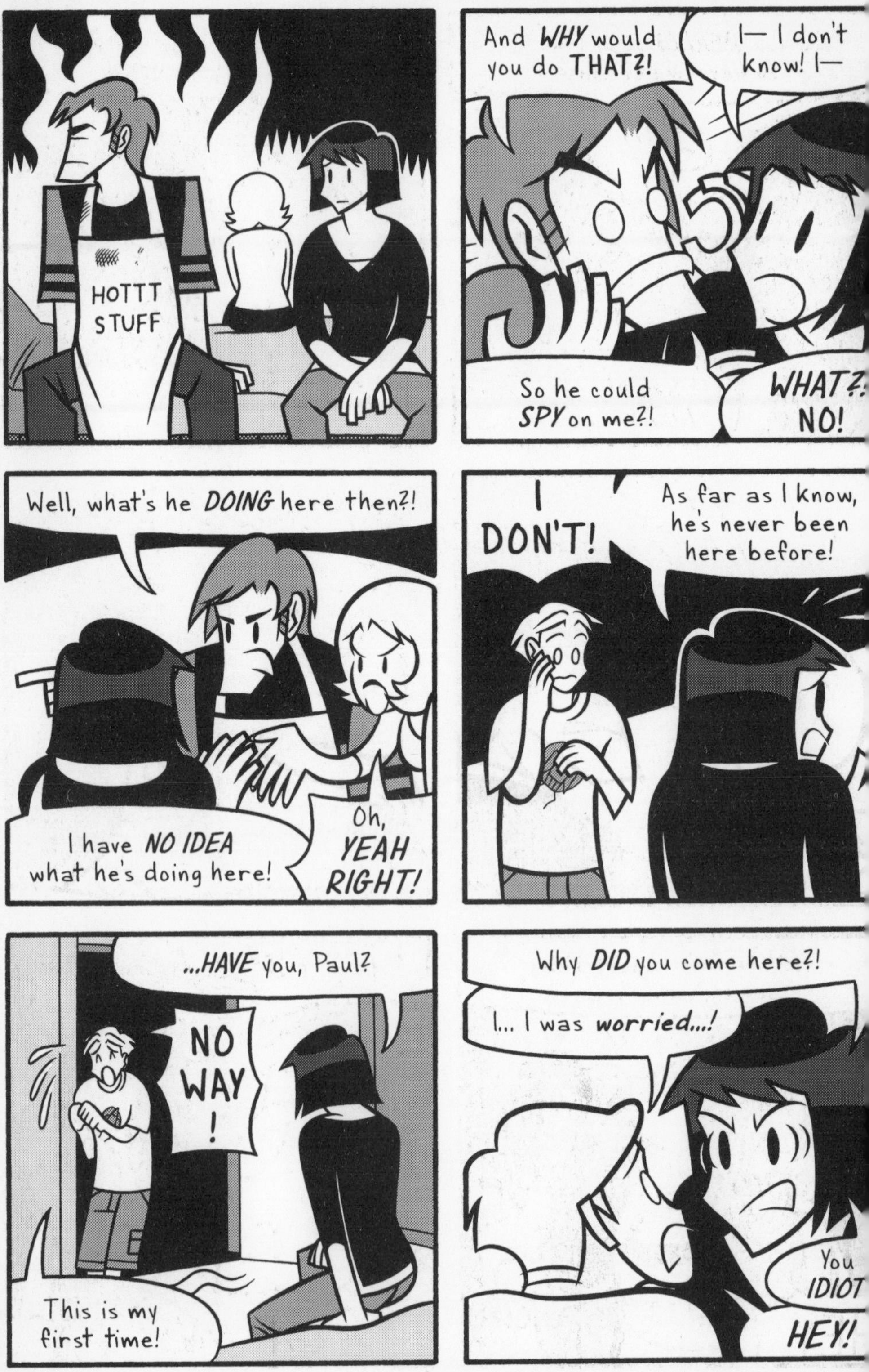
HOTTT STUFF
And WHY would you do THAT?!
I— I don't know! I—
So he could SPY on me?!
WHAT?! NO!
Well, what's he DOING here then?!
I have NO IDEA what he's doing here!
Oh, YEAH RIGHT!
I DON'T!
As far as I know, he's never been here before!
...HAVE you, Paul?
NO WAY!
This is my first time!
Why DID you come here?!
I... I was worried...!
You IDIOT
HEY!

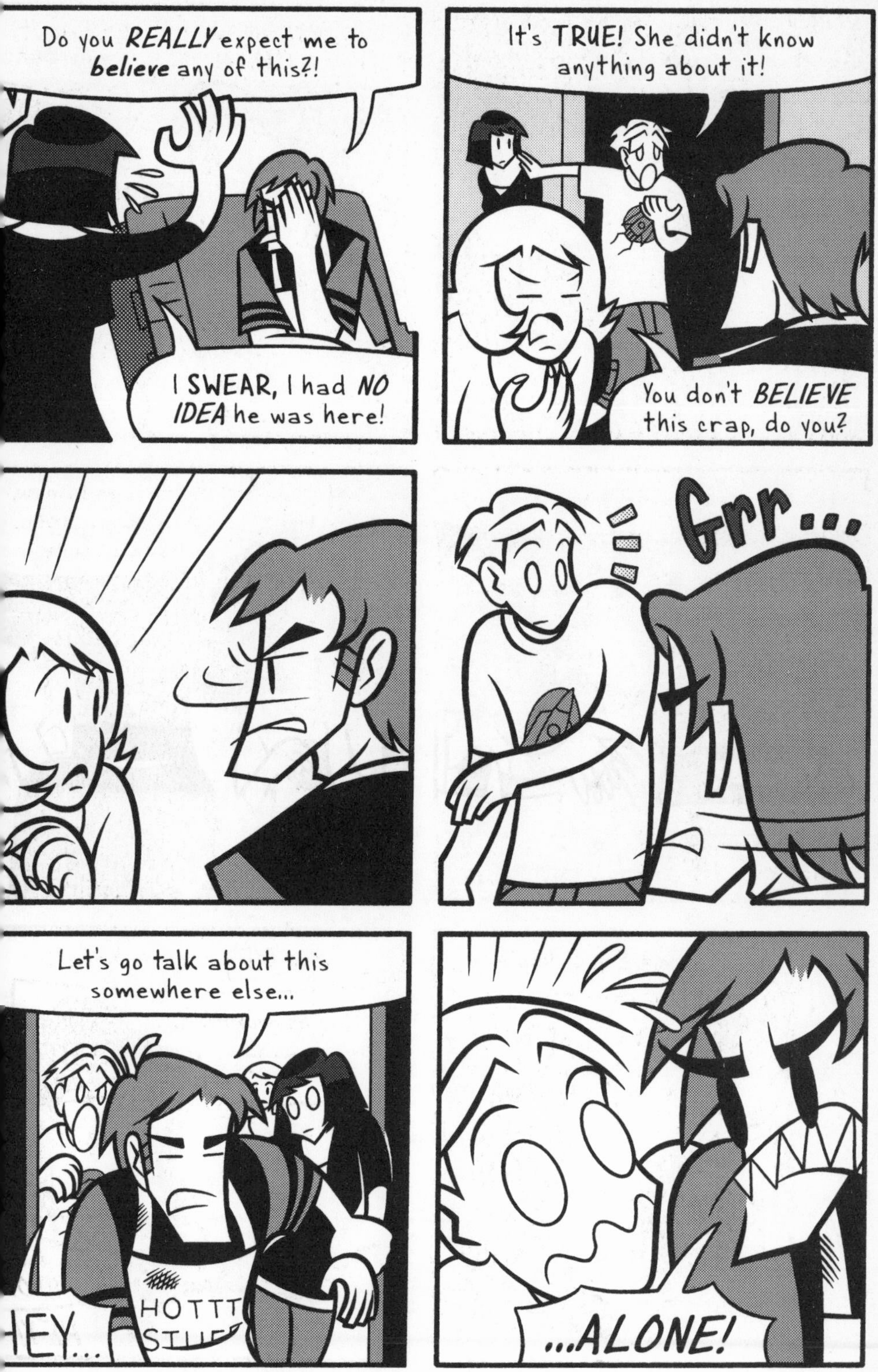
Do you REALLY expect me to believe any of this?!
I SWEAR, I had NO IDEA he was here!
It's TRUE! She didn't know anything about it!
You don't BELIEVE this crap, do you?
Grr...
Let's go talk about this somewhere else...
HOTTT STUFF
HEY...
...ALONE!

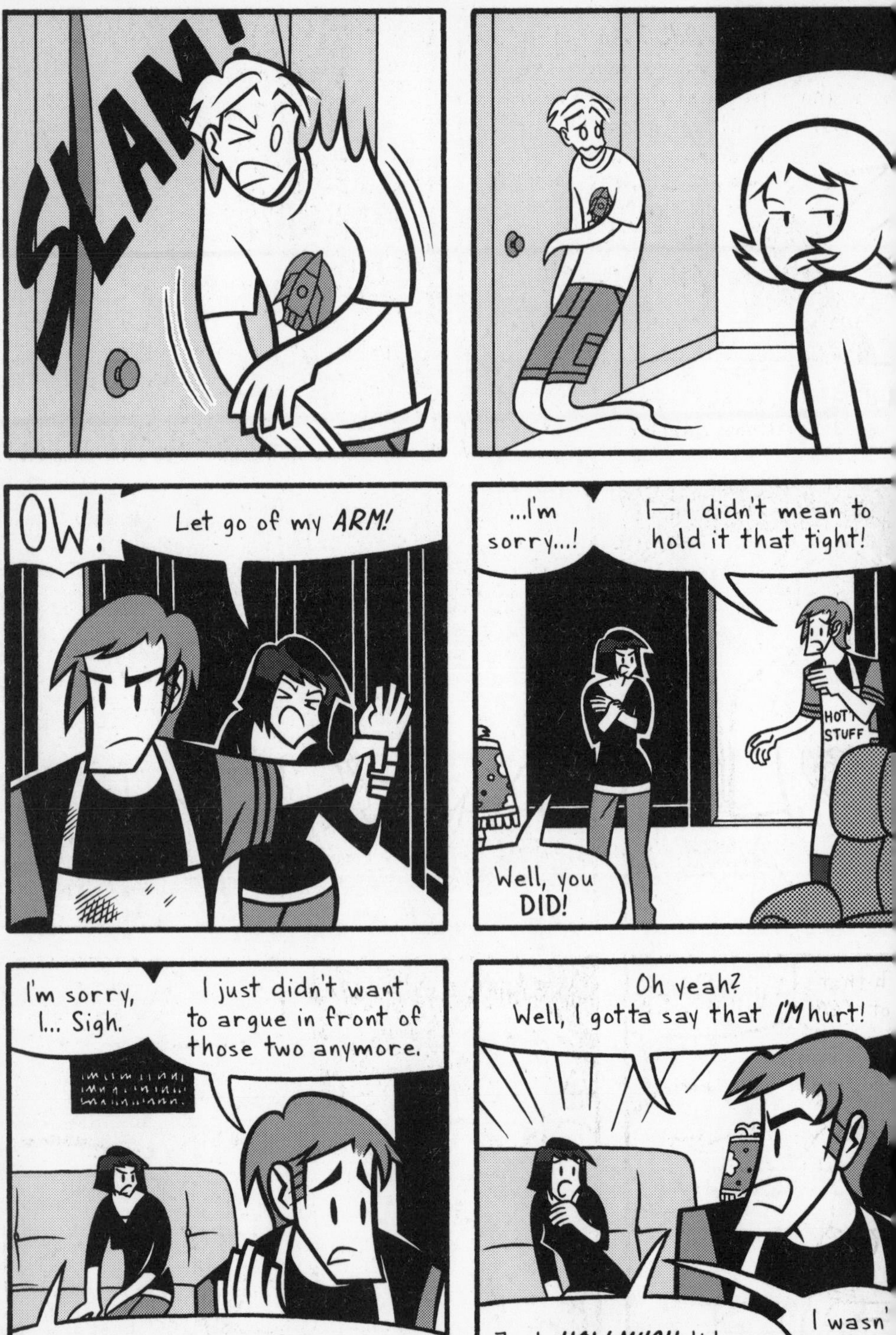
SLAM!
OW!
Let go of my ARM!
...I'm sorry...!
I— I didn't mean to hold it that tight!
HOT STUFF
Well, you DID!
I'm sorry, I... Sigh.
I just didn't want to argue in front of those two anymore.
Well, I didn't like it either, but you don't see me HURTING anyone!
Oh yeah? Well, I gotta say that I'M hurt!
Just HOW MUCH did you plan on LYING to me?!
I wasn' LYING, just...

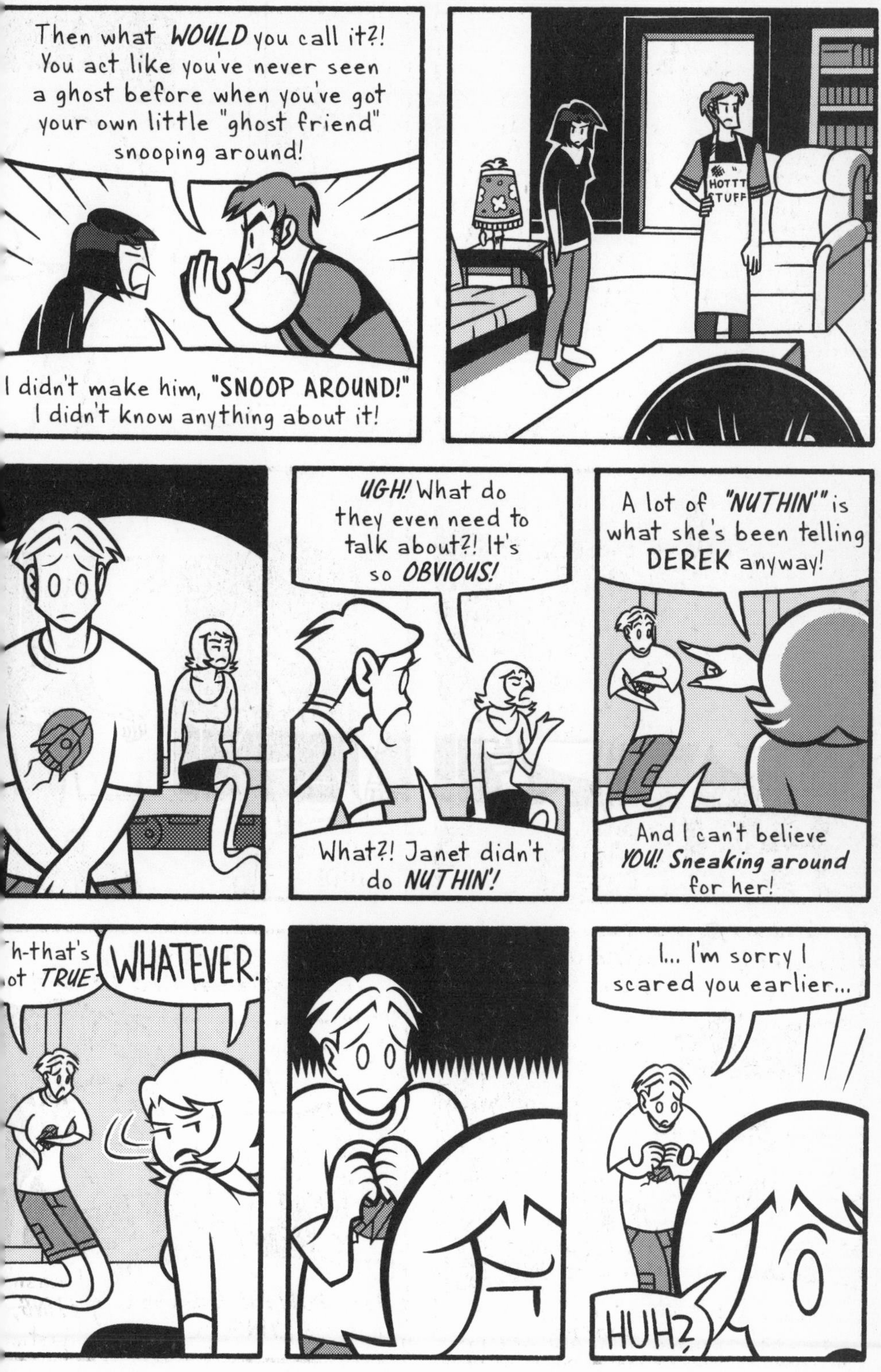
Then what WOULD you call it?! You act like you've never seen a ghost before when you've got your own little "ghost friend" snooping around!
I didn't make him, "SNOOP AROUND!" I didn't know anything about it!
HOTTT STUFF
UGH! What do they even need to talk about?! It's so OBVIOUS!
What?! Janet didn't do NUTHIN'!
A lot of "NUTHIN'" is what she's been telling DEREK anyway!
And I can't believe YOU! Sneaking around for her!
h-that's ot TRUE
WHATEVER.
I... I'm sorry I scared you earlier...
HUH?

N-no biggie... Don't worry about it.

It's kind of stupid to be scared by a ghost when you *ARE* one, anyway...

Heh... Yeah... I guess. But I've never seen any ghosts other than you.

Are you kidding me?! You neither?

Nuh-uh, you're the first!

It's kind of weird...

WAIT ...!

You mean you haven't either?

NOPE!

Sigh...

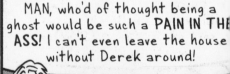

MAN, who'd of thought being a ghost would be such a **PAIN IN THE ASS!** I can't even leave the house without Derek around!

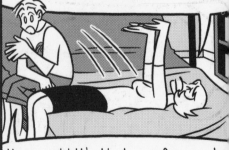

Hey, yeah! It's that way for me too

It's not so bad though... Janet always gets me tons of books and games and there's TV and hanging out and stuff!

BLECCCCH!

Well, *I CAN'T STAND IT!*

I had my own life before this happened!

Now everything is, *"Derek this"* and, *"Derek that!"*

I can't just live vicariously through *DEREK!*

And I knew it! I *KNEW* it! I'm *AGING!* I *TOLD* Derek I was getting wrinkles, but *NO...*

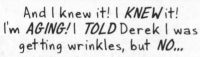

I just wish I knew why I'm still here... Should I have some sort of *"GHOST MISSION"* or something like that?

dunno, I don't really think about it...

WHAT DO YOU MEAN YOU DON'T THINK ABOUT IT! You've had like **12 YEARS** to *THINK* about it!

I don't know... There's always stuff to do... and I *LIKE* being around Janet...

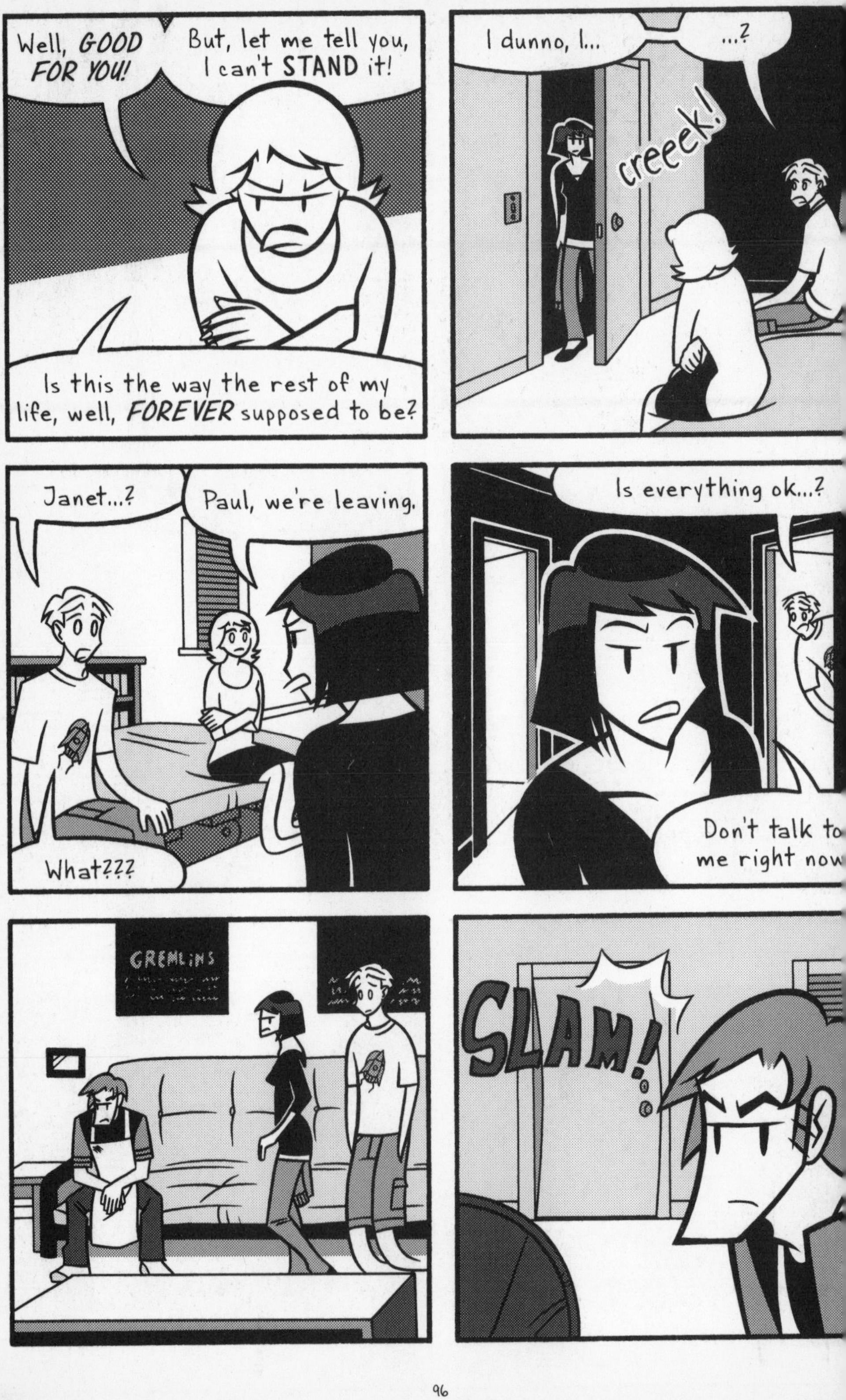
Well, GOOD FOR YOU!
But, let me tell you, I can't STAND it!
Is this the way the rest of my life, well, FOREVER supposed to be?
I dunno, I...
...?
creeek!
Janet...?
Paul, we're leaving.
What???
Is everything ok...?
Don't talk to me right now
GREMLINS
SLAM!

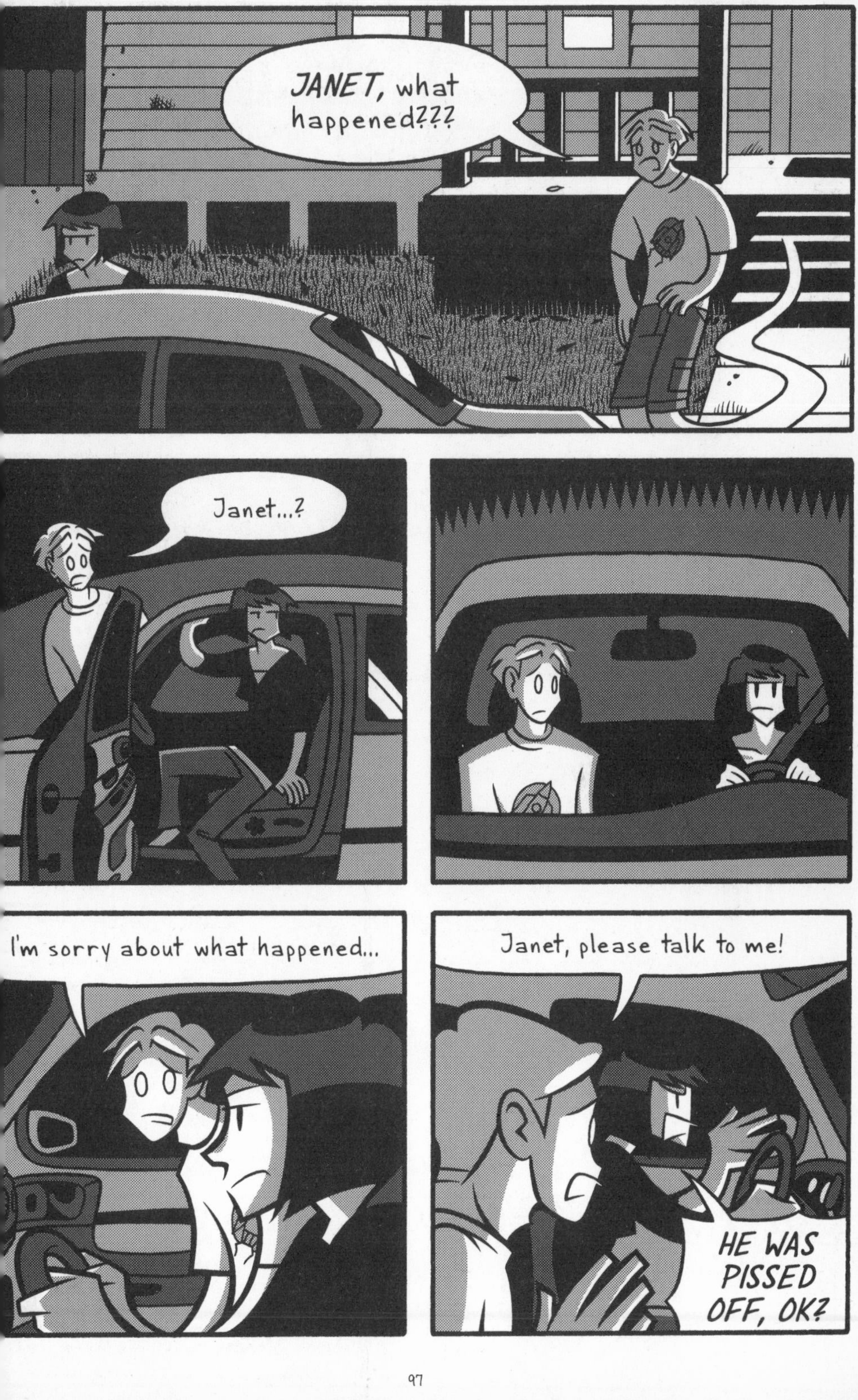

JANET, what happened???
Janet...?
I'm sorry about what happened...
Janet, please talk to me!
HE WAS PISSED OFF, OK?

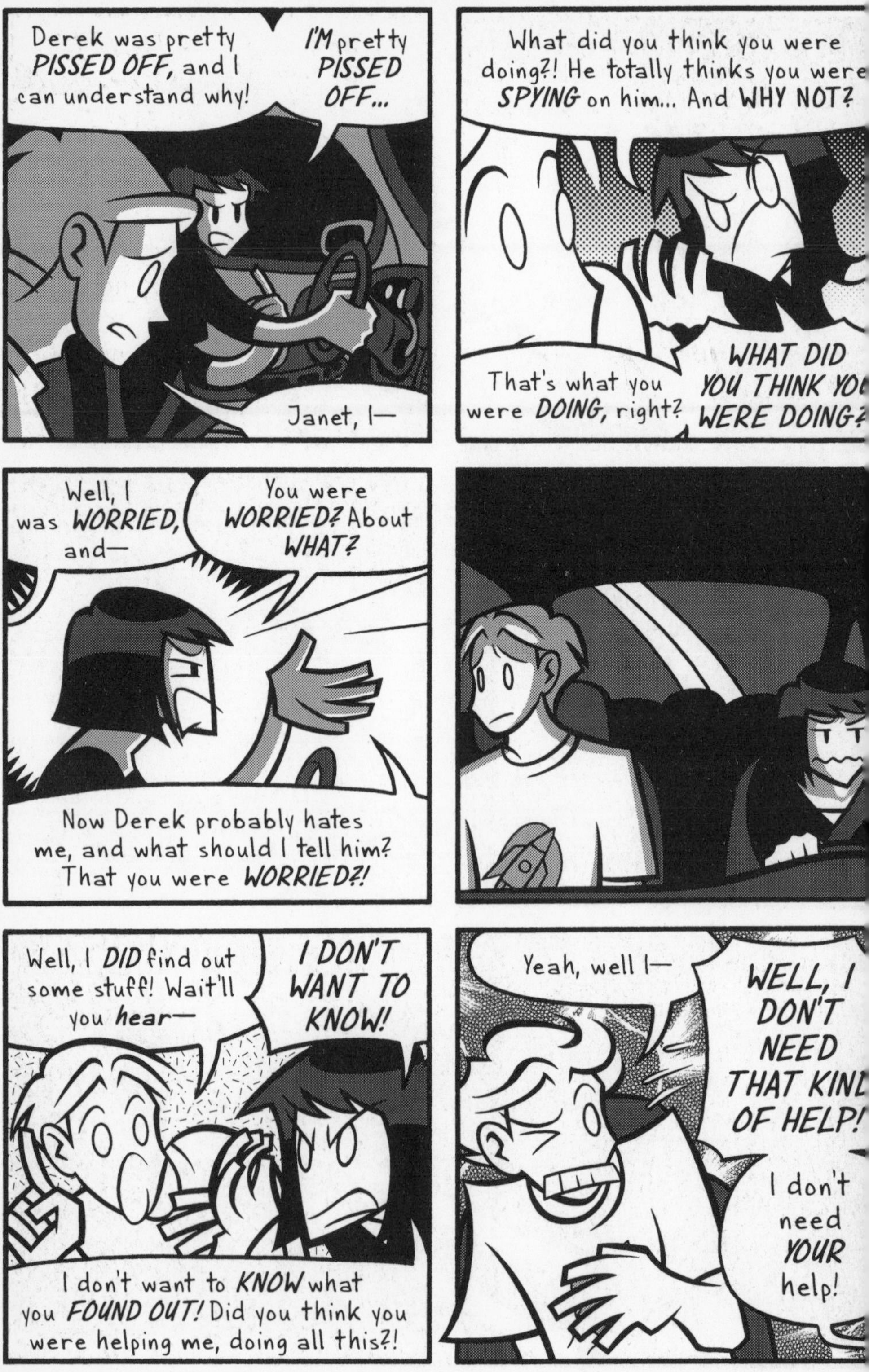
Derek was pretty PISSED OFF, and I can understand why!
I'M pretty PISSED OFF...
Janet, I—
What did you think you were doing?! He totally thinks you were SPYING on him... And WHY NOT?
That's what you were DOING, right?
WHAT DID YOU THINK YOU WERE DOING?!
Well, I was WORRIED, and—
You were WORRIED? About WHAT?
Now Derek probably hates me, and what should I tell him? That you were WORRIED?!
Well, I DID find out some stuff! Wait'll you hear—
I DON'T WANT TO KNOW!
I don't want to KNOW what you FOUND OUT! Did you think you were helping me, doing all this?!
Yeah, well I—
WELL, I DON'T NEED THAT KIND OF HELP!
I don't need YOUR help!

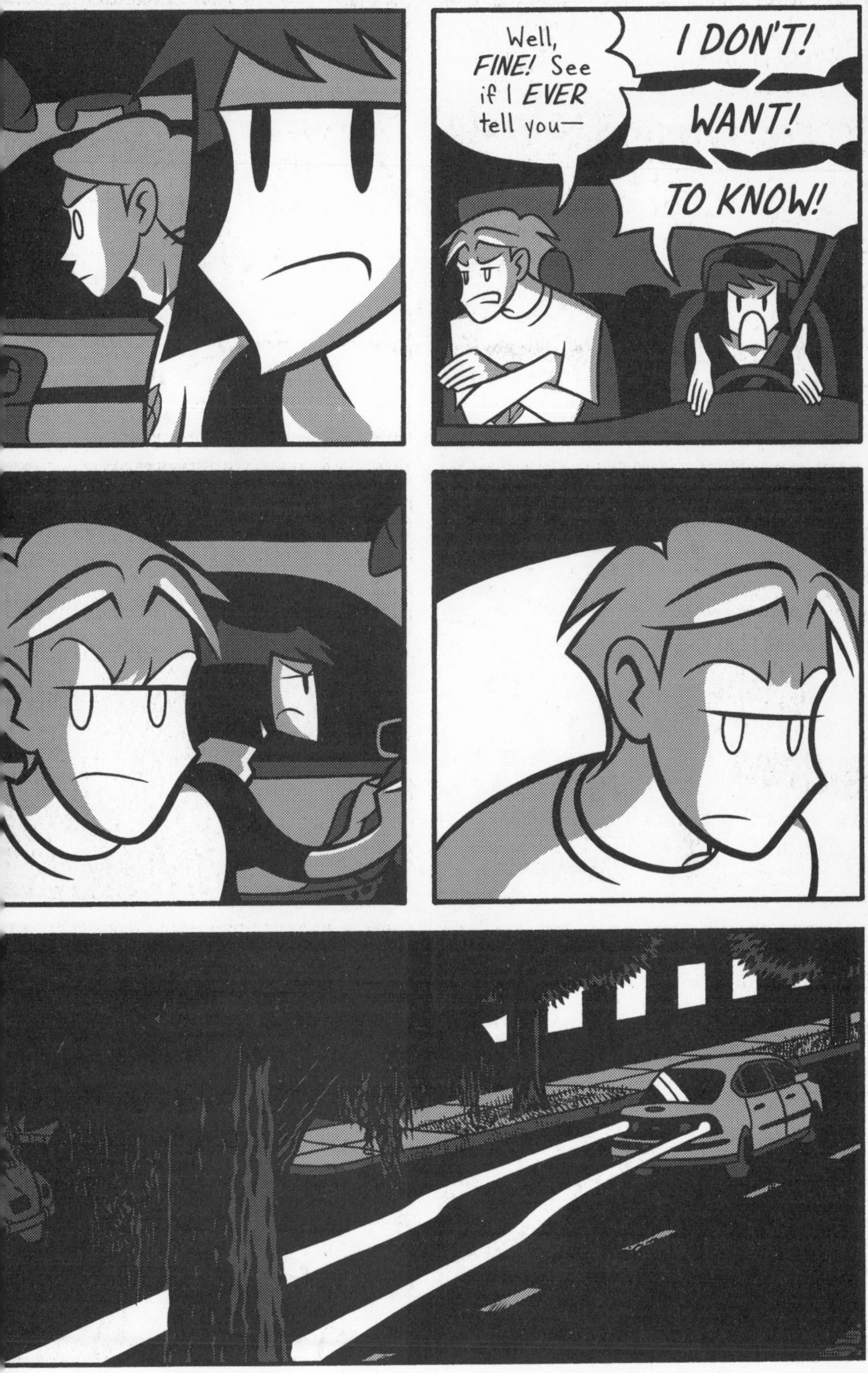
Well, FINE! See if I EVER tell you—
I DON'T!
WANT!
TO KNOW!

Chapter 6

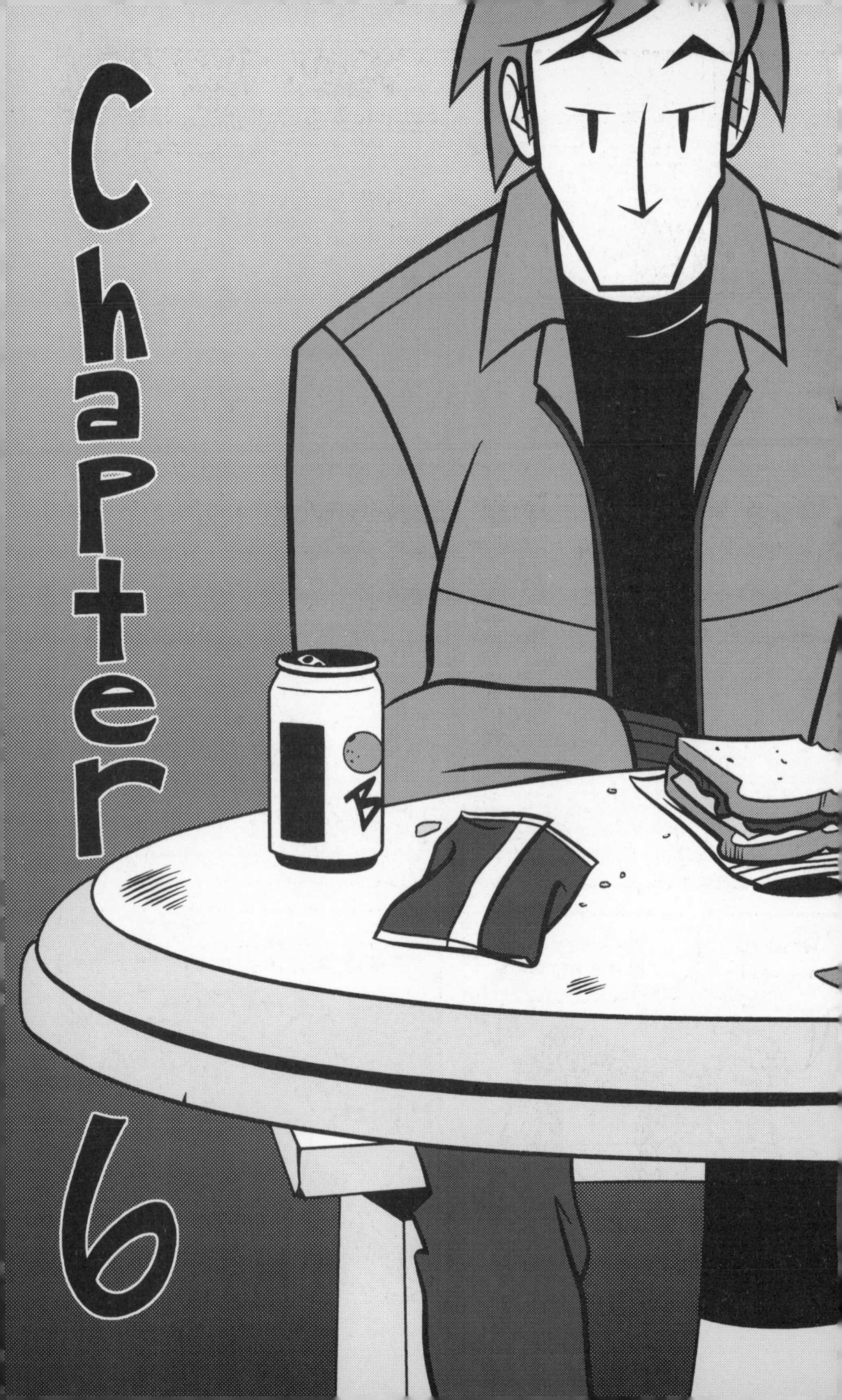

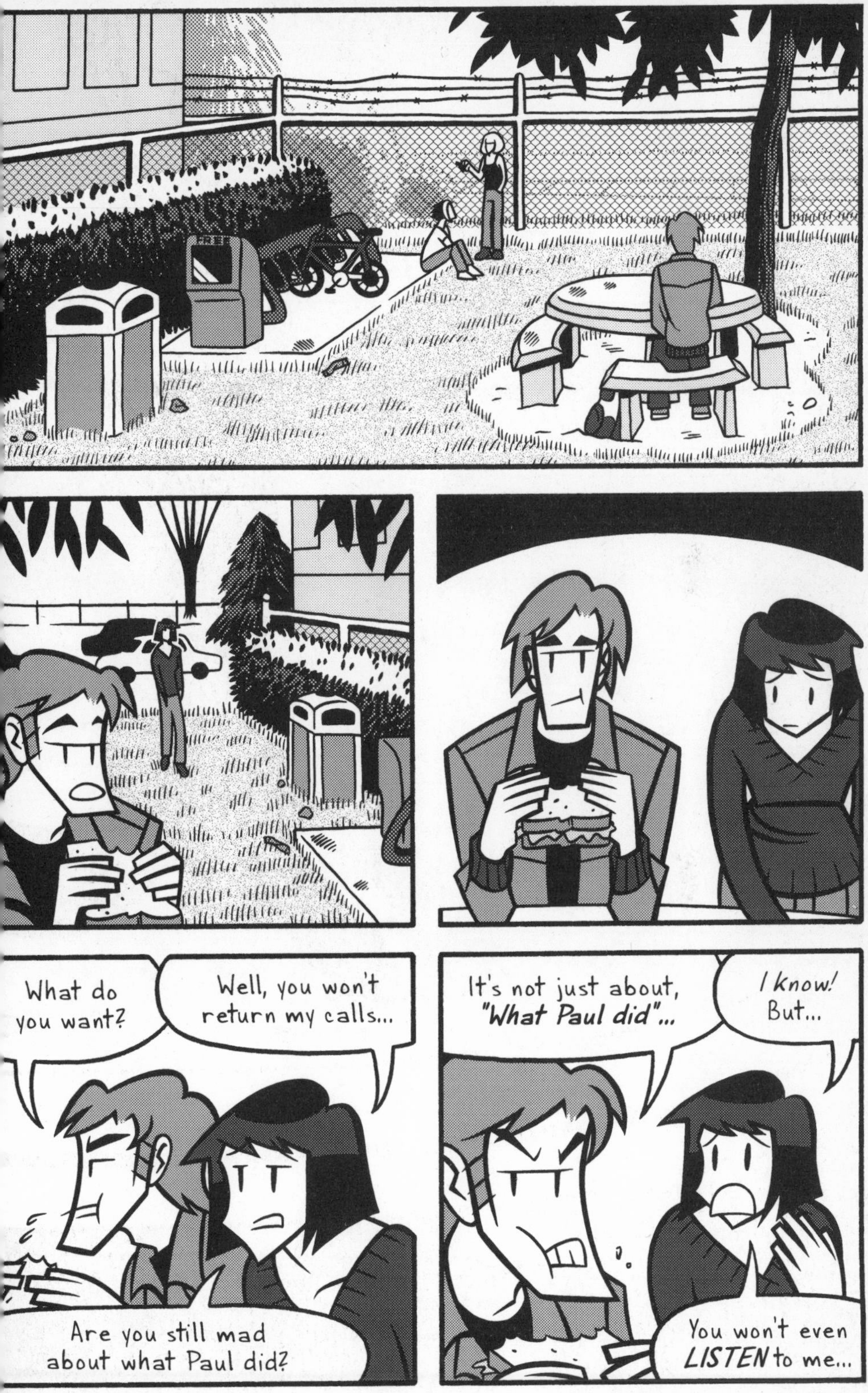

What do you want?
Well, you won't return my calls...
Are you still mad about what Paul did?
It's not just about, "What Paul did"...
I know! But...
You won't even LISTEN to me...

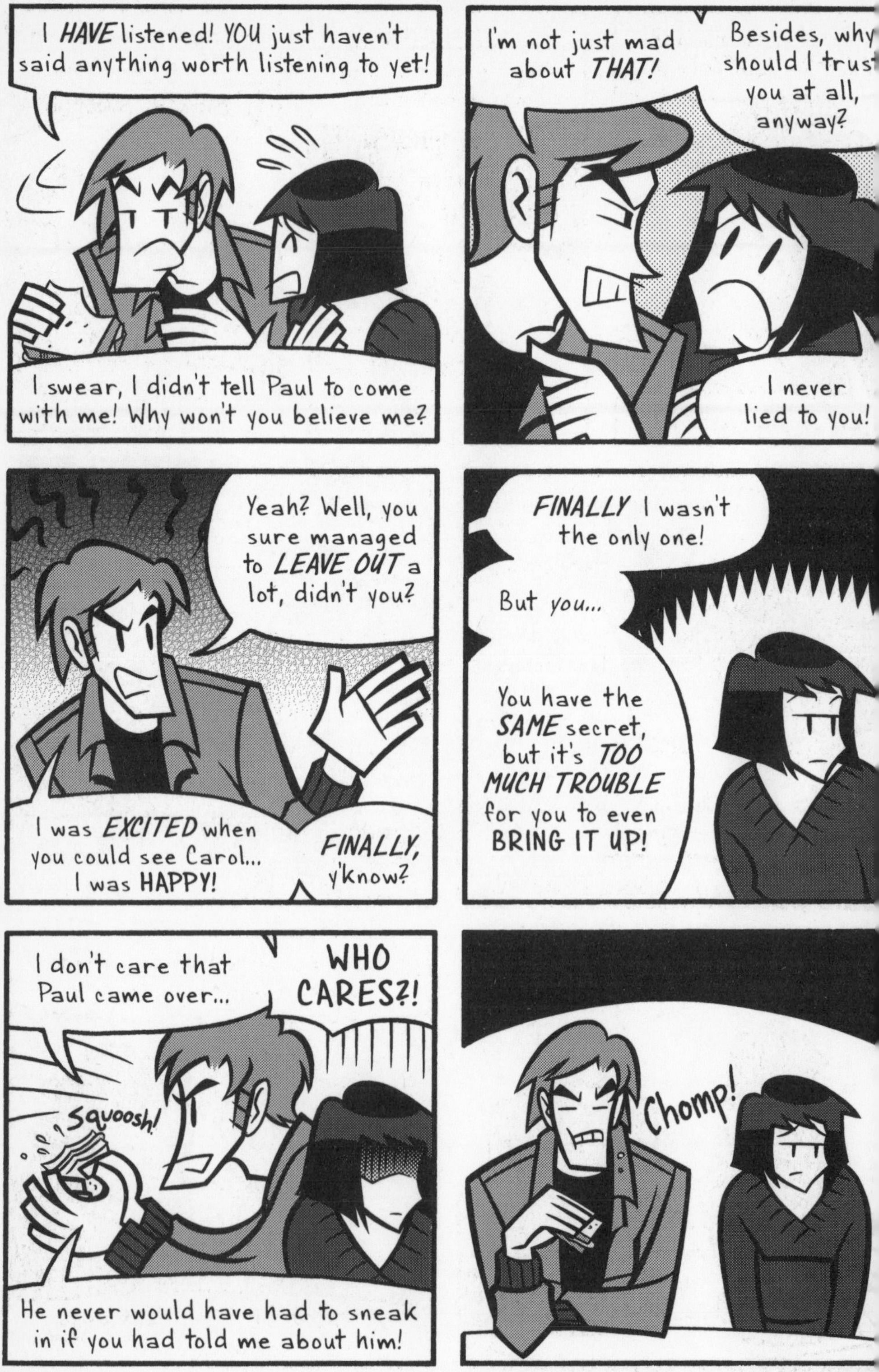
I HAVE listened! YOU just haven't said anything worth listening to yet!
I swear, I didn't tell Paul to come with me! Why won't you believe me?
I'm not just mad about THAT!
Besides, why should I trust you at all, anyway?
I never lied to you!
Yeah? Well, you sure managed to LEAVE OUT a lot, didn't you?
I was EXCITED when you could see Carol... I was HAPPY!
FINALLY, y'know?
FINALLY I wasn't the only one!
But you...
You have the SAME secret, but it's TOO MUCH TROUBLE for you to even BRING IT UP!
I don't care that Paul came over...
WHO CARES?!
Squoosh!
He never would have had to sneak in if you had told me about him!
Chomp!

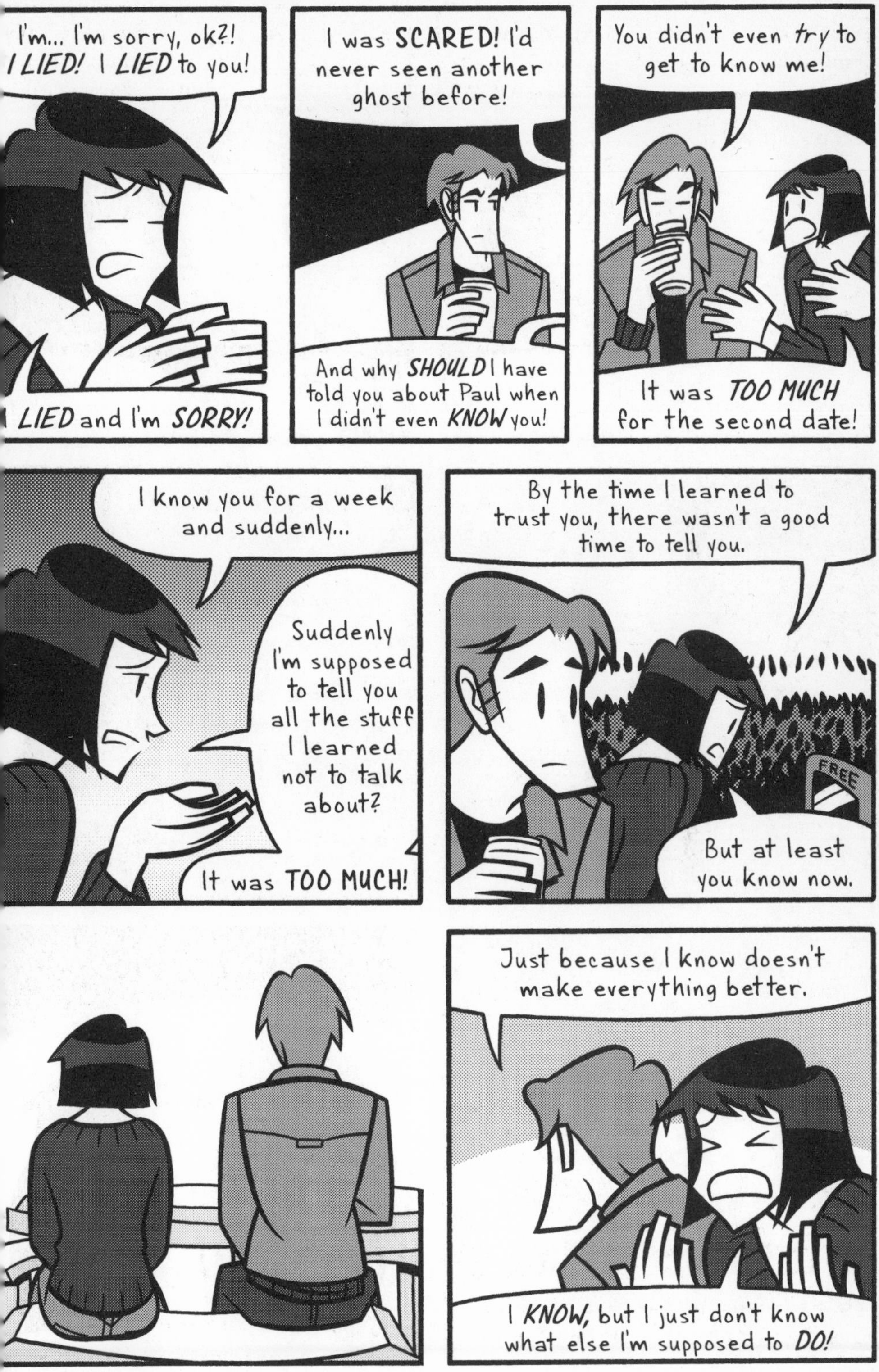
I'm... I'm sorry, ok?! I LIED! I LIED to you!
LIED and I'm SORRY!
I was SCARED! I'd never seen another ghost before!
And why SHOULD I have told you about Paul when I didn't even KNOW you!
You didn't even try to get to know me!
It was TOO MUCH for the second date!
I know you for a week and suddenly...
Suddenly I'm supposed to tell you all the stuff I learned not to talk about?
It was TOO MUCH!
By the time I learned to trust you, there wasn't a good time to tell you.
FREE
But at least you know now.
Just because I know doesn't make everything better.
I KNOW, but I just don't know what else I'm supposed to DO!

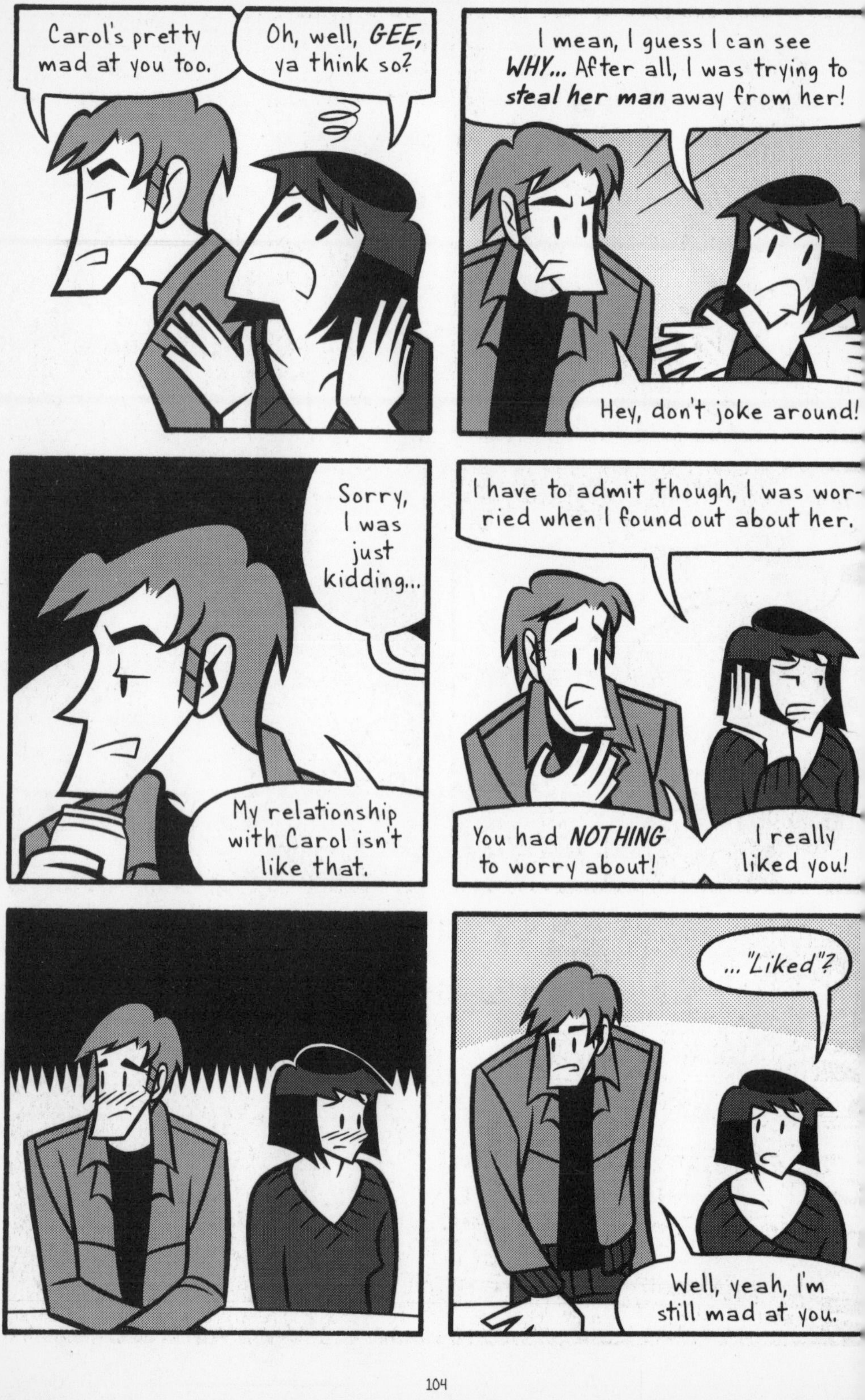
Carol's pretty mad at you too.
Oh, well, GEE, ya think so?
I mean, I guess I can see WHY... After all, I was trying to steal her man away from her!
Hey, don't joke around!
Sorry, I was just kidding...
My relationship with Carol isn't like that.
I have to admit though, I was worried when I found out about her.
You had NOTHING to worry about!
I really liked you!
..."Liked"?
Well, yeah, I'm still mad at you.

I got to get to class...

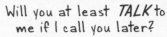

Will you at least *TALK* to me if I call you later?

Yeah, sure...

I gotta get going.

Seeya 'round.

Seeya...

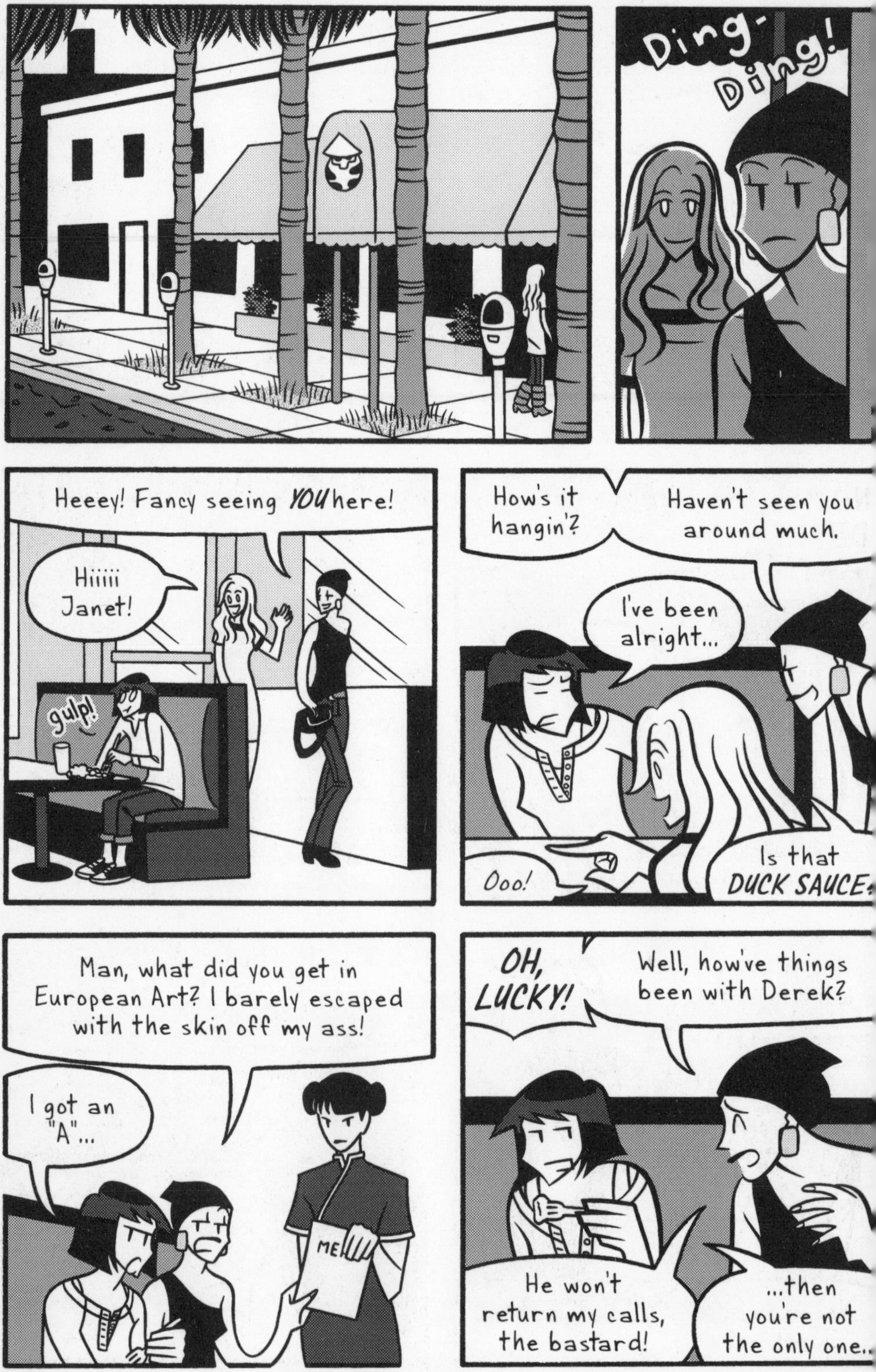

Ding-
Ding!
Heeey! Fancy seeing YOU here!
Hiiiii Janet!
gulp!
How's it hangin'?
Haven't seen you around much.
I've been alright...
Ooo!
Is that DUCK SAUCE?
Man, what did you get in European Art? I barely escaped with the skin off my ass!
I got an "A"...
ME
OH, LUCKY!
Well, how've things been with Derek?
He won't return my calls, the bastard!
...then you're not the only one...

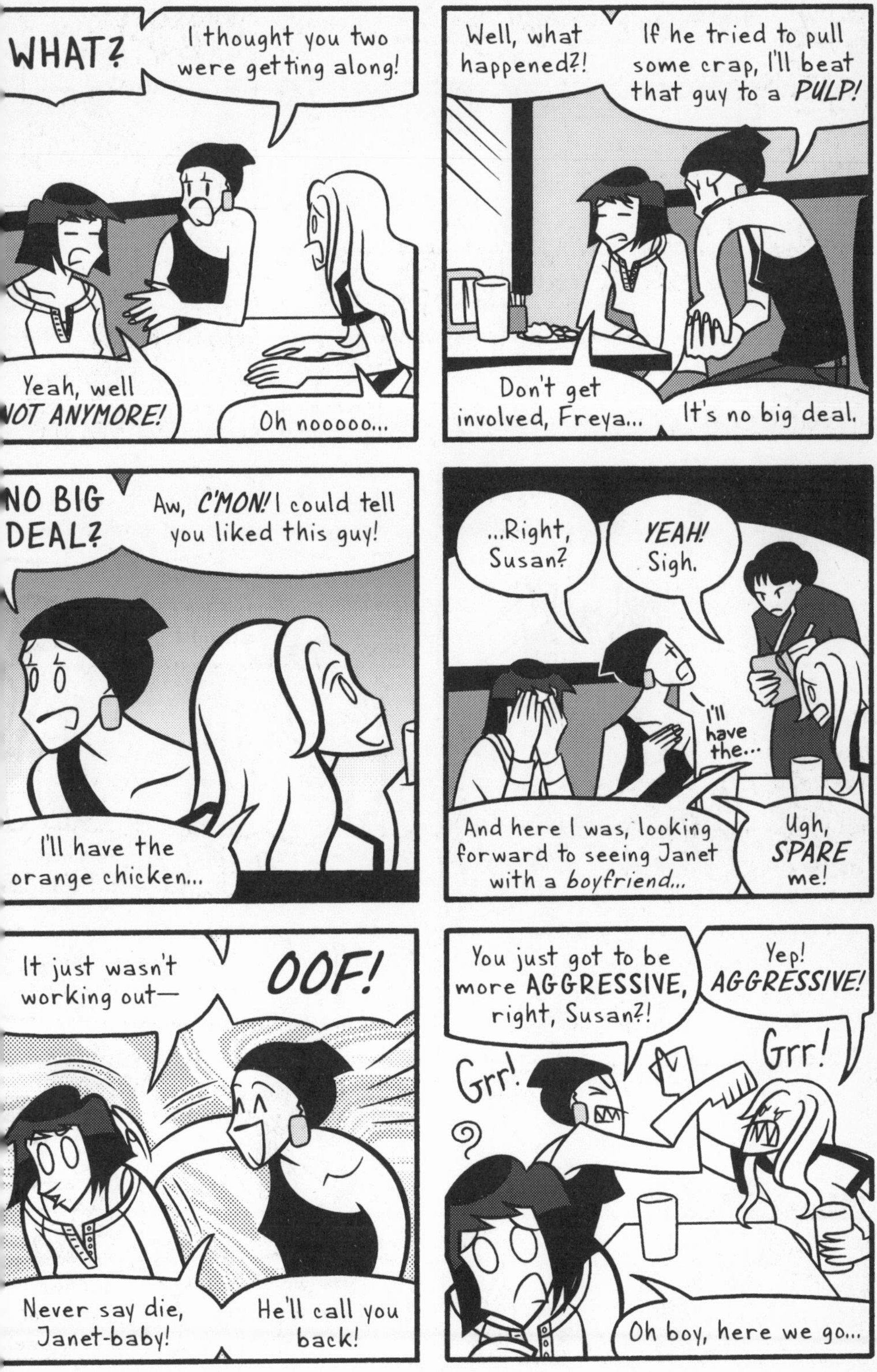
WHAT?
I thought you two were getting along!
Yeah, well NOT ANYMORE!
Oh nooooo...
Well, what happened?!
If he tried to pull some crap, I'll beat that guy to a PULP!
Don't get involved, Freya...
It's no big deal.
NO BIG DEAL?
Aw, C'MON! I could tell you liked this guy!
I'll have the orange chicken...
...Right, Susan?
YEAH! Sigh.
I'll have the...
And here I was, looking forward to seeing Janet with a boyfriend...
Ugh, SPARE me!
It just wasn't working out—
OOF!
Never say die, Janet-baby!
He'll call you back!
You just got to be more AGGRESSIVE, right, Susan?!
Yep! AGGRESSIVE!
Grr!
Grr!
Oh boy, here we go...

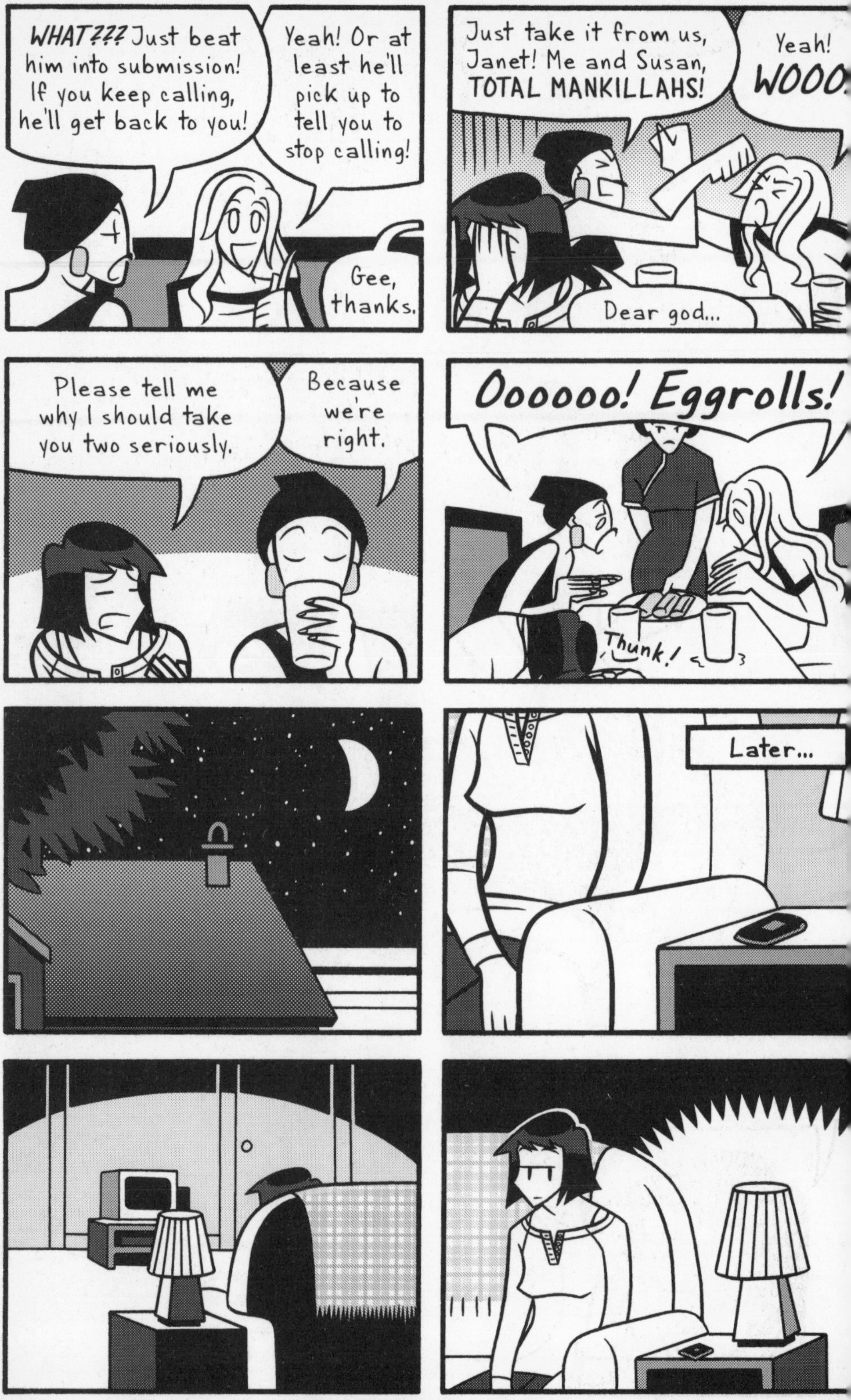
WHAT??? Just beat him into submission! If you keep calling, he'll get back to you!
Yeah! Or at least he'll pick up to tell you to stop calling!
Gee, thanks.
Just take it from us, Janet! Me and Susan, TOTAL MANKILLAHS!
Yeah! WOOO
Dear god...
Please tell me why I should take you two seriously.
Because we're right.
Oooooo! Eggrolls!
Thunk!
Later...

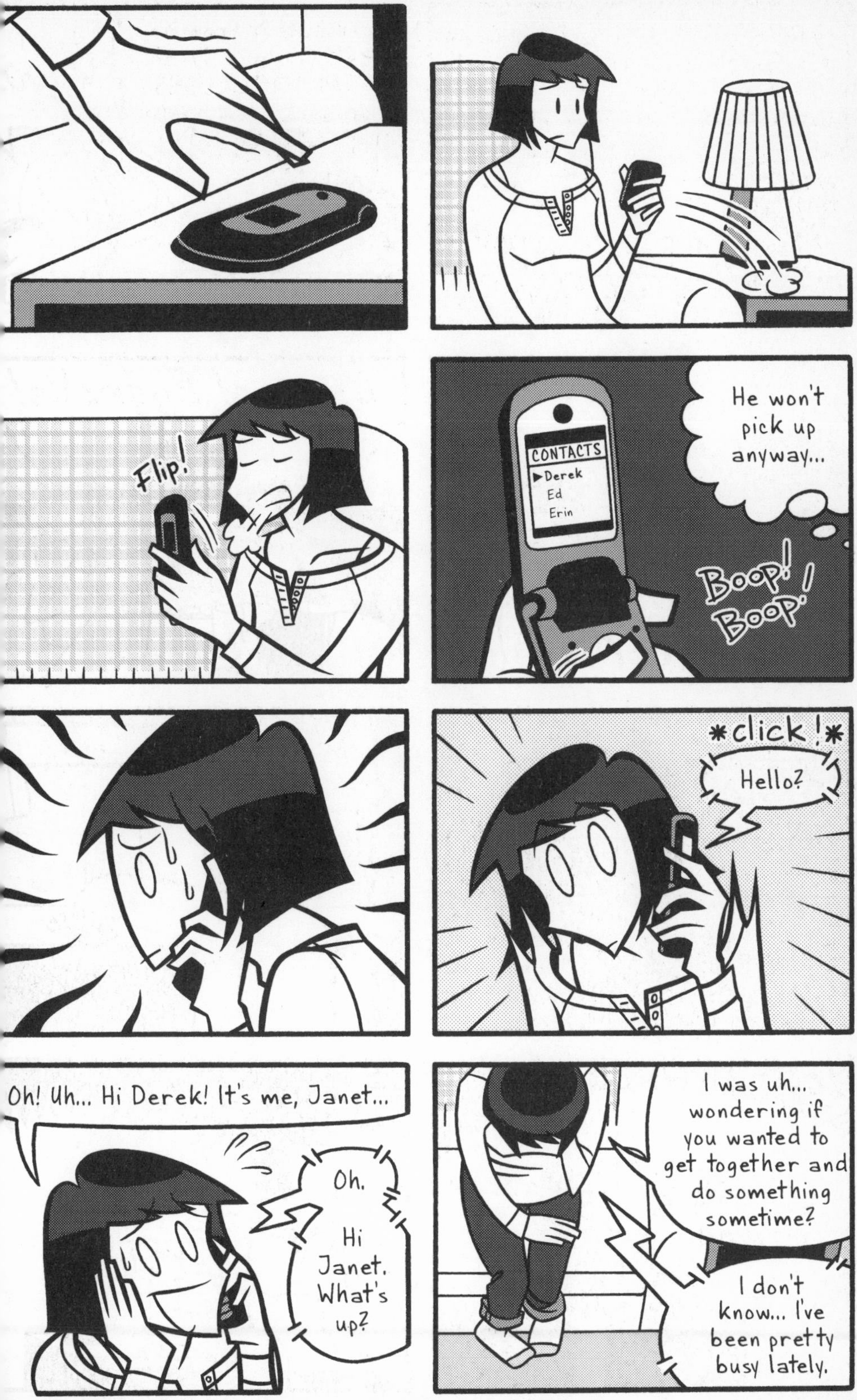

He won't pick up anyway...
CONTACTS
▶Derek
Ed
Erin
Flip!
Boop! Boop!
click!
Hello?
Oh! Uh... Hi Derek! It's me, Janet...
Oh.
Hi Janet. What's up?
I was uh... wondering if you wanted to get together and do something sometime?
I don't know... I've been pretty busy lately.

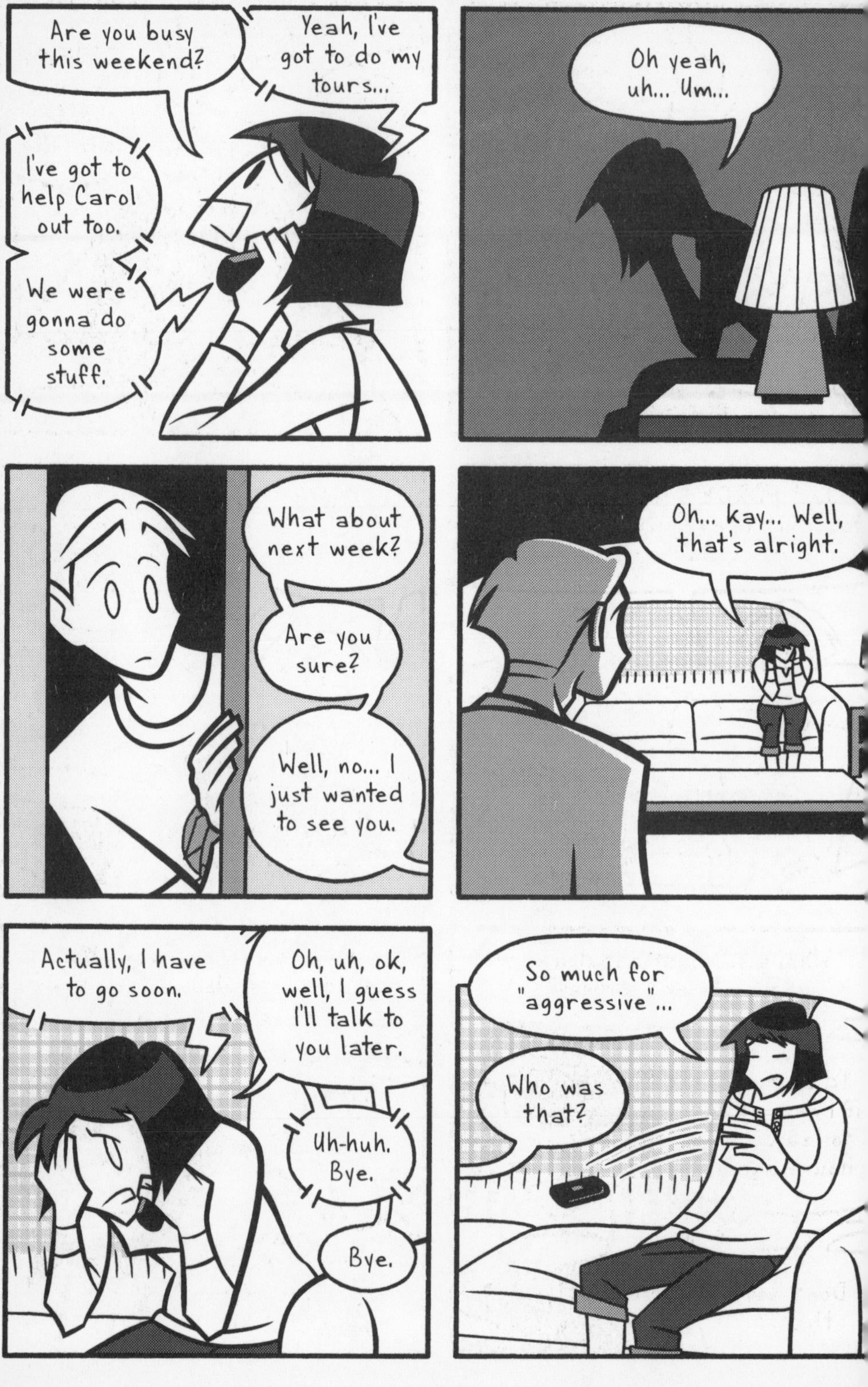

Are you busy this weekend?
Yeah, I've got to do my tours...
I've got to help Carol out too.
We were gonna do some stuff.
Oh yeah, uh... Um...
What about next week?
Are you sure?
Well, no... I just wanted to see you.
Oh... kay... Well, that's alright.
Actually, I have to go soon.
Oh, uh, ok, well, I guess I'll talk to you later.
Uh-huh. Bye.
Bye.
So much for "aggressive"...
Who was that?

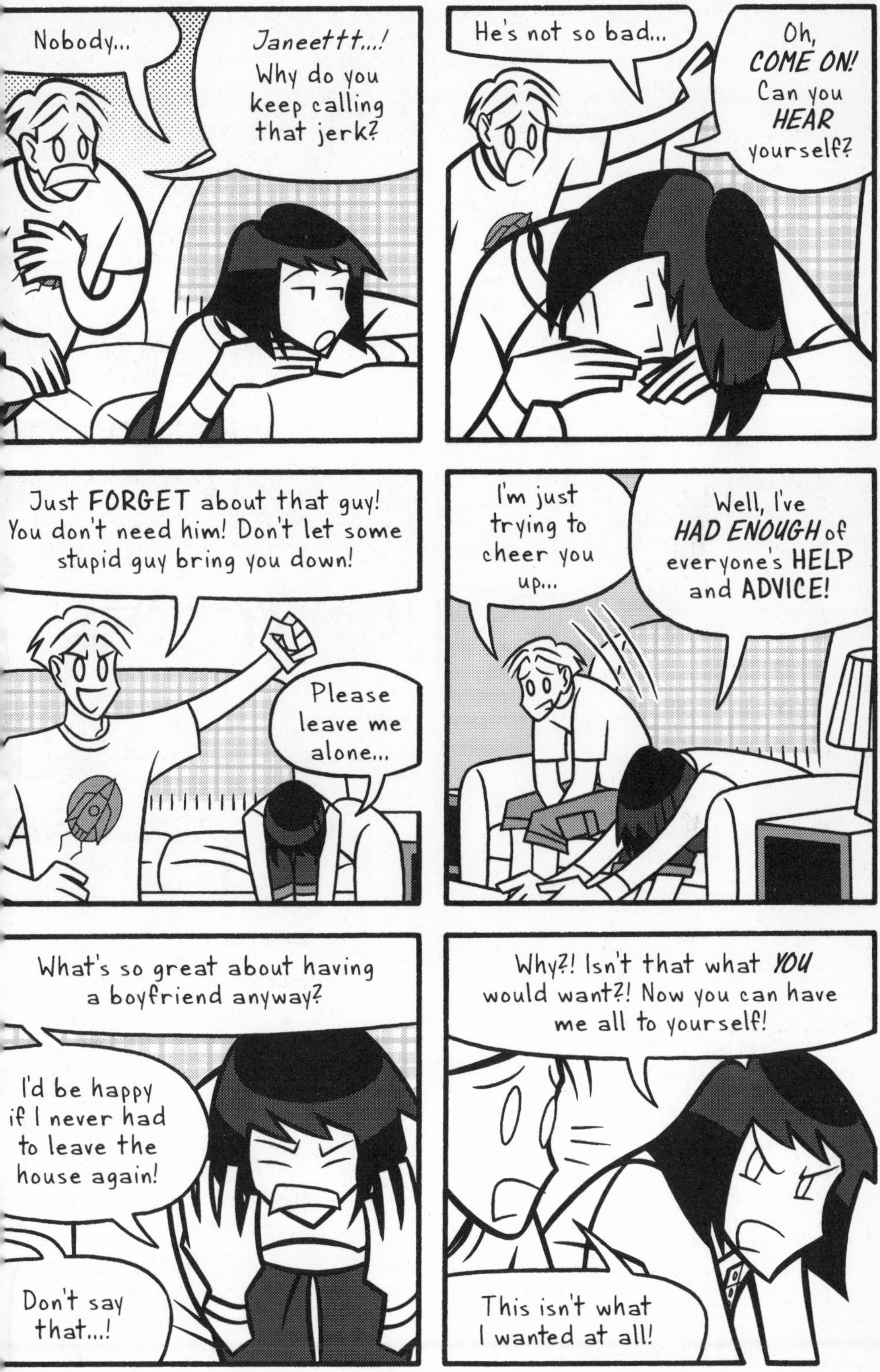
Nobody...
Janeettt...! Why do you keep calling that jerk?
He's not so bad...
Oh, COME ON! Can you HEAR yourself?
Just FORGET about that guy! You don't need him! Don't let some stupid guy bring you down!
Please leave me alone...
I'm just trying to cheer you up...
Well, I've HAD ENOUGH of everyone's HELP and ADVICE!
What's so great about having a boyfriend anyway?
I'd be happy if I never had to leave the house again!
Don't say that...!
Why?! Isn't that what YOU would want?! Now you can have me all to yourself!
This isn't what I wanted at all!

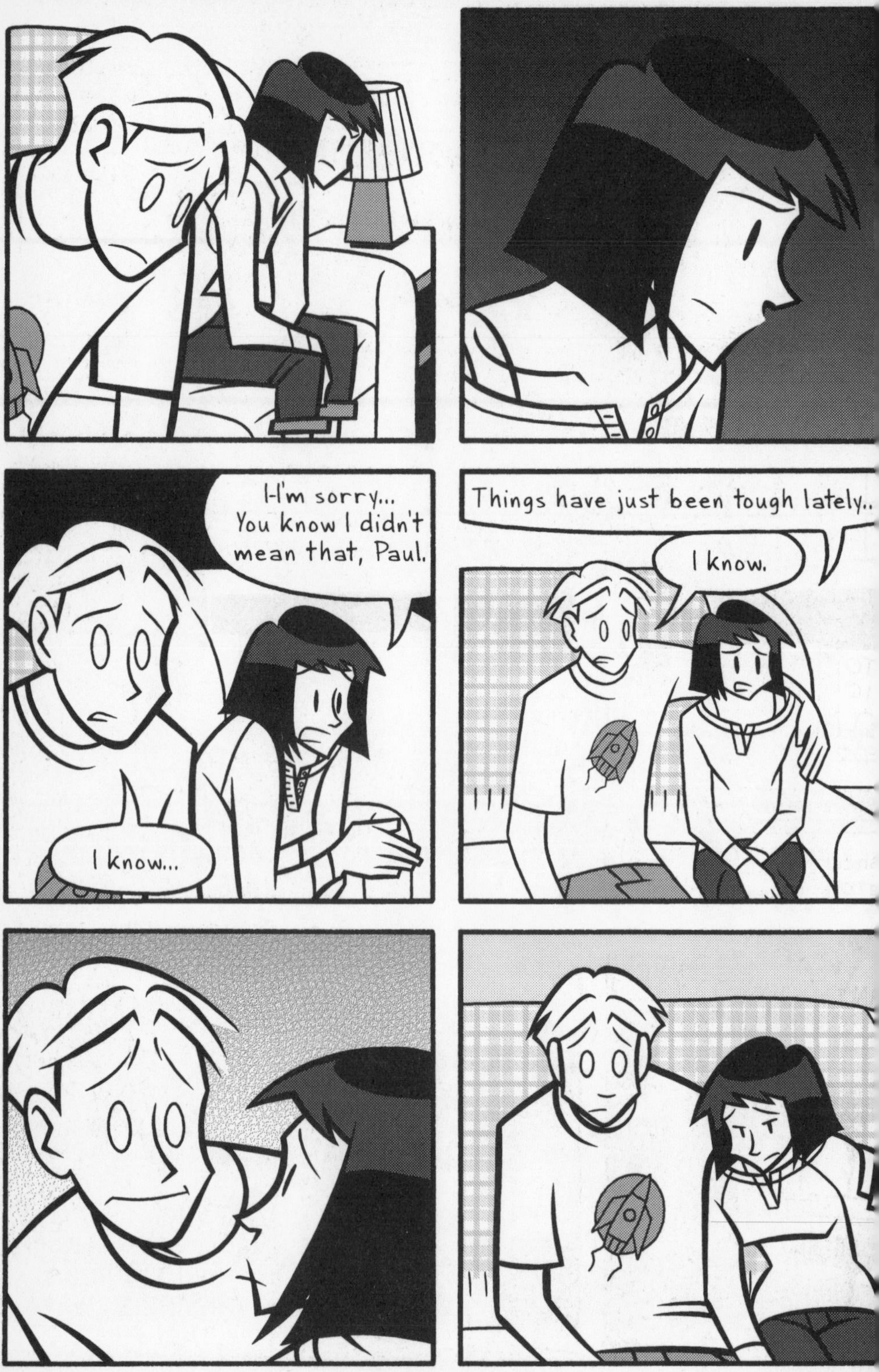

I-I'm sorry... You know I didn't mean that, Paul.
I know...
Things have just been tough lately..
I know.

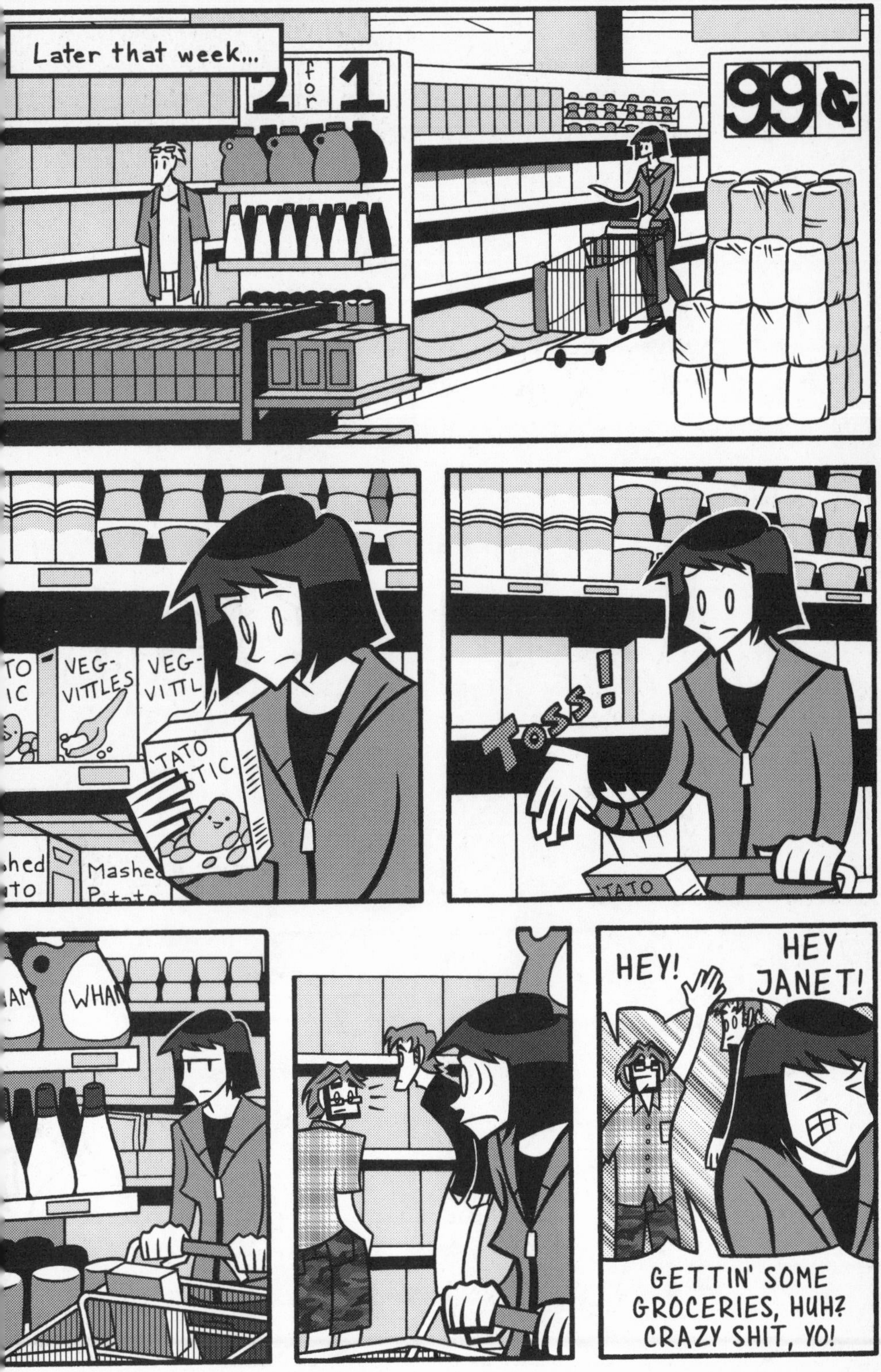
Later that week...
2 for 1
99¢
VEG-VITTLES
VEG-VITTL
'TATO
TIC
Mashed Potato
TOSS!
'TATO
WHAM
HEY!
HEY JANET!
GETTIN' SOME GROCERIES, HUH? CRAZY SHIT, YO!

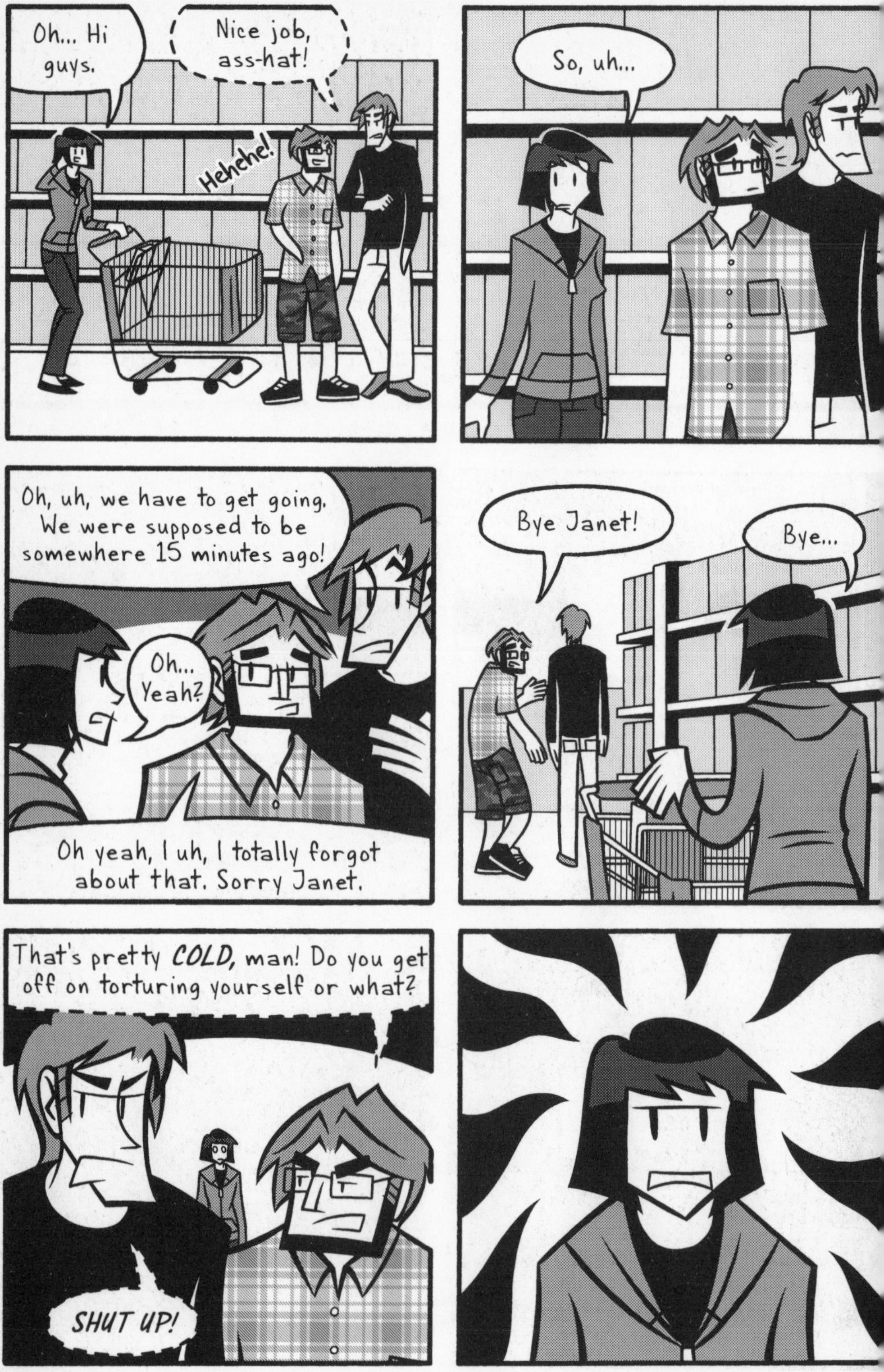
Oh... Hi guys.
Nice job, ass-hat!
Hehehe!
So, uh...
Oh, uh, we have to get going. We were supposed to be somewhere 15 minutes ago!
Oh... Yeah?
Oh yeah, I uh, I totally forgot about that. Sorry Janet.
Bye Janet!
Bye...
That's pretty COLD, man! Do you get off on torturing yourself or what?
SHUT UP!

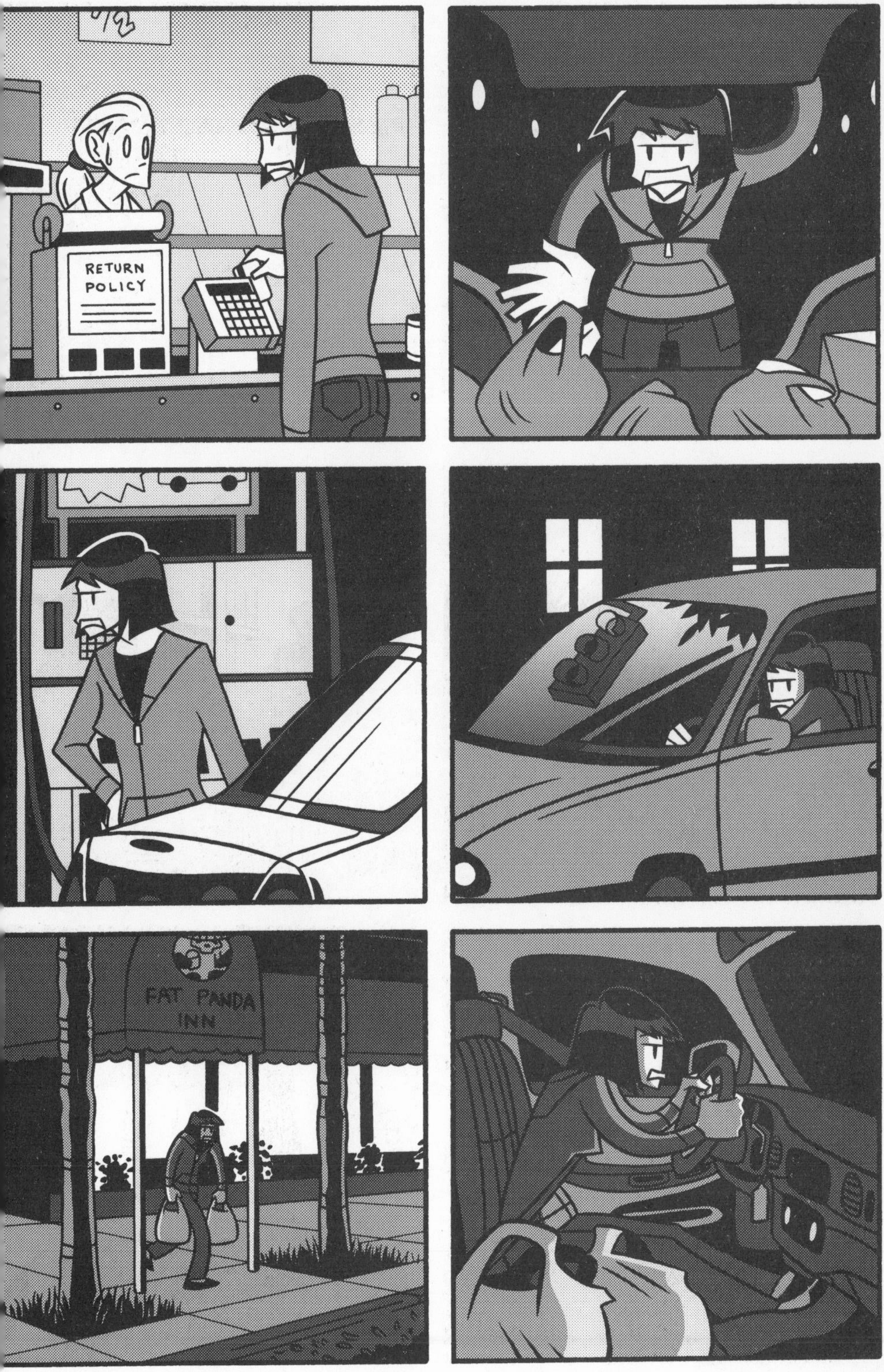
RETURN POLICY
FAT PANDA INN

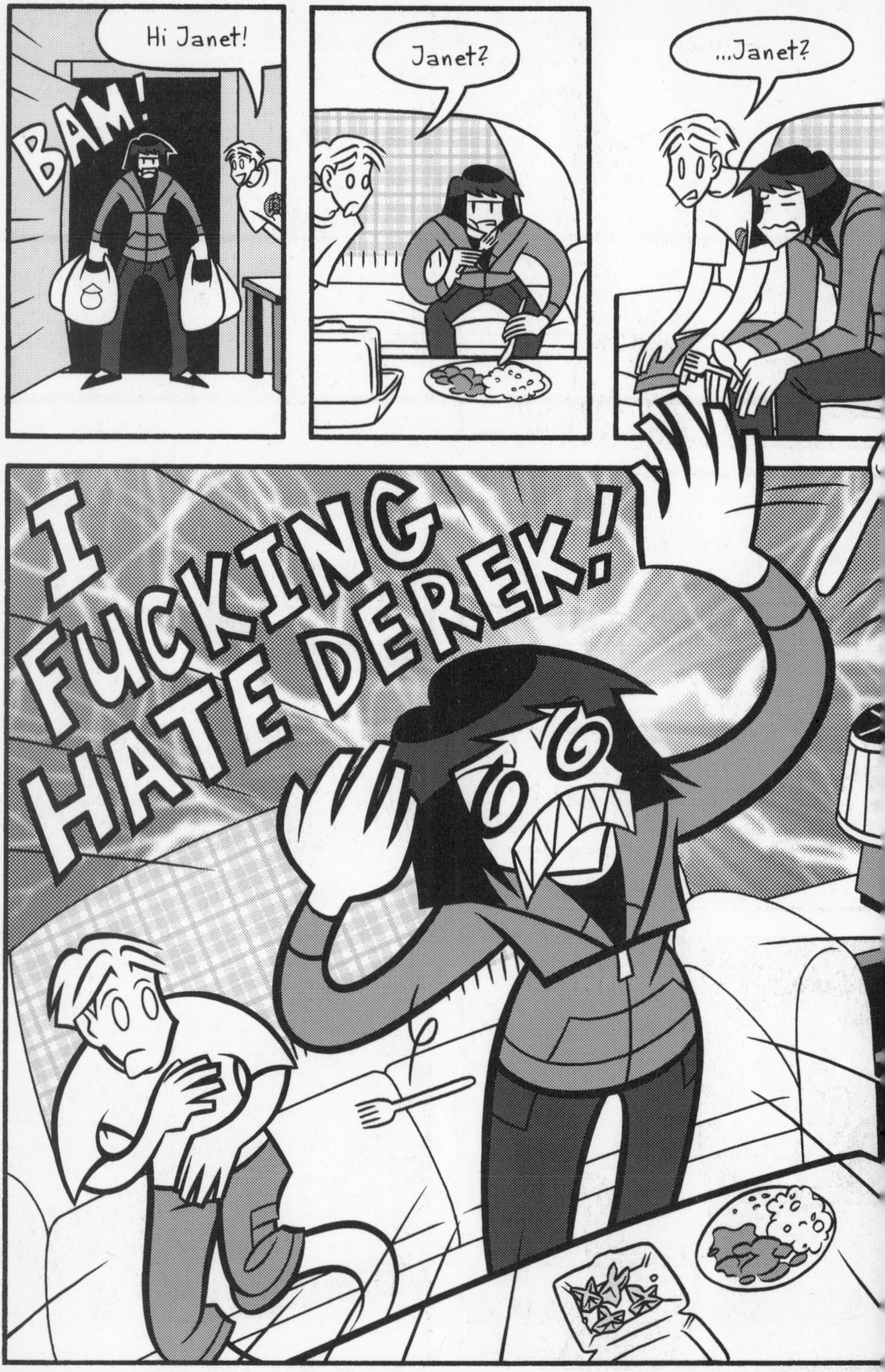
BAM!
Hi Janet!
Janet?
...Janet?
I FUCKING HATE DEREK!

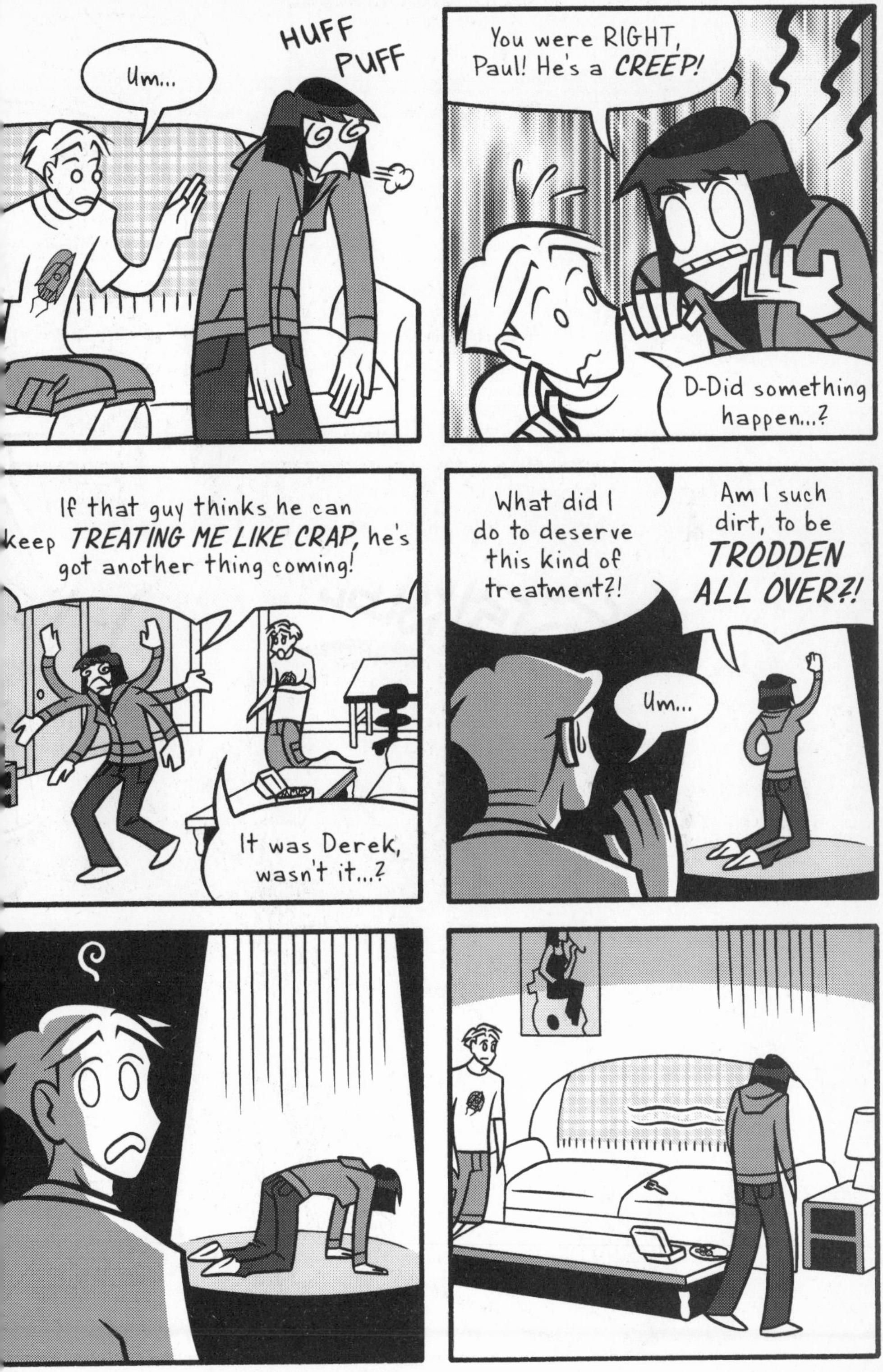

Um...
HUFF
PUFF
You were RIGHT, Paul! He's a CREEP!
D-Did something happen...?
If that guy thinks he can keep TREATING ME LIKE CRAP, he's got another thing coming!
It was Derek, wasn't it...?
What did I do to deserve this kind of treatment?!
Am I such dirt, to be TRODDEN ALL OVER?!
Um...

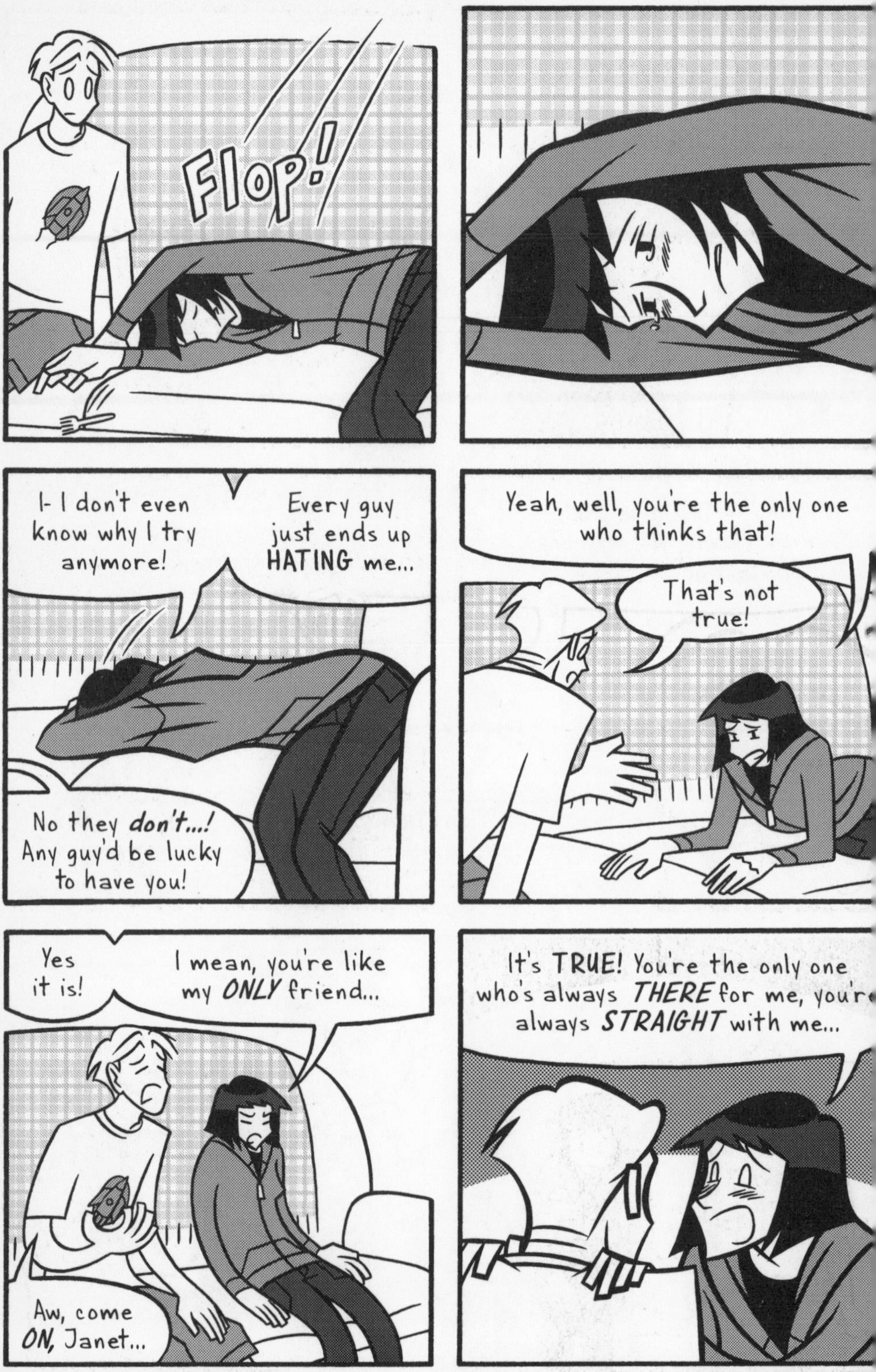
FLOP!
I- I don't even know why I try anymore!
Every guy just ends up HATING me...
No they don't...! Any guy'd be lucky to have you!
Yeah, well, you're the only one who thinks that!
That's not true!
Yes it is!
I mean, you're like my ONLY friend...
Aw, come ON, Janet...
It's TRUE! You're the only one who's always THERE for me, you'r always STRAIGHT with me...

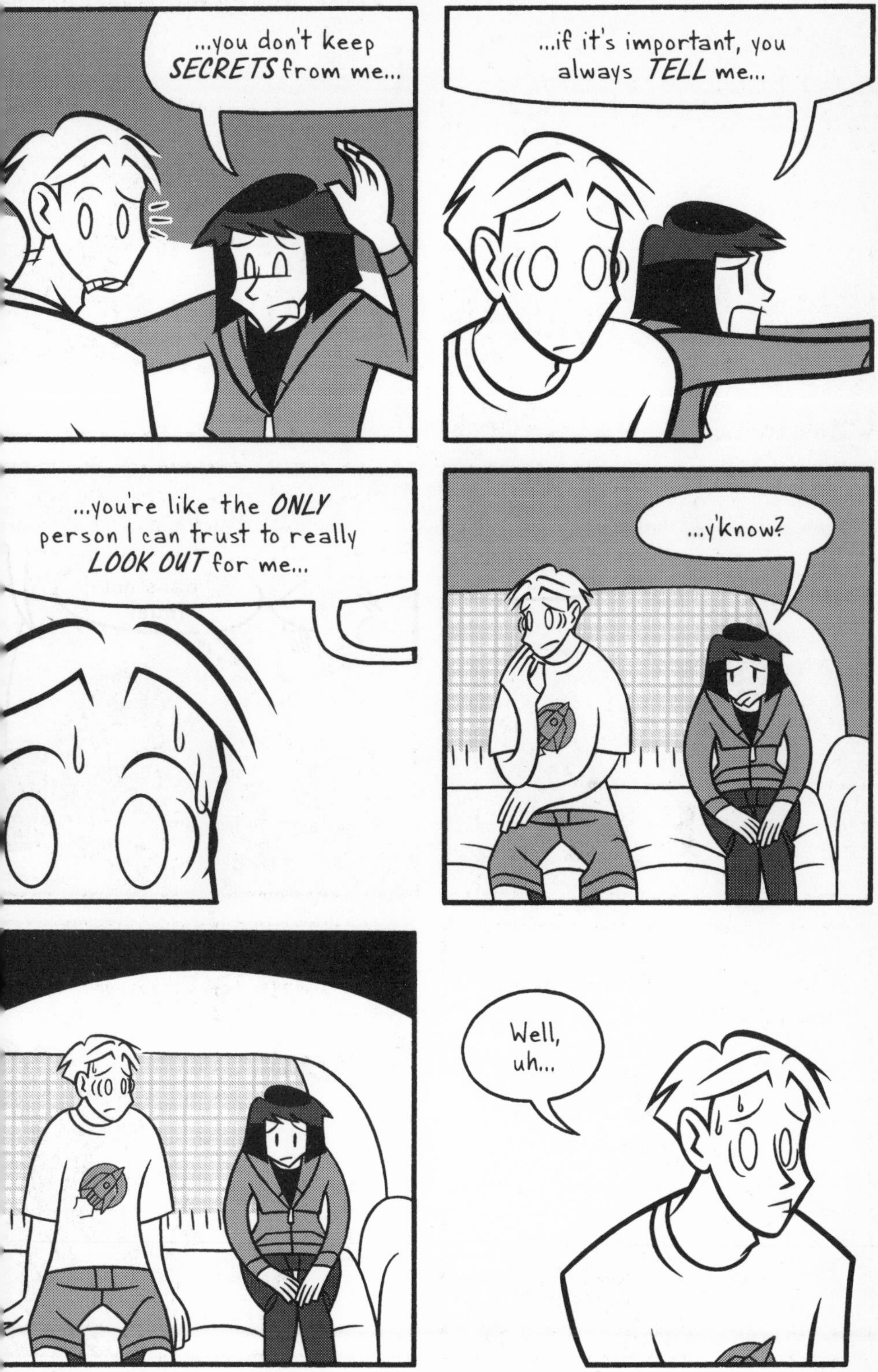
...you don't keep
SECRETS from me...
...if it's important, you
always TELL me...
...you're like the ONLY
person I can trust to really
LOOK OUT for me...
...y'know?
Well,
uh...

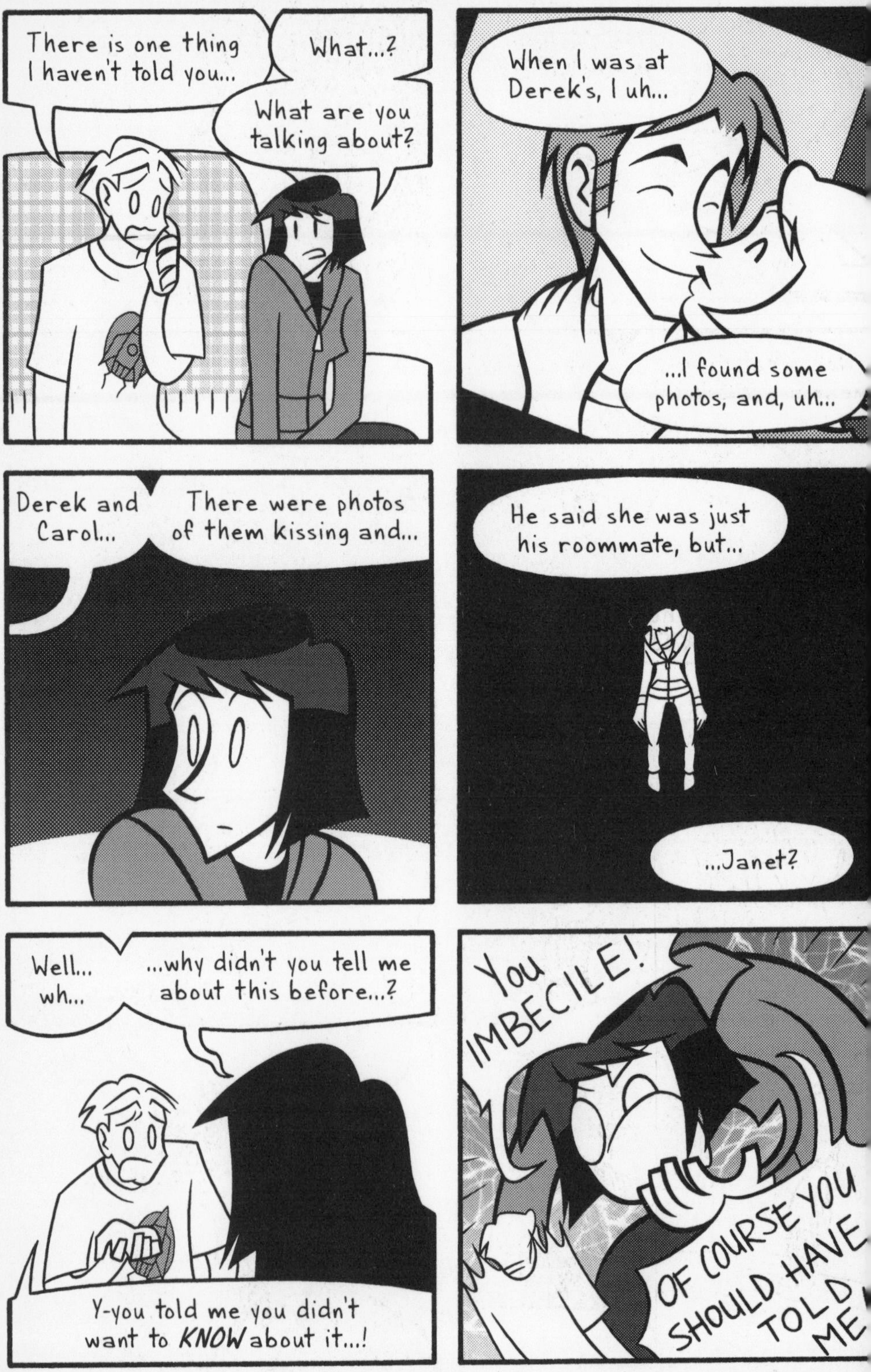

There is one thing I haven't told you...
What...?
What are you talking about?
When I was at Derek's, I uh...
...I found some photos, and, uh...
Derek and Carol...
There were photos of them kissing and...
He said she was just his roommate, but...
...Janet?
Well... wh...
...why didn't you tell me about this before...?
Y-you told me you didn't want to KNOW about it...!
You IMBECILE!
OF COURSE YOU SHOULD HAVE TOLD ME

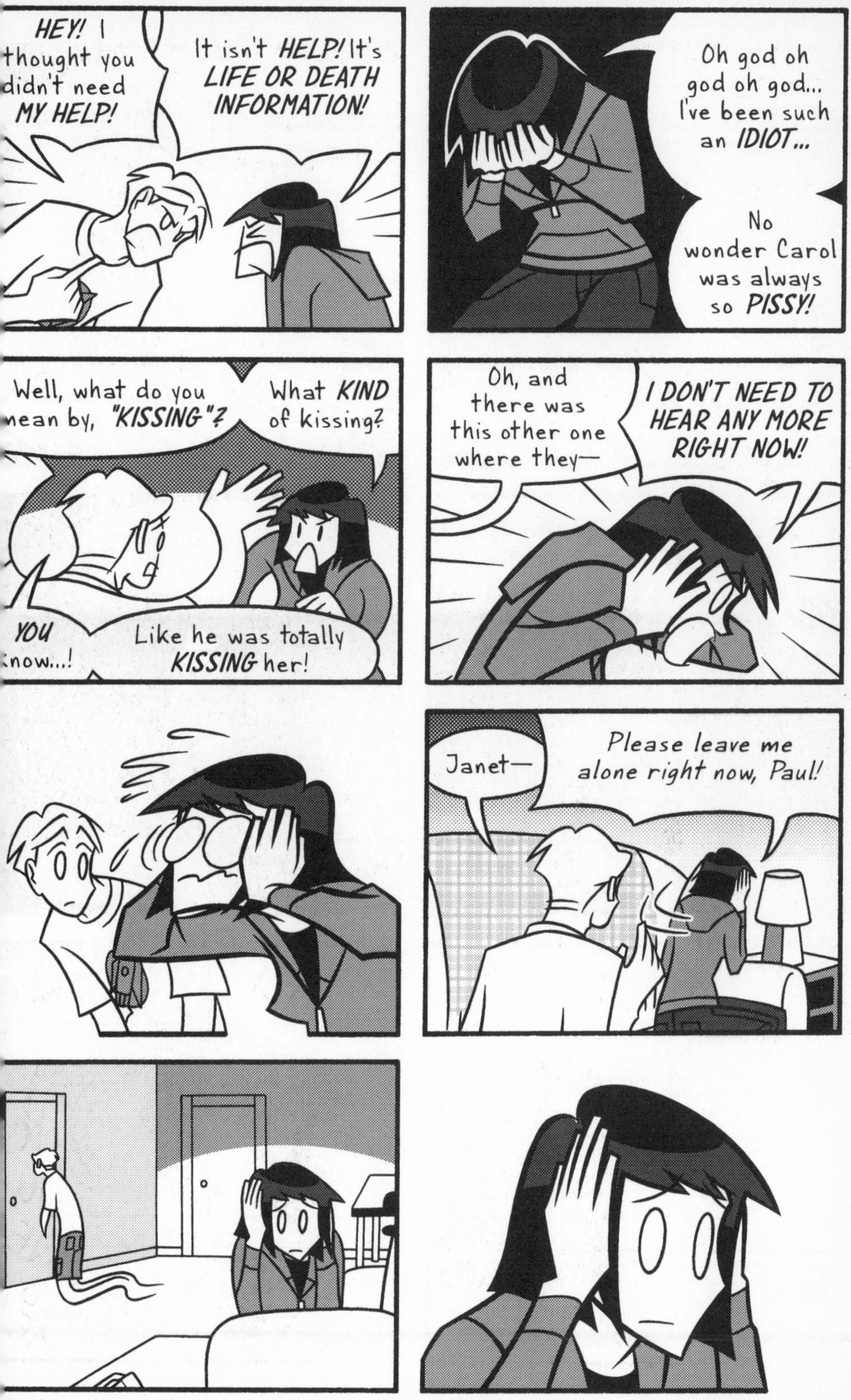
HEY! I thought you didn't need MY HELP!
It isn't HELP! It's LIFE OR DEATH INFORMATION!
Oh god oh god oh god... I've been such an IDIOT...
No wonder Carol was always so PISSY!
Well, what do you mean by, "KISSING"?
What KIND of kissing?
YOU know...!
Like he was totally KISSING her!
Oh, and there was this other one where they—
I DON'T NEED TO HEAR ANY MORE RIGHT NOW!
Janet—
Please leave me alone right now, Paul!

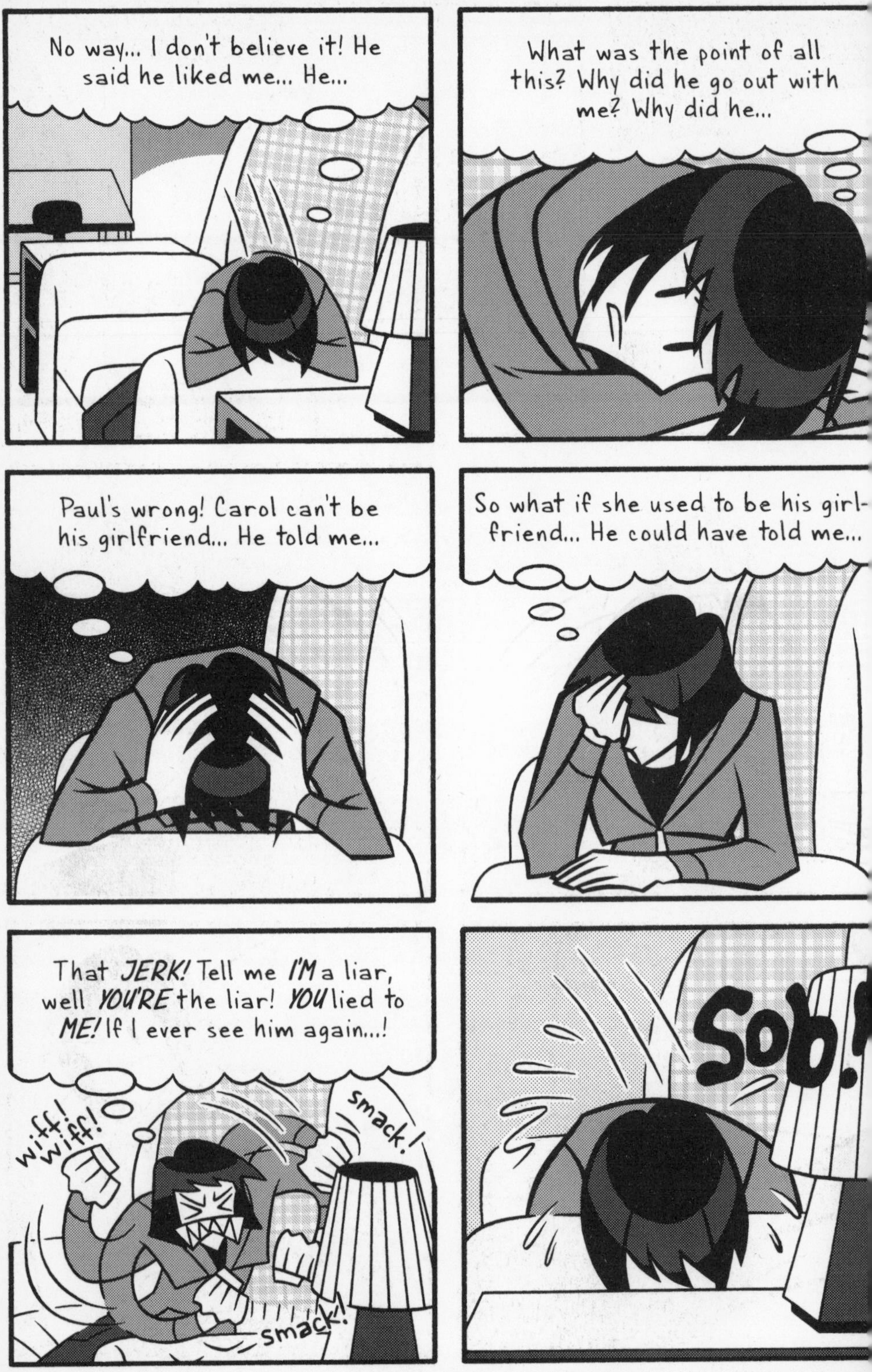
No way... I don't believe it! He said he liked me... He...
What was the point of all this? Why did he go out with me? Why did he...
Paul's wrong! Carol can't be his girlfriend... He told me...
So what if she used to be his girl-friend... He could have told me...
That JERK! Tell me I'M a liar, well YOU'RE the liar! YOU lied to ME! If I ever see him again...!
wiff! wiff!
smack!
smack!
Sob!

Rustle!
Rustle!

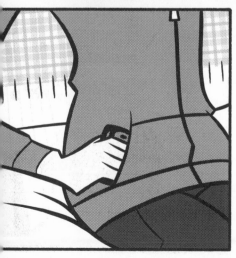

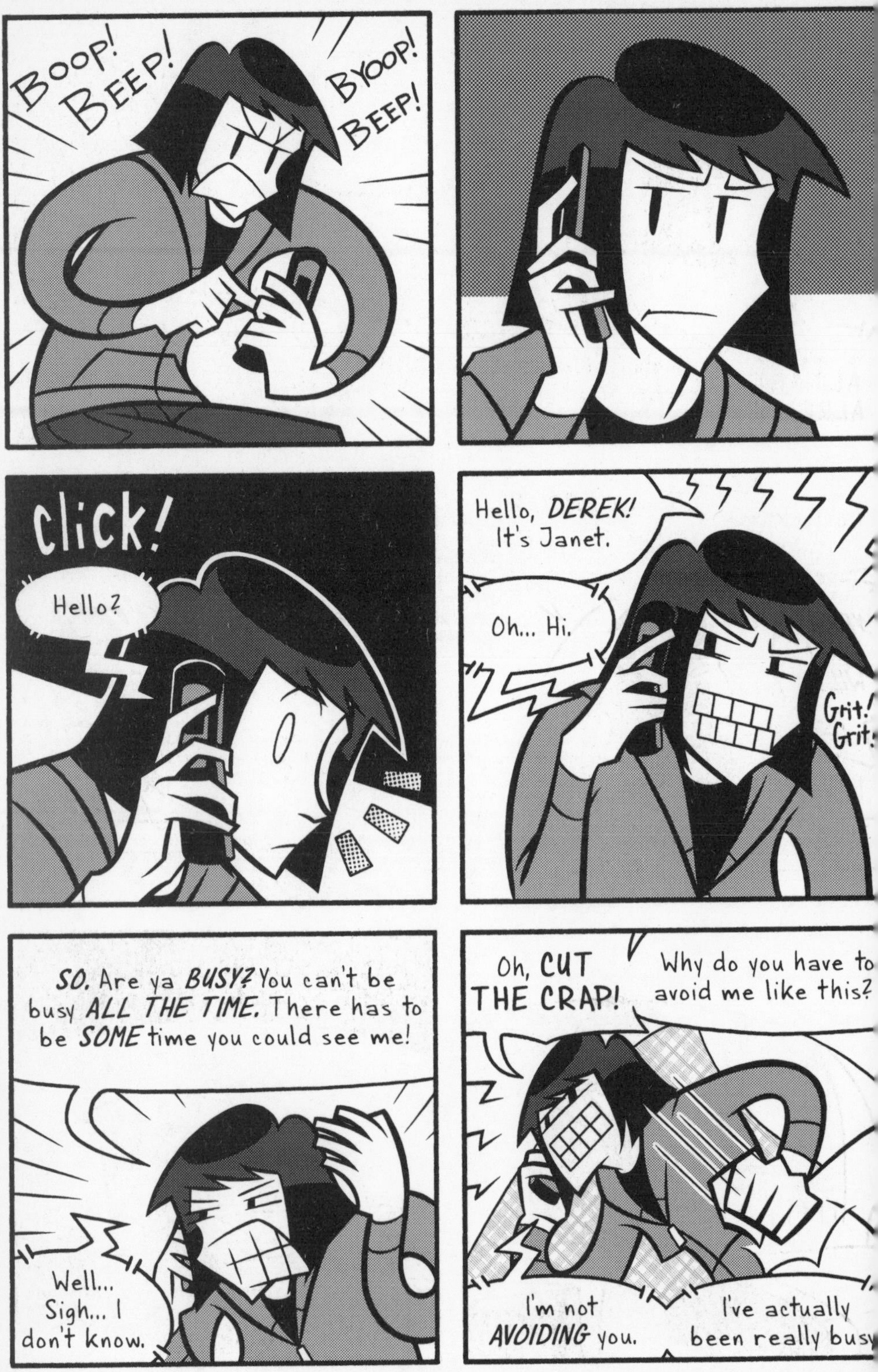
BOOP! BEEP!
BYOOP! BEEP!
Click!
Hello?
Hello, DEREK! It's Janet.
Oh... Hi.
Grit! Grit!
SO. Are ya BUSY? You can't be busy ALL THE TIME. There has to be SOME time you could see me!
Well... Sigh... I don't know.
Oh, CUT THE CRAP!
Why do you have to avoid me like this?
I'm not AVOIDING you.
I've actually been really bus

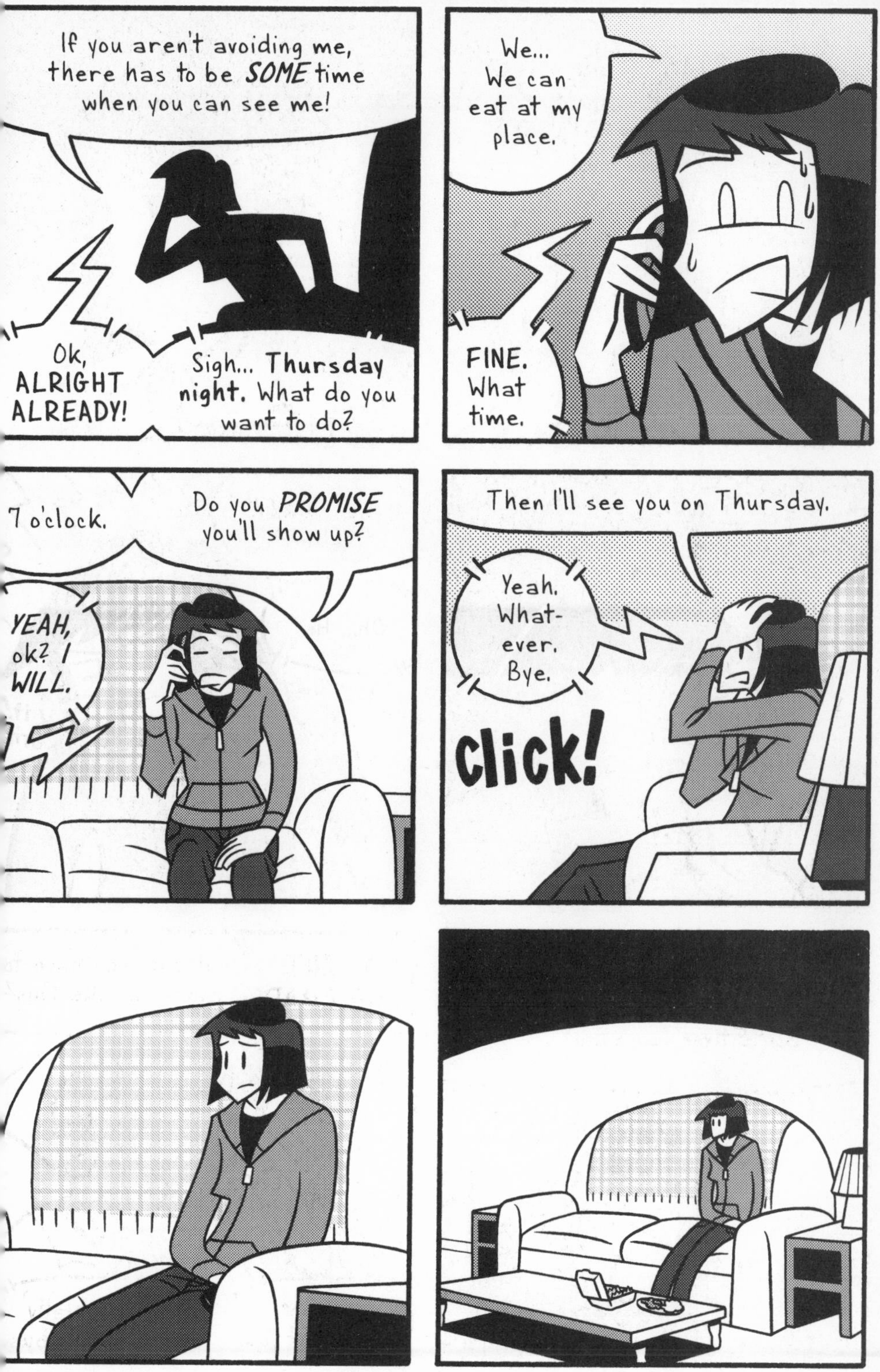
If you aren't avoiding me, there has to be SOME time when you can see me!
Ok, ALRIGHT ALREADY!
Sigh... Thursday night. What do you want to do?
We...
We can eat at my place.
FINE. What time.
7 o'clock.
Do you PROMISE you'll show up?
YEAH, ok? I WILL.
Then I'll see you on Thursday.
Yeah. What-ever. Bye.
Click!

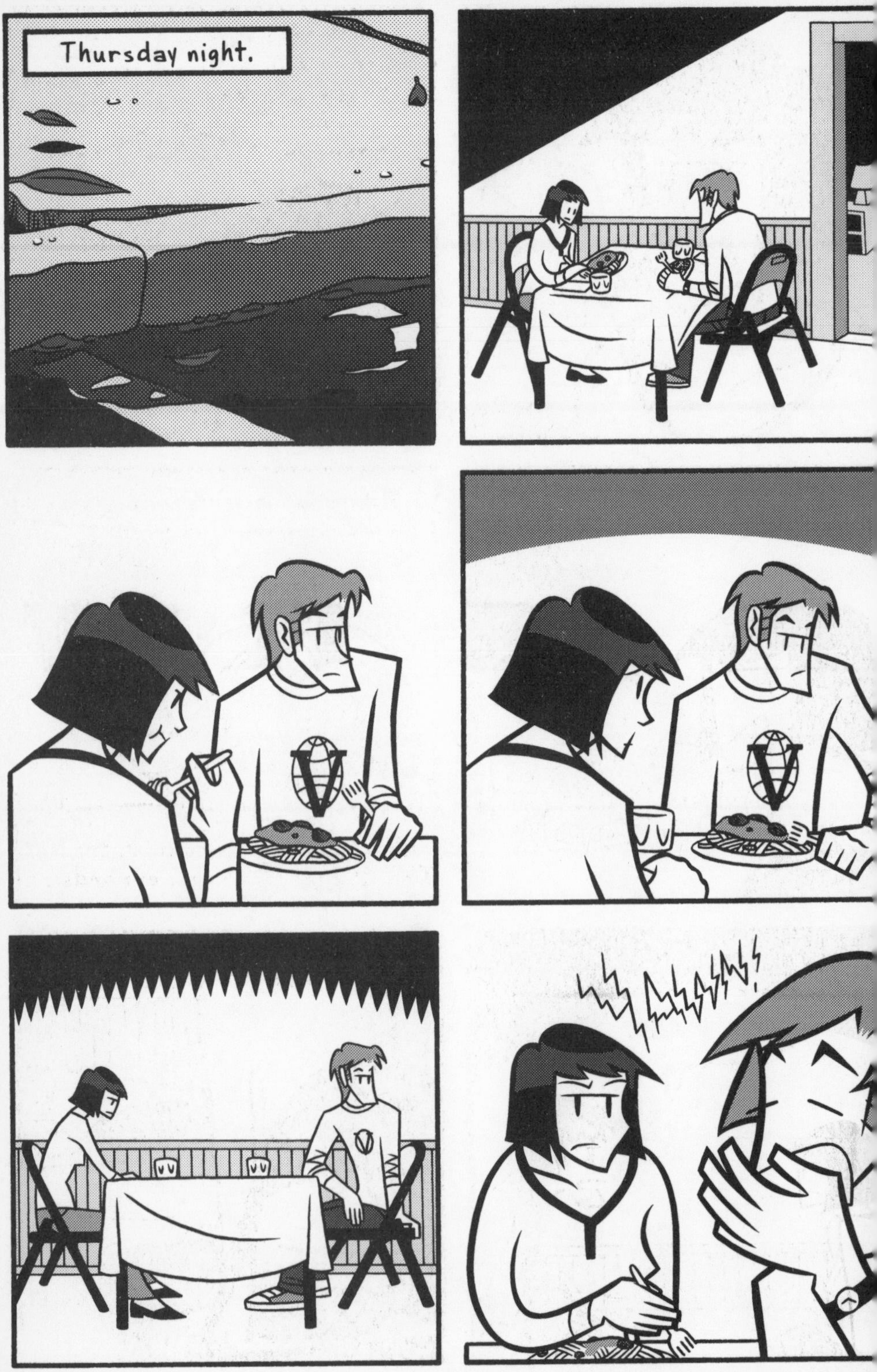
Thursday night.
SHHHMAAAAAHHHH!

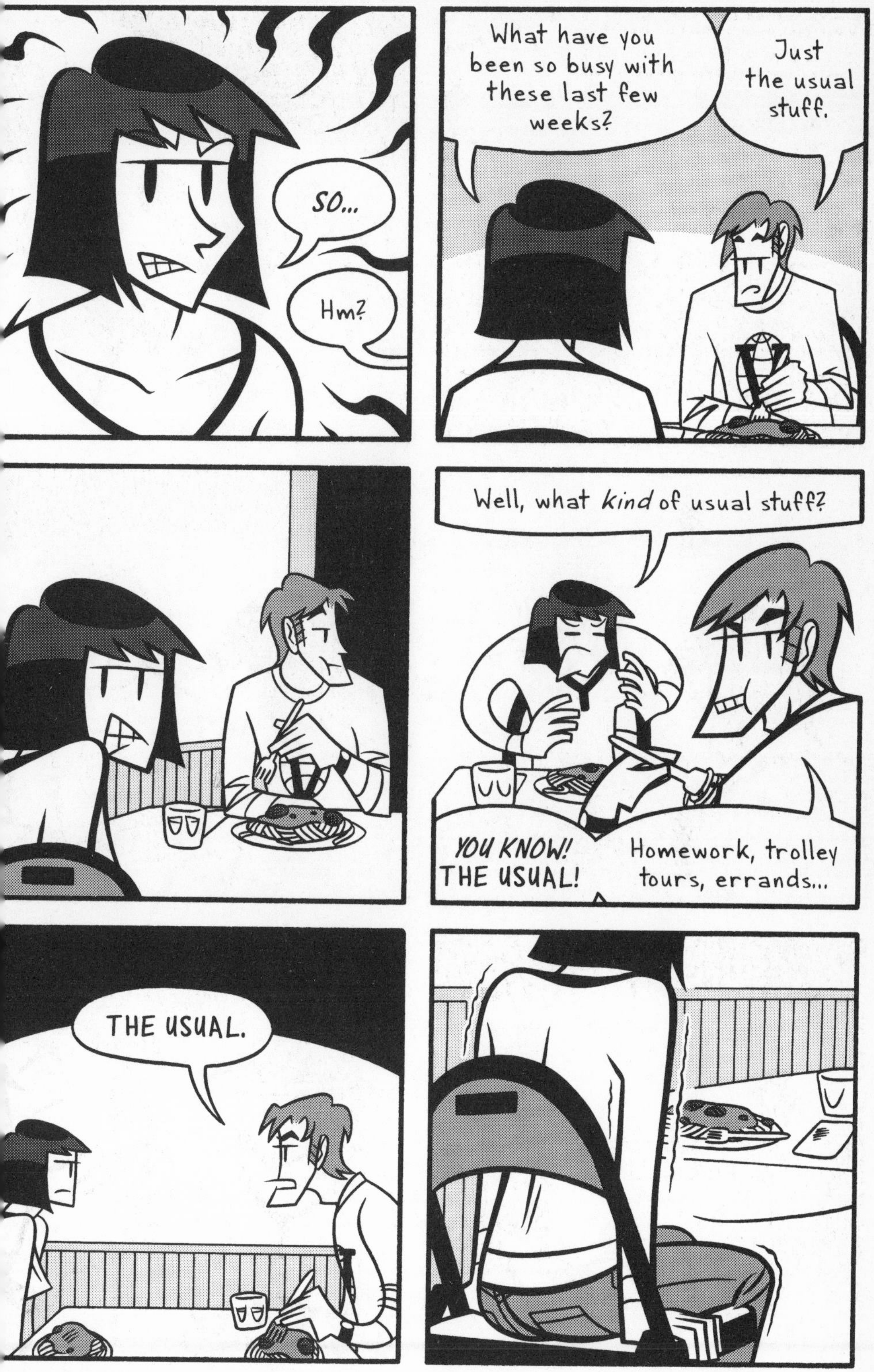
SO...
Hm?
What have you been so busy with these last few weeks?
Just the usual stuff.
Well, what *kind* of usual stuff?
Homework, trolley tours, errands...
YOU KNOW! THE USUAL!
THE USUAL.

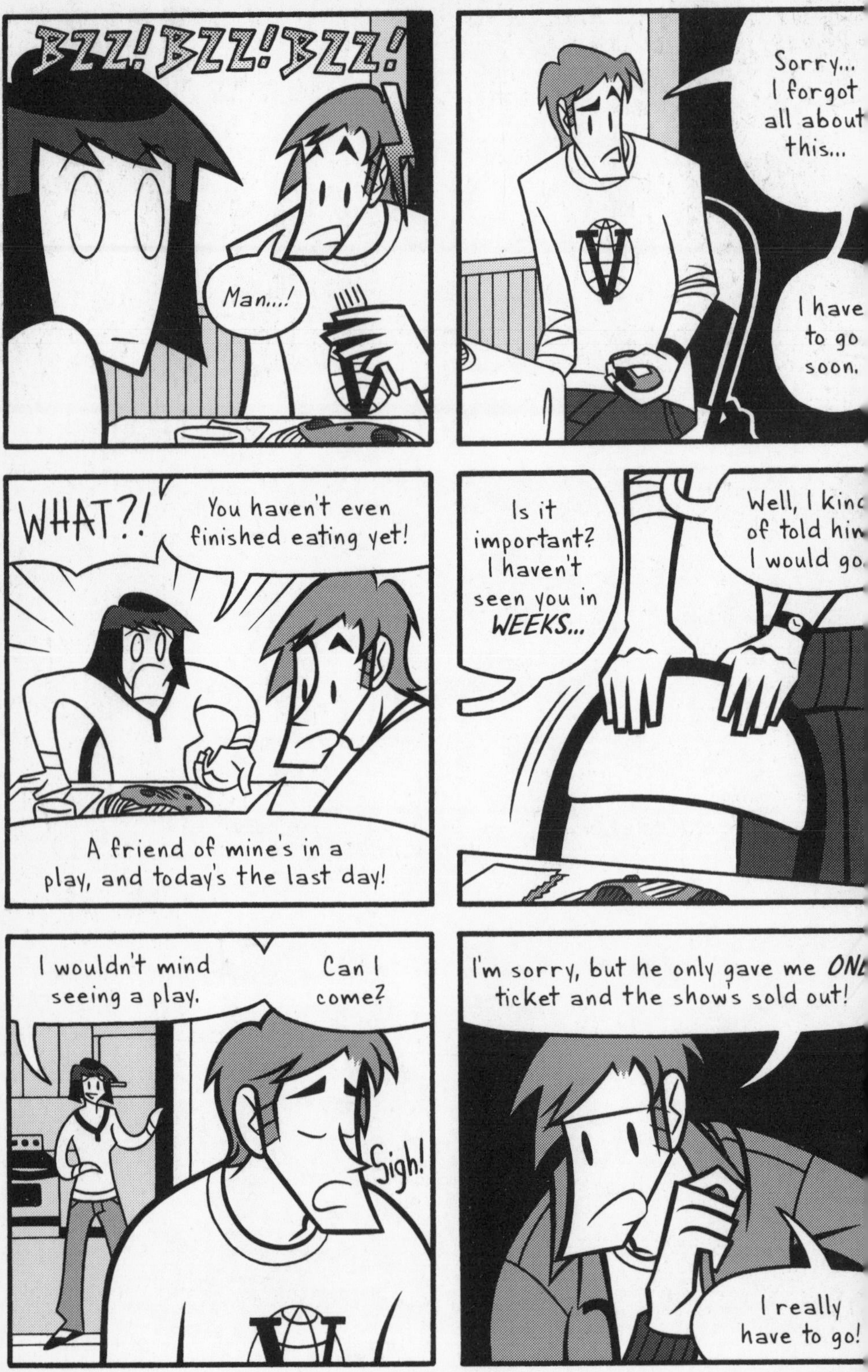
BZZ! BZZ! BZZ!
Man...!
Sorry... I forgot all about this...
I have to go soon.
WHAT?!
You haven't even finished eating yet!
A friend of mine's in a play, and today's the last day!
Is it important? I haven't seen you in *WEEKS...*
Well, I kin of told hi I would go
I wouldn't mind seeing a play.
Can I come?
Sigh!
I'm sorry, but he only gave me *ON* ticket and the show's sold out!
I really have to go!

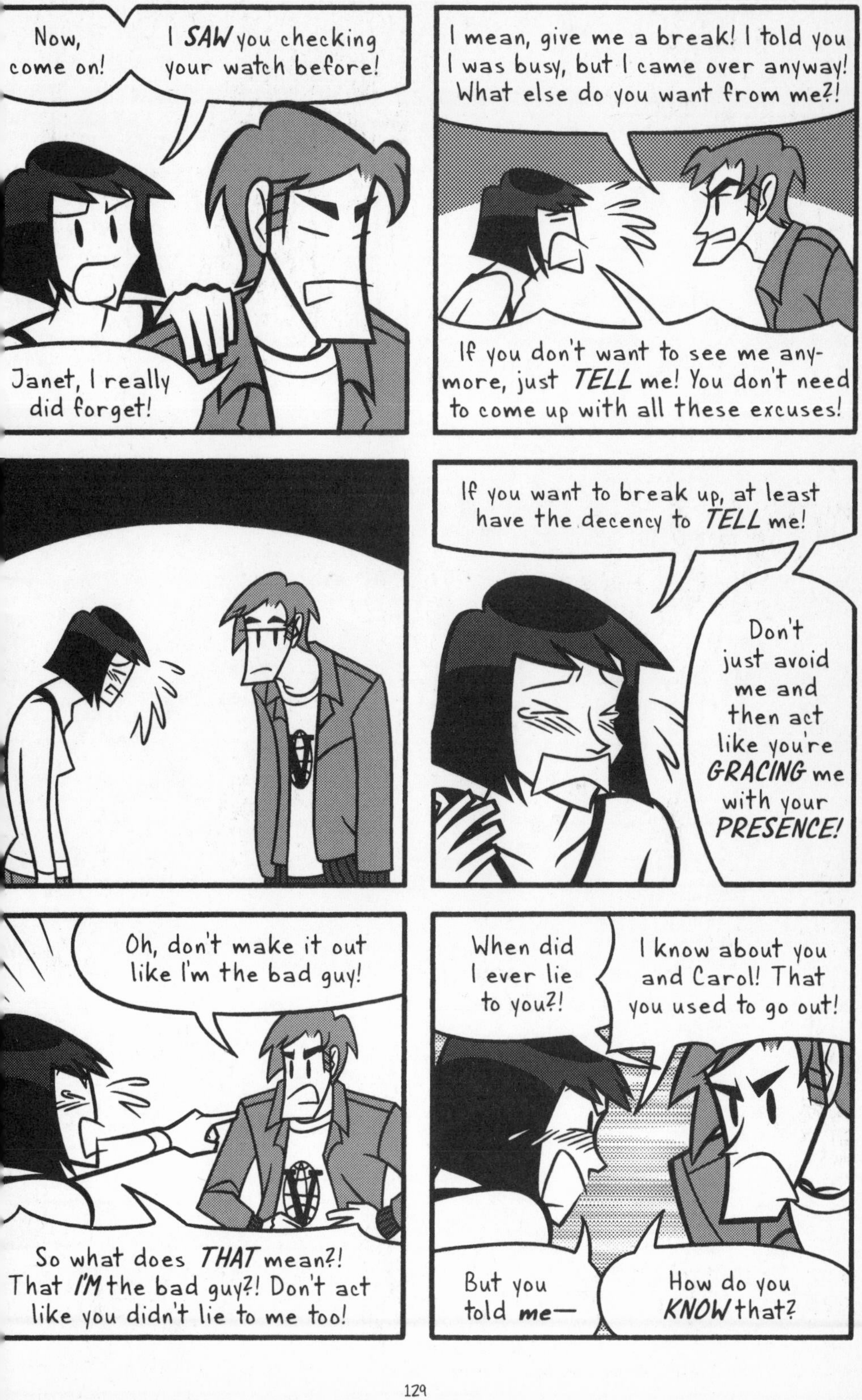
Now, come on!
I SAW you checking your watch before!
Janet, I really did forget!
I mean, give me a break! I told you I was busy, but I came over anyway! What else do you want from me?!
If you don't want to see me anymore, just TELL me! You don't need to come up with all these excuses!
If you want to break up, at least have the decency to TELL me!
Don't just avoid me and then act like you're GRACING me with your PRESENCE!
Oh, don't make it out like I'm the bad guy!
So what does THAT mean?! That I'M the bad guy?! Don't act like you didn't lie to me too!
When did I ever lie to you?!
I know about you and Carol! That you used to go out!
But you told me—
How do you KNOW that?

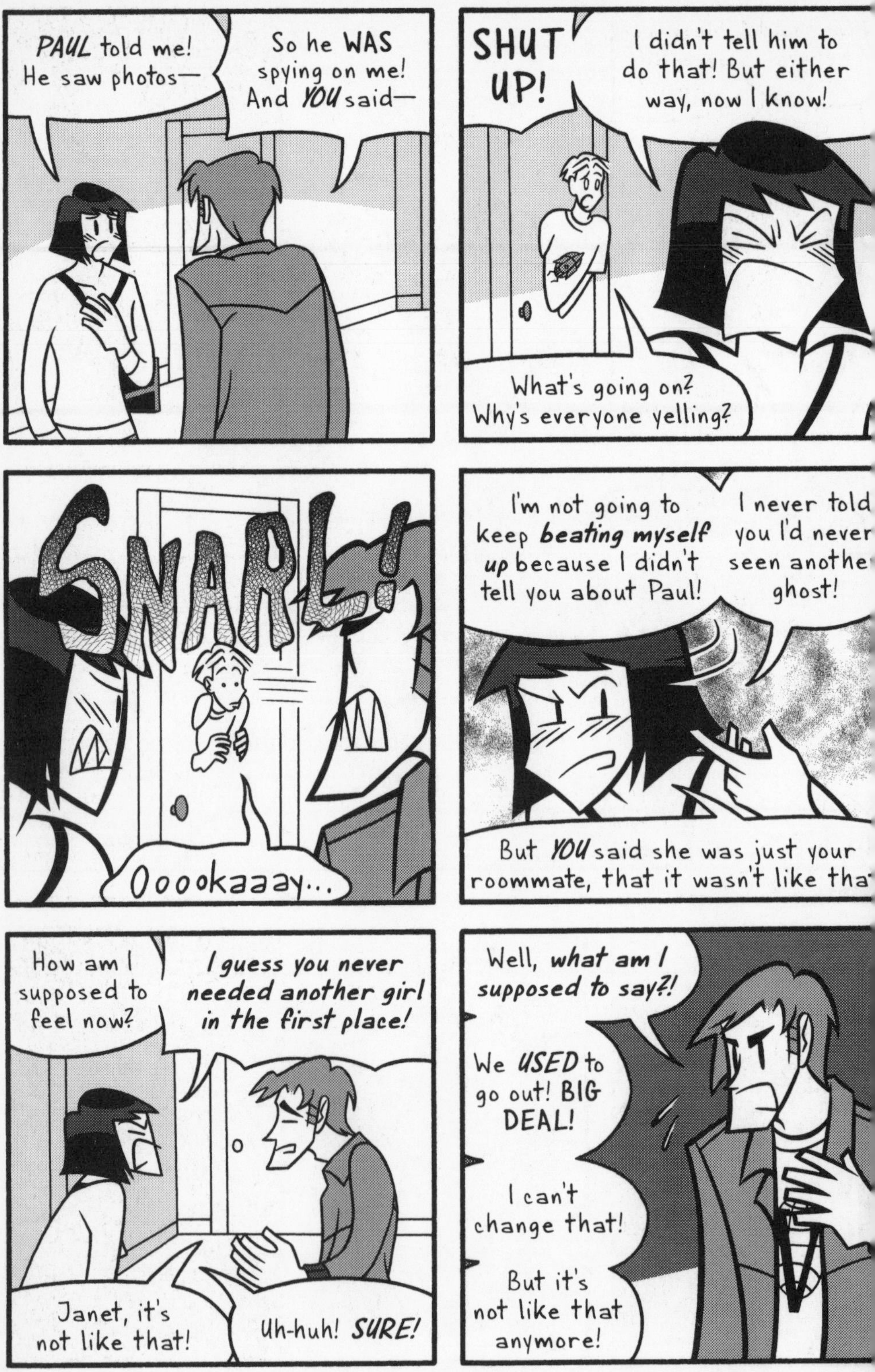

PAUL told me! He saw photos—
So he WAS spying on me! And YOU said—
SHUT UP!
I didn't tell him to do that! But either way, now I know!
What's going on? Why's everyone yelling?
SNARL!
Ooookaaay...
I'm not going to keep beating myself up because I didn't tell you about Paul!
I never told you I'd never seen anothe ghost!
But YOU said she was just your roommate, that it wasn't like tha
How am I supposed to feel now?
I guess you never needed another girl in the first place!
Janet, it's not like that!
Uh-huh! SURE!
Well, what am I supposed to say?!
We USED to go out! BIG DEAL!
I can't change that!
But it's not like that anymore!

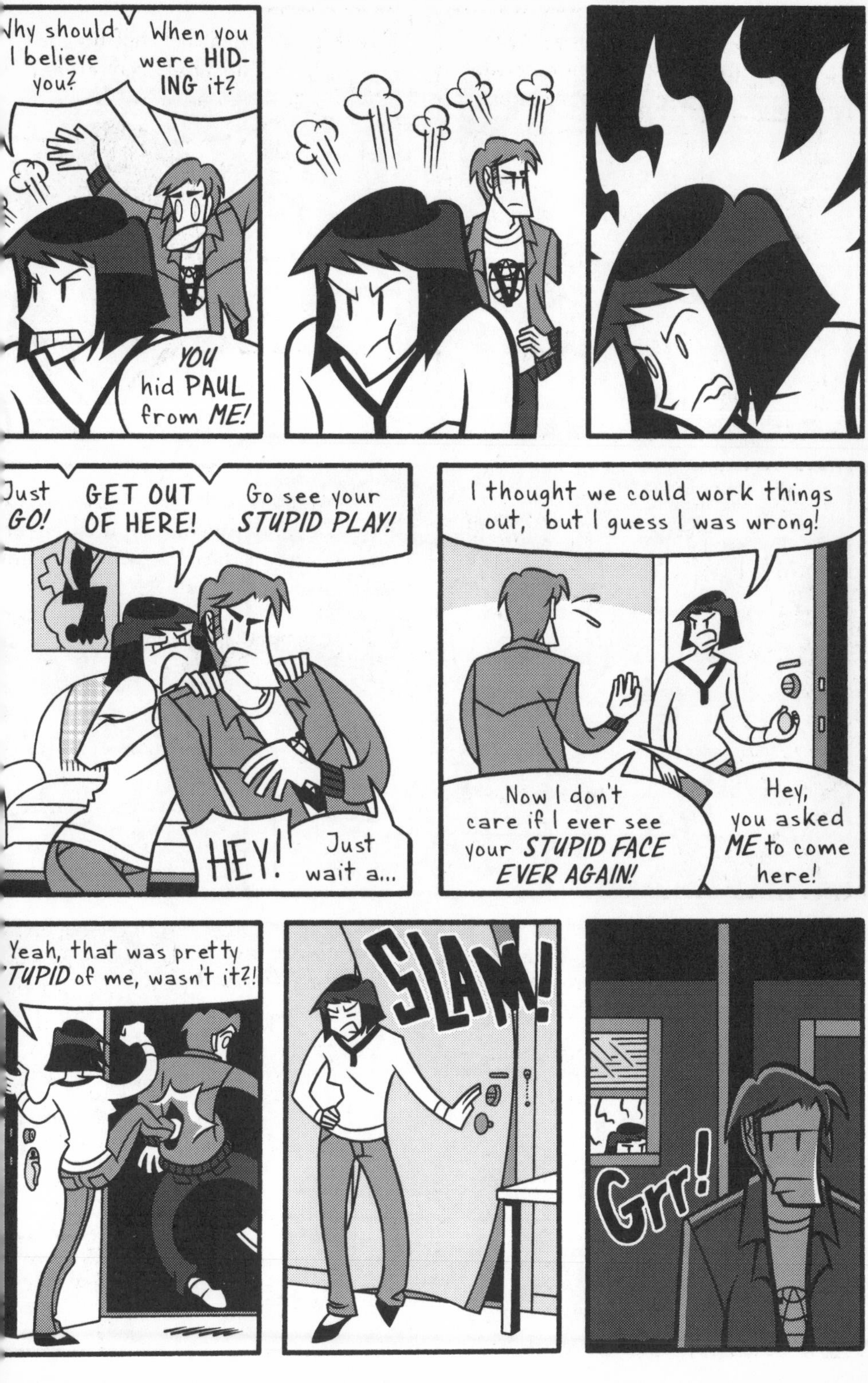

Why should I believe you?
When you were HIDING it?
YOU hid PAUL from ME!
Just GO!
GET OUT OF HERE!
Go see your STUPID PLAY!
HEY!
Just wait a...
I thought we could work things out, but I guess I was wrong!
Now I don't care if I ever see your STUPID FACE EVER AGAIN!
Hey, you asked ME to come here!
Yeah, that was pretty STUPID of me, wasn't it?!
SLAM!
Grr!

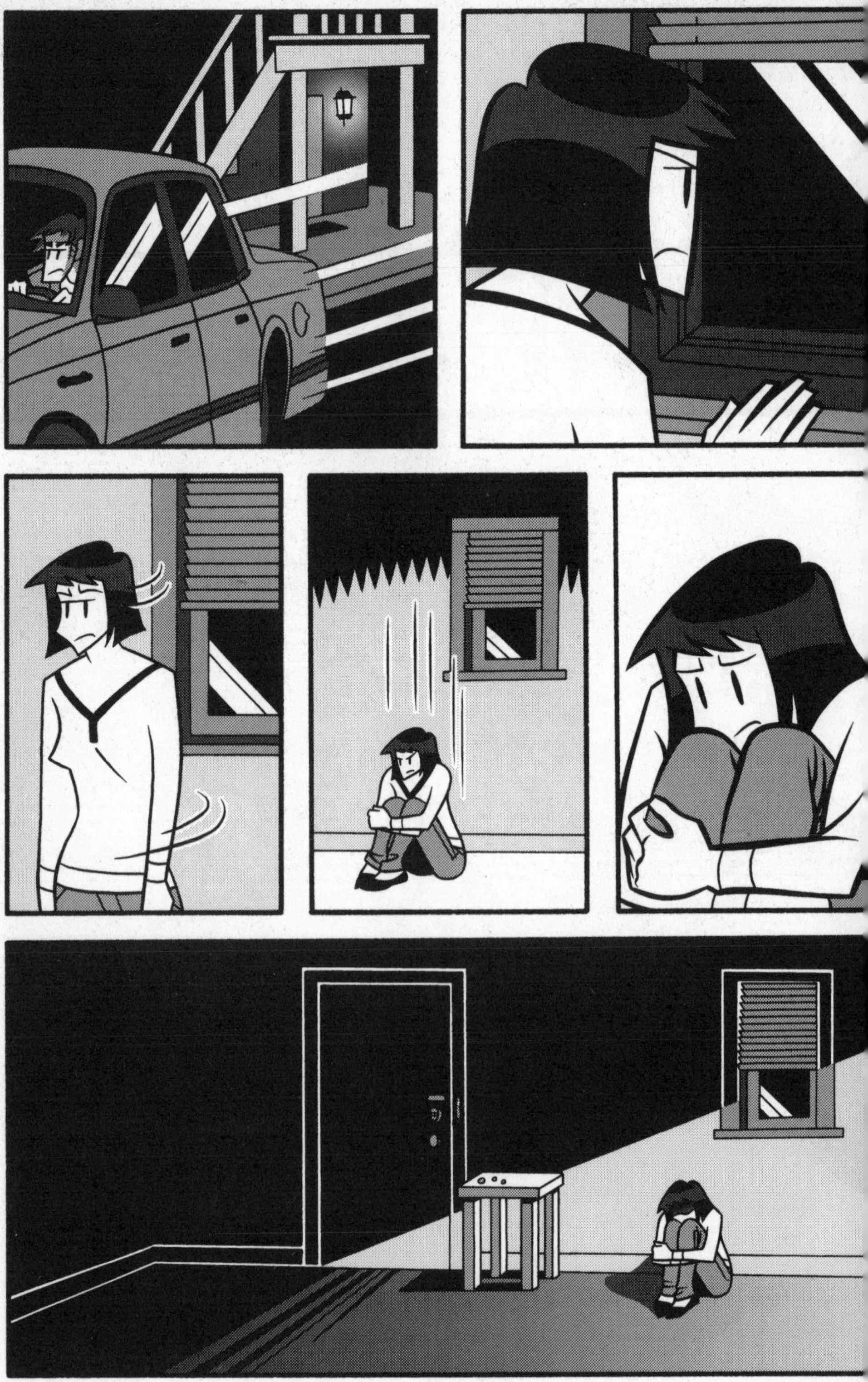

Chapter 7

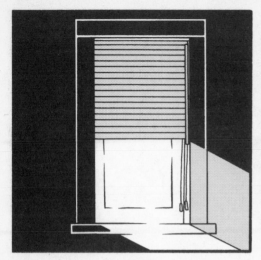
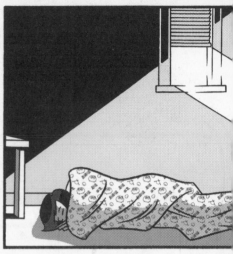

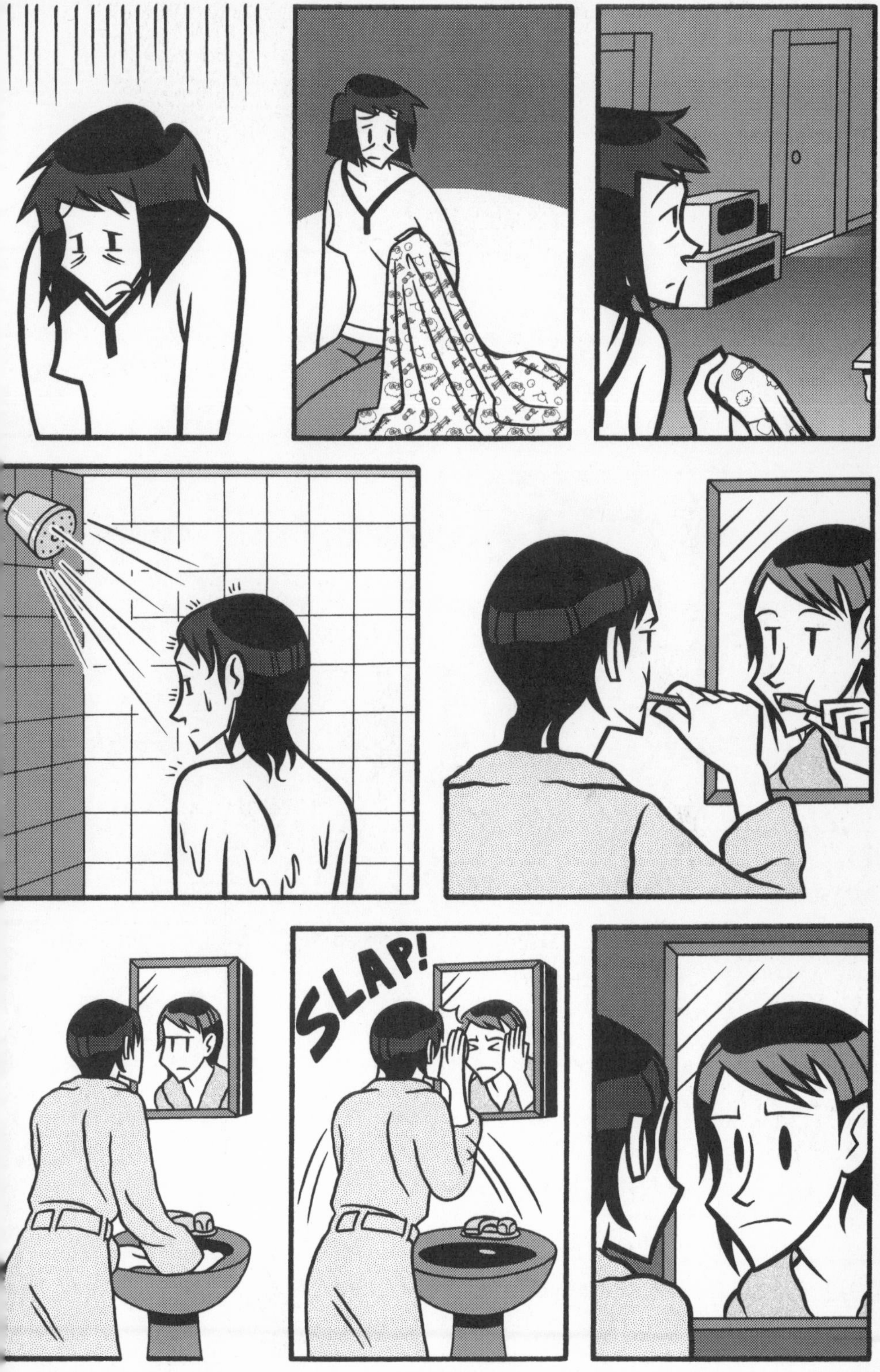
SLAP!

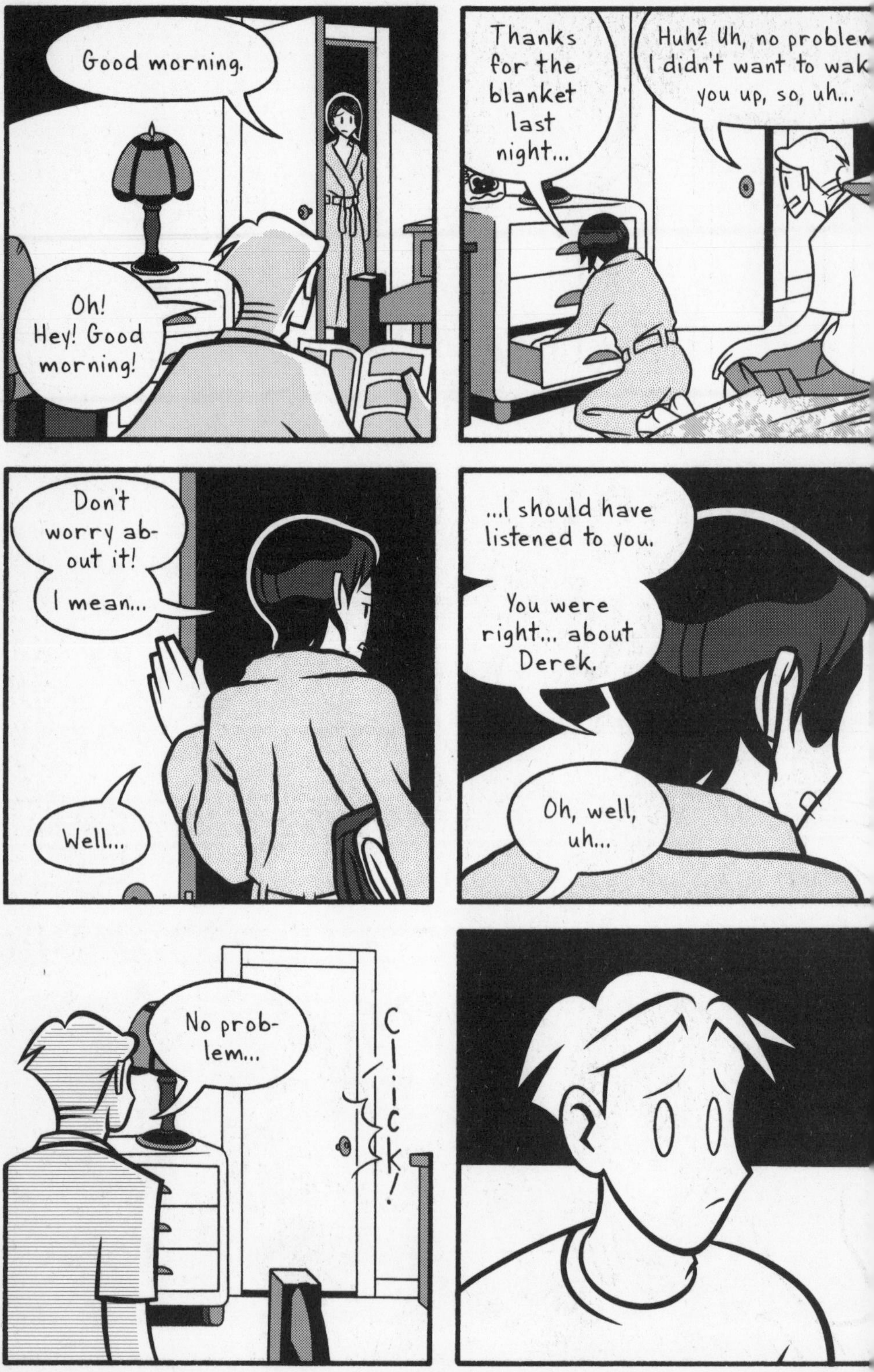

Good morning.
Oh! Hey! Good morning!
Thanks for the blanket last night...
Huh? Uh, no problem. I didn't want to wak you up, so, uh...
Don't worry about it! I mean...
Well...
...I should have listened to you. You were right... about Derek.
Oh, well, uh...
No problem...
Click!

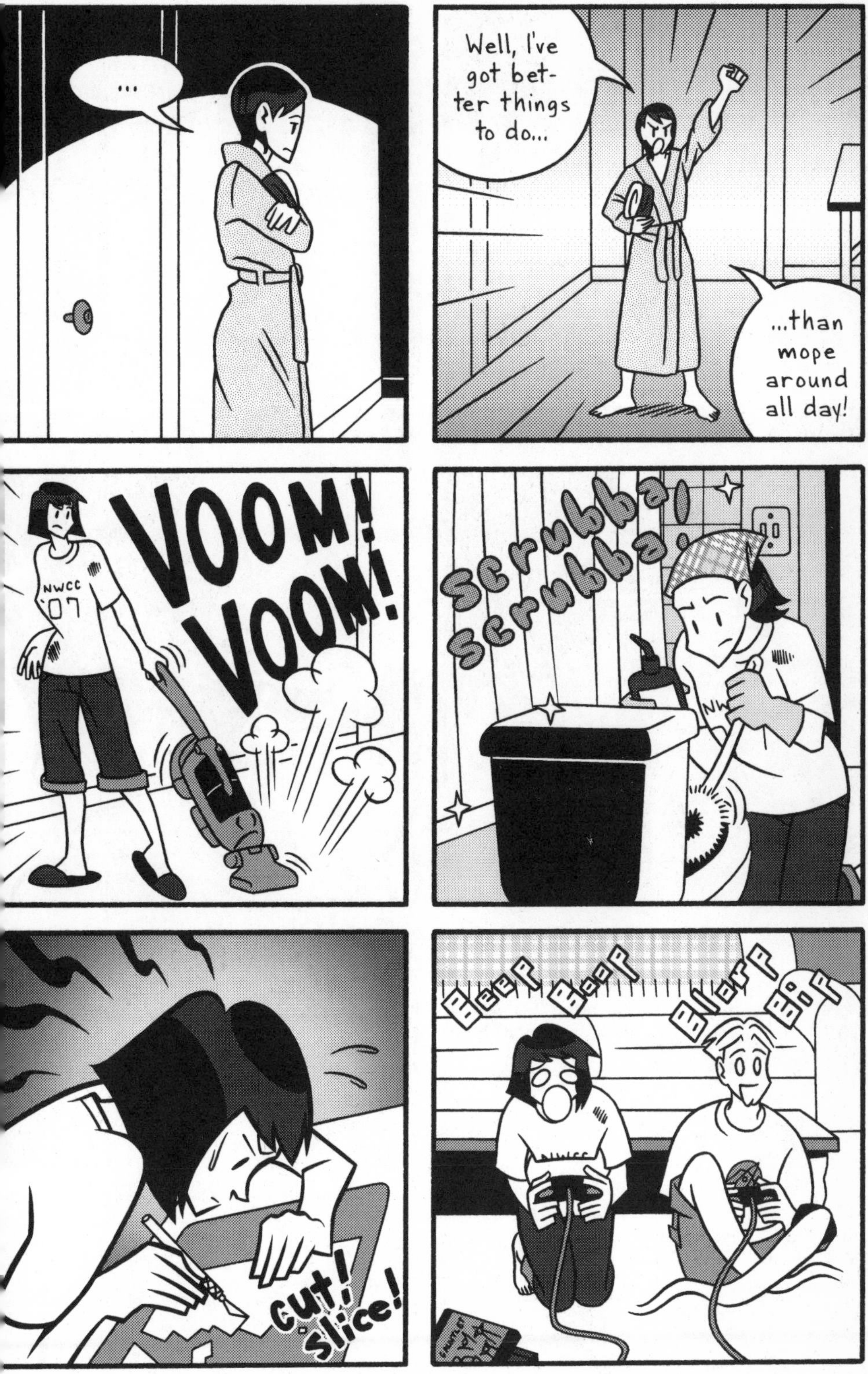
...
Well, I've got bet-ter things to do...
...than mope around all day!
VOOM! VOOM!
NWCC '07
Scrubba! Scrubba!
Cut! Slice!
Beep Boop
Blorp Bip

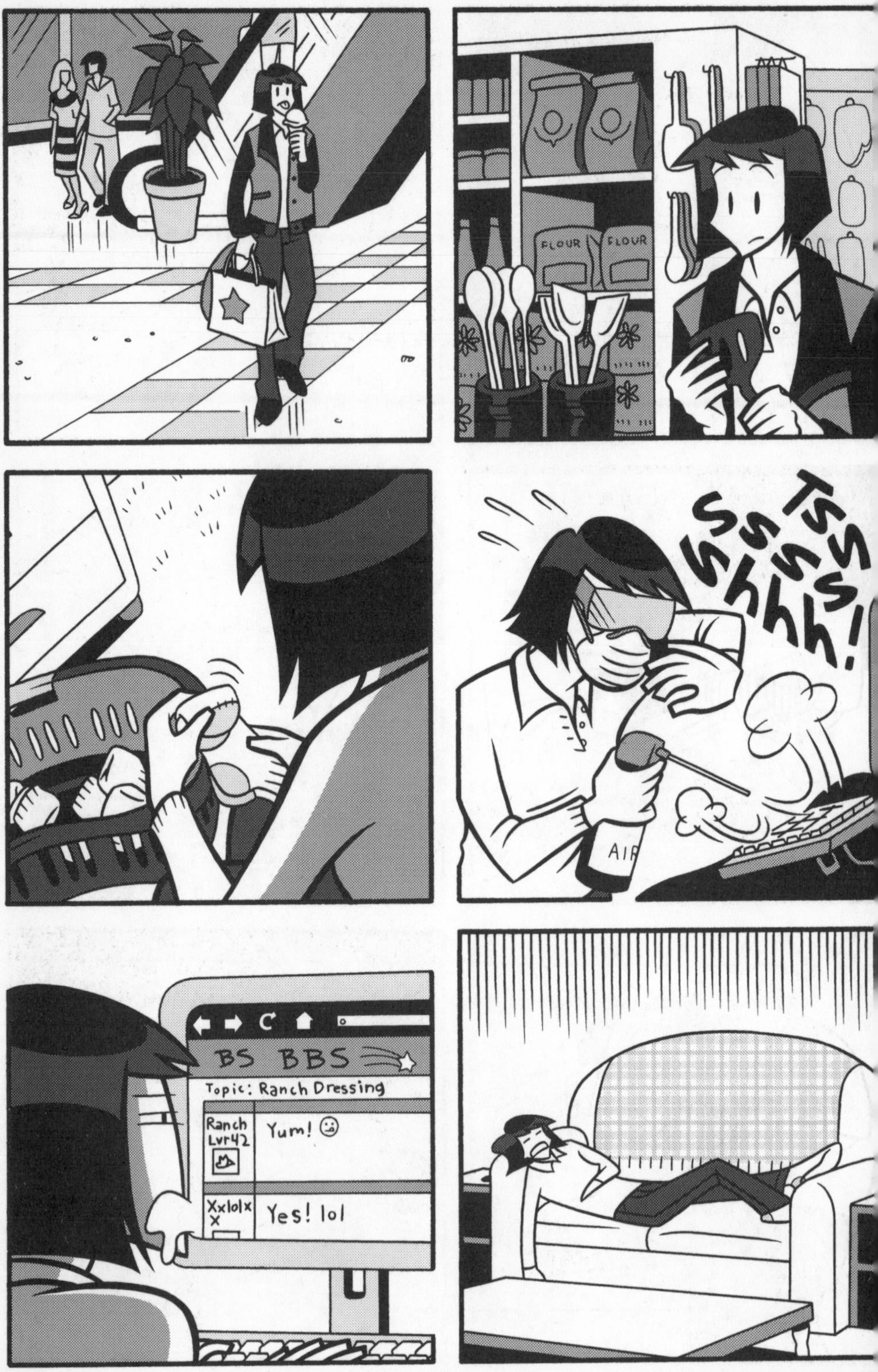
FLOUR
FLOUR
TSSSSSShhh!
AIR
BS BBS
Topic: Ranch Dressing
Ranch Lvr42
Yum!
Xxlolx x
Yes! lol

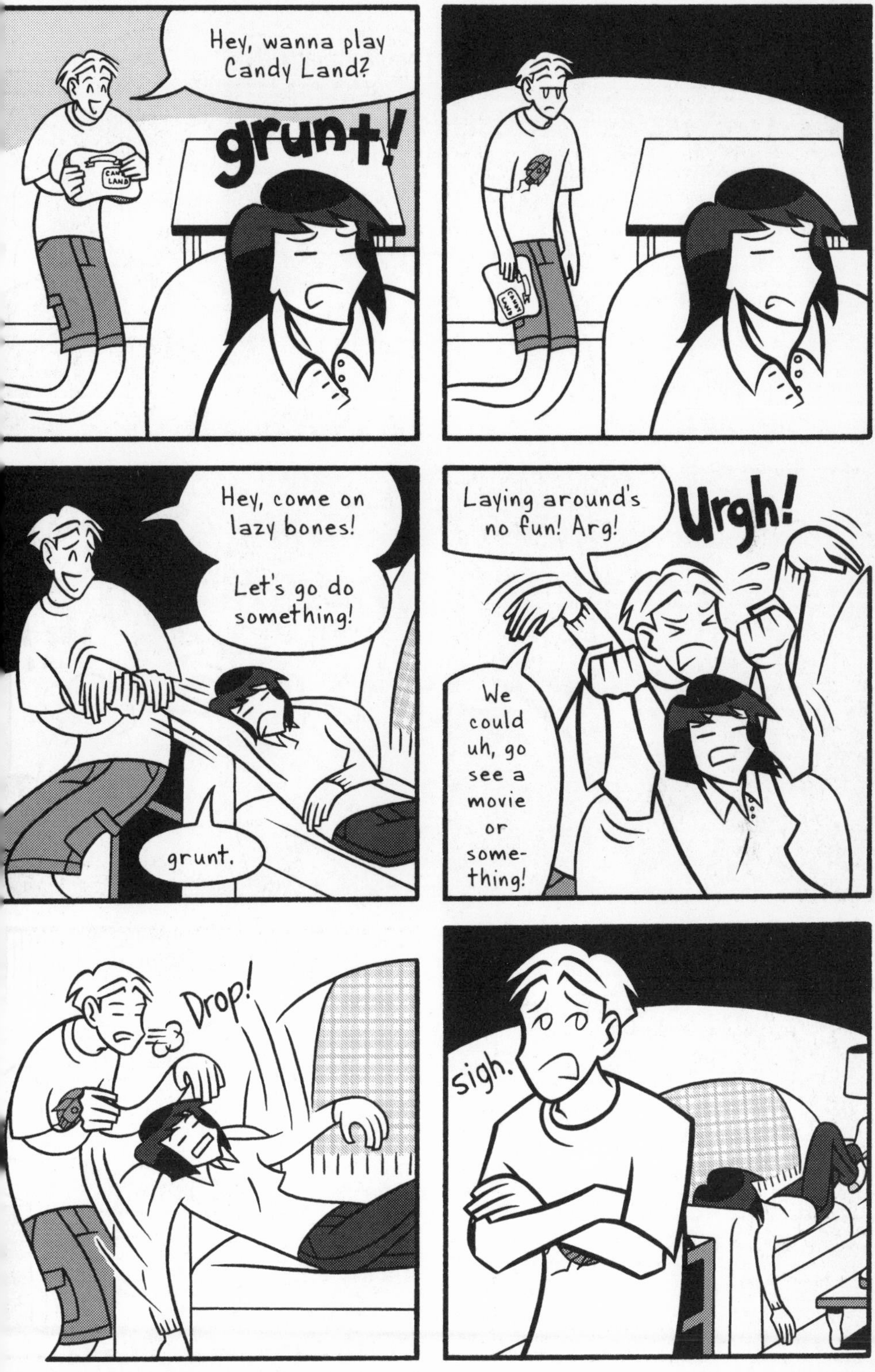
Hey, wanna play Candy Land?
grunt!
CANDY LAND
Hey, come on lazy bones!
Let's go do something!
grunt.
Laying around's no fun! Arg!
Urgh!
We could uh, go see a movie or something!
Drop!
sigh.

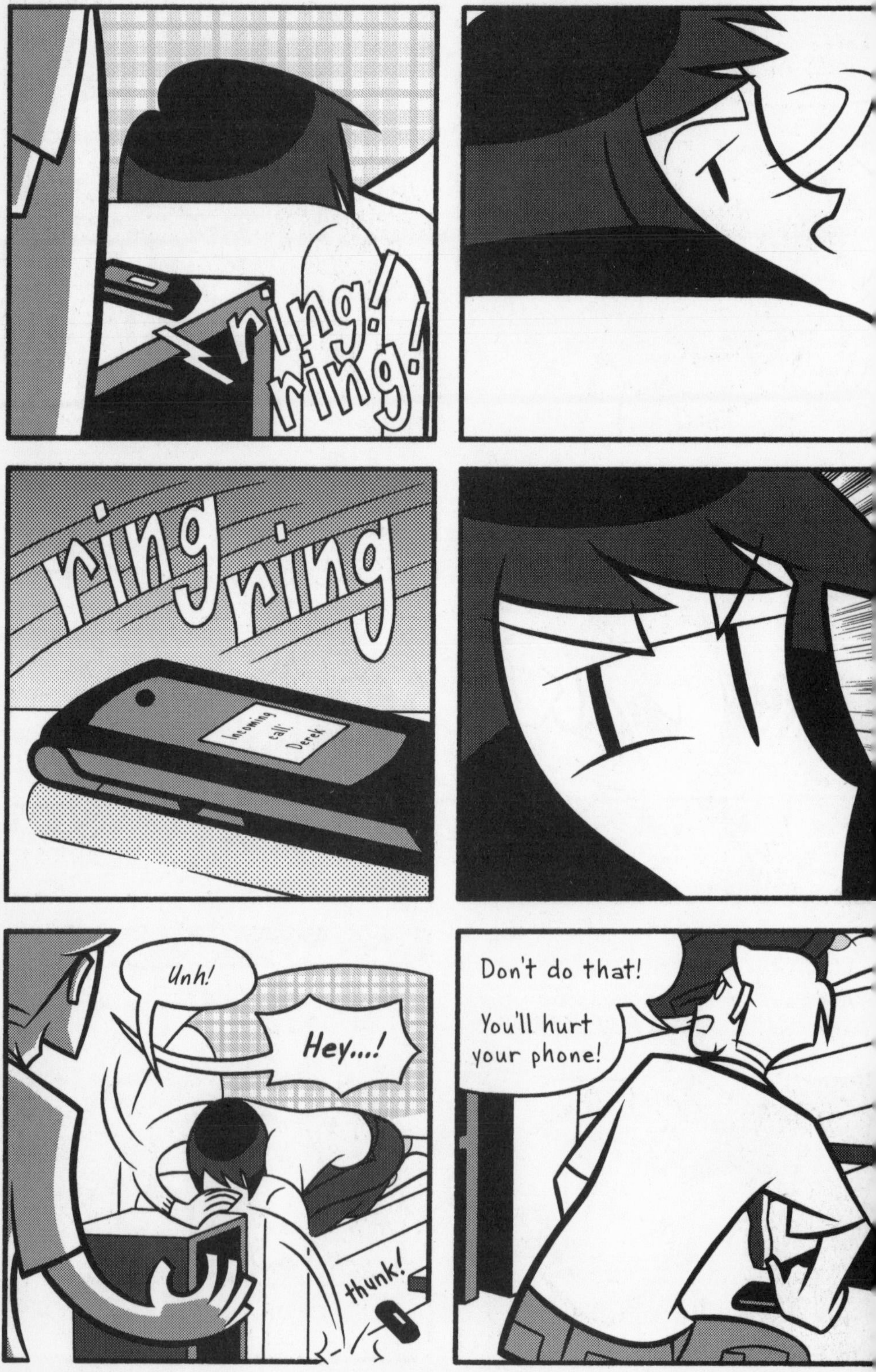
ring! ring!
ring ring
Incoming call: Derek
Unh!
Hey...!
thunk!
Don't do that!
You'll hurt your phone!

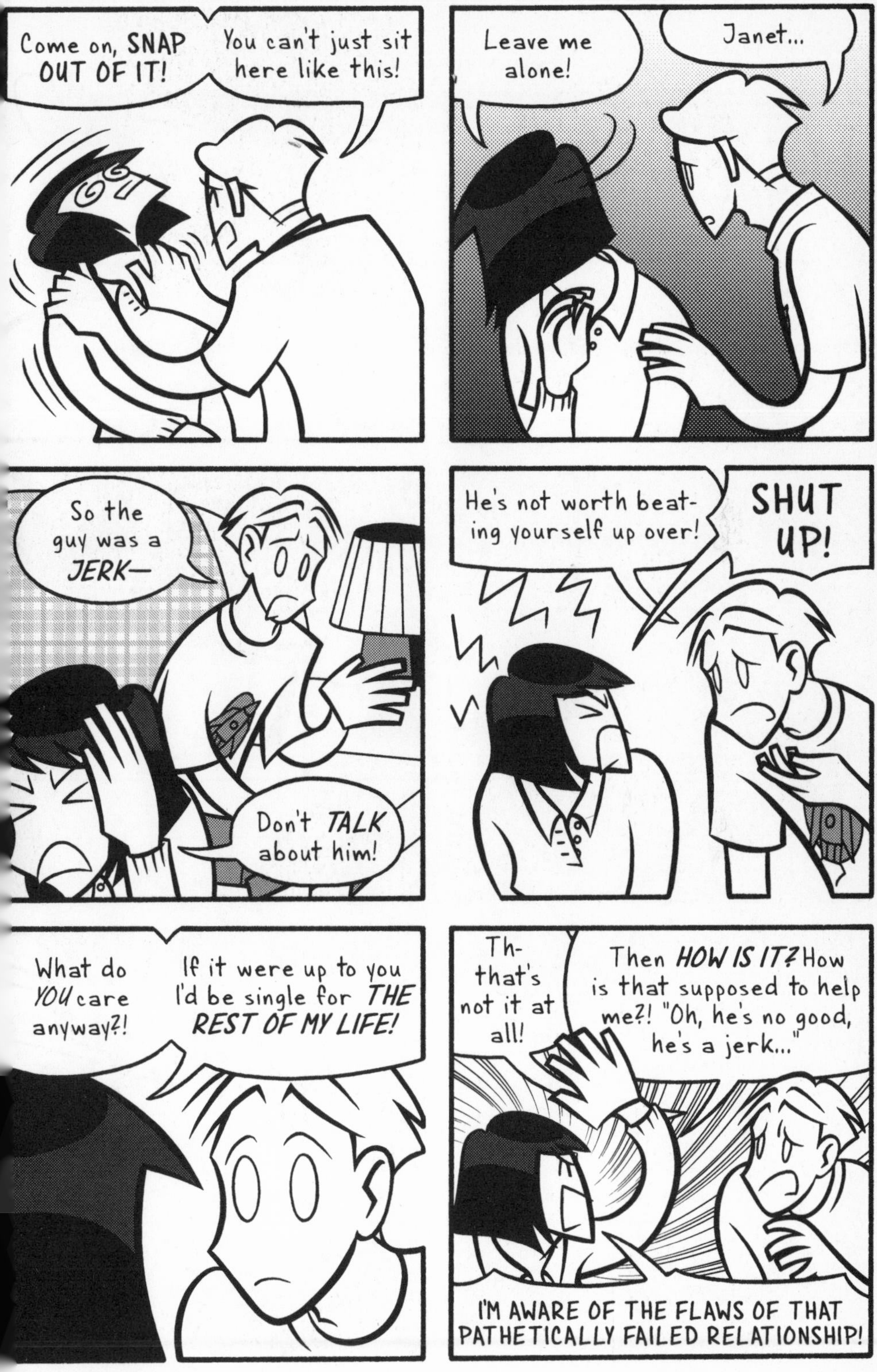
Come on, SNAP OUT OF IT!
You can't just sit here like this!
Leave me alone!
Janet...
So the guy was a JERK—
Don't TALK about him!
He's not worth beat-ing yourself up over!
SHUT UP!
What do YOU care anyway?!
If it were up to you I'd be single for THE REST OF MY LIFE!
Th- that's not it at all!
Then HOW IS IT? How is that supposed to help me?! "Oh, he's no good, he's a jerk..."
I'M AWARE OF THE FLAWS OF THAT PATHETICALLY FAILED RELATIONSHIP!

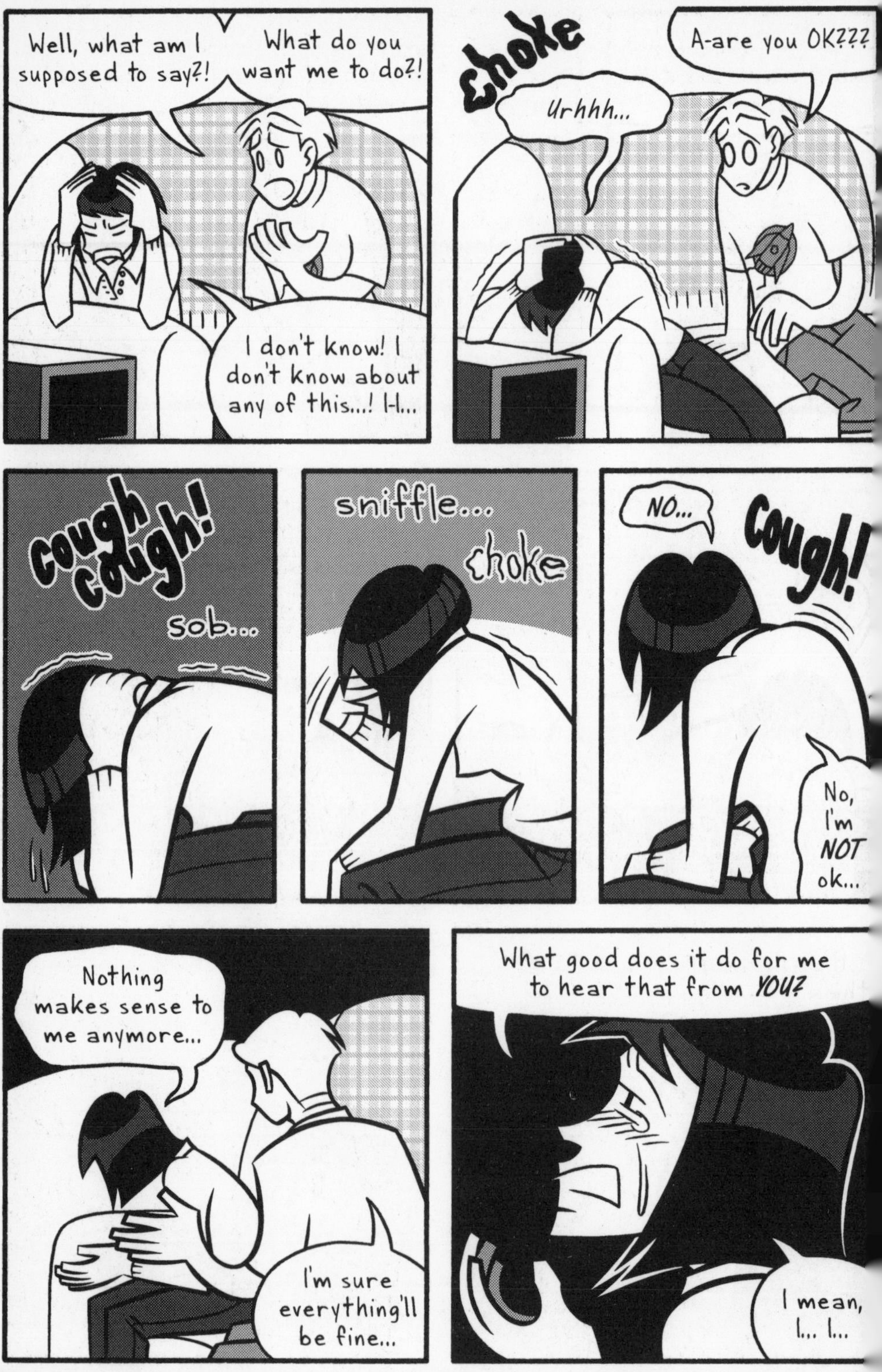

Well, what am I supposed to say?!
What do you want me to do?!
I don't know! I don't know about any of this...! I-I...
Choke
Urhhh...
A-are you OK???
cough cough!
sob...
sniffle...
choke
NO...
Cough!
No, I'm NOT ok...
Nothing makes sense to me anymore...
I'm sure everything'll be fine...
What good does it do for me to hear that from YOU?
I mean, I... I...

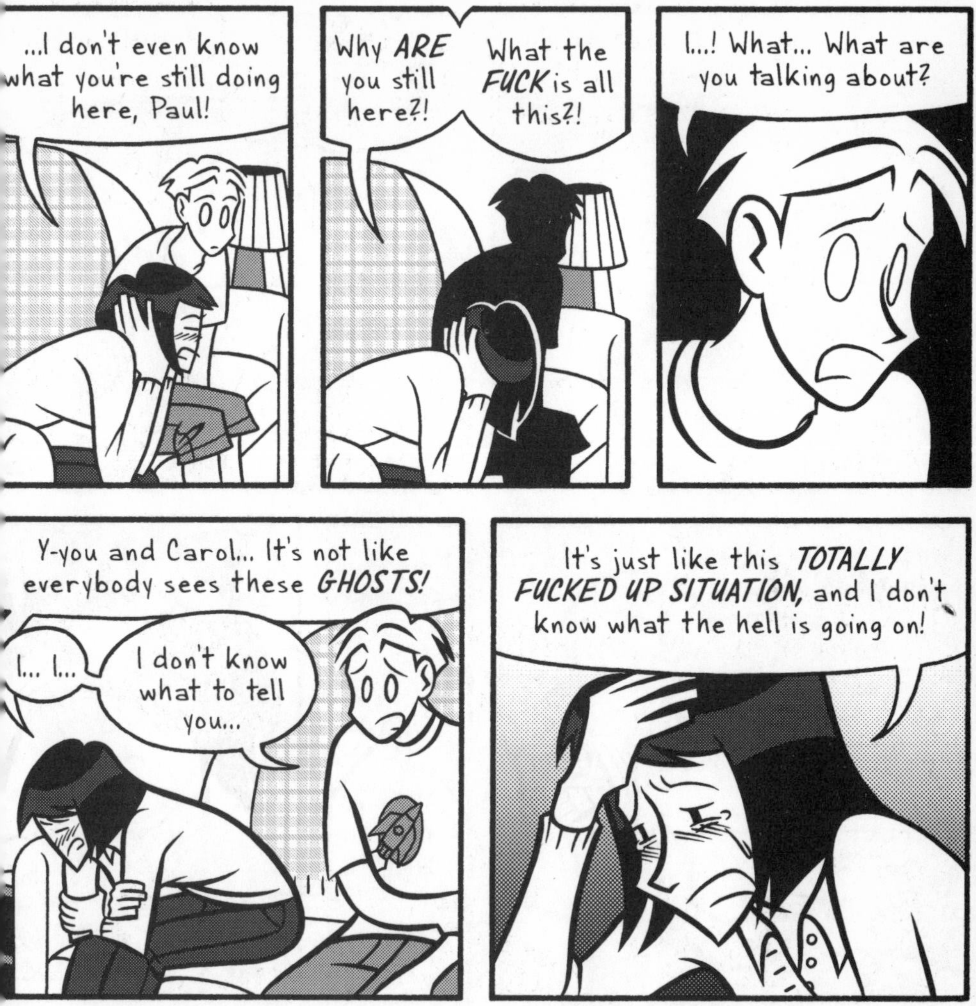

...I don't even know what you're still doing here, Paul!
Why ARE you still here?!
What the FUCK is all this?!
I...! What... What are you talking about?
Y-you and Carol... It's not like everybody sees these GHOSTS!
I... I...
I don't know what to tell you...
It's just like this TOTALLY FUCKED UP SITUATION, and I don't know what the hell is going on!
It's... I... I don't think it's so bad...
I mean, I like being with you, and...
I like being with you too, but, y'know...
Don't you ever wonder why you're still here?
...
Yeah.
Some-times
...

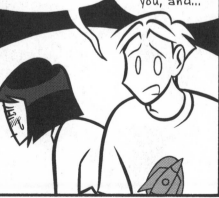

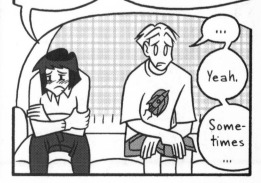

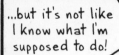...but it's not like I know what I'm supposed to do!

I've just had to accept all this and hope it works out...

Well, things *AREN'T* working out!

Nothing's changed! I don't want to just keep *HOPING*...

What are we supposed to *do?*

How should *I* know?!

I'm frustrated *too*, y'know?

I mean, every day your life keeps going!

You keep *LIVING!*

All I get to do is *WATCH!*

Even if I look older now, I may as well still be that 8 year old kid!

I get lonely sometimes, I get *bored*...

And when I can't even cheer you up when you're like this, I just feel worthless...

How can you say that?!

What would I do without you?!

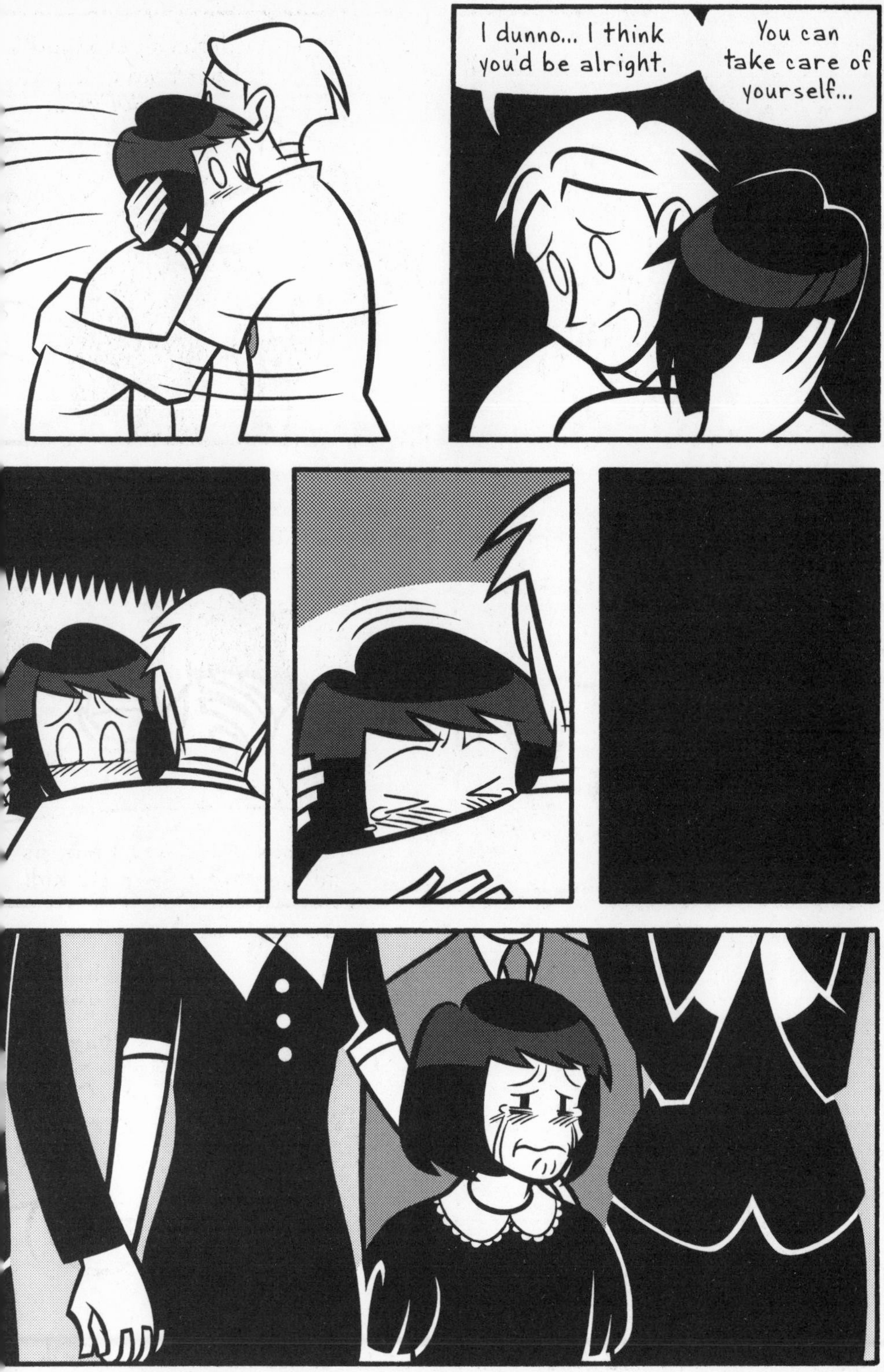
I dunno... I think you'd be alright.
You can take care of yourself...

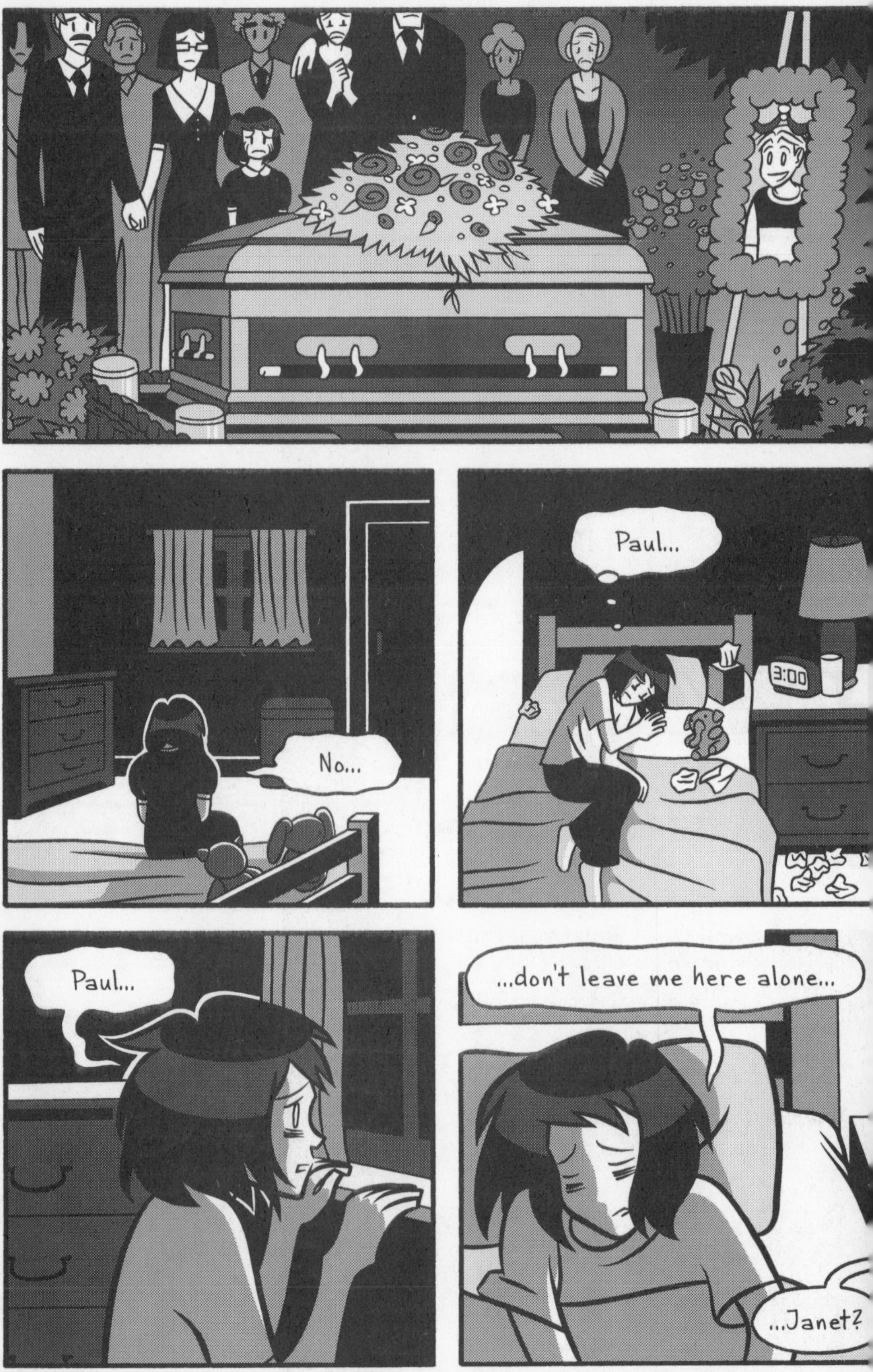
No...
Paul...
Paul...
...don't leave me here alone...
...Janet?

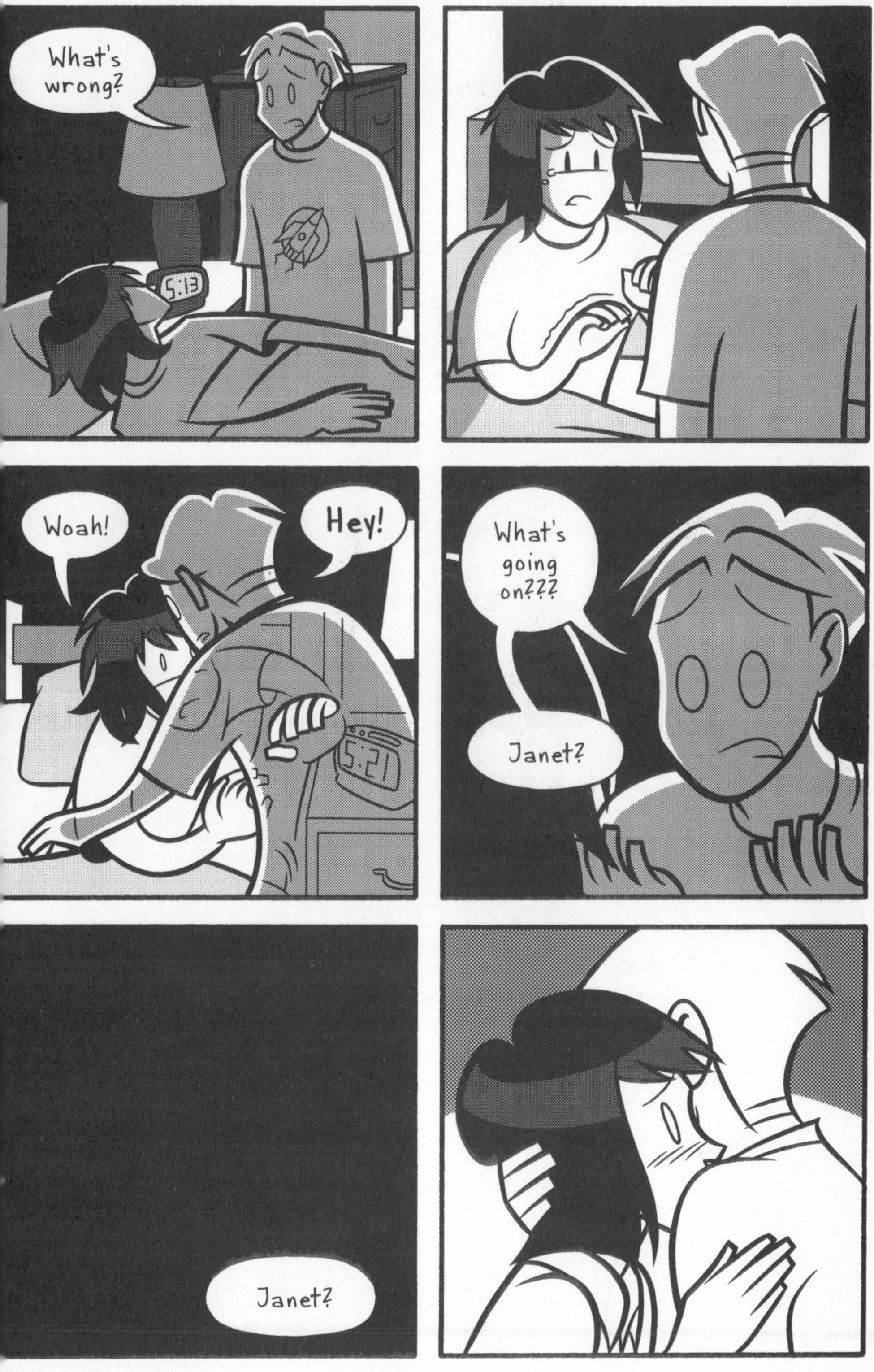
What's wrong?
Woah!
Hey!
What's going on???
Janet?
Janet?

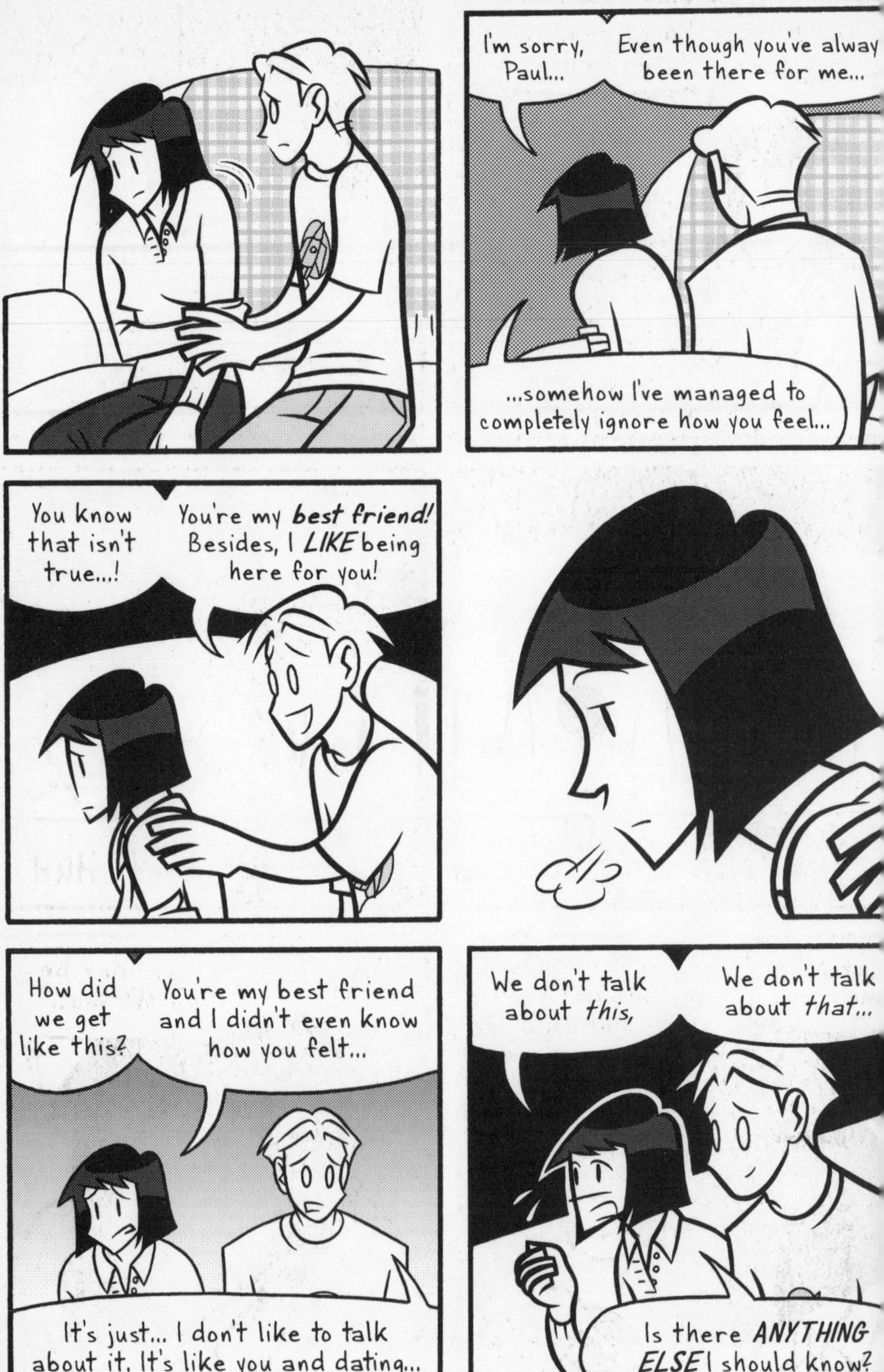
I'm sorry, Paul...
Even though you've alway been there for me...
...somehow I've managed to completely ignore how you feel...
You know that isn't true...!
You're my best friend! Besides, I LIKE being here for you!
How did we get like this?
You're my best friend and I didn't even know how you felt...
It's just... I don't like to talk about it. It's like you and dating...
We don't talk about this,
We don't talk about that...
Is there ANYTHING ELSE I should know?

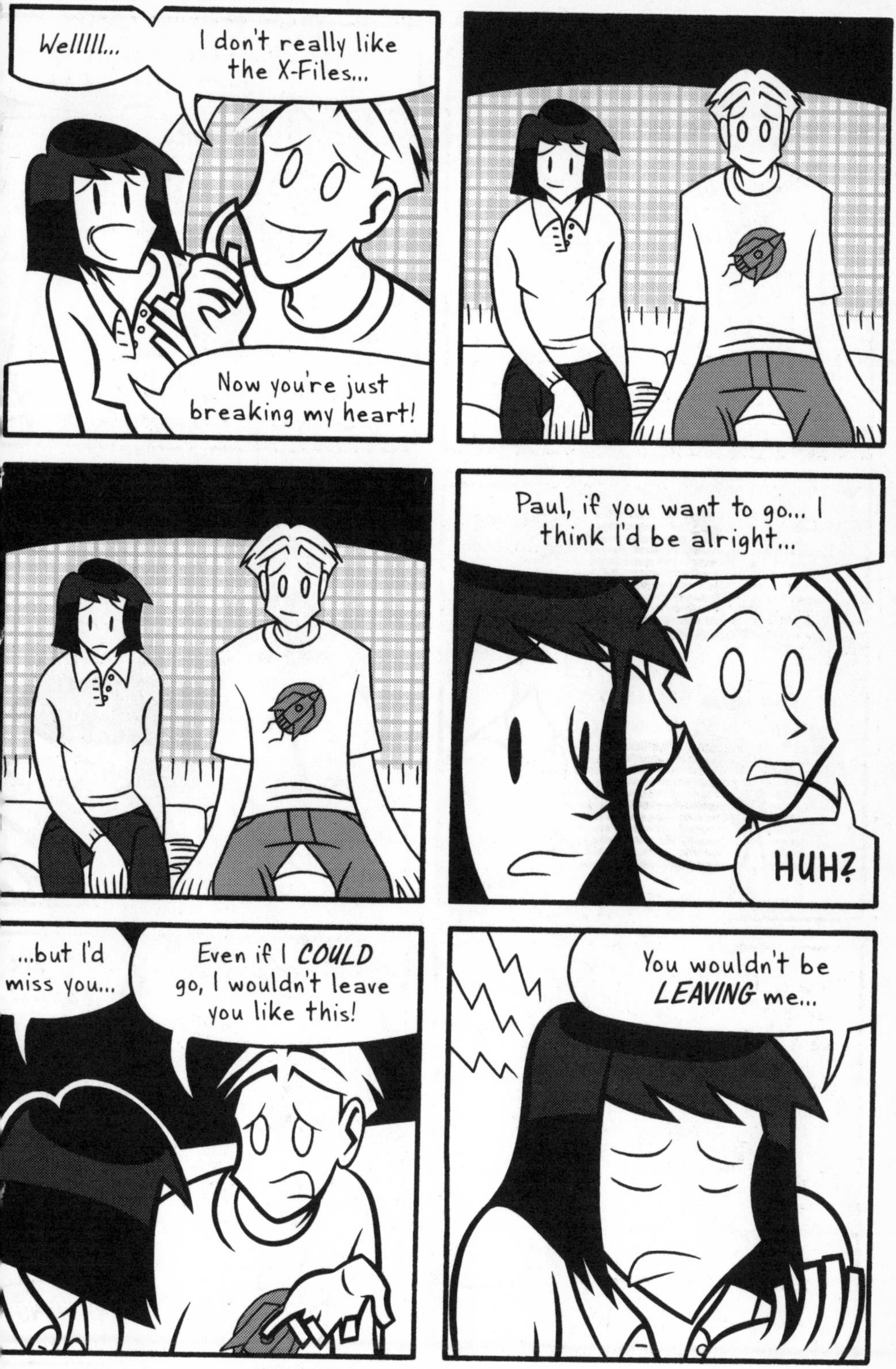
Wellllll...
I don't really like the X-Files...
Now you're just breaking my heart!
Paul, if you want to go... I think I'd be alright...
HUH?
...but I'd miss you...
Even if I COULD go, I wouldn't leave you like this!
You wouldn't be LEAVING me...

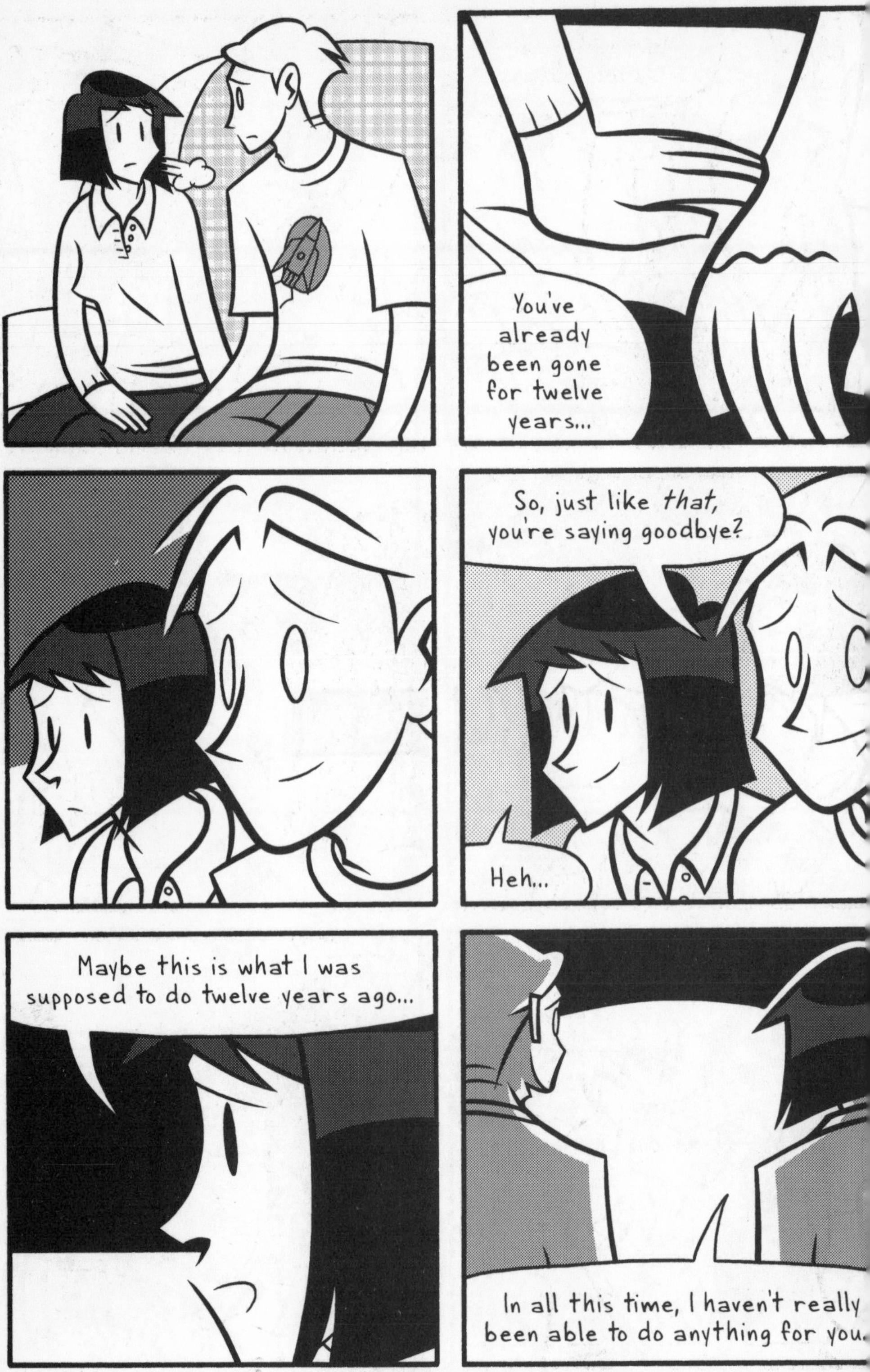
You've already been gone for twelve years...
So, just like *that,* you're saying goodbye?
Heh...
Maybe this is what I was supposed to do twelve years ago...
In all this time, I haven't really been able to do anything for you.

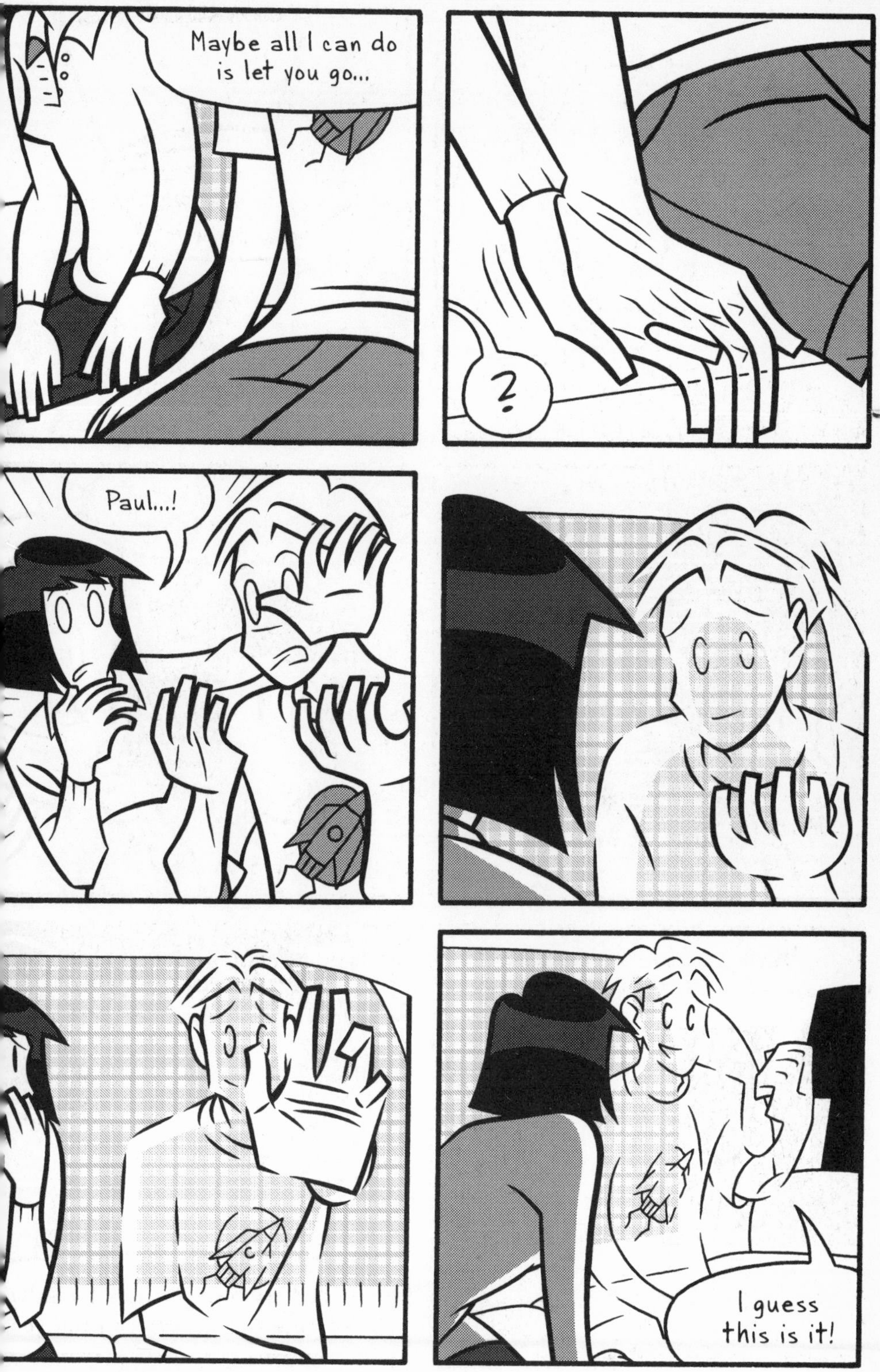
Maybe all I can do is let you go...
?
Paul...!
I guess this is it!

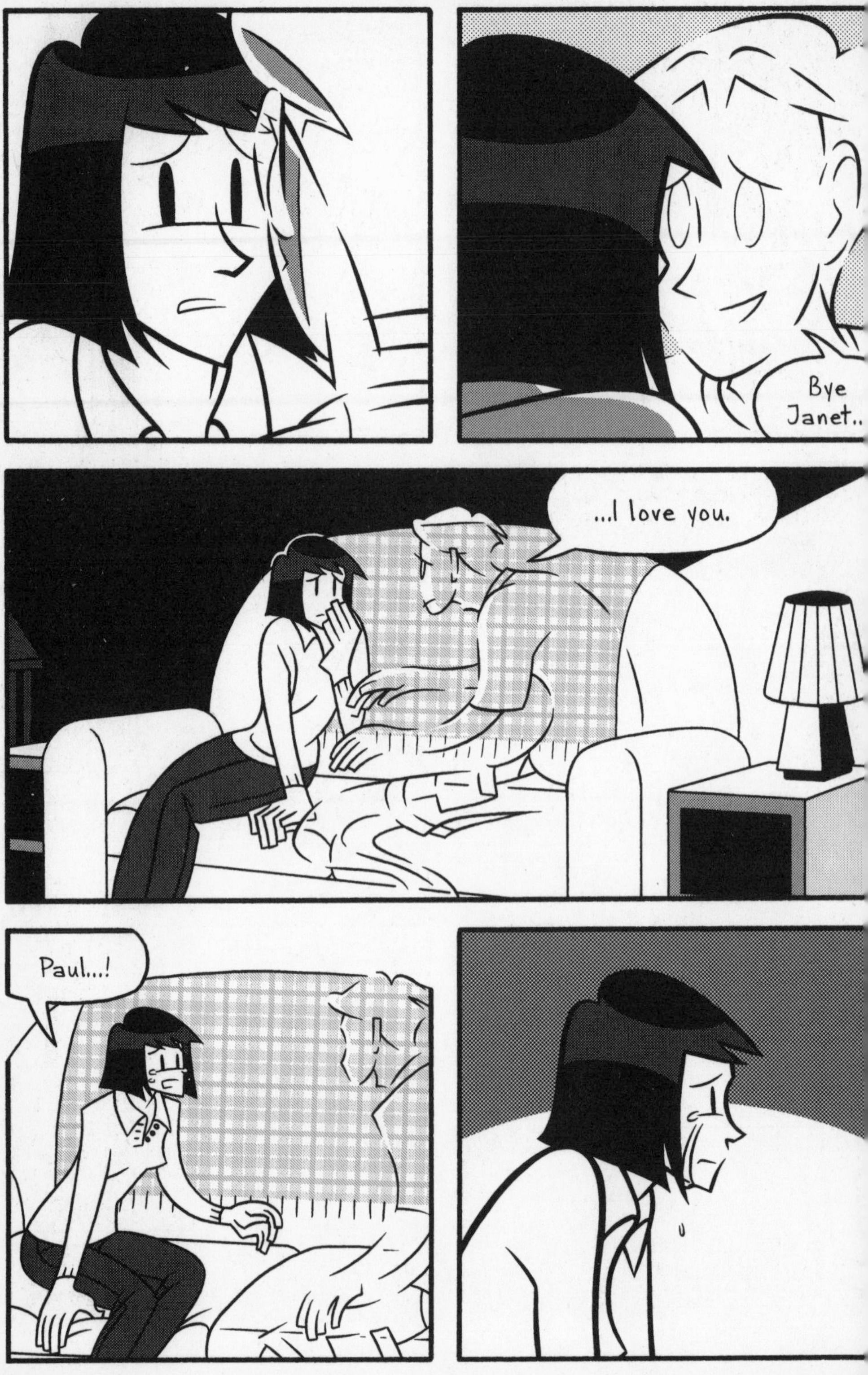
Bye Janet..
...I love you.
Paul...!

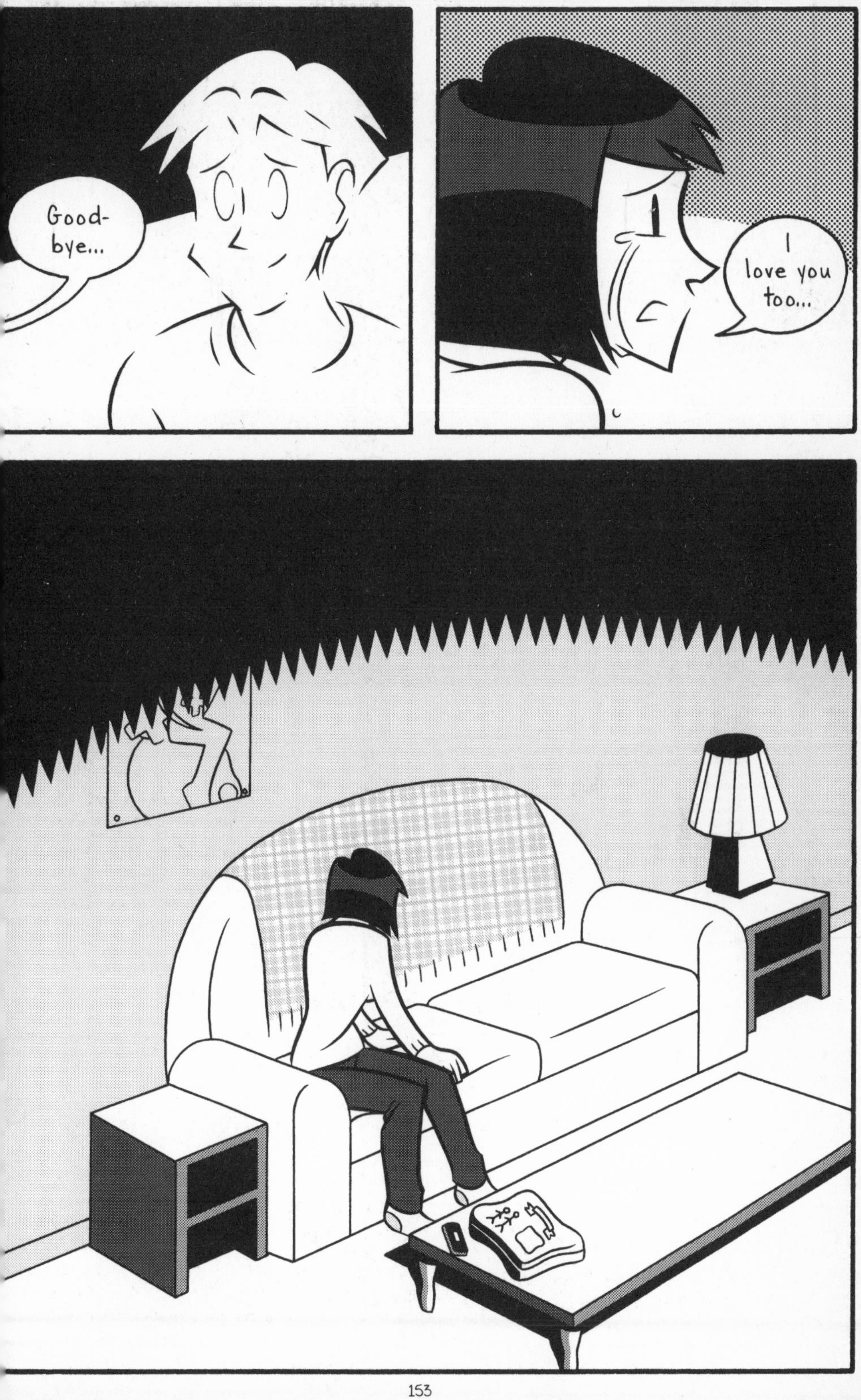
Good-bye...
I love you too...

Chapter 8

ring ring!

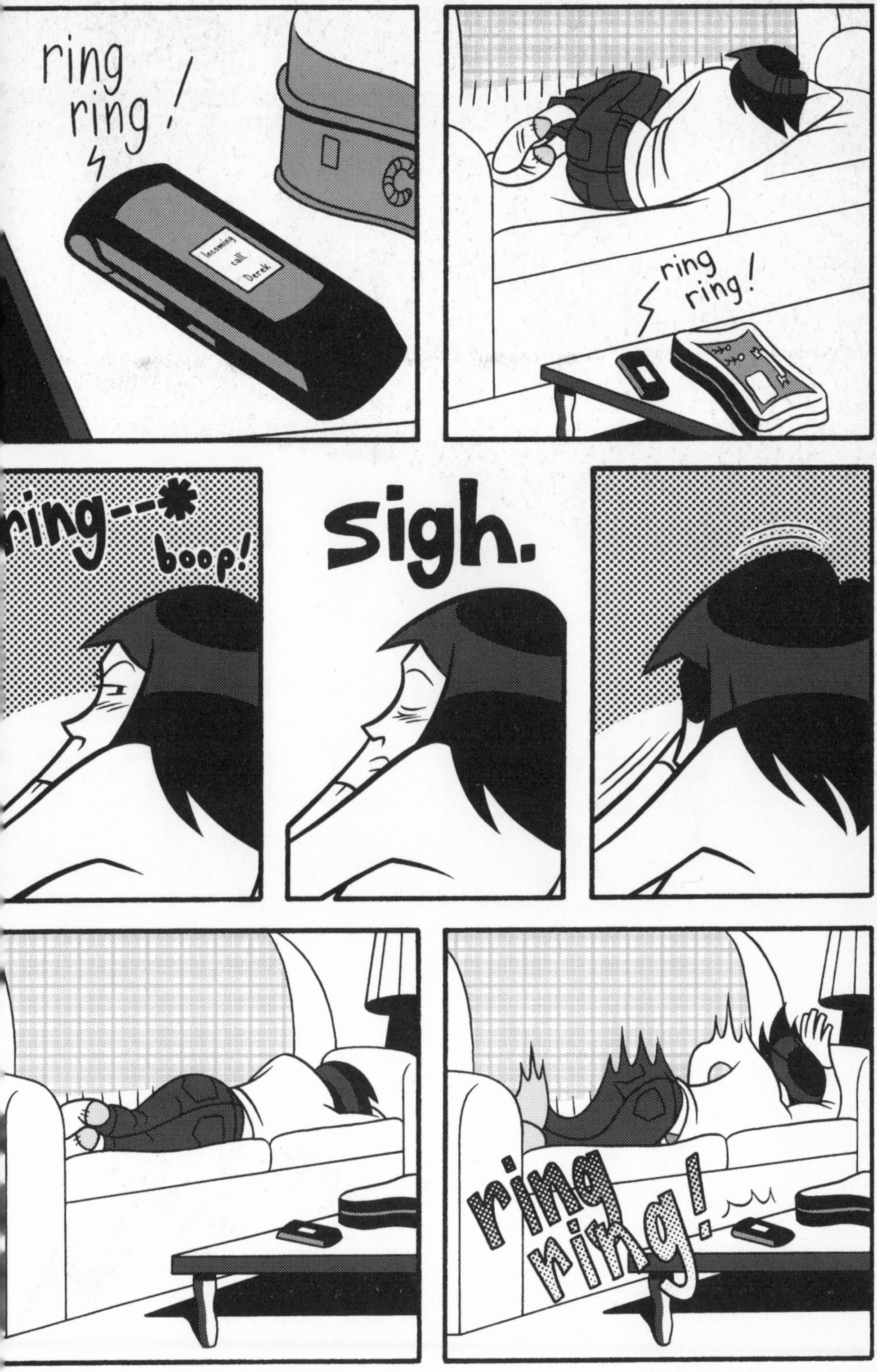
ring
ring!
Incoming call Derek
ring
ring!
ring--*
boop!
Sigh.
ring
ring!

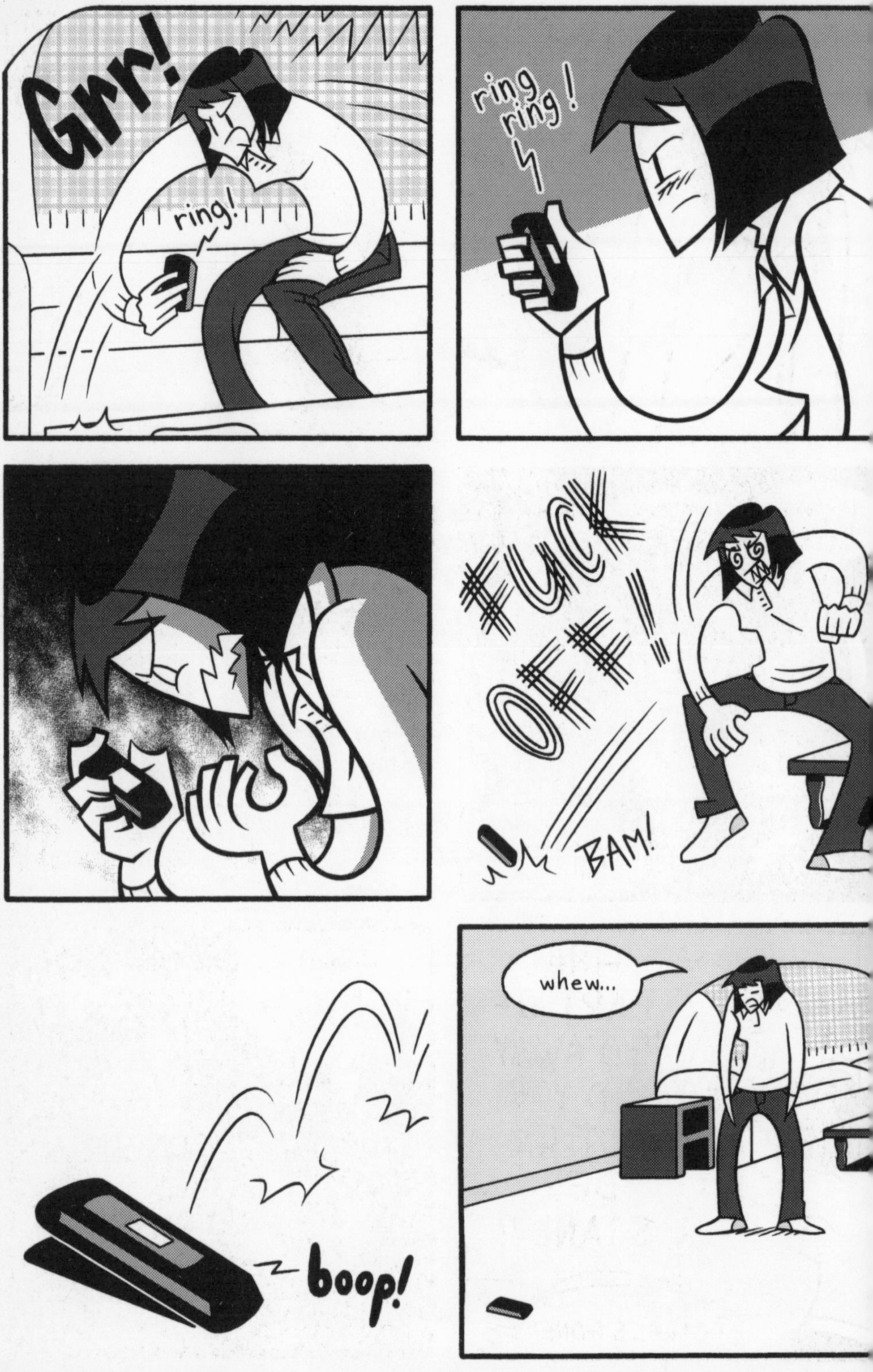
Grr!
ring!
ring ring!
#FUCK OFF#!
BAM!
boop!
whew...

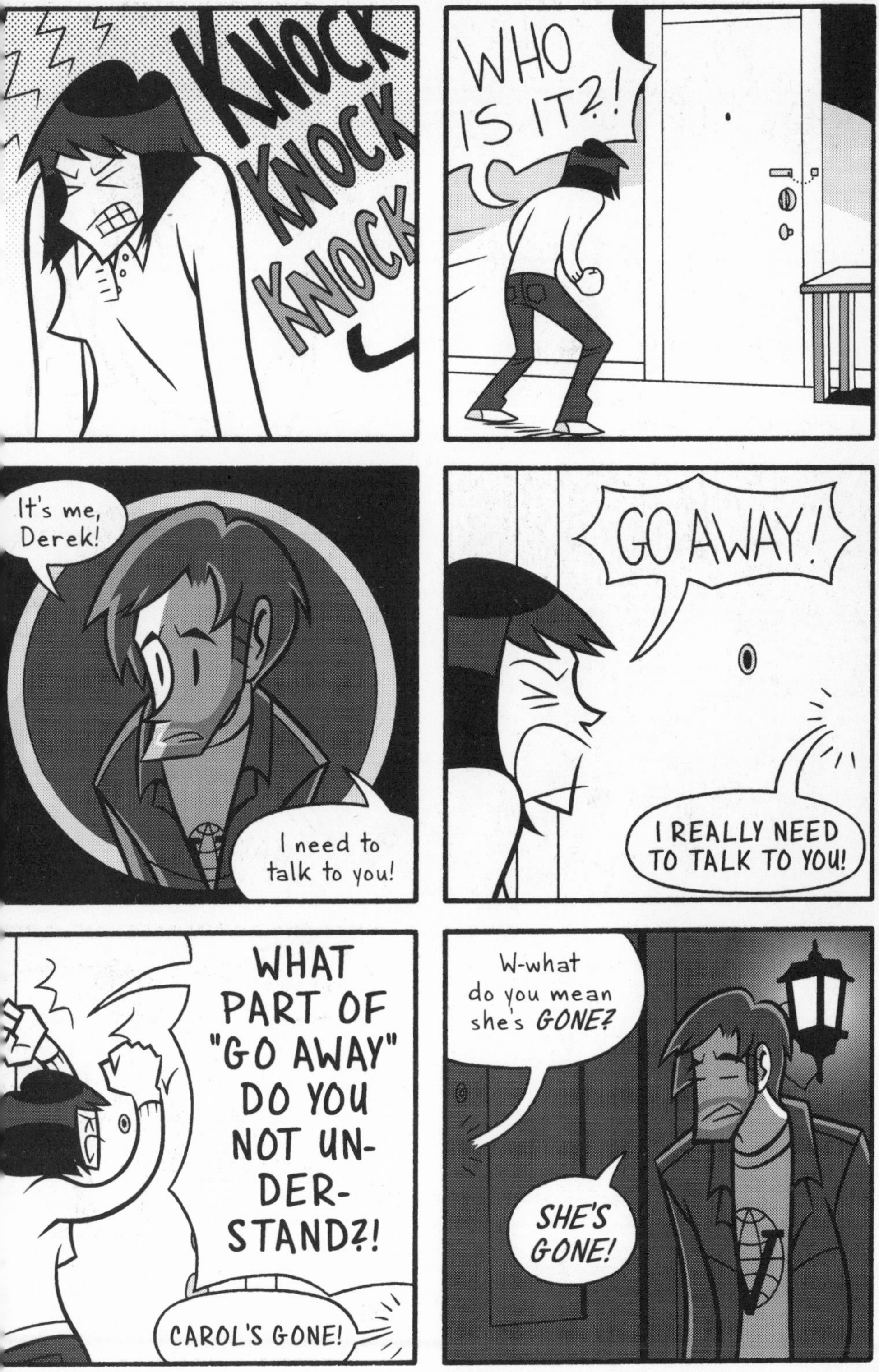
KNOCK
KNOCK
KNOCK
WHO IS IT?!
It's me, Derek!
I need to talk to you!
GO AWAY!
I REALLY NEED TO TALK TO YOU!
WHAT PART OF "GO AWAY" DO YOU NOT UN-DER-STAND?!
CAROL'S GONE!
W-what do you mean she's GONE?
SHE'S GONE!

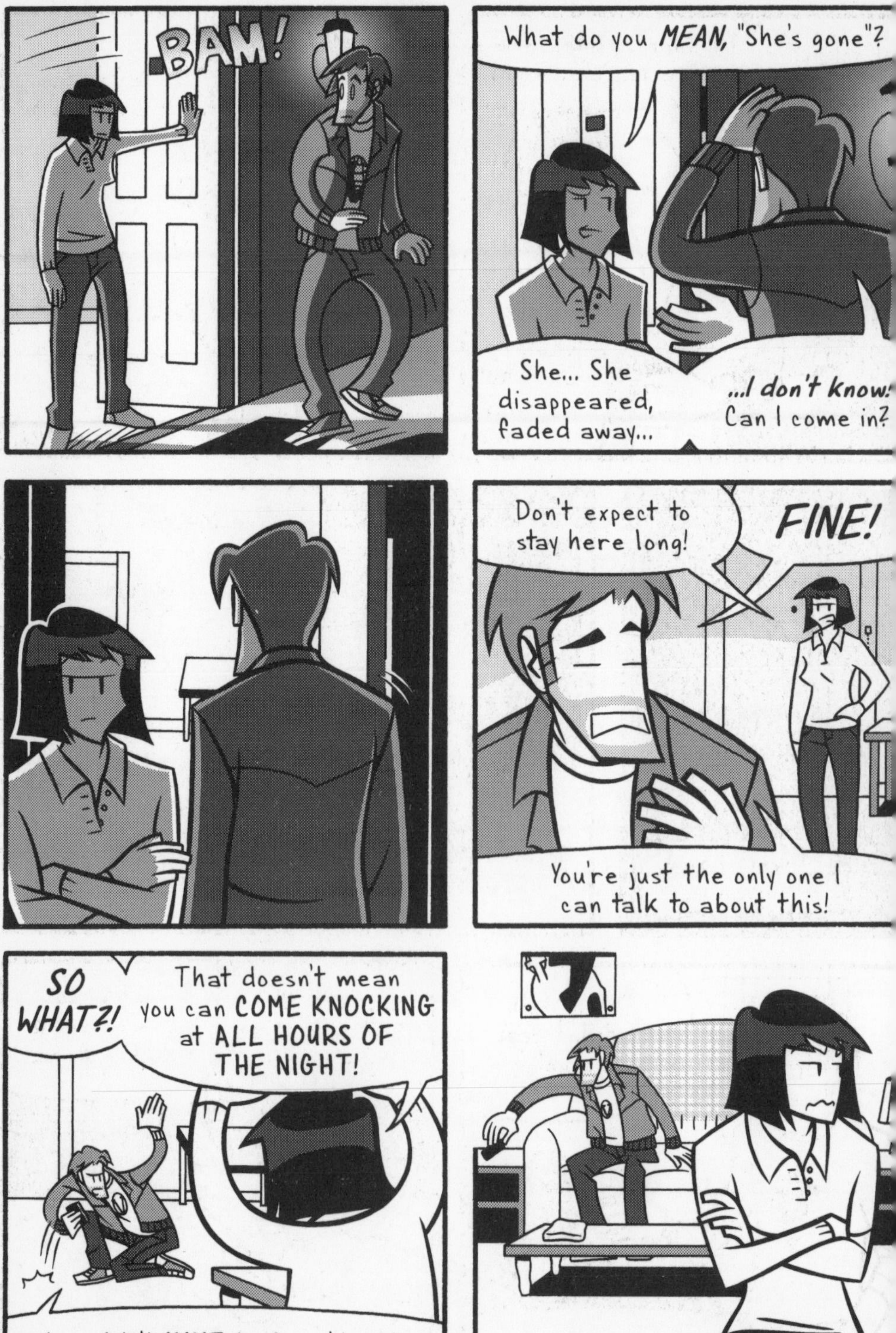
BAM!
What do you MEAN, "She's gone"?
She... She disappeared, faded away...
...I don't know.
Can I come in?
Don't expect to stay here long!
FINE!
You're just the only one I can talk to about this!
SO WHAT?!
That doesn't mean you can COME KNOCKING at ALL HOURS OF THE NIGHT!
I wouldn't HAVE to if you'd just PICK UP YOUR DAMN PHONE!

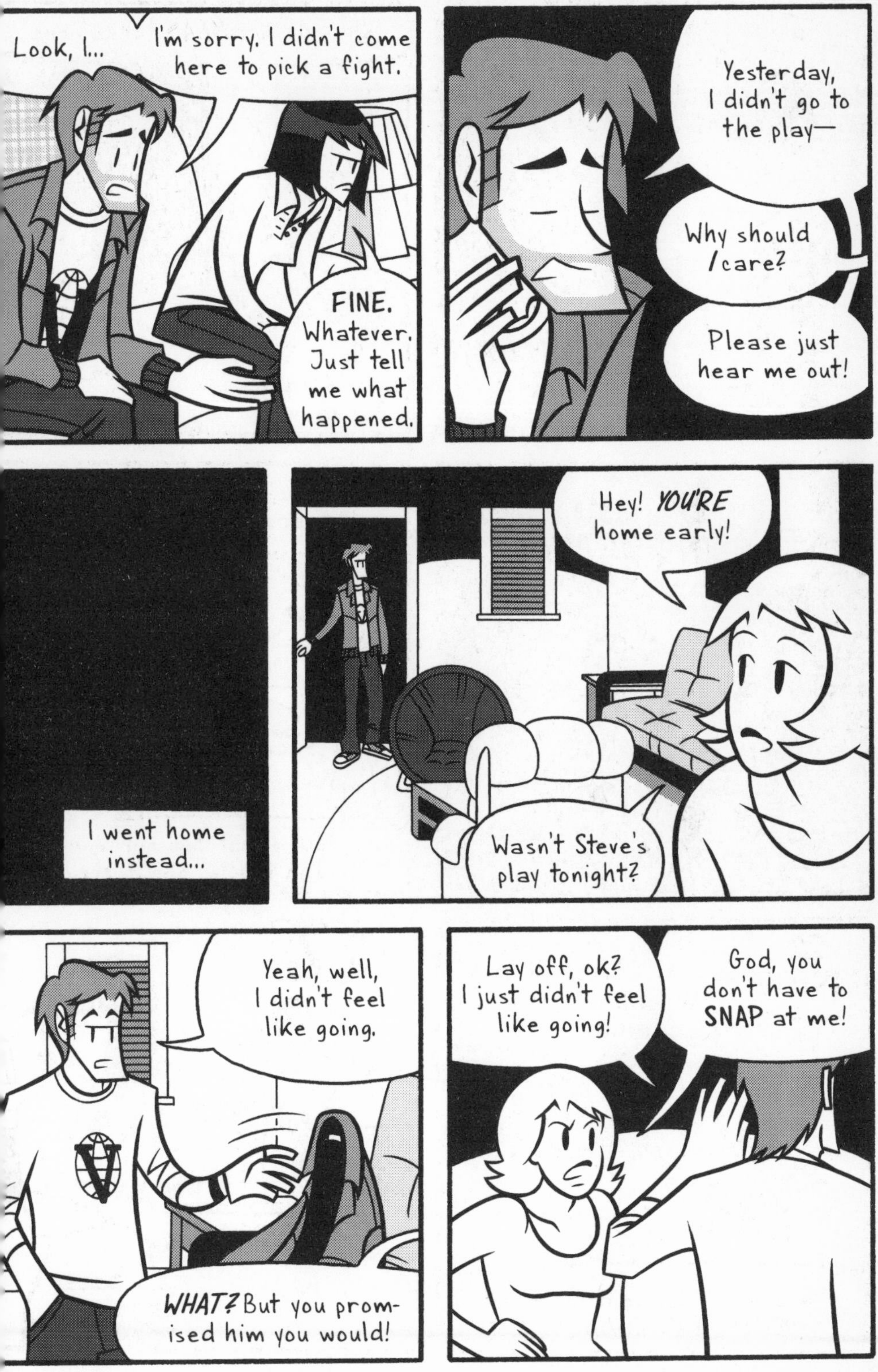
Look, I...
I'm sorry. I didn't come here to pick a fight.
FINE. Whatever. Just tell me what happened.
Yesterday, I didn't go to the play—
Why should I care?
Please just hear me out!
I went home instead...
Hey! YOU'RE home early!
Wasn't Steve's play tonight?
Yeah, well, I didn't feel like going.
WHAT? But you promised him you would!
Lay off, ok? I just didn't feel like going!
God, you don't have to SNAP at me!

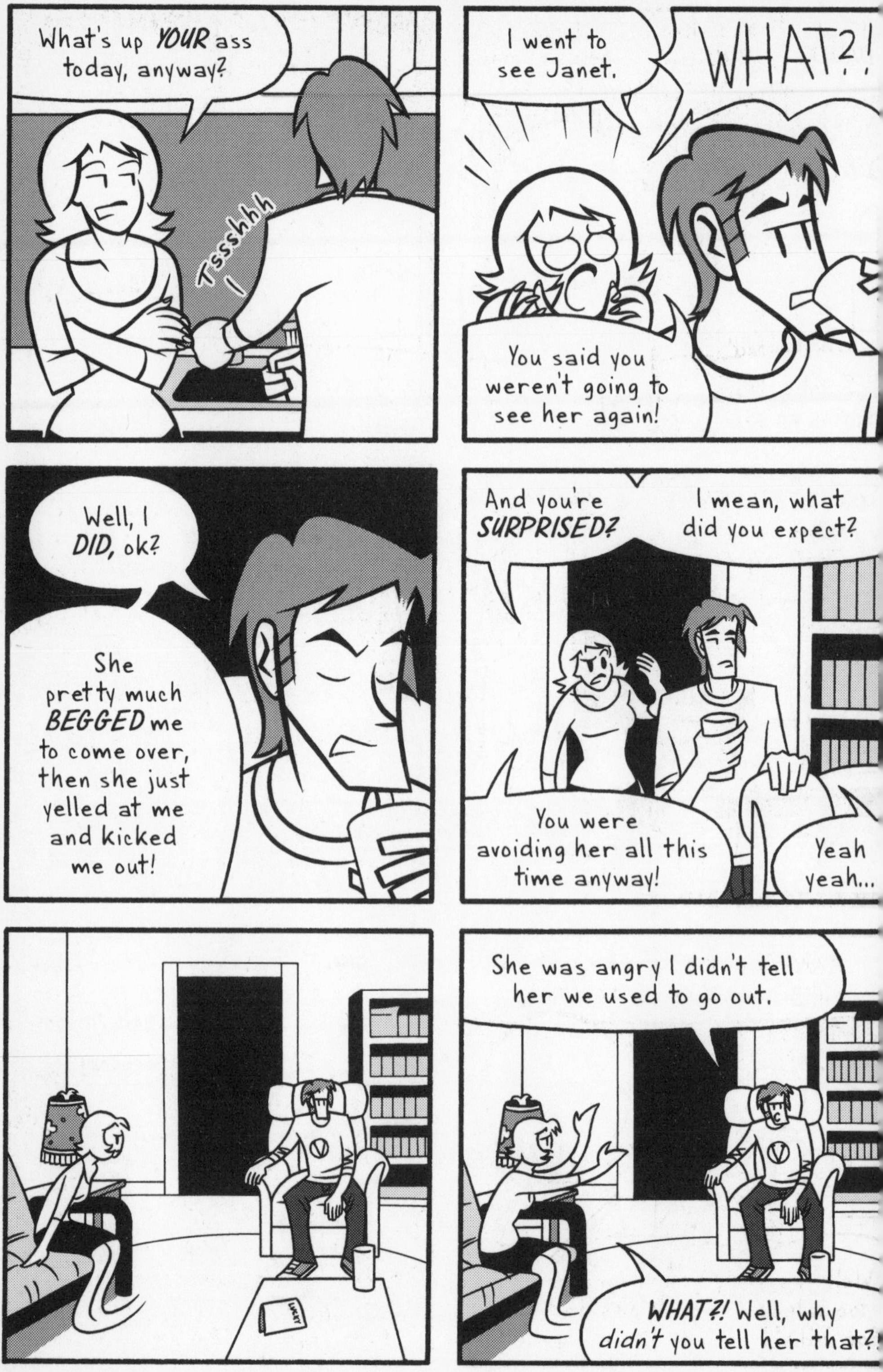
What's up YOUR ass today, anyway?
Tssshhh
I went to see Janet.
WHAT?!
You said you weren't going to see her again!
Well, I DID, ok?
She pretty much BEGGED me to come over, then she just yelled at me and kicked me out!
And you're SURPRISED?
I mean, what did you expect?
You were avoiding her all this time anyway!
Yeah yeah...
She was angry I didn't tell her we used to go out.
WHAT?! Well, why didn't you tell her that?!

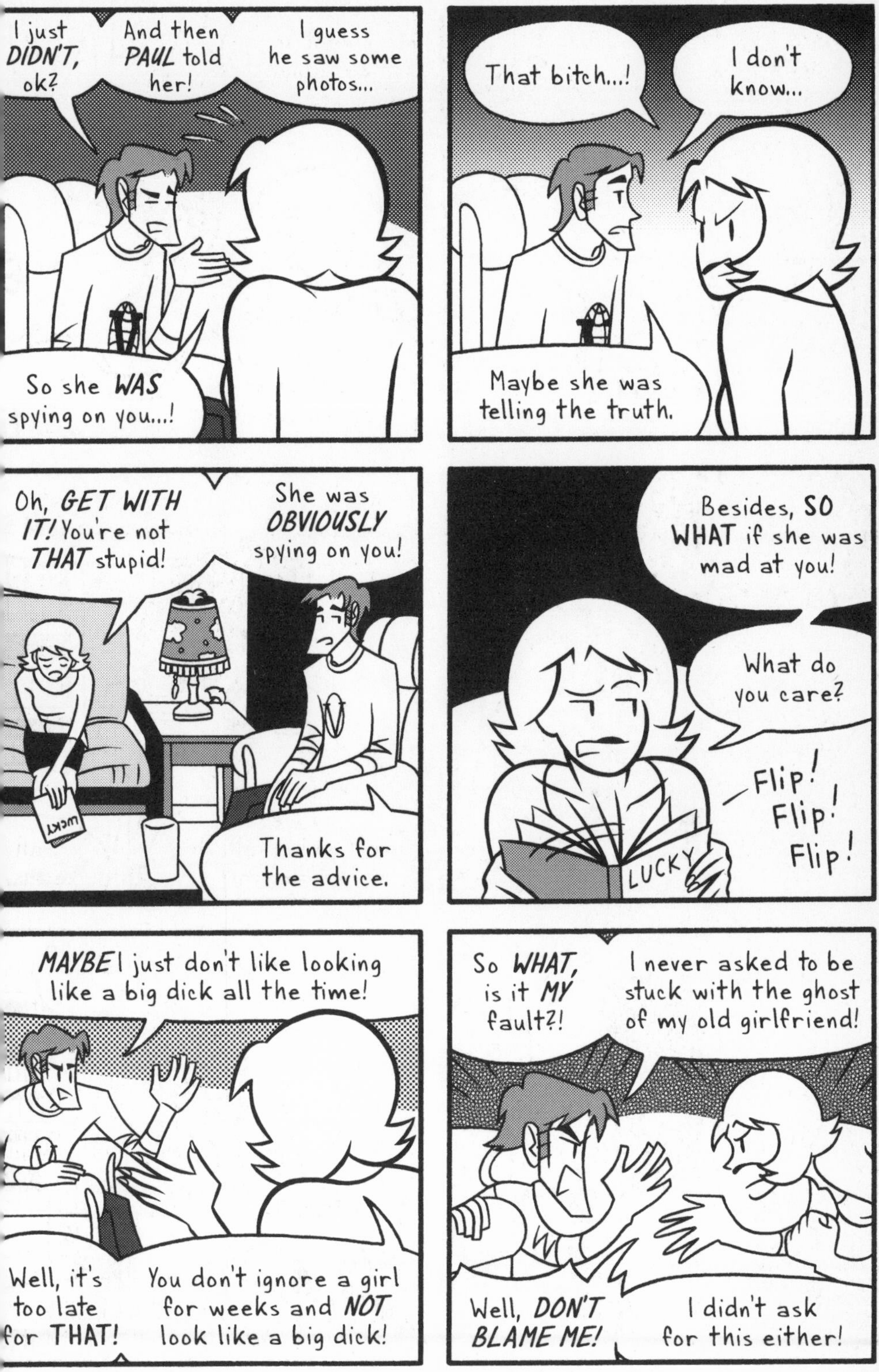
I just DIDN'T, ok?
And then PAUL told her!
I guess he saw some photos...
So she WAS spying on you...!
That bitch...!
I don't know...
Maybe she was telling the truth.
Oh, GET WITH IT! You're not THAT stupid!
She was OBVIOUSLY spying on you!
Thanks for the advice.
LUCKY
Besides, SO WHAT if she was mad at you!
What do you care?
Flip! Flip! Flip!
LUCKY
MAYBE I just don't like looking like a big dick all the time!
Well, it's too late for THAT!
You don't ignore a girl for weeks and NOT look like a big dick!
So WHAT, is it MY fault?!
I never asked to be stuck with the ghost of my old girlfriend!
Well, DON'T BLAME ME!
I didn't ask for this either!

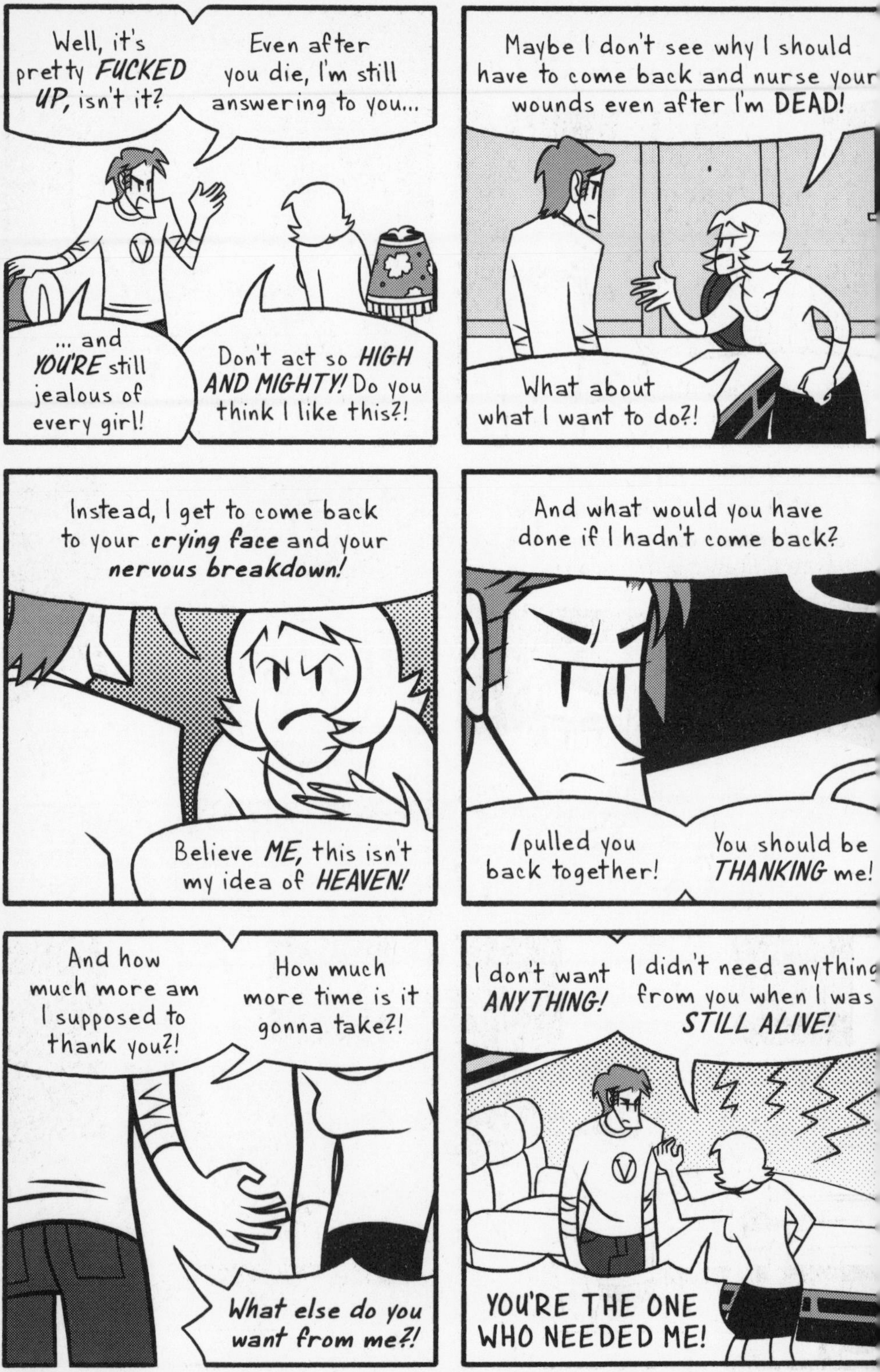

Well, it's pretty FUCKED UP, isn't it?
Even after you die, I'm still answering to you...
... and YOU'RE still jealous of every girl!
Don't act so HIGH AND MIGHTY! Do you think I like this?!
Maybe I don't see why I should have to come back and nurse your wounds even after I'm DEAD!
What about what I want to do?!
Instead, I get to come back to your crying face and your nervous breakdown!
Believe ME, this isn't my idea of HEAVEN!
And what would you have done if I hadn't come back?
I pulled you back together!
You should be THANKING me!
And how much more am I supposed to thank you?!
How much more time is it gonna take?!
What else do you want from me?!
I don't want ANYTHING!
I didn't need anything from you when I was STILL ALIVE!
YOU'RE THE ONE WHO NEEDED ME!

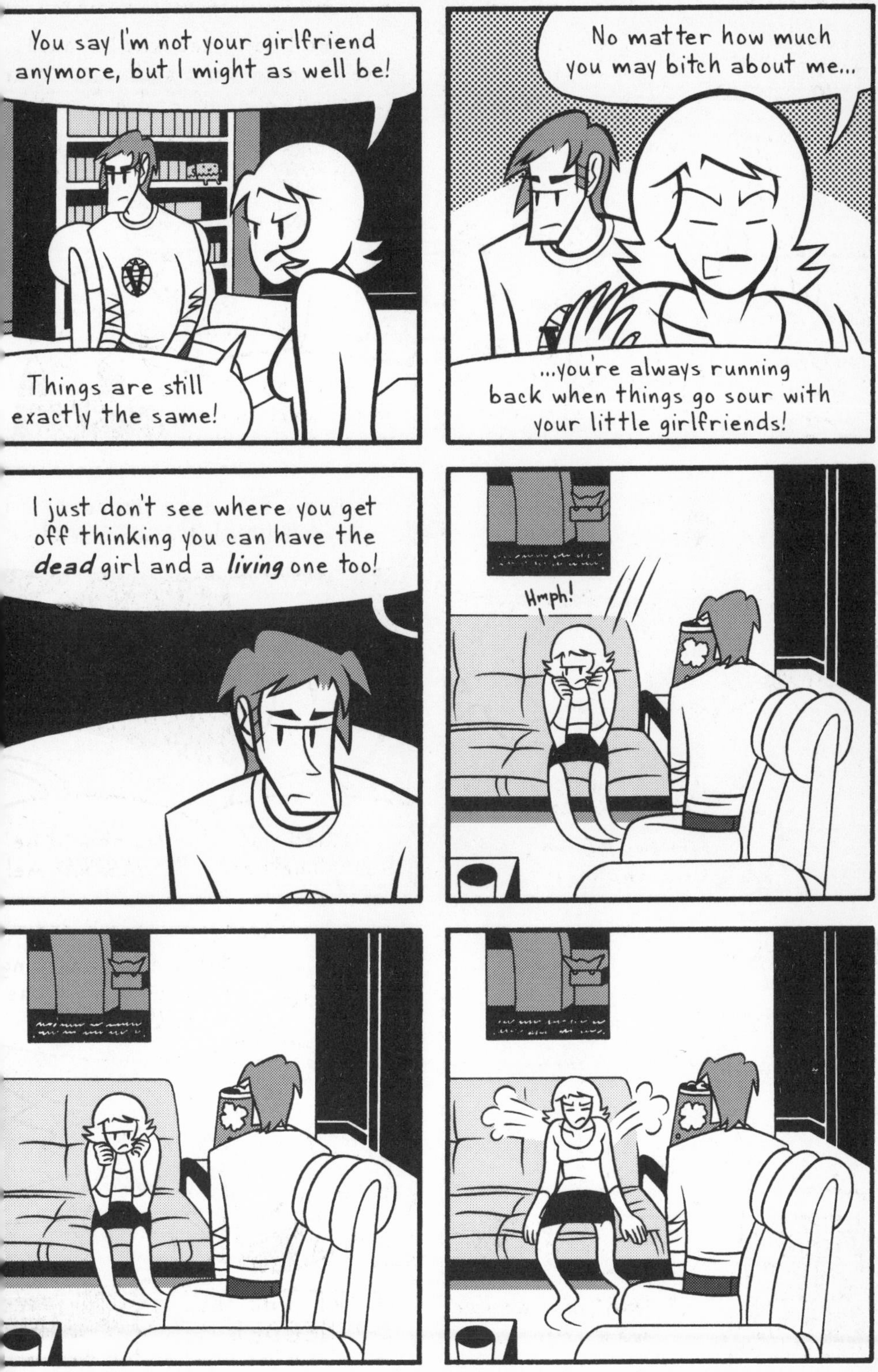
You say I'm not your girlfriend anymore, but I might as well be!
Things are still exactly the same!
No matter how much you may bitch about me...
...you're always running back when things go sour with your little girlfriends!
I just don't see where you get off thinking you can have the *dead* girl and a *living* one too!
Hmph!

...You're right.

HUH?

You're right! I *know* you don't want to be here. You make that clear pretty much *EVERY DAY*...

But still, you're a big help.

Y'know, I think we really used to love each other, but well...

...I don't know. Things weren't even that good back then.

Hey, you don't need to tell me

Nothing's really changed...

Here I am, still holding on to something that's already gone...

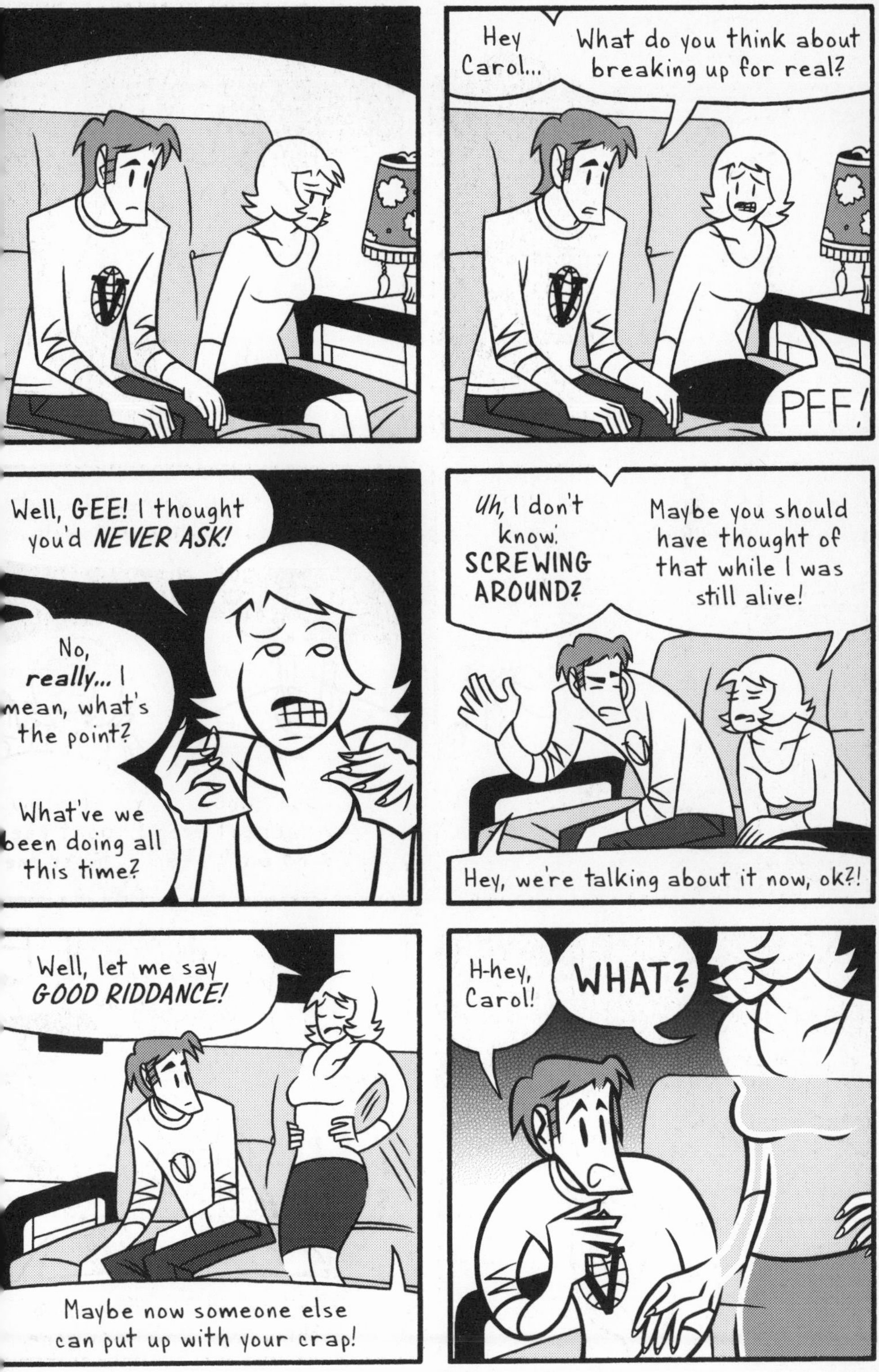
Hey
Carol...
What do you think about breaking up for real?
PFF!
Well, GEE! I thought you'd *NEVER ASK!*
No, ***really...*** I mean, what's the point?
What've we been doing all this time?
Uh, I don't know. SCREWING AROUND?
Maybe you should have thought of that while I was still alive!
Hey, we're talking about it now, ok?!
Well, let me say *GOOD RIDDANCE!*
Maybe now someone else can put up with your crap!
H-hey, Carol!
WHAT?

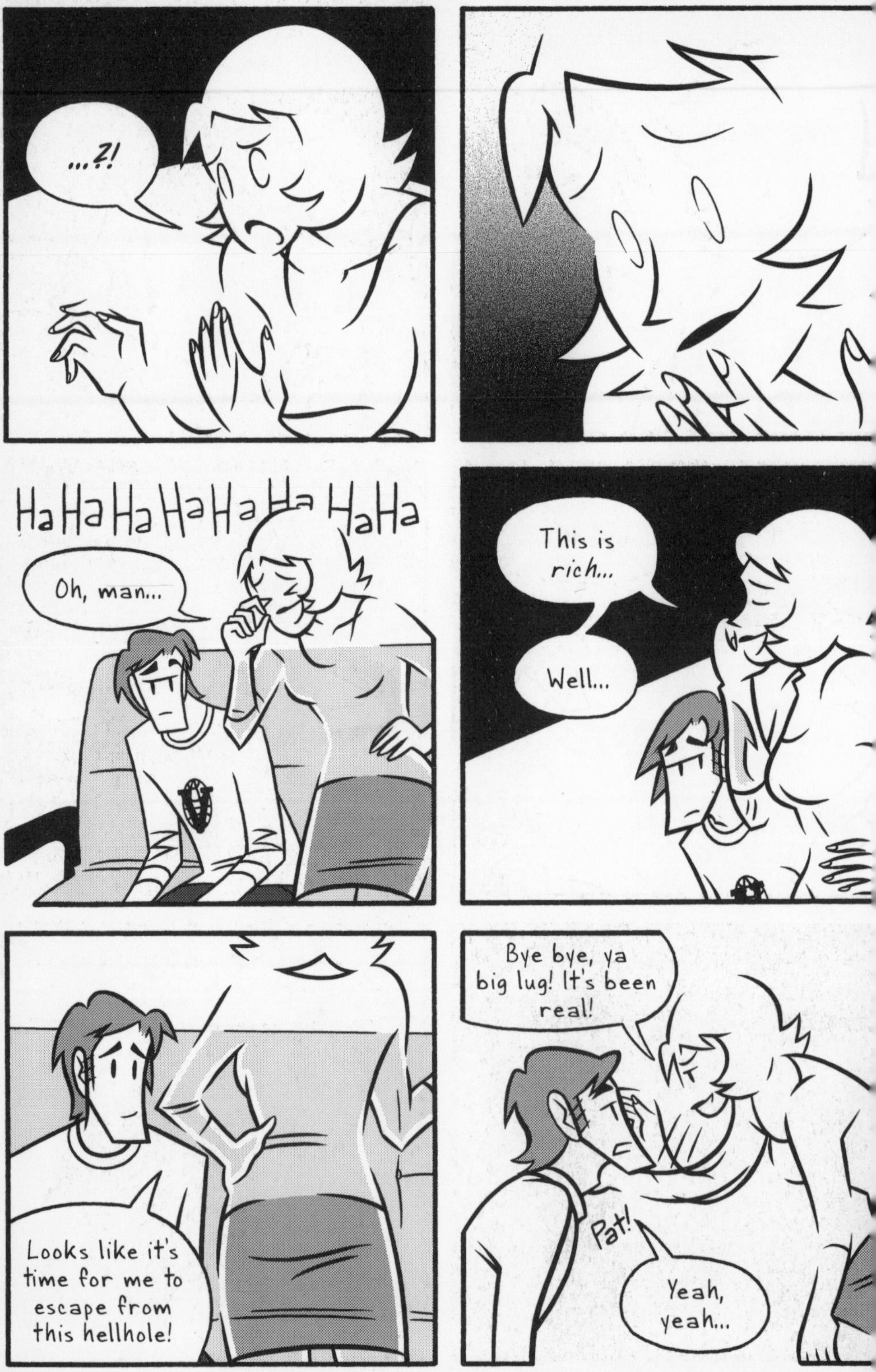
...?!
HaHaHaHaHaHaHaHaHa
Oh, man...
This is rich...
Well...
Looks like it's time for me to escape from this hellhole!
Bye bye, ya big lug! It's been real!
Pat!
Yeah, yeah...

...Take care of yourself this time, ok?

Yeah...

You too, Carol.

Goodbye...

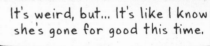

It's weird, but... It's like I know she's gone for good this time.

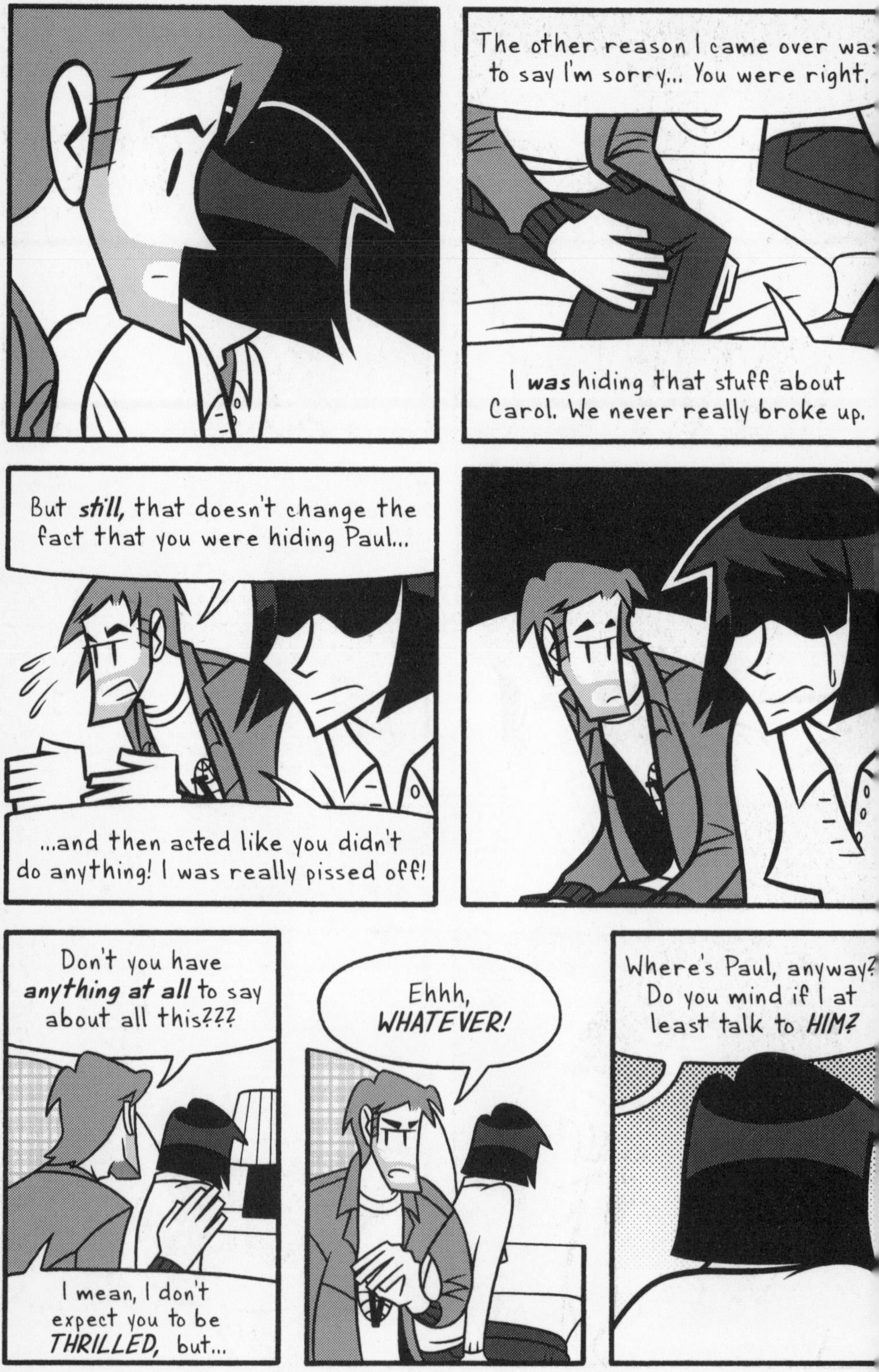
The other reason I came over was
to say I'm sorry... You were right.
I was hiding that stuff about Carol. We never really broke up.
But still, that doesn't change the fact that you were hiding Paul...
...and then acted like you didn't do anything! I was really pissed off!
Don't you have anything at all to say about all this???
I mean, I don't expect you to be THRILLED, but...
Ehhh, WHATEVER!
Where's Paul, anyway? Do you mind if I at least talk to HIM?

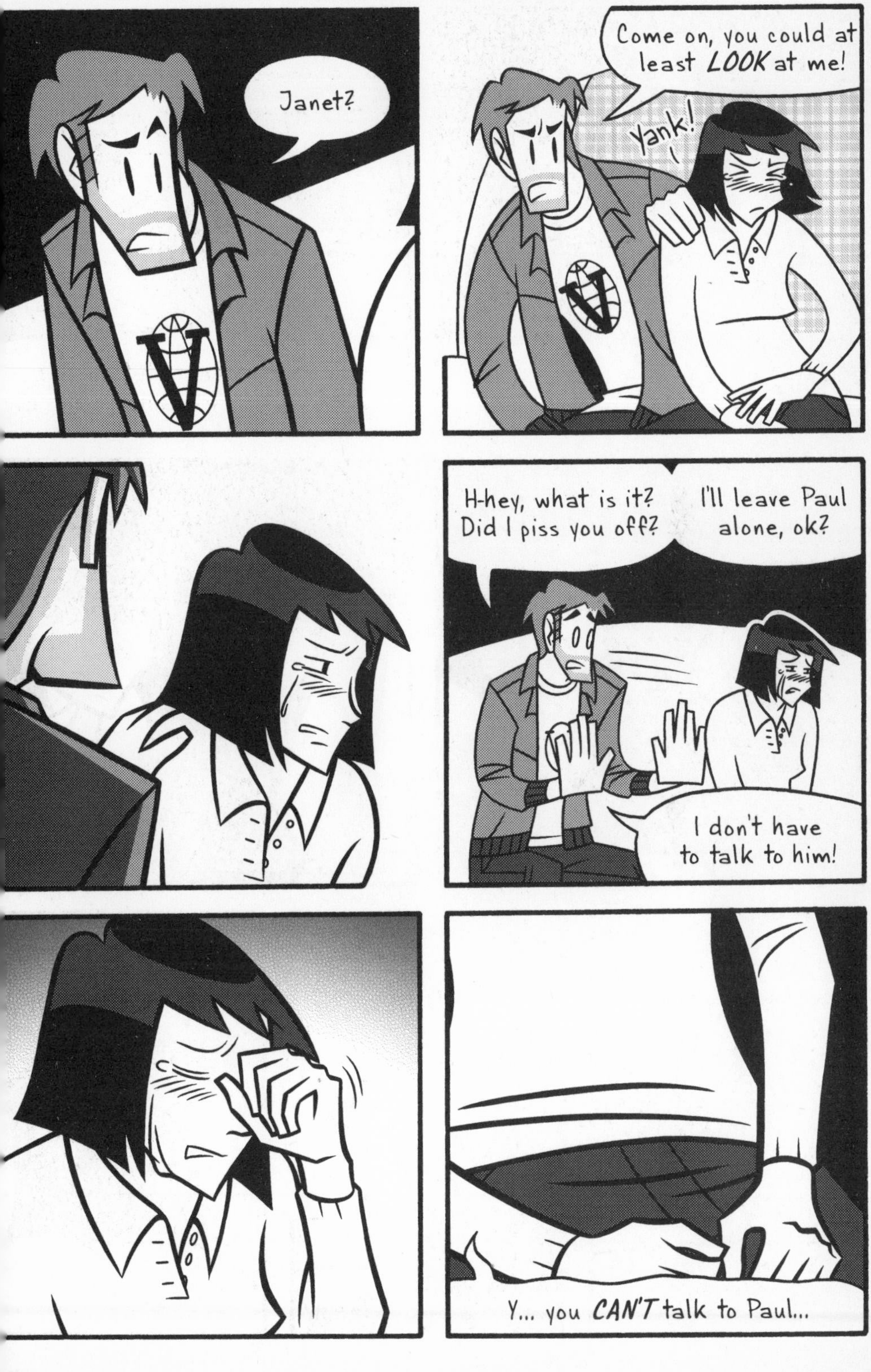

Janet?
Come on, you could at least LOOK at me!
yank!
H-hey, what is it? Did I piss you off?
I'll leave Paul alone, ok?
I don't have to talk to him!
Y... you CAN'T talk to Paul...

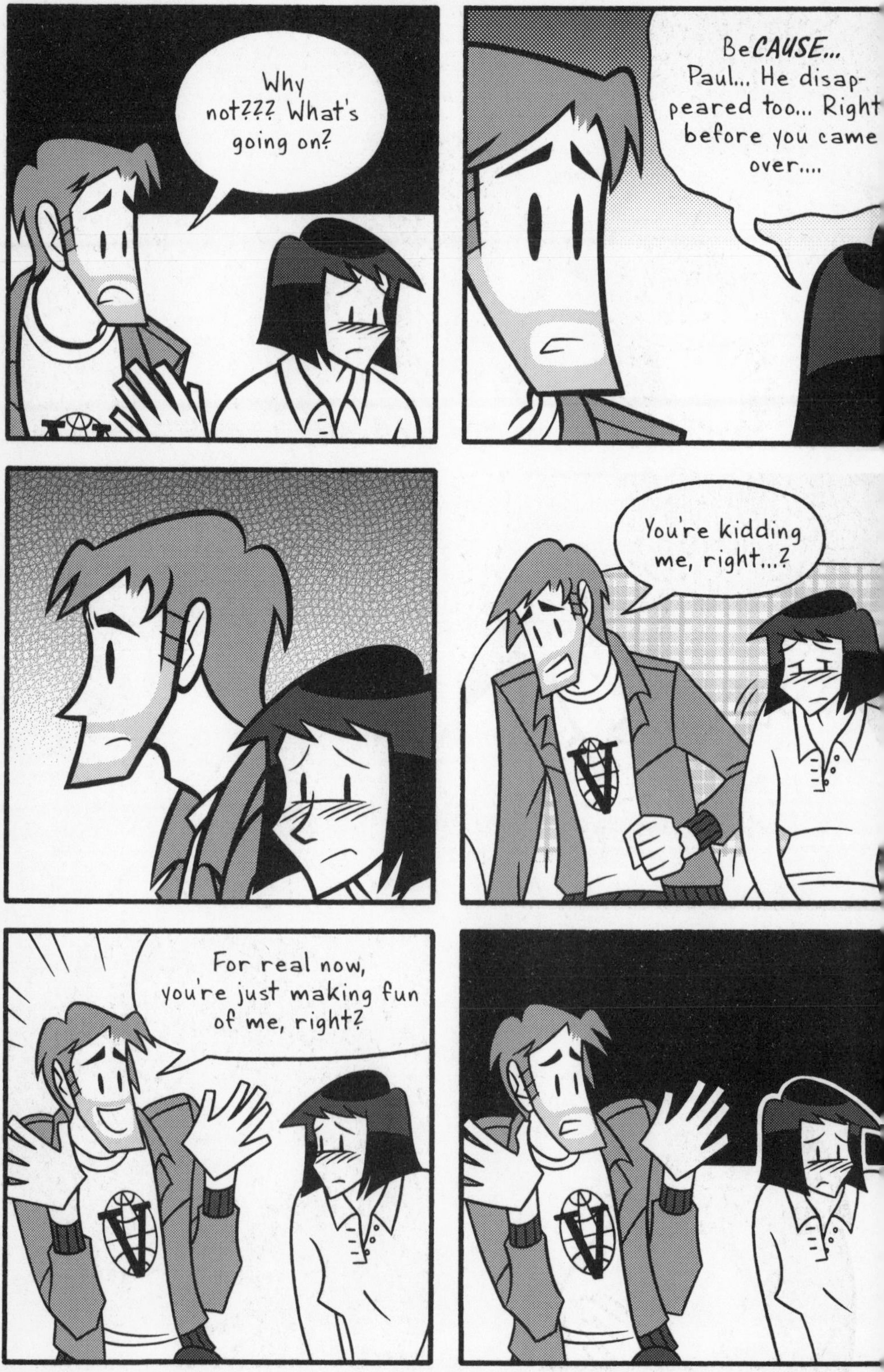
Why not??? What's going on?
BeCAUSE... Paul... He disappeared too... Right before you came over....
You're kidding me, right...?
For real now, you're just making fun of me, right?

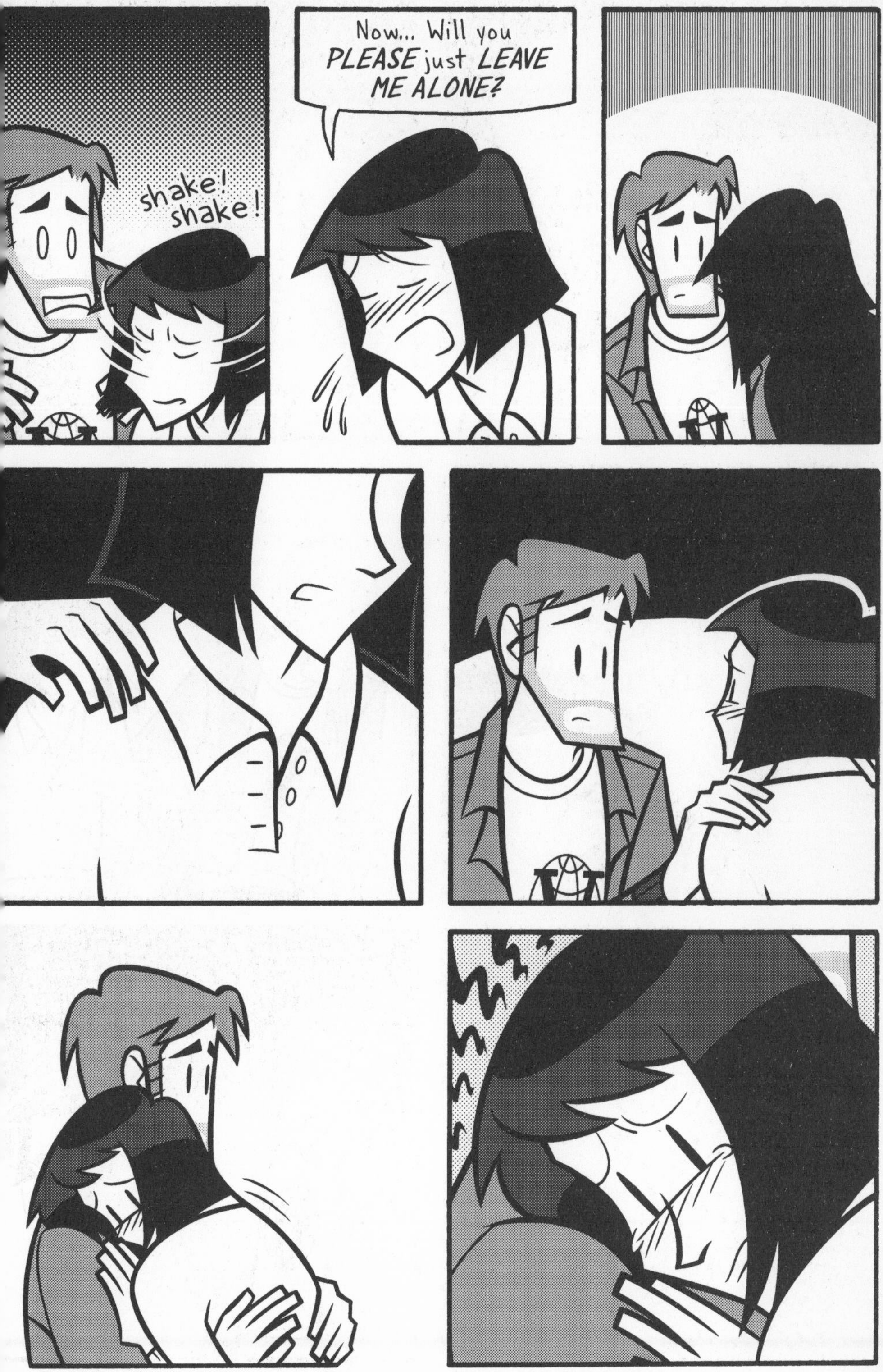
shake! shake!
Now... Will you PLEASE just LEAVE ME ALONE?

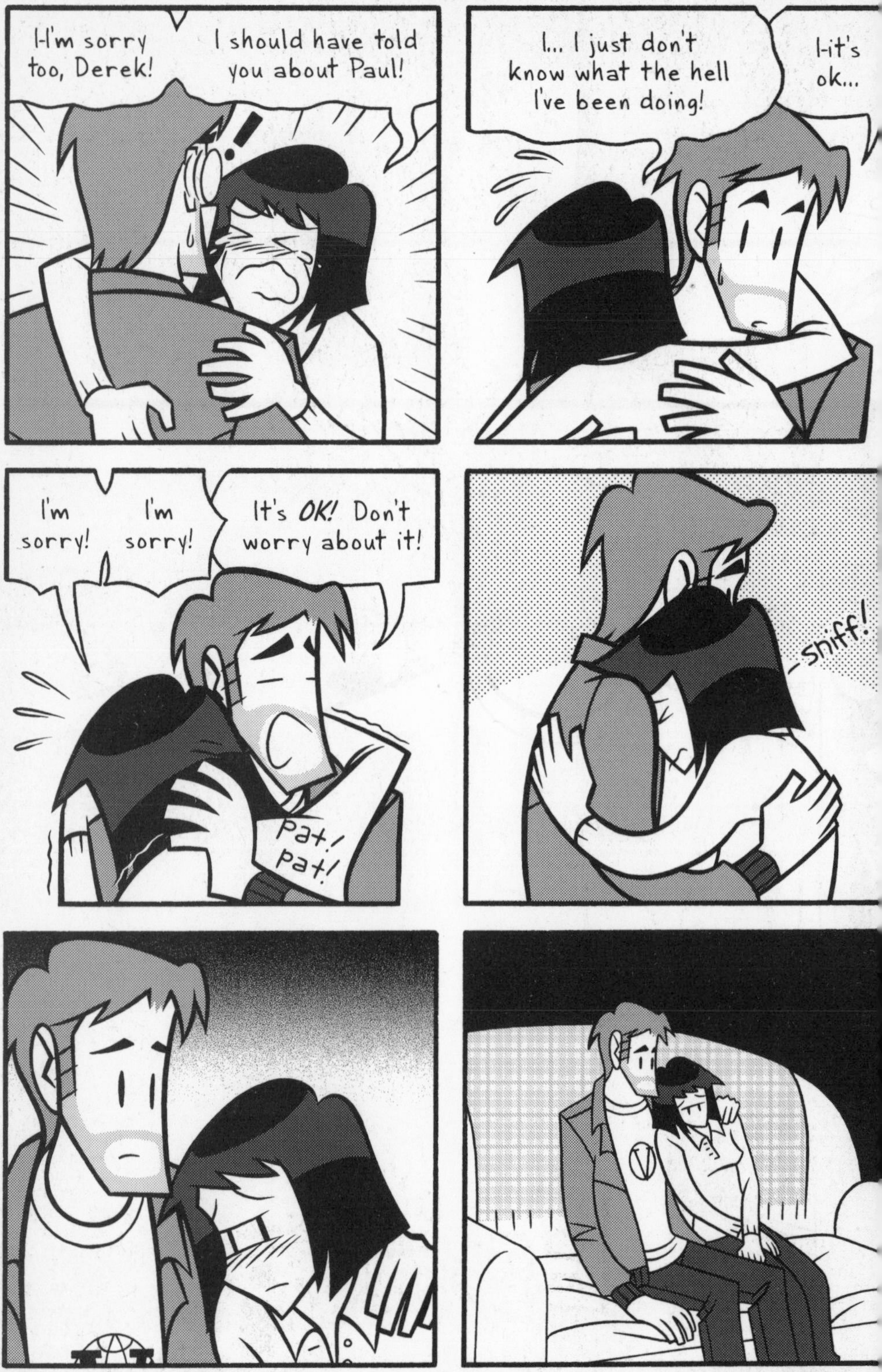
I-I'm sorry too, Derek!
I should have told you about Paul!
I... I just don't know what the hell I've been doing!
I-it's ok...
I'm sorry!
I'm sorry!
It's *OK!* Don't worry about it!
Pat! Pat!
shiff!

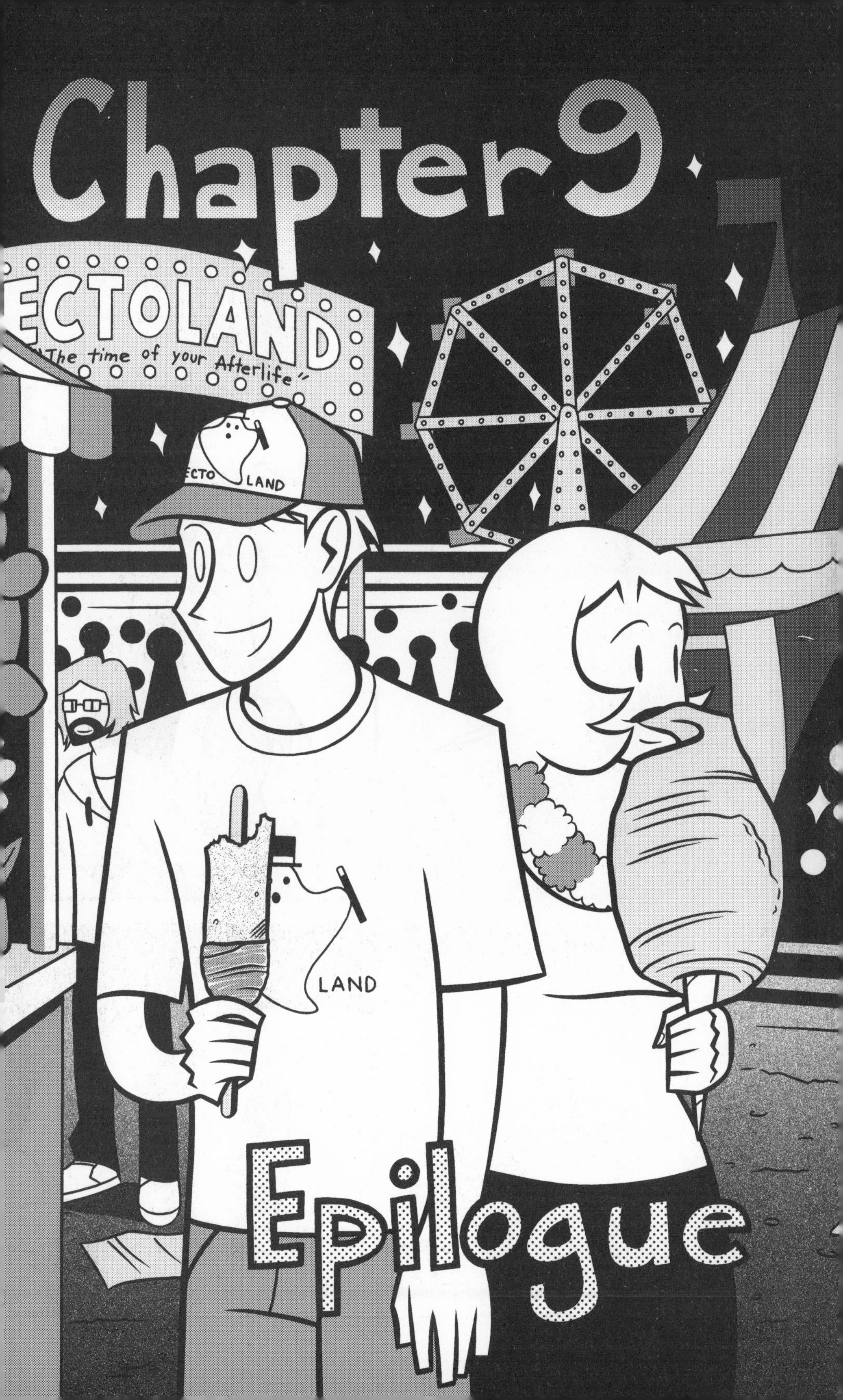
Chapter 9
ECTOLAND
"The time of your Afterlife"
ECTO LAND
LAND
Epilogue

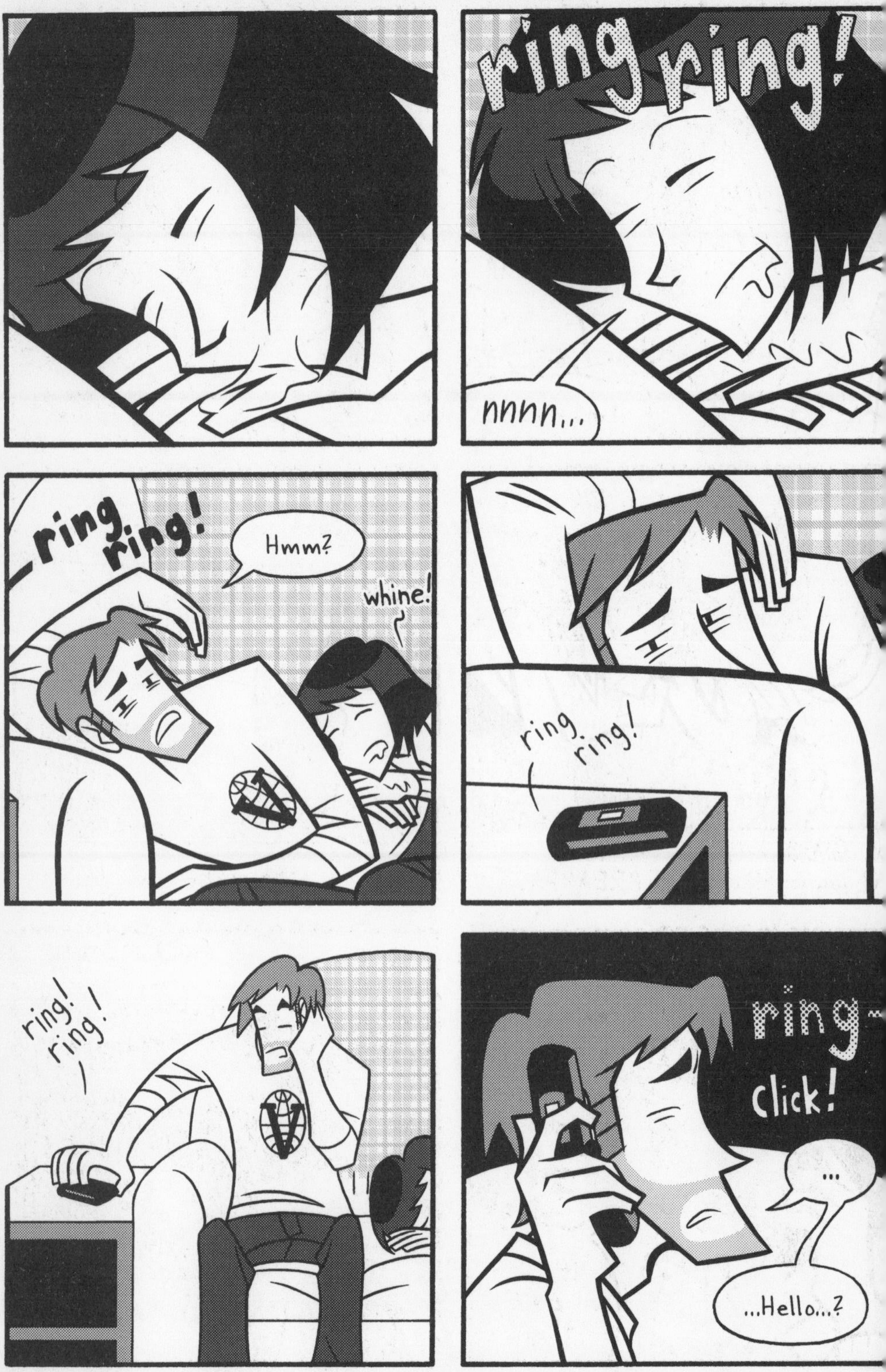
ring ring!
nnnn...
ring ring!
Hmm?
whine!
ring ring!
ring! ring!
ring-
click!
...
...Hello...?

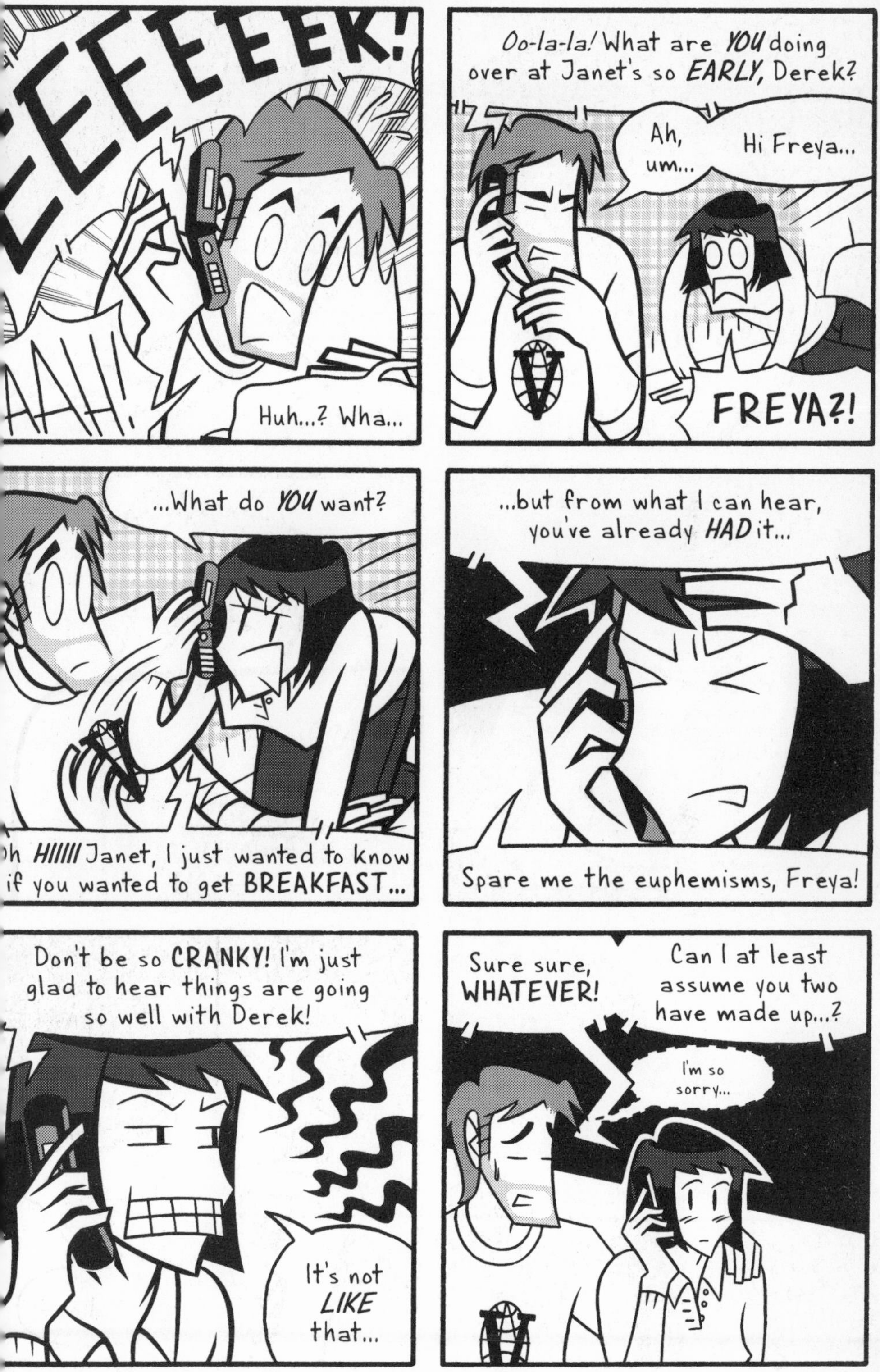
EEEEEEK!
AAH!
Huh...? Wha...
Oo-la-la! What are YOU doing over at Janet's so EARLY, Derek?
Ah, um...
Hi Freya...
FREYA?!
...What do YOU want?
h HI!!!! Janet, I just wanted to know
if you wanted to get BREAKFAST...
...but from what I can hear, you've already HAD it...
Spare me the euphemisms, Freya!
Don't be so CRANKY! I'm just glad to hear things are going so well with Derek!
It's not LIKE that...
Sure sure, WHATEVER!
Can I at least assume you two have made up...?
I'm so sorry...

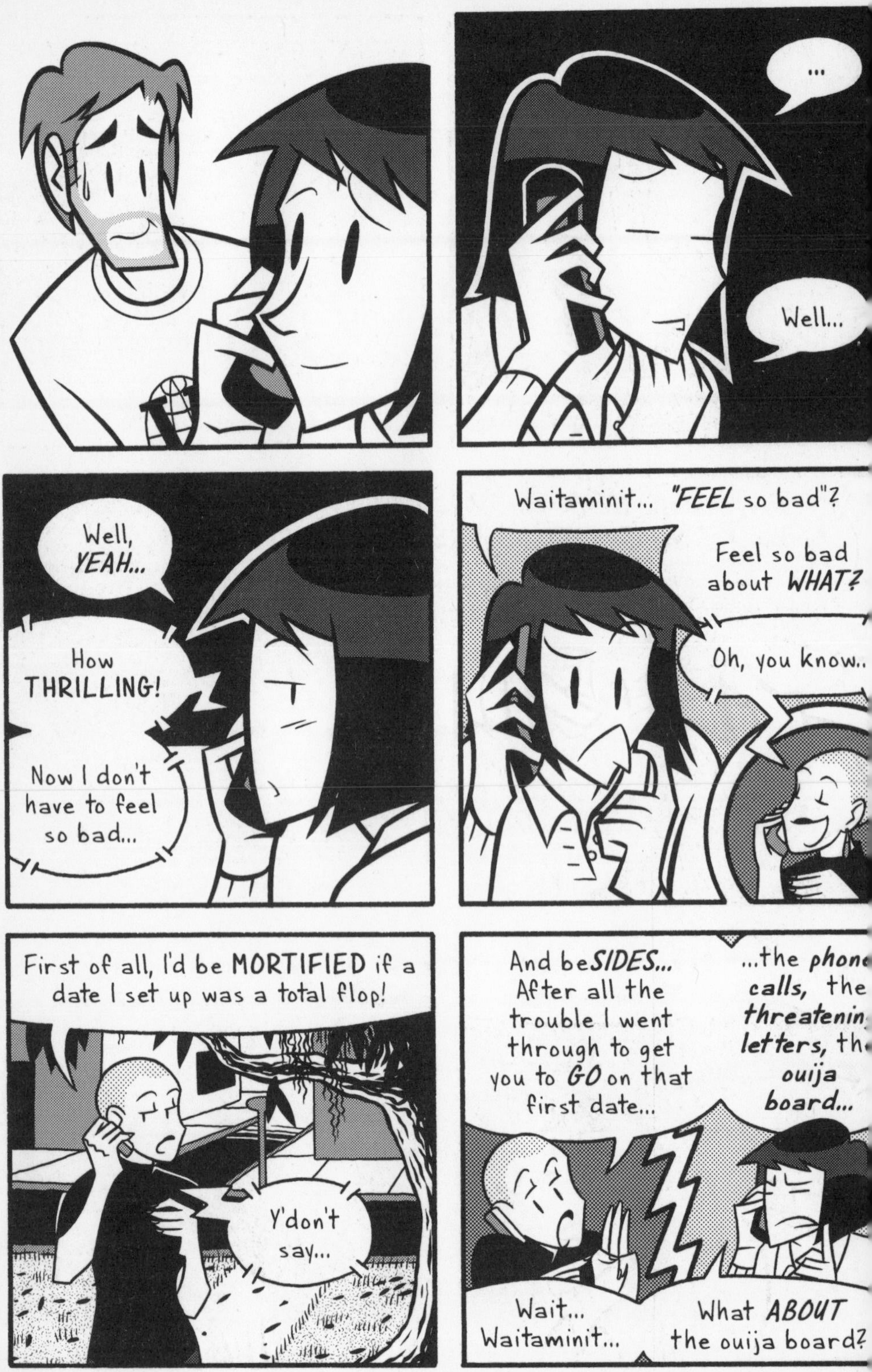
...
Well...
Well,
YEAH...
How
THRILLING!
Now I don't
have to feel
so bad...
Waitaminit... "FEEL so bad"?
Feel so bad
about WHAT?
Oh, you know..
First of all, I'd be MORTIFIED if a
date I set up was a total flop!
Y'don't
say...
And beSIDES...
After all the
trouble I went
through to get
you to GO on that
first date...
...the phone
calls, the
threatening
letters, the
ouija
board...
Wait...
Waitaminit...
What ABOUT
the ouija board?

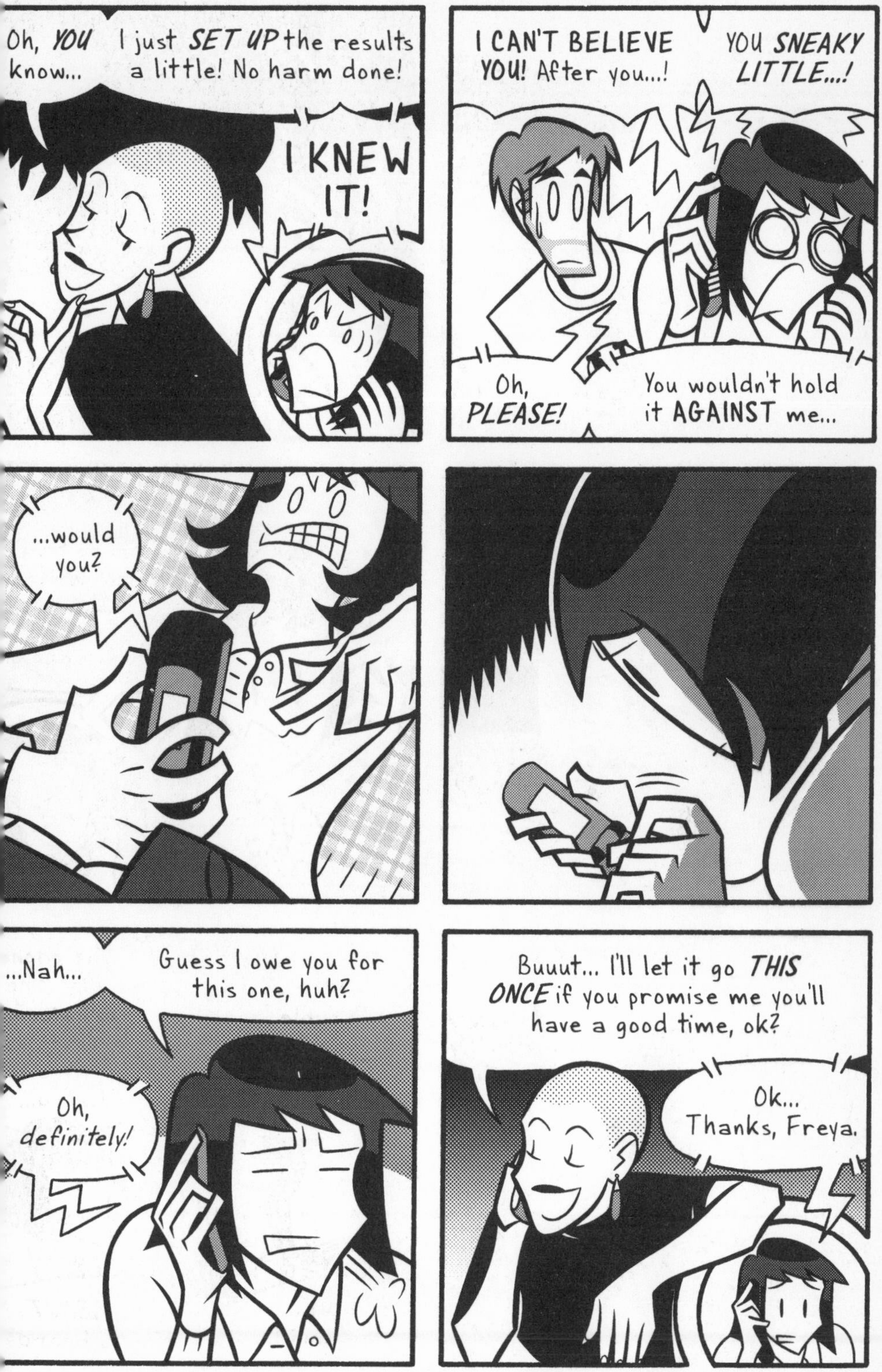
Oh, YOU know...
I just SET UP the results a little! No harm done!
I KNEW IT!
I CAN'T BELIEVE YOU! After you...!
YOU SNEAKY LITTLE...!
Oh, PLEASE!
You wouldn't hold it AGAINST me...
...would you?
...Nah...
Guess I owe you for this one, huh?
Oh, definitely!
Buuut... I'll let it go THIS ONCE if you promise me you'll have a good time, ok?
Ok... Thanks, Freya.

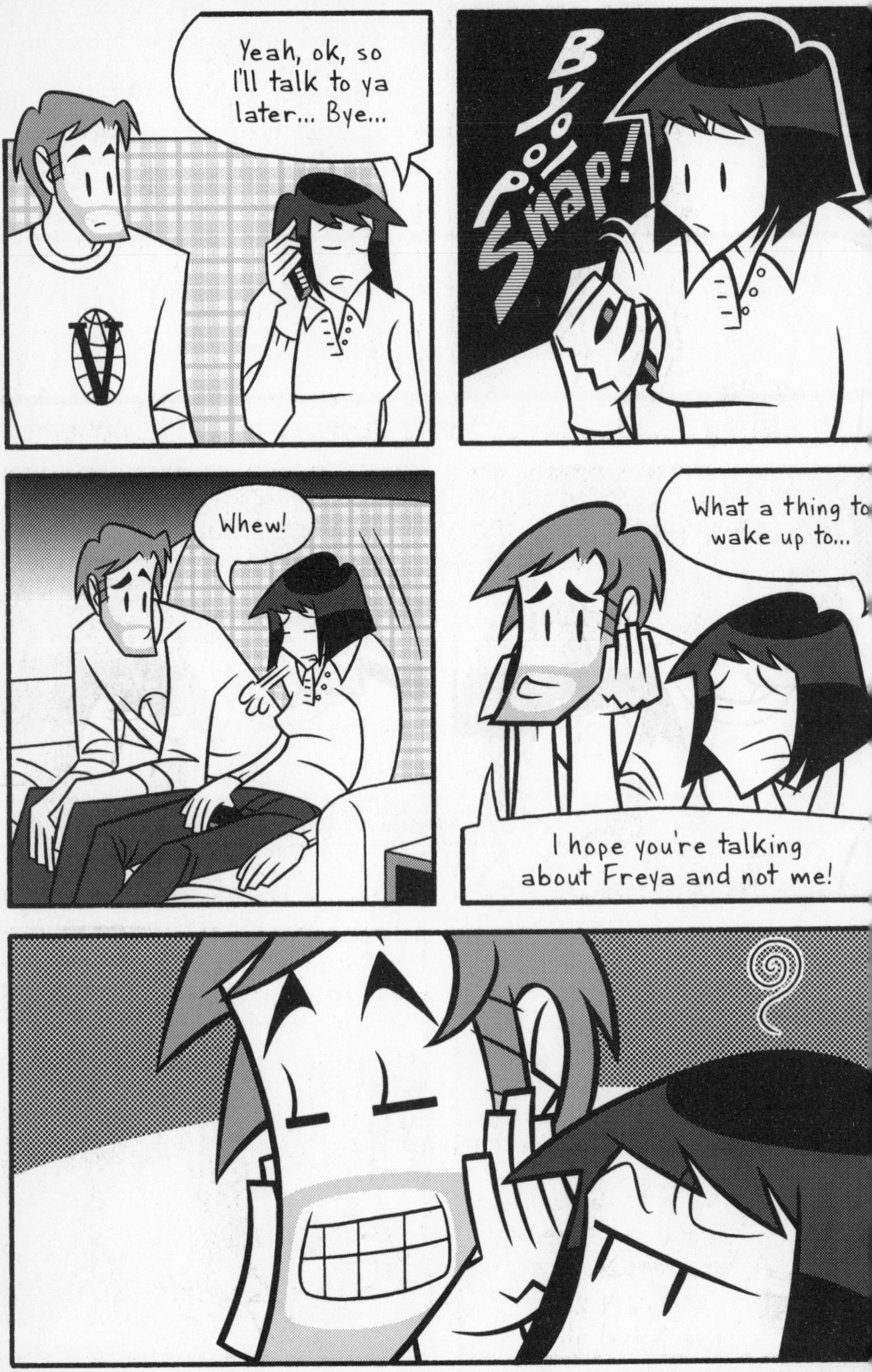

Yeah, ok, so I'll talk to ya later... Bye...
Byoo-doop Snap!
Whew!
What a thing to wake up to...
I hope you're talking about Freya and not me!

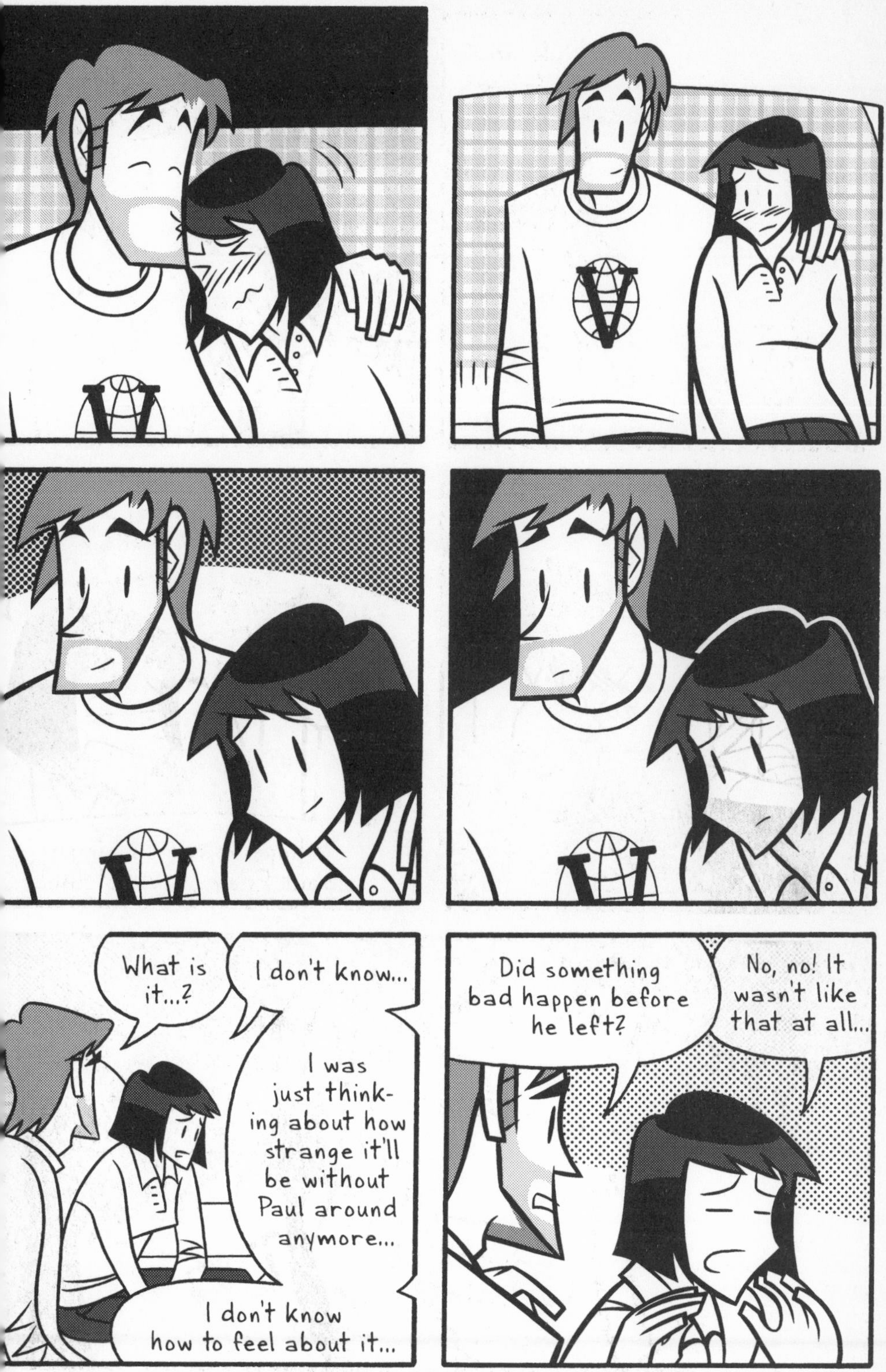
What is it...?
I don't know...
I was just thinking about how strange it'll be without Paul around anymore...
I don't know how to feel about it...
Did something bad happen before he left?
No, no! It wasn't like that at all...

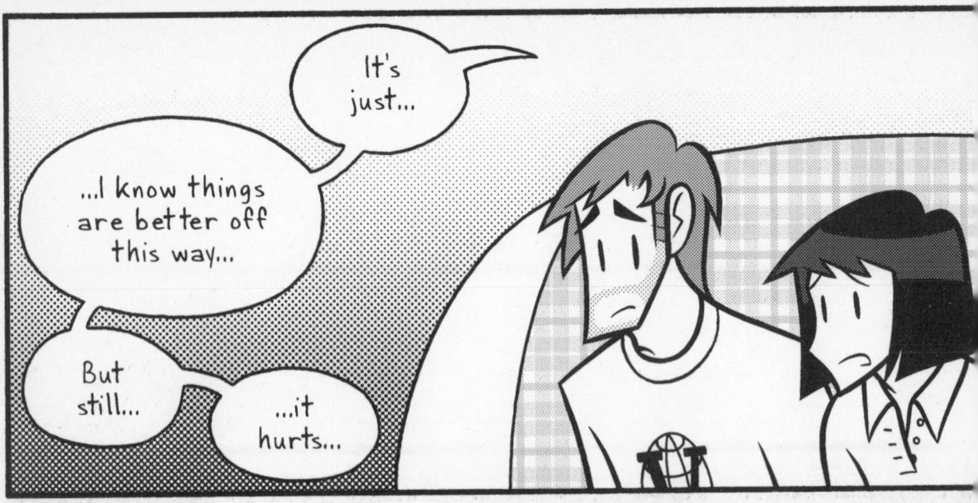
It's just...
...I know things are better off this way...
But still...
...it hurts...

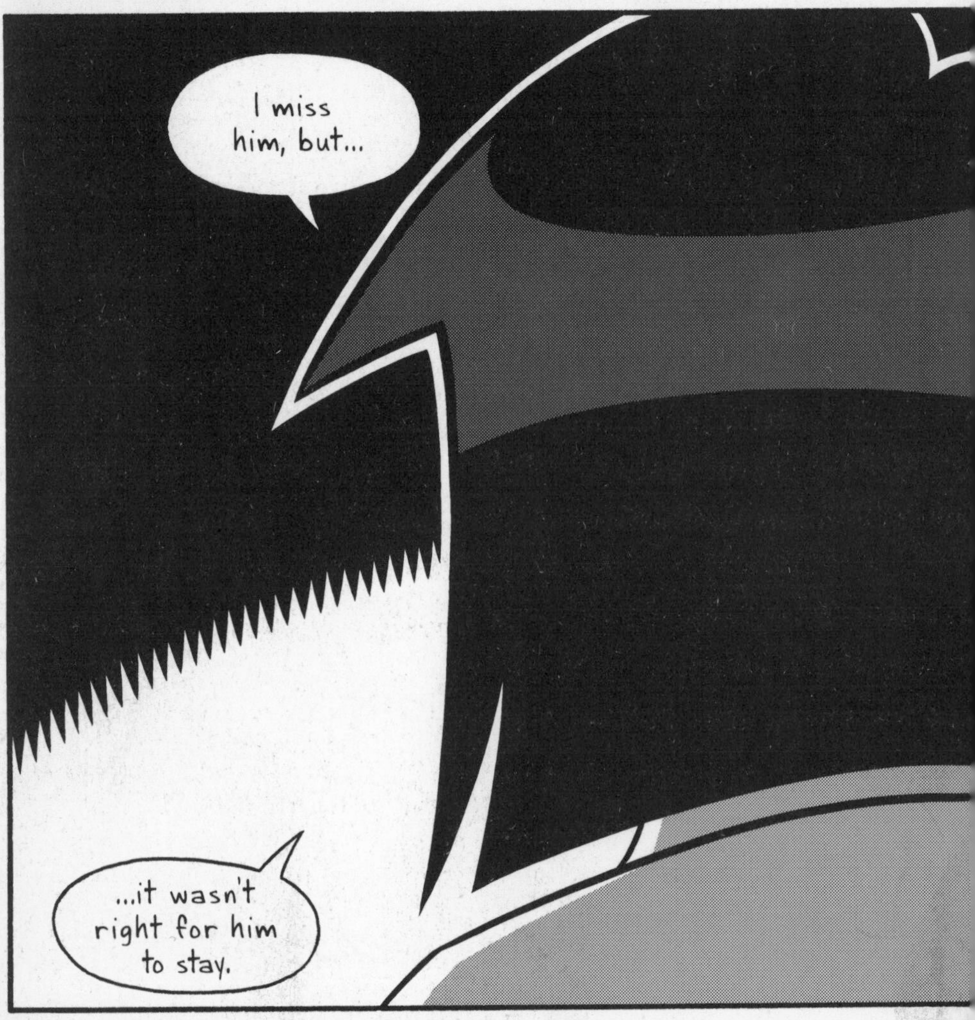
I miss him, but...
...it wasn't right for him to stay.

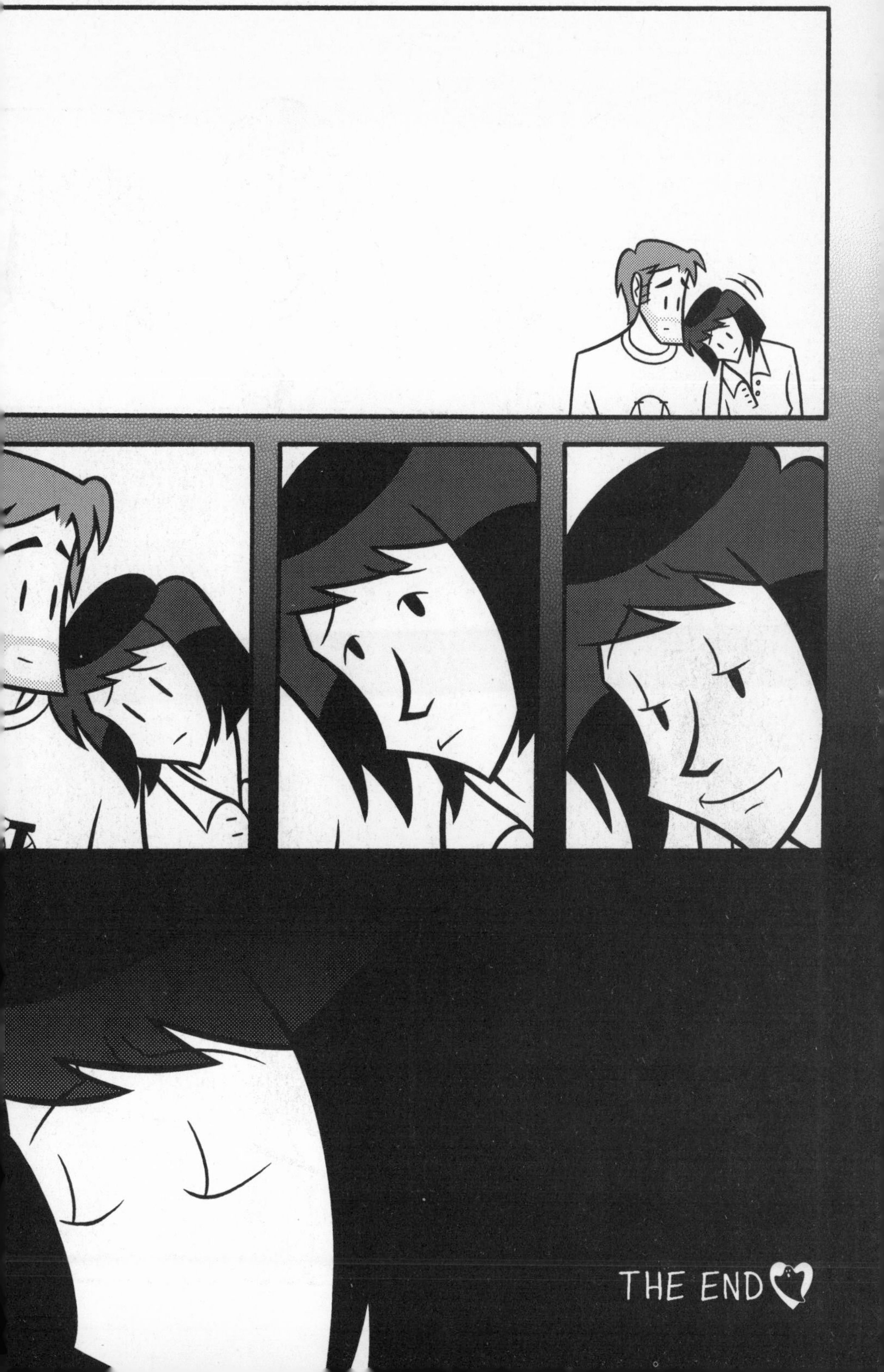
THE END

Illustration by Kyle Magnan · www.kylemagnan.com

Renee Lott

Raised on rice in the wilds of the Ozark Mountains, Renee Lott first became enamored with sequential art after acquiring an issue of *Betty & Veronica* that had flown out of the bed of a passing pick-up truck. After scrawling pictures in the dirt for 25 years, she felt it was time to make her professional debut.

Special thanks to:

James Lucas Jones and the rest of the **Oni Press crew**: Without your help and dedication, this book wouldn't exist!

Dad: Without your support, I'm sure this book would have taken twice as long to finish and I might have starved (or at least slowly wasted away and lived in a hovel)!

Kyle: You put up with me every day, looked over every page of the book, helped edit the material on every level, and even brought me tasty food...! I couldn't have done it without your help!

Other books from Oni Press

Courtney Crumrin and the Night Things
by Ted Naifeh

Gray Horses
by hope larson

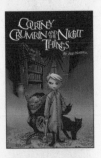

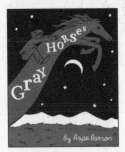

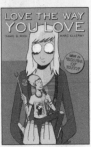

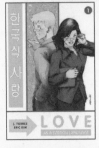

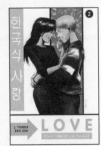

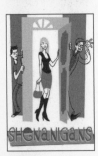

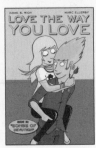

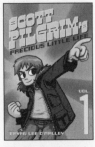

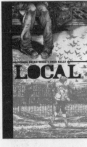

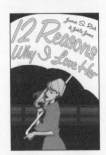

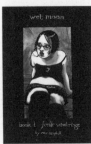

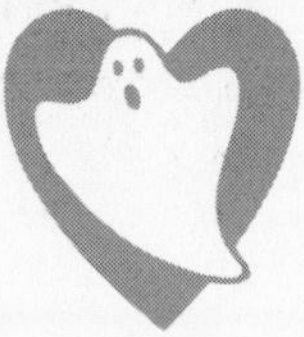

COURTNEY CRUMRIN - VOL. 1: THE NIGHT THINGS
By Ted Naifeh
128 pages · digest · B&W interiors
$11.95 · ISBN 978-1-929998-60-9

GRAY HORSES
By Hope Larson
112 pages · 7"x9" · 2-color interiors
$14.95 · ISBN 978-1-932664-36-2

BRIAN WOOD · RYAN KELLY
LOCAL

1
한국식 사랑
J. TORRES
ERIC KIM
LOVE

2
한국식 사랑
J. TORRES
ERIC KIM
LOVE

LOCAL - DELUXE HARDCOVER
By Brian Wood & Ryan Kelly
384 pages · hardcover · B&W interiors
$29.99 · ISBN 978-1-934964-00-2

LOVE AS A FOREIGN LANGUAGE: COLLECTED EDITION - VOL. 1
By J. Torres & Eric Kim
200 pages · digest · B&W interiors
$11.95 · ISBN 978-1-932664-41-6

LOVE AS A FOREIGN LANGUAGE: COLLECTED EDITION - VOL. 2
By J. Torres and Eric Kim
200 pages · digest · B&W interiors
$11.95 US ·ISBN 978-1-932664-58-4

LOVE THE WAY YOU LOVE
JAMIE S. RICH
MARC ELLERBY

JAMIE S. RICH
MARC ELLERBY
LOVE THE WAY YOU LOVE
"SONGS OF DEVOTION"

SCOTT PILGRIM'S PRECIOUS LITTLE LIFE
VOL. 1
BRYAN LEE O'MALLEY

LOVE THE WAY YOU LOVE - SIDE A
By Jamie S. Rich & Marc Ellerby
200 pages · digest · B&W interiors
$11.95 ·ISBN 978-1-932664-66-9

LOVE THE WAY YOU LOVE - SIDE B
By Jamie S. Rich & Marc Ellerby
200 pages · digest · B&W interiors
$11.95 · ISBN 978-1-932664-95-9

SCOTT PILGRIM - VOL. 1: SCOTT PILGRIM'S PRECIOUS LITTLE LIFE
By Bryan Lee O'Malley
168 pages · digest · B&W interiors
$11.95 ·ISBN 978-1-932664-08-9

SHENANIGANS

Jamie S. Rich
& Joëlle Jones
12 Reasons Why I Love Her

wet moon
book 1 feeble wanderings

SHENANIGANS
By Ian Shaughnessy & Mike Holmes
168 pages · digest · B&W interiors
$14.95 · ISBN 978-1-932664-55-3

12 REASONS WHY I LOVE HER
By Jamie S. Rich & Joëlle Jones
144 pages · 6x9 B&W interiors
$14.95 · ISBN 978-1-932664-51-5

WET MOON - VOL. 1: FEEBLE WANDERINGS
By Ross Campbell
168 pages · 6x9 · B&W interiors
$14.95 · ISBN 978-1-932664-07-2

Oni Press

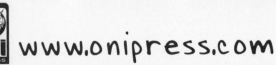

www.onipress.com

For more information on these and other fine Oni Press comic books and graphic novels, visit www.onipress.com. To find a comic specialty store in your area, call 1-888-COMICBOOK or visit www.comicshops.us.